QUESTIONS
OF THE
FRENCH REVOLUTION

QUESTIONS
OF THE
FRENCH REVOLUTION

A HISTORICAL OVERVIEW

JACQUES SOLÉ

Incorporating work by Donald M. G. Sutherland
Translated from the French by Shelley Temchin

With a foreword by Eugen Weber

PANTHEON BOOKS
NEW YORK

All rights reserved under International and Pan-American Copyright
Conventions. Published in the United States by Pantheon Books, a
division of Random House, Inc., New York, and simultaneously in Canada by Random House of Canada Limited, Toronto. Originally published
in France as *La Révolution en Questions* by Éditions du Seuil. Copyright
© 1988 by Éditions du Seuil.

Library of Congress Cataloging-in-Publication Data

Solé, Jacques.
[Révolution en questions. English]
Questions of the French Revolution : a historical overview /
Jacques Solé ; foreword by Eugen Weber ; translated from the French
by Shelley Temchin.
p.   cm.
Translation of: La Révolution en questions.
Bibliography: p.
Includes index.
ISBN 0-394-58001-X ISBN 0-679-72563-6 (pbk.)
1. France—History—Revolution, 1789–1799. 2. France—History—
Revolution, 1789–1799—Influence. 3. France—History—Revolution,
1789–1799—Social aspects. I. Title.
DC148.S6713 1989
944.04—dc19   89-42556

With special thanks to Donald M. G. Sutherland for his kind permission
to cite extensively his excellent book *France 1789–1815: Revolution
and Counterrevolution*, (© copyright 1985 by D. M. G. Sutherland;
London, William Collins, 1985; New York, Oxford University Press,
1985) and the many invaluable arguments he presents therein.
                                                    —Jacques Solé

Book Design by Anne Scatto

Manufactured in the United States of America

In memory of André Latreille,
with gratitude for his teaching and his friendship.

"He who serves the revolution plows the sea."

—*Bolívar*

"Revolutions are the barbarous form of progress."

—*Jaurès*

CONTENTS

FOREWORD

by Eugen Weber

Everything that you would like to know about the French Revolution, and everything you should ask if you knew what to ask—that is what Jacques Solé offers in this handy compendium.

Ever since 1789, the Revolution has inspired a stream of accounts and interpretations. As 1989 drew near, the stream became a torrent, a river, a flood. Two hundred years after the Estates-General were summoned, not a day passes without the appearance of one or more titles dedicated to some aspect of that fateful year and of its successors. Not even specialists can keep up with what has been, and continues to be, published. As for interested nonspecialists, they find it hard to tell the essential from the inessential, the wheat from the chaff. It was time for a review of what is known about the Revolution, of where we stand after much thinking, rethinking, and debate. Not another interpretation of the Revolution, but a presentation and comparison of the major contemporary positions concerning it. That is what makes this book so welcome.

Solé avoids theory because theories tend to be self-verifying. Those who wield them have to show that things happened the way they happened because they had to happen that way. The fact that they happened proves that they were bound to happen. It also demonstrates that the theorist's theory is valid. This leaves no room for contingency, for choice, for chance, for the intervention of individual men and women, who are treated as flotsam on the tide of inevitable trends. Solé prefers a more pragmatic approach, which may be why he often quotes what the French call Anglo-Saxon historians—mostly English ones—who tend to fragment The Revolution into an unruly crowd of individual, local, and factional conflicts, rivalries, initiatives, and aspirations. This latter approach deprives us of comfortable interpretations that purport to explain everything, but brings us a little closer to messy every day realities.

What this means in practice you can tell by a glance at the table of contents, which features not affirmations, but queries. How valid are familiar explanations? How much water do they hold? Was the Revolution a culmination of the Enlightenment, and Napoleon the last of the enlightened despots? or was it an early manifestation of romanticism, and Napoleon simply romanticism on horseback? Did the Revolution reflect the wishes of a majority of the French, or the fantasies and passions of a minority? The spirit of the Enlightenment was elitist. From Robespierre to Lenin, radical revolutionaries would be elitist too. Then, were the people for the Revolution or against it? Who *were* "the people"? Whoever they were, when we can locate them, they seem to think first of their own interests—local, particular, personal, familial—and only reluctantly heed what politicians describe as the general interest.

Relations between particular and general interest seem to have been as tenuous as relations between revolutionary formulae and popular need. Revolutionaries called for virtue, dedication, and civic spirit. The mass of the French faced poverty, hunger, violence, and fear as endemic as deprivation. In 1789, 40 percent of the kingdom's population depended on charity, two out of every five men, women, and children. There was little that revolutionary enthusiasm could do about this. The balance between a growing population and insufficient resources remained murderously unstable until it was solved by demographic decline in the later nineteenth century.

Solé concludes that the Revolution did not change the fate of the poor, of women, or of children. It hardly ushered in an age of reason, either. It proclaimed far-reaching principles—civil equality, national sovereignty, public liberties, a secular state—but proved less effective in applying them than in hindering their application. Did it at least promote social equality, stanch that cascade of contempt of superiors for inferiors that Mirabeau denounced? Rather, it fed the passion critics attribute to the French for that version of equality in which being as good as your fellows is demonstrated by putting them down.

Was the Revolution carried out against despotism or designed to make despotism more efficient? Was it a bourgeois uprising against the oppressive nobility? But who were the nobles? Just bourgeois who had made it, or their offspring. And nobles were as prominent in advancing the cause of revolution and revolutionary change as nonnobles. Solé suggests that, far from being a triumph of the bourgeoisie, the Revolution permitted its aristocratization; that was what the bourgeoisie had wanted and that is what the more successful among them got, more swiftly and in greater numbers than under the monarchy. So 1789 orginated less the sovereignty of the people than the sovereignty of the rich. Not Marx's harbingers of industrial revolution, but landowners and owners of urban real estate who represented riches under the old regime and continued to represent it under the new; the Revolution did not accelerate industrial changes but delayed them.

Did the Revolution unite the country or polarize it? Did people take sides for ideological reasons, or did new political slogans sharpen old cleavages, clan, and communal rivalries? Were old conflicts resolved in a new spirit of fraternity, or simply exacerbated—as between peasants and burghers, or Protestants and Catholics? Alexis de Tocqueville has drawn attention to the contrast between benign words and violent acts. The guillotine, its introduction inspired by considerations of humanity, efficiency, and equality (Louis XVI himself intervened to improve the shape of the blade), proves that the road to terror is paved with good intentions. The determination to democratize democracy soon skidded off the humanitarian highway in aberrant directions. Too often insistence on unity expressed itself by exclusion or elimination: The call for unanimity became denunciation of nonconformity. Minted, like "vandalism" to describe revolutionary destruction, the terms *"Terror,"* *"terrorism,"* *"terrorist,"* were coined in the 1790s.

Did the Revolution represent a break? No question. It set out to revolutionize time and space. For some years, the seven-day week and the twenty-four-hour day were officially replaced by more "rational" divisions based on the decimal system. Even the months received new, evocative names like floréal or brumaire. More lasting would be the new administrative entities drawn up to replace historic regions like Flanders and Burgundy. There have been many revolutions in France since 1789, but the creation of departments, and in due course of prefects, to run departments, has not been challenged. The revolutionary restructuring of life went further: Local customs, dialects, weights and measures, were to be replaced by national measures, nationally valid legislation, one national language. Local particularisms and particular privileges were suppressed. Ancient servitudes and inequalities, already on the wane, were abolished. Subjects became citizens. And the monarchy itself was unmade.

Innovations were so radical, the revolutionary experience so traumatic, that it took some time before commentators like Tocqueville could observe that the Revolution was also a continuation of earlier trends, that Republic and Empire perfected that for which royalty had striven.

Centralization became tighter, bureaucrats more numerous, administration more intrusive, the new citizen more effectively harnessed to the state than the old subject had been. In the end, the relation of continuity and change seems best reflected in the tricolor flag that combines the white of the royal household with the red and blue colors of revolutionary Paris.

So, despite what it dreamed of, despite what it promised, the Revolution did not abolish the state, or the exploitation of man by man, or social and economic inequalities. State powers, which many French had hoped to whittle down, were reinforced; taxes, against which the Revolution had been a revolt, were increased; men proclaimed free and equal were more strictly policed and more sharply differentiated; woman under the new laws were even less free and equal than they had been before 1789. And there were more political prisoners after the Bastille fell than there had ever been before the Revolution.

One reason things got out of hand may have been the youth of the players: The best-known figures of the 1790s were in their thirties, except for those in their twenties, like Napoleon. Camille Desmoulins died at 34, Danton at 35, Robespierre at 36, Saint-Just at 27. More important than age was inexperience. The English and American gentlemen who made successful revolutions in the seventeenth and eighteenth centuries were used to public affairs. The French were not and seldom had time to gather enough experience.

One revolutionary innovation has not been sufficiently noted. As the Revolution snowballed, as rebellion called for repression and conspiracy inspired constraint, as terror spawned counterterror, the ruling classes were exposed to violence and brutality hitherto reserved for the masses alone. Minds, life-styles, philosophies long insulated from most of the cruelties and humiliations of everyday life could never again ignore them. In France as in no other land, conflict became a normative value. This state of affairs would lend its own strange coherence to two centuries of French history in which crisis is chronic but never catastrophic—at least, no more catastrophic than the founding catastrophe had been.

Meanwhile, the chaos wrought by the revolutionary avalanche, by the revolutionary inability to stop revolution, opened the way to despotism vastly greater than that of the monarchy. The dream of popular participation gave way to the reality of popular apathy, troubled only by economic tremors. A supposedly liberating experience convinced large numbers of French that only absolute government and strong administration could produce stability and maintain it. *Also* that government and administrators, always in quest of more order, efficiency, and justice, could and should be challenged in the name of more perfect order, efficiency, and justice. Hence the schizophrenic French attachment to both authoritarianism and rebellion.

The aggressive defensiveness of the Revolution involved war, both civil and foreign. The Franco-French war shows little sign of abating. The attractions of foreign war waned more quickly, but they should not be minimized. War waged for glory and profit had always been popular. Napoleon showed that it could be made to pay, built a brilliant career on it, and left behind an enduring fascination with military glory. Militarism and the glorification of military virtues from childhood on dimmed only in the twentieth century.

So the Revolution did not achieve all it set out to achieve. Indeed, like the men who marched off to the Hundred Years' War, the French of 1789 could scarcely be expected to know how finely and how long the Mixmaster of revolution would go on grinding.

Solé knows that. He knows that there was a France that lived the Revolution and a France that (as the Abbé Sieyès said) simply survived it. He acknowledges the difference between words and deeds, between those who do and those who have things done to them. He misses neither the meanness of great occasions nor the greatness of horrid enterprises. His book is informed and up-to-date, his bibliography is a treasure trove, his views are clear, his approach is impartial (and when he is partial he is straightforward), his writing is a pleasure to read. And now, here is his book to be read.

QUESTIONS
OF THE
FRENCH REVOLUTION

INTRODUCTION

For historians today, the French Revolution isn't quite what it used to be. For a long time they had an appealing analysis of the great event of 1789. This major episode in the rise of the bourgeoisie of the Western world originated with the gradual weakening of the feudal aristocracy as a result of the development of capitalism. The flowering of Enlightenment thought was the intellectual reflection of these economic and social changes, with the crisis of the *ancien régime* monarchy the consequence of its inability to deal with them.

The Revolution of 1789 was thus viewed as the victory of the bourgeoisie, backed by the common people, after imprudent provocation by the aristocracy. The resulting new order at first reflected its dual origins, but was soon forced to cope with both the spread of the revolutionary spirit and clashes with the rest of Europe. A second French Revolution therefore began in 1792, and led to the proclamation of the Republic, the dictatorship by the Committee of Public Safety, and the Terror. The fall of Robespierre left the ruling bourgeoisie unable to form a stable political system until Napoleon's 1799 coup d'état.

Bonaparte was, however, able to build new structures on the foundations laid by the Revolution, which had destroyed the old corporative society. In a world divided between the spread of revolutionary ideas and reactionary ones, the France of liberty and equality offered to the peoples of the world the image of their future.[1]

These views, to which most of the general public still subscribes, are part of a tradition favorable to the Revolution. Liberals and socialists alike have continually viewed it as both necessary and beneficial. Such was the opinion, from the start, of Barnave and Madame de Staël. Under the Restoration, Mignet, Thiers, and Guizot saw the events of 1789 as the foundation of the inevitable ascendancy of the bourgeoisie.

Romantic historians, such as Michelet, added to this image the popular and national dimensions of the Revolution. During the Third Republic, this epic transfiguration led directly to Aulard's interpretation, which identified the history of the French Revolution with the continuing growth of democratic ideas in the nineteenth century.

These liberal, and later republican, views were eventually joined by the socialist interpretation, which was more favorable to the Jacobins and more tolerant of the exigencies of the Terror. At the turn of the century, Jaurès added Marxist theories concerning the importance of economic and social phenomena to these political analyses.

Sanctioned by the Sorbonne and spread by textbooks, the detailed and stirring saga of the revolutionary events of 1789 to 1794 dominated France's historical consciousness for the first half of the twentieth century. How many readers of Mathiez would not identify with Saint-Just or Robespierre? After 1917, or even more after World War II, how many people viewed the Russian revolution and its inevitable universal triumph as the long-awaited fulfillment of the prophetic promises of 1793?

All of which goes to show how profoundly these deeply ingrained mental habits have been shaken by the historiographic reevaluation that is now taking place.

We are indebted, above all, to English and American researchers for providing a totally new perspective during the last twenty years on the origins, the course, and the outcome of the Revolution. The dynamism of university departments in the United States and Great Britain is now bearing fruit in these as in other disciplines. To take offense for narrowly nationalistic reasons would be foolish.[2]

For a long time the only fresh perspective on the French Revolution was the theory that it was one episode in a vast upheaval that shook aristocratic societies in countries of European culture on both sides of the Atlantic toward the end of the eighteenth century. A more fruitful approach was the frontal assault led by Alfred Cobban, starting in 1955, against the classic interpretation of 1789. This English historian refused to characterize as "bourgeois" a revolution that was never led by representatives of mercantile or industrial capitalism. He argued, furthermore, that the major division throughout the entire revolution was not between the bourgeoisie on one hand and the aristocracy or the lower classes on the other, but rather between the countryside and the city.[3]

The wealth of studies and theories that have poured in from across the Channel and the Atlantic in the last twenty years has totally reshaped our understanding of the events that occurred in France between 1787 and 1799. We no longer believe, for example, in the image of a decadent and backward-looking "feudal" nobility, nor in a long struggle waged against it by an "enlightened" bourgeoisie. We have learned to see the links between the urban and rural popular uprisings of the revolutionary period and long-standing traditions of dissent and revolt under the *ancien régime*. We have become skeptical about both the reformist nature of the French monarchy and the reactionary character of the aristocracy during the eighteenth century.[4]

Today, we realize more clearly that the groups responsible for the major revolutionary episodes that began in 1789 were in the minority, and that they often encountered strong opposition in many areas of the country. Indeed, the more radical the Revolution became, the more enemies it made, and ultimately the masses were mobilized as much against it as for it. Viewed from this perspective, it is the counterrevolution, along with the reactions it provoked, that seems to constitute the major political event of the revolutionary period.

The leaders of the counterrevolution were plunged into a general crisis that they had in large part created and over which they could exercise only partial control at the cost of often indiscriminate violence. Their inability to guide the Revolution into lawful, constitutional channels led to the establishment of a dictatorship by Napoleon. Molded even more by this fragmentation of power than by the principles of 1789, he was ever mindful, in his authoritarian reshaping of the government, of the struggle against enemies from both within and without that originated in the period of the Terror.[5]

Thus viewed without prejudices, the revolutionary period seems less the glorious inception of a new order than the most wrenching and chaotic sort of civil war. Indeed, this objective observation has been put forth in more polemical terms by certain schools of historiography that have been hostile to the Revolution from the outset. They have denounced it, by turns, as avoidable and destructive. Hence, on the first point, the convenient hypothesis, advanced early on by Rivarol and Barruel, of a factional or Masonic plot. This conspiracy theory, part of a universally prevalent political mythology, resurfaced at the beginning of this century, when Augustin Cochin saw the mechanistic influence of the intellectual societies as the source of the revolutionary discourse and activities that dominated France from 1788 to 1794.[6]

The major critique of the Revolution, however, is to be found in the writings of Taine between 1876 and 1893. The author of *The Origins of Contemporary France* simultaneously pilloried popular anarchy and the Jacobin and Napoleonic dictatorships. More a biologist in some ways than a sociologist, this pessimist believed that the flaws of the *ancien régime* led inevitably to its downfall and the regrettable foundation of the modern state.[7] Not all of his analysis was taken up by his followers, who taught veneration for monarchy to the likes of *L'Action Française*. Among them, Gaxotte contrasted the achievements of the fading royalty with the stupidity of the "communistic" system of 1793.[8]

It is no accident that these distortions are being echoed in today's newspapers and television programs. Despite its brief political victory in 1981, the left has relinquished its long-standing dominance over the French intellectual scene. Its traditional worship of the Revolution is, inevitably, backfiring. And with sensitivities heightened around the time of the bicentennial, many people speak of the de-Christianizing and terrorist activities of the 1790s in the tones of a Joseph de Maistre taking on Satan.

Disillusionment over the lackluster or horrific outcomes of twentieth-century revolutions makes this task even easier. Yet it would be wrong to use the recent research on the Revolution of 1789 indiscriminately for this purpose. Scratching the surface of the icon has only made its grandeur and importance shine forth more brightly, since for better or for worse, a good part of our ideological divisions and our political aspirations were born in that astonishing decade.

Rather than dwell on fruitless disputes, it would be useful to indicate how far our knowledge about this period has progressed in a short time. Such are the welcome results of research enriched by the efforts of many historians. The public at large knows them mainly for their more or less heated disputes, which in France have set supporters of the traditional interpretation, linked in one way or another to Marxism, against François Furet and his associates. The author of *Penser la Révolution française* has done more than spread the theories of Cobban and his successors. On the basis of his extensive knowledge of nineteenth- and twentieth-century historiography, he calls for us to stop either venerating or vilifying 1789.[9]

Following the lead of Tocqueville's attempt to conceptualize the French Revolution as a phenomenon embodying both continuity and discontinuity,[10] he reaps the fruits of the rich crop of new interpretations by historians of the English-speaking world over the last two decades. Relatively unscathed by the ideological traditions of the struggle between communism and its adversaries, they have been more sensitive than we to the significance of happenstance and regional variations, the importance of the popular counterrevolution, and the large numbers of individuals and groups disillusioned with the Revolution.

This type of reevaluation, at once more concrete, individual, and attentive to the multiple contradictions of a society that was far from the influence of the great Parisian stage, seems more useful than our usual discussions of the Revolution as a class phenomenon or debates over the origins of "revolutionary discourse." Such research has nothing in common with current attempts by those who are eager to forget the Revolution and bury it once and for all. As alive as ever, this period still gives rise to scholarly debates that show how rich and lively the field remains.

This book is meant to summarize these debates. Its sole aim is to spread information, findings, and theories that are now generally available only in works intended for specialists. On the occasion of the celebration of the bicentennial, objective information seems more important than hollow polemics, for our understanding of the Revolution cannot be enhanced by sweeping pronouncements or ideological confrontations. This modest contribution to the dissemination of recent studies of the Revolution is intended to show their convergence. Brought down from its mythic pedestal and restored to its complex reality, the French Revolution is all the more interesting to those who seek a better understanding of one of the major sources of modern history.

UNDERLYING CAUSES?

1. A TRIUMPH
OF THE ENLIGHTENMENT?

The theory of the intellectual origins of the French Revolution shared by historians from Barruel to Tocqueville to Mathiez has been significantly revised since Daniel Mornet's pioneering study of 1933.[1] French sociocultural historians have recently contributed to this reinterpretation. We may wonder, as they do, whether the ideas of the philosophes, *linked as they were with modes of thought characteristic of the elites, had penetrated the mentality of the French people on the eve of 1789. One might also question the revolutionary nature of these ideas. Were they the source of the psychological upheaval that hastened the downfall of the* ancien régime?

WAS ENLIGHTENMENT THOUGHT AN INTEGRAL PART
OF THE FRENCH MENTALITY
ON THE EVE OF THE REVOLUTION?

This is doubtful, and we tend to agree with Donald Sutherland's conclusion that its influence on eighteenth-century society was very limited.[2] Even among the minority capable of absorbing these ideas, professional, religious, and historical issues remained the major cultural preoccupations. Both in the provinces and in Paris, religious works were more widely read than those of the *philosophes*. As for the intellectual tastes of the popular classes, they inclined rather to the supernatural, the amazing, and the fantastic. The educated nobility was the only group within the population capable of understanding and supporting Enlightenment philosophy, and it did so. It was to this group, for the most part, that the great writers of the eighteenth century owed their success. The *Encyclopédie* was originally an aristocratic enterprise. It was the aristocratic members of the provincial *parlements* who were the first to encourage these new intellectual forays.

Until the eve of the Revolution, most of the population, bourgeois as well as popular class, remained untouched by Enlightenment philosophy, which had little to do with its concrete concerns. The Catholic religion remained, for the most part, the dominant influence in the lives of such people. It would be correct only to say that the small minority that led the revolutionaries of 1789 were the utilitarian and desacrilizing inheritors of eighteenth-century philosophy. This philosophy did indeed triumph in the new order, thanks to the enlightened elite that founded a liberal and representative regime. But the ideals of the country as a legal entity bore little resemblance to the realities of the country as it actually was.

A number of recent studies seem to confirm this apparent paradox. They show how little the *philosophes* influenced the profoundly conservative bourgeoisie, right up to the spring of 1789, and indicate that the *philosophes'* social impact was limited to the educated portion of the aristocracy.[3] It is misleading, in this regard, to view their critical stance as an attack on the principle of this class's dominant position. Although the salons, the academies, and the intellectual establishment as a whole had been won over to the new philosophy, public opinion remained generally untouched by it, if not hostile toward it. Focusing only on the Parisian facade of French life, historians have for too long considered it representative of the entire nation which, in the provinces, remained very traditionalist.[4]

Daniel Mornet realized this in 1928, when he pointed out the reactionary resistance of many segments of the aristocracy, the bourgeoisie, and the popular classes to the enlightened snobbery of the worldly and the great.[5] Paying little heed to Enlightenment thought, they stuck to the catechism. Unconcerned with the new ideas, they respected and reproduced familial and patriarchal traditions.

How insignificant eighteenth-century philosophy, which reached only a few thousand readers, seems as a social phenomenon in comparison with the weight of the past! An elite minority pitted logic and reason against popular superstitions that it scorned but could not destroy. These superstitions, entrenched, for example, in rural folklore and tacitly condoned by the church, constituted the essence of the country's culture. The rationalism of the *philosophes* was thus first and foremost an assault on the views of the majority of the French people. It was forced to admit, in the *Encyclopédie*, that it was unable to make any profound changes. Despite its "vigilant mobilization" against entrenched attitudes, the philosophical movement remained, on the eve of the Revolution, an elitist utopia whose "complacent and self-congratulatory optimism" should not obscure the narrowness of its social base.[6]

The *cahiers* of 1789 reflect this cultural heterogeneity and the negligible impact, in quantitative terms, of Enlightenment thought. The over-whelming majority of the French remained untouched by it within their parishes. It was traditional institutions more than the new rationalism that molded their political attitudes. Far from inspiring them to seek general renewal, these encouraged them to fall back on timeworn customs. Averse to radicalism and highly conservative, such was apparently the character of the French people at the time when its leaders were about to plunge it into the greatest of its revolutions. Ill-equipped to initiate or even foresee it, the people found it, for this very reason, extremely difficult to accept. Its leaders, from the summer of 1789 on, were always aware of the gap separating them from a "silent majority" that could neither comprehend nor share their programs or their principles. Throughout its course, the Revolution was never able to bridge this psychological chasm between the French people and its would-be representatives.[7]

The leaders' slighting of the deeply religious character of the people was another source of this split. Louis XVI's France allowed only a very limited aristocratic and intellectual elite the luxury and possibility of nonbelief. Both in the cities and the countryside, the religious faith of the bourgeois and popular classes remained intact. Although less fervent than it might have been under the preceding reign, it was barely scratched by the influence of the *philosophes*. We know that the new philosophy hardly reached the masses, whose need for faith, as evidencd by the regularity of its expression, remained constant. Ceremonies and processions were still their most popular entertainments, fostering social cohesiveness under the guiding hand of the clergy. Young people and the populace as a whole flocked to a Catholic faith that retained a surprising vitality in late-eighteenth-century France. Religion was respected and believers were legion, while Voltaire had less of a following than was once believed. This religious identity was, for the majority of the populace, an element of their basic traditionalism. The success of attempts at so-called secularization, including some by the clergy, should not be overestimated. To forget that the French Revolution involved a nation resolutely opposed to the de-Christianizing trends of the day is to misunderstand it totally. The Abbé Grégoire, future member of the Convention and head of the Constitutional Church, was no friend of the *philosophes*, but rather a disciple of Saint Paul. In Lorraine, he had presided over one of the parishes that were so central to the life of the people. Rooted in the sacraments, the conformity of the humble was echoed by that of the many prominent personages who, when faced with death, for example, abandoned the "old Baroque sensibility" to write poignantly mystical professions of faith.[8]

Describing certain areas of Provence in the century of the *philosophes*, Michel Vovelle has discerned a pattern of secularization of the popular mentality after 1750. It would be a mistake to extrapolate from this to the rest of France and its people. Marseilles does not explain Strasbourg, any more than an urban elite can serve as a model for the analysis of the primarily rural masses. Before as well as after 1789, and for a long time thereafter, popular faith was a decisive component of the complex mixture that constituted the French mentality.[9]

Historians of eighteenth-century French Catholicism certainly find rifts but no fundamental crisis. Beyond the philosophical verbiage, they discover much rigor and a great deal of militancy. The conflict between the faithful and the *philosophes* is less significant in this regard than the surprising success of the religious offensive. Preaching by parish priests, work by nuns, and parish proselytizing were all part of a profound Christianizing trend. Always spectacular and filled with pathos, these last remained extremely popular. In Louis XVI's France, the jubilee year of 1776 would again see a triumph of piety. The conversion of non-believers and the strengthening of religious spirit were also characteristic of the era of the *philosophes*. The book market gives evidence of this, dominated as it was on the eve of 1789 by the reprinting of religious works in the hundreds of thousands. These down-to-earth works nourished a simple and unaffected piety that was mindful of official responsibilities and inspired by the Holy Scripture, and concerned with both the inner and the outer life. More than a secularization of faith, the eighteenth century saw a secularization of sainthood. "In the shadow of the new churches" chapels flourished. The kingdom embodied a whole geography and sociology of the sacred. These pious traditions were shaken by a revolution that was fiercely opposed by many of the faithful, who were certainly in the majority in most of the rural areas and among women. Alongside the conformist masses, who undoubtedly outnumbered the nonobserving and the "enlightened" Catholics, the driving force of this national piety was the new intensity of religious fervor, most pronounced among the common people, but rich and diverse and growing more and more powerful as 1789 approached. Discreet and silent, this often overlooked upsurge was to make the counterrevolution the most important event of the French Revolution.[10]

By comparison, in quantitative terms the ideas of the *philosophes*, which lacked cohesiveness, true daring, and an authentic audience, seemed to have little impact on the eve of 1789,[11] when the irrationalism of the occultists gained more adherents than Enlightenment rationalism. The latter addressed only the aristocratic values of a culture opposed to the traditionalist aspirations of the immense majority of the French people, who were totally indifferent, for example, to the prestige of free thinking.[12] The often highly elitist membership of the Masonic lodges confirms this schism, characteristic of French history, between enlightened society and society in general. It has perhaps never been so pronounced as it was just before the Revolution.[13]

Toulouse, then, was undoubtedly not the only center of religious zealotry opposed to the spread of the lewd "enlightened" literature that was bent on destroying respect for the monarchy and religion.[14] And the association of professional historians, for whom 1789 represented the end of a world, was probably not the only intellectual group to feel profoundly alienated from the superficial, declamatory, and duplicitous philosophers of the "Enlightenment."[15] D'Alembert, who was in a sense their leader, was justified in echoing with dismay his good friend Frederick II's judgment that "France, with all its touted philosophers, is one of the most superstitious and least advanced nations in Europe."[16]

WAS ENLIGHTENMENT THOUGHT REVOLUTIONARY?

The traditional ideology of the *ancien régime* was complex and contradictory. It regarded the kingdom as composed not of individual subjects, but of different groups, each with its own privileges. Royal power, at the apex of the state, constituted the only unifying element in this disparate whole. The absolutism of the monarchy was the outgrowth of this situation and was sanctioned by its religious nature and sacred character.

Its institutional structure rested on a juridical pyramid that assigned everyone a rank, defining claims within a hierarchical system. The king was absolute only insofar as he recognized countless privileges, and his power remained limited by their reclamation. The recent development of administrative centralization, while it reinforced royal authority, was often at odds with the corporative bases of the society on which the monarchy rested.

It was in this context that the *philosophes* became part of the ideological constellation of the French elite. They opposed the monarchical tradition on a certain number of essential points, supporting the secularization and rationalization of world views and of the social order and the challenging of all privileges. A whole sector of the *ancien régime* elite enthusiastically embraced the ideas of the *philosophes* with little awareness of this apparent contradiction.

These sophisticated elements in the ruling class, present in all the dominant sectors of the state, were particularly well represented within its bureaucracy. They were thirsty for concepts of reason and natural law that could be used to justify the tasks of standardization and the eradication of privileges. Turgot's momentary success, early in Louis XVI's reign, symbolized this meeting of minds. His successors, no less reform-minded than he, were unable to find an ideological frame of reference anywhere but in the ideas of the *philosophes*, which had already gained a secure following at the heart of the *ancien régime* well before the explosion of 1789. Members of the *parlements*, likewise, defended their privileges in the name of a universally adopted "philosophical" vocabulary.

Two opposing ideologies thus coexisted without apparent contradiction in the French political system on the eve of the Revolution. The one put forth by the *philosophes* competed on equal footing with the traditional monarchical one. This contrast between ideological inconsistency and political stability could have lasted a long time, as it did in England. The former was not, in itself, a factor in revolutionary upheaval.[1]

This analysis by William Sewell, Jr., seems to be confirmed by the equally paradoxical role that the foremost scholars attribute to French public opinion of the late *ancien régime*. They reject the notion that the elite's progressive adherence to Enlightenment thought was a decisive element in the political crisis that broke out starting in 1787. The upsurge in informed criticism did not in any way rock the traditional monarchical order until the last minute. The groups that could have been affected by it, and which were most concerned with the public interest, were favorably treated by the ruling administration, which indeed could not see healthy, reformist thought as a revolutionary threat.[2]

On the question of tolerance of Protestants, for example, the *parlements* had by 1770 been converted to the ideas of the *philosophes*. On this point and others, the *philosophes* had won over the privileged aristocracy rather than conveyed some hypothetical bourgeois challenge to them.[3] It might even be said that in the face of the pronounced decline in the number of French lawyers who were political theorists, the eighteenth century replaced them, little by little, in the highest state circles, with Montesquieu and his disciples. Far from upsetting the traditional order, their prestige tended rather to reinforce it.[4]

By 1971, Robert Darnton considered the standard theory associating Enlightenment thought with revolutionary ideology outmoded.[5] He observed that the elitism of Enlightenment thought was by no means favorable to the subversion of society, but rather that it supported a program of liberal reforms that would preserve the hierarchy, not destroy it. D'Alembert admired clear distinctions of rank and felt that superiority conferred by birth should be respected. Voltaire, in his *Philosophical Dictionary*, associated the *philosophes* with "privileged souls" opposed to the mentality of the "bourgeois families." Wholly aristocratic, as Richet has shown,[6] eighteenth-century liberalism made no claim to be an adversary of the seignioral and monarchical regime.

Concentrating only on attacks directed against Enlightenment philosophy and its practitioners, a whole historiographical tradition has wrongly reduced them to a sort of political party rising up against the "feudal" royalty. This anachronism, which attributes intellectual origins to the French Revolution, is itself the product of the events of 1789 and the search for theoretical justifications that are to a greater or lesser degree mythical. It is difficult to discern, in the cultural milieu shared by the *philosophes*, diverse ideologies that would have set hypothetical supporters of a "rising bourgeoisie" against the defenders of a "dominant nobility."[7]

The liberalism of the eighteenth century was the common property of the entire elite that, before 1789, envisioned for it no applications outside the context of the traditional order. Attributing a revolutionary calling to the thought of the *philosophes* is a throwback to an approach that has been rejected by the majority of historians who study ideas and society. They have long realized that the surest way to misunderstand the philosophers of the Enlightenment is to study them in relation to the Revolution that followed them. Indifferent to the new preoccupations of the latter, and imbued with monarchical conservatism and conformism, the *philosophes* could not have paved the way for revolution.[8]

Daniel Roche has demonstrated this with regard to the academies of provincial France.[9] He has described a local intellectual elite steeped in notions of public service, civic participation, and social integration. The nobility played its role within this urban assemblage that included the clergy, lawyers, and doctors, but not businessmen. The outlook of these societies was neither aristocratic nor bourgeois, but rather administrative and utilitarian, within the framework of a traditional order in need of rational management—something which the royal bureaucracy, incidentally, also attempted to provide. This interpretation is a total departure from the prevailing view formerly held by historians of the "bourgeois" *philosophes*. It views the ideas of the *philosophes* as the work of an exclusive group that was perfectly integrated into the established hierarchy. Theirs was an ideology of modernization, not of revolution. Their political views reflected rather than contested absolutist norms. It thus seems questionable to link the collapse of the *ancien régime* monarchy with the spread of Enlightenment discourse, which in itself contained nothing threatening to the traditional order. So we must look elsewhere for the sources of the revolutionary cataclysm.[10]

As Mounier wisely pointed out in 1801, neither the *philosophes* nor their readers were responsible for it. The lawyers who in every jurisdiction in the kingdom played an important role during the prerevolutionary crisis, no doubt resembled for the most part those of the Béarn, who were intelligent, reform-minded, and staunch supporters of the "conservative liberalism of a society of elites." The more they supported the spread of Enlightenment thought, the more hesitant they were, in general, about the Revolution.[11] Panckoucke, an educated book-dealer who was responsible for and profited from the publication of the *Encyclopédie*, viewed the upheaval of 1789 primarily as "a collapse of established values." The new ideological and cultural radicalism was not at all to the taste of this reformer. Having helped to shape the *philosophes'* audience, he had not anticipated the direction the infernal machine he had helped set in motion would take. Hume, moreover, like Montesquieu and Gibbon, believed that the French monarchy of the *ancien régime* was the most favorable society for men of letters that history had ever seen.[12]

Even on the ideological level, the Revolution of 1789 resulted more from the political experience acquired during the two years that preceded it than from the influence of undemocratic, highly monarchical, philosophical writings. Their aim was to reconstruct the human spirit, not the government. Taken out of its moderate ideological context, the vocabulary of the *philosophes* was exploited by revolutionaries who changed its meaning. The conditions and results of this process were impossible to predict in the early 1780s and in some cases even in the spring of 1789.[13]

Uninterested in utopian fantasies, the critical and rationalist spirit of the eighteenth century hardly lent itself to the fanatical excesses that characterized its end. Late in Louis XV's reign and during Louis XVI's time it produced, in Linguet, an intelligent advocate of a strong state and an enemy of destructive revolution. This nonconformist philosopher, who died on the scaffold in 1794, shared in general the utilitarian, humanitarian, and reformist ideas of the *philosophes*. These coexisted, in him, with an extremely traditional conception of political order.[14]

The encyclopedists, contrary to the opinion of Burke, Taine, and Cochin, were by no means precursors of Jacobinism. Those who survived the *ancien régime* for the most part proved, under the Terror, to be moderates strongly opposed to the revolutionary frenzy. Many suffered directly for this or resisted courageously. Naigeon, a friend of Diderot's for the last twenty years of his life, was contemptuous of the Committee of Public Safety and considered Robespierre worse than Nero.[15]

Then there is the myth of a Holbachian coterie spreading this philosophical radicalism in prerevolutionary Paris. According to Barruel, the anti-Christian Baron Holbach, along with his educated friends, was the center of a veritable political conspiracy. This counterrevolutionary fabrication, with its Rousseauian overtones, has been dutifully repeated by historians from Tocqueville to Naville. According to them, the secret influence of deeply committed atheists set the stage for the downfall of the monarchy. Scholars today are unable to reconcile this mysterious conspiracy with the totally apolitical speculations of the harmless intellectuals who made up this supposed sect.[16] Those who lived long enough to see the Revolution that was attributed to them were for the most part horrified by its outcome. The materialist thinkers of the eighteenth century were firmly rooted in the traditional state. They disliked the "vulgar masses" and did not understand violence. Robespierre, who hated them, was correct in thinking that the Revolution had been accomplished without and even despite them.[17]

The Freemasons, who have sometimes, since Barruel, been credited with laying the ideological groundwork for the 1789 conflagration, would have been prevented from doing so by the profoundly conformist tendencies of their elitist membership. The mythology of the secret societies, based on belated denunciations by administrations late in the *ancien régime*, was invented to account for the revolutionary upheaval that could not be explained by anything but some unfathomable conspiracy. Divided and complex, the Masonic brotherhood was basically a social organization that could not have played this political role. Gerard Gayot has depicted the majority of its members as "taken aback, speechless or hostile" to the "awesome invasion of democracy in 1789." For their activities were, above all, an expression of the eighteenth-century elite's penchant for joining associations. They never intended to disrupt either the state or religion. Ambivalent toward the *philosophes*, often insensitive to the idea of equality, the fifty thousand Frenchmen who joined lodges under Louis XVI in no way contributed to his fall. They had organized in order to prosper within the framework of the traditional monarchy. In 1790, the Social Contract Lodge of Paris denounced the social struggles to come. Dispersed by the Revolution, its members were not so much its authors as its victims. They had dreamt of peace and harmony, not civil war. In Provence, for example, the Masonic lodges had simply been superimposed on the old network of the brotherhoods of penitents. The ways in which the France of the *ancien régime* became secularized and bourgeois had nothing to do with its political collapse. And Masonic ideology foreshadowed the future republican slogans less clearly than did Fénelon in his *Télémaque*.[18]

Rousseau's thought offers a final example of the ambiguous and ultimately innocuous character of Enlightenment philosophy in the sociopolitical realm. Starting in the 1760s, Jean-Jacques's influence contributed above all to the formation of the pre-Romantic sensibility, which was virtuous, no doubt, but above all irrationalist and maudlin. Far from posing the questions addressed by the Revolution and undermining the existing order, Rousseau, who favored neither science nor modernity, was incapable of proposing a new one. The aristocrats took up his ideas enthusiastically in their struggle against the Revolution in the early 1790s. All of which shows the extent to which Rousseauian thought had become contradictory and incoherent. Inevitably invoked during the Revolution, Jean-Jacques had neither sought nor caused it, and for good reason. His memory was used, successively, by the different parties, and served the petty nobility of the Constituent Assembly as well as the Thermidorean enemies of anarchy. These ambiguities crop up again today in depictions of Rousseau as a precursor of totalitarianism or, on the contrary, as the fierce apostle of liberty. What they have in common is that they ignore the real Jean-Jacques, in his complexity and within the bounds of his historical experience, who was fortunate enough to die unaware of what others were to make of his ideas.[19]

DID A REVOLUTIONARY MENTALITY EXIST ON THE EVE OF 1789?

This seems unlikely, given that until around 1787 public opinion was still very unpoliticized and much more concerned with other subjects. Moreover, because it was so deeply divided, its impatience with the inability of the government to keep pace with social developments failed to crystallize into any particular grievances. Even the English model, which had long been highly regarded, was no longer universally admired after the serious defeat inflicted on British institutions by the American Revolution.[1]

Robert Darnton has studied the only intellectual circles that fostered a revolutionary mentality. The "gutter Rousseaus" of Louis XVI's France took over the *provocateurs'* role previously occupied by the Enlightenment *philosophes* who had been so perfectly integrated into the existing order. These literary bohemians produced pamphlets that spoke more directly to the public than the great writers had and did more to undermine its certainties and habits.

Alongside the pensioners and those who benefited in different capacities from official patronage and its charity, prerevolutionary Paris teemed with literary people far removed from the world of the courtiers. These "literary insurrectionists," denounced by D'Alembert as hostile to the establishment, were described by Mallet du Pan as mistaking their "facility for talent" and dying of starvation or being reduced to begging when they were unable to produce and sell their pamphlets. Voltaire placed these "poor hacks," eager provincials who flooded Paris, on a rung below prostitutes. Under the National Convention, they were often to be found presiding over its deliberations and its bloodiest actions.

Before coming into their glory, they had vegetated for a long time, seething with hatred for the tyranny of the aristocrats who dominated the realm of letters. Marat, Brissot, and Cara thus became revolutionaries and Jacobins thanks to resentment born in the "depths of the intellectual dregs" in which they stagnated. Confronted with a cultural and literary system ruled by privilege, these drifting lampooners and schemers shared the difficult existence of the marginals and the displaced, at the opposite pole from those fortunate souls who monopolized the salons. Their egalitarianism was spawned by bitter failure, their aggressivity bent on wreaking vengeance on a system that had reduced them to "poverty and degradation." Before being destroyed by the Revolution, "high society" was undercut by the scatological tracts and "scurrilous libel" that issued from this milieu, whose sociopolitical influence was much more pernicious than that of the *philosphes*. This rabble was raised to power in journalism and government by the events of 1789 and given the opportunity to satisfy some of its appetites.[2]

Brissot, future leader of the Girondins, had served as a police informer under Louis XVI.[3] The clandestine clique of lampooners and pamphleteers had likewise kept a public that was eager to learn of the alleged orgies of Marie-Antoinette and her prelates supplied with pornographic works. The revolutionary explosion that spewed from this literary cesspool retained its crude diatribes against the monarchy and the church. Masters of defamation, these founders of a counterculture were calling for a cultural revolution against the *ancien régime* that soon materialized.[4] A whole network of drifting propagandists, circulating on the fringes of society, had helped set off their intellectual time bomb. Their books, secretly passed from hand to hand and largely forgotten today, blackened the most august of reputations. In them, more than in the tomes of the *Encyclopédie*, are to be found the roots of the psychological crisis that attacked the "absolute" monarchy in the last twenty years of its existence.[5]

This ideological assault had been led not by the leaders of the Enlightenment, but by the motley crew of "literary Bohemians" beneath them. It was taken up, during the 1770s, by those "insurrectionary" journalists who politicized and radicalized theater criticism. From Fréron to Grimm and La Harpe the established conservative intellectuals were horrified by the insolent, vulgar, and uncouth manner of the philistines who flocked around Mercier. Along with Linguet and others, in his *Parisian Tableau* he shocked official France with his decadence. By 1789, this preoccupation with uncovering the vices of the great became the guiding principle of revolutionary journalism. Marat, long a nonpracticing physician and a failed writer who placed himself above Lavoisier and Newton, had the audacity to claim, in his moment of triumph in January 1793, that he had plumbed all the workings of the human mind on the subjects of morality, philosophy, and politics and culled the best from them all." This demagogue, in his histrionic megalomania, was accurately summing up the immensity of the ambitions and aspirations of his ilk.[6]

Early in his unfinished fragments on the course of the Revolution, Tocqueville evokes the "violent and uncertain agitation of the human spirit" that characterized its beginnings. He depicts the intelligentsia of Europe as a whole as being in the grip not of philosophical illumination, but of "irregular, incoherent, and bizarre movements." He saw in this the "symptoms of a new and extraordinary malady that would have terrified contemporary witnesses if they had been able to understand it." A mixture of idealistic optimism about the future of humanity and exaggerated condemnation of the corruption of contemporary society, of disgust with the present and vague yearning for total change, constituted, in fact, the essence of the revolutionary mentality among many intellectuals. Present in Louis XVI's France as in the rest of the Western world, this yearning explains the popularity of secret societies and the taste for the supernatural that had a much stronger impact at the time than the heritage of the *philosophes*. On the eve of 1789 occultists and visionaries came closer than they to satisfying the widespread demand for absolute regeneration. Dreams, illusions, enthusiasm for the marvelous and the inexplicable, and the delirium of mystical imaginations account for the Revolution more than rational calculations. According to the author of *The Ancien Régime and the Revolution*, a decidedly apocalyptic perspective ("the voice of John crying out in the wilderness that a new day was at hand") accounts for the malaise of many people who, unjustifiably, found their condition "unbearable," and sought to escape it by means of a movement that was as yet undefined. "The year 1787" gave this passion "a precise goal" and a reason for action. To judge from this passage, the Revolution was born not of the secular, objective evolution of ideas, but of the sudden politicization of over-whelming anxiety.[7]

Historians often underestimate the irrational roots of 1789, although they were demonstrated long ago. The popularity in Paris in the 1780s of the practice of healing by "animal magnetism," introduced by the Austrian doctor Mesmer, is a case in point. This lucrative charlatanism became a way to crystallize and popularize aspirations toward social renewal. A canny application of fashionable science to the contemporary taste for the invisible and the imaginary, Mesmerism prospered thanks to the Society for Universal Harmony, supported by the Lyons lawyer Bergasse and the Strasbourg banker Kornmann. It reinforced the political concerns of the literary bohemians in opposing the privileged profes-sionals of the government-backed academies. In the course of this new struggle, radical writers such as Brissot, Marat, and Cara attacked the dominant society from a perspective based not on nature or reason, but on their opposite. In this atmosphere many future revolutionaries de-voted more energy to their enthusiasm for Mesmer than to plans for rebuilding their country on more lucid bases. The end of the *ancien régime* was engineered by men driven, like Cagliostro and Mesmer, not by the ideas of the *philosophes*, but by visions of an earthly paradise.[8] Saint-Martin, who embodied the prerevolutionary occultist tendencies, remained a staunch believer in the "divine rupture" that occurred in 1789. He saw in this manifestation of recovered energy a premonition of the "reintegration" he favored.[9]

Some viewed the revolutionary events as confirmation of their reli-gious aspirations. In Paris in 1780, the Jansenist lawyer Lepaige carefully recorded the crucifixion ceremonies of his sect of convulsionaries. This ancient system of prophecy thus coexisted with new definitions, hardly more serious, of human happiness. On the eve of 1789, the former, which sympathized with Mesmerism, confined itself to awaiting the imminent annunciation of colossal disasters, but in 1792 in Lyons it spawned a group that linked these with the course of the Revolution.[10] Prophetesses like Suzette Labrousse and Catherine Théot saw in them, on the contrary, the fulfillment of promises of regeneration. Living evi-dence of the persistence in eighteenth-century France of millenarianism, these two women had calmly awaited this inevitable event. After it occurred, Suzette left for Rome, as we know, to explain it to the pope, whereas Catherine applied the traditions of popular piety to the celebration of Robespierre's regime.[11]

The elite certainly had more specific things to worry about. The pre-revolutionary Freemasons, for example, have been credited with a system of values that was already democratic, as shown, in particular, by the names of the lodges, which often vaunted aspirations toward patriotism, liberty, and equality. The discussions held there lent a clearly "progressive" flavor to the socializing of the brothers. Keith Baker even goes so far as to see in their ideology and structure the direct antecedents of the revolutionary clubs and societies.[12]

The American Revolution provided powerful support for this tendency. The extent of its influence throughout the intellectual community of Europe has been well documented, and France was no exception. In 1784, French readers made a great success of Crèvecoeur's *Lettres*, which were dedicated to La Fayette and depicted the American farmer as the archetype of the new man freed of the chains of despotism and aristocracy. This naively subversive and vaguely Rousseauian ideology slipped into a kingdom that had been instrumental in the birth of the new republic, and which celebrated, with Franklin, the creation of a country that was at long last free and virtuous. This wave of approval had no truly decisive political influence. But it impelled many to view the United States as a laboratory for social renewal at a time when this view held great appeal. The utopian longing so dear to such men as Turgot and Condorcet could thus be nourished at a distant but recent source.[13]

But we may well wonder whether its presence among the *philosophes* was a manifestation of rationalism or its opposite. It was accompanied by an anguished outcry over the frightening death sentence hanging over a society threatened by inevitable demographic decline. The Revolution was in this sense an irrational reaction by some of its harbingers to an imaginary and therefore all the more dreaded danger. This dynamic view animates the pages Diderot added in the 1770s to Raynal's *Histoire*, which contrasts the happiness and virtue of savages threatened by European expansion with the baseness of the powerful, the clergy and the colonizers. These declamations reached their height in a program of reforms addressed to Louis XVI, which denounced, willy-nilly, the greed of courtiers and those who were bilking the country. These frenetic outbursts, heralds of a desirable liberation, spoke to the passions more than to reason. Preaching disrespect and antagonism to tyranny, they were appeals to enthusiasm and energy, and were not intended to be models of moderation or objectivity.[14]

At his death, Diderot, more than ever the destroyer and enemy of idols, expressed the spirit of a whole segment of society in the 1780s. His hatred of despotism and the aristocracy, especially the forms they took in France, bore witness to the ongoing humiliation felt by philosophers outraged by a society that did not recognize the legitimacy or power of intellectuals. This was at a time when, in the realm of art, the heroism celebrated by David echoed this demand for recognition, already a quasi-republican theme. Here the fruits of philosophical teachings joined the resentments of the literary world and the aspirations of the new generation. In all areas, from science to aesthetics, the views of the "cultivated public" about the current state of affairs were becoming politicized and radicalized. But this upsurge of civic virtue, in which love of country competed with hatred of the powerful and their vices, resulted less from the triumph of ideological propaganda than from a change in focus of intellectual passions.[15]

The cases of Brissot and Robespierre, for example, show that this was true for a number of future leaders of the Revolution. In 1780, the former had explained to a more realistic friend his absolute scorn for contemporary institutions. He considered even the most monstrous theories preferable, feeling they could hardly be more absurd or terrible. As for Robespierre, Robert Palmer concludes that after surveying his modest prospects as a provincial lawyer, he manifested early on certain characteristics of the revolutionary mentality (such as class hatred, intolerance, certainty of being right, and the polemical habit of seeing the interplay of great principles in trivial incidents). Future events were to give these obsessions ample opportunities for expression.[16]

2. A DEFEAT
OF DESPOTISM?

The political origins of the French Revolution have long been under-estimated in favor of intellectual and socioeconomic ones. This tendency has recently been reversed, and historians are more and more placing the crisis undergone by the monarchy of the ancien régime *at the top of the list of causes of the upheaval of 1789. Opinion is not unanimous, however, either on the exact nature or the inevitable character of its outcome.*

WAS THE MONARCHY CAPABLE
OF REFORM BEFORE 1787?

Royal government placed on its leader, who had absolute power, a formidable burden, which Louis XVI was clearly unable to bear. His lack of self-confidence prevented him from making any bold initiatives. Isolated within the petty circles of the court, he gave in to its influence without ever attempting to overcome it. Dependent, like his predecessors, on the quality of his advisers, he always chose them from within a narrow circle, with the exception of the Genevan banker Necker, who was soon dismissed for the originality of his political views. The stranglehold of tradition doomed the monarchical system to reliance on those ministers who were the most unswervingly conservative. By definition, the attitudes imposed on them by their careers led them to reject any significant innovation in the established order.

The government's inertia was reinforced by the conditions of its operation, which was entirely dependent on royal favor. Continuing personal rivalries took precedence, even within the council, over collective responsibility. The ministers spent most of their energy convincing the king or queen of their superiority over their colleagues. Although Maurepas was able to guide Louis XVI through these machinations from

1774 to 1781, the spirit of intrigue revived after him, and Calonne's downful in 1786, for example, was impatiently anticipated by his rivals.

Out-of-favor ex-ministers also tried to mobilize public opinion against their successors, as Necker did, after 1781, against Calonne. This sharpening of rivalries, which aggravated difficulties, was itself increased by the tensions between the different ministerial departments and the relatively anarchic character of their representation and participation in the various councils of the government. The ambitious group of *maîtres des requêtes*, from whose ranks were recruited the *intendants* who dominated the provinces, made up the backbone and the recruitment pool of the government.

Their authority had been weakened since Louis XIV's reign by indecisiveness at the upper levels. The bureaucracy, moreover, was unable to handle its expanded work load, which made it more dependent on local authorities. Noble governors, unrepresentative provincial estates, and a system of municipal organization that was heterogeneous and had little real independence from the state, all added to the unwieldiness of government organization.

Louis XVI's authority, ultimately rested on the tacit consent of his subjects. For he had even fewer policemen than administrators. A constabulary force of four thousand men was expected to maintain order in the entire kingdom, with a patrol of fewer than one hundred carrying out this task in the city of Lyons. Paris itself allotted its police lieutenant a force of slightly over three thousand.

Although the army was there to back up these means of social discipline, the government had to exercise determination and firmness to maintain them in times of crisis. These were two qualities utterly lacking in Louis XVI, who had inherited a system riddled with permanent indecisiveness and absolute inefficiency. These defects of the tottering *ancien régime*, "the tyranny of weakness" to use François Bluche's term,[1] existed at all levels and were not dependent on the personality of the leaders, who were prisoners of the administrative apparatus they served. Clumsily and needlessly bureaucratic and rigid, it was unable to change or to work more quickly. These internal weaknesses were all the more significant insofar as the government encountered opposition that had been weakened but not eliminated by Louis XIV.

This bleak picture, recently painted by William Doyle,[2] seems to be contradicted by the major victories scored by the monarchy during the eighteenth century. When, in 1771, Louis XV directed his chancellor, Maupeou, to dismiss the *parlements* and thus provoked a violent ideological battle in the country, it was monarchist propaganda, supported by Voltaire, that won out against the futile historical pretensions of the class of royal officeholders. Their cause seemed lost until Louis XVI restored them upon his accession to the throne.[3]

William Doyle has shown that after this episode the members of the *parlements*, contrary to general opinion, never again posed a threat to the government. Hard hit by Maupeou's reforms, they were neither able nor eager to use their recall to undermine the actions of the government. The first president, d'Aligre, boasted to Vergennes in 1782 about this perfect—and unprecedented—accord. The following year a provincial magistrate lamented that the members of the Parisian *parlement*, "sapped by the pleasures of the voluptuous life" and "guided by ambition," obeyed "with blind deference the wishes of the King." A *fermier général* correctly noted that from 1774 to the end of 1786 "the *parlement* . . . had . . . been as obsequious as possible to all the desires of the ministers." Less apparent in the provinces, this docility was nonetheless an important source of support for the government during most of the reign of Louis XVI, who, until 1787, had nothing to fear from the irreparably weakened opposition of the *parlements*.[4]

Other studies have confirmed the importance of the ministerial party among the oldest members of the *parlement* of Paris, as well as the basically conservative attitude of these aristocratic supports of the seignorial regime. Traditionalists rather than revolutionaries, these magistrates above all supported the preservation of the old political and social order. They were in no way an obstacle to the government, and a certain number of them justified absolutism as a way of counterbalancing the authority of the privileged. They opposed the universal institution of the provincial assemblies as recommended by Necker, which they saw as unduly favoring the landed gentry of the provinces. Their concept of administrative secrecy derived from Louis XIV's, and the most serious of them no doubt agreed with the one who told the young Pasquier in late 1787 that "the day France has an Estates-General it will also have a terrible revolution." The majority of the nobles of the robe were certainly even more opposed to this prospect than the nobles of the sword, and they did not always condemn despotism.[5]

Under Turgot, the French monarchy attempted, between 1774 and 1776, to modernize and incorporate the spirit of the Enlightenment. In his famous *Mémoire sur les municipalités*, offered as a projected "constitution" for the renovation of the old structures of state and society, this minister, on the contrary, saw the provincial assemblies at the apex of the system as a means of strengthening royal government, not weakening it. Much less in favor of the principle of political absolutism itself than his physiocrat friends, Turgot nonetheless felt, like Voltaire, that the traditional power structure was the only possible agent of reform in France. This administrator could never envision a way for his country to function without the legislative monopoly of the king. He neither understood nor approved of the checks and balances used by the English constitution, which were later taken up by the American republic. As a writer with occasionally utopian tendencies, he saw political reality primarily in terms of an executive who was all-powerful and thus better armed against the privileged classes. For Turgot, this was the only way to avoid a revolution whose effects would probably be worse than the abuses it was trying to eliminate.[6]

The absolutist model thus remained the main focus of not only the reformers but also the conservatives of the 1770s. Both sought in it a solution to apparently irreconcilable contradictions. Turgot's career fitted into this traditional framework. Although it may well have been a financial and debt crisis that finished off the reign of Louis XVI, Turgot was simply confronted with the most crucial of the problems his predecessors had faced for centuries.[7]

The Austrian ambassador to Paris judged, in 1783, that the king was merely exacerbating the situation by his fear of the "geniuses" who were urging him to place inept people within the ministry rather than capable ones, and to endure ongoing disunity. In such a system, "the initiators of reforms could only be the enlightened minsters and their assistants as long as they enjoyed the support" of the king. Surrounded, since the middle of the eighteenth century, by strongly antagonistic competing interests, they never found in Louis XVI, who feared opposition within the court, the unflagging support they needed. The French political struggle at the end of the *ancien régime* revolved around the unresolvable conflict between privilege and despotism. Unable to surmount this, the king could be neither totally autocratic, which would have been contrary to his principles, nor truly constitutional insofar as public opinion, powerless and hopelessly divided, offered no real help in finding a peaceful solution to the crisis.[8]

This pessimistic view of the only institution from which the French, prior to 1789, could expect leadership is confirmed by the most recent study of its activities in the provinces. Contrary to what Tocqueville thought, and judging, at any rate, by the case of Provence, Louis XV and Louis XVI's *intendants* were not so much enlightened, reformist agents of a central government committed to the public interest as they were the spokesmen of a resolutely conservative local elite. Socioeconomic innovation was not their concern, and their activities scarcely

reached beyond the narrow circle of the ruling class. Forever pandering
to this class, powerless and unpopular, these inheritors of Louis XIV's
bureaucracy presided over a disintegrating royal administration.[9]

The state it served seemed henceforth unable to direct society toward
any specific program. Its financial difficulties, which were to lead to its
downfall, were symptomatic of the depth and extent of this "organic
crisis," to use Gramsci's term. We know that Calonne informed Louis
XVI of the seriousness of the budgetary deficit in August 1786. This
situation was to be expected under the *ancien régime* and its sources
were no mystery. But the government was suddenly caught with no way
out of its truly desperate straits. Neither cutbacks in spending, nor tax
increases, bankruptcy, nor new loans were possible. Having concealed
this situation for three years, it now had to deal with it. Calonne had
no intention of changing the financial organization of the monarchy,
which relied heavily on the cooperation of businessmen. He proposed
instead an overall unification and streamlining of the system that would
finally bring the state the money it needed.[10]

This new attempt to solve the budget deficit by means of sociopolitical
reforms has been praised by many historians as a particularly lucid and
courageous approach. John Bosher, in a key study of French finance
between 1770 and 1795, challenges this judgment by asserting that the
ancien régime's troubles in this area were above all administrative, as
the outcome of the Revolution, moreover, demonstrates. In the traditional system, the king was the client of his financial officers, a large
part of whose dealings did not concern the state. It was they, moreover,
who furnished most short-term credit, necessitated by the multiplicity
of treasuries and the quantity of hidden money. The king's credit thus
amounted to that of his own officers. The monarchy's true financial crisis
did not derive from the problem of balancing the budget; it resulted
from a kind of administration that made the king dependent on spec-
ulative fortunes, which had themselves been depleted in 1787 by the
economic crisis.

According to John Bosher, Calonne never understood how unhealthy
it was that private initiative lay at the heart of public finances. Necker,
on the contrary, had begun to reform administrative finance, which was
a first step toward its rationalization and nationalization. After Calonne,
Brienne carried on this effort intended to establish ministerial control of
the budget and the foundations of a governmental bureaucracy. As we
shall see, legislation enacted under the Revolution was the logical outcome of this reformist trend, which, before 1789, had already attempted
to convert the French financial system of contractual relations between
the Crown and businessmen to one involving a hierarchy of salaried

officials. This was an attempt to save the state from capitalist domination. The first *commis des finances* (bureaucratic tax administrators) were intelligent civil servants who thus laid the foundations for the modern system under Louis XVI, and three of the four were to serve under Napoleon.[11]

Michel Bruguière has recently confirmed the singular modernism of the later period of the *ancien régime* in financial matters. Its ministers worked to limit the purchase of offices, rationalize the treasury, and reduce the role of the royal court. These structural reforms brought major technical progress. By instituting new procedures for decision making, supervision, and appeals, they reinforced centralized power at just the time and in the precise area where it was soon to give way. Gaudin and Mollien, Napoleon's ministers of finance and the treasury, were already in charge, under Louis XVI, of direct taxes and relations with the *Ferme Générale*. Their associates, likewise salaried officials, shared their "government employees' disdain for others' money." The technocracy survived the Revolution; unable to modernize France before 1789, it became indispensable to the state thereafter.[12]

This puts Necker in a new light. His reputation as grave digger of the *ancien régime* earned the Swiss banker much scorn from historians. It seems indisputable that he was a progressive minister, unlike his successor, Calonne, who was often a narrow-minded reactionary. His ideas concerning government reform seem on a par with Turgot's, and his 1781 *Compte rendu*, which reported a satisfactory state of royal finances during the American Revolution, is now considered credible. The loans negotiated by Necker were, indeed, by no means catastrophic. Beyond this curious switch in ministerial reputations, the present rehabilitation of Madame de Staël's father by an entire school of historiographers serves to remind us that the prerevolutionary crisis was only partly a matter of financial technicalities. Conflicting interests, ambitions, and ideologies exploited these for their own ends in the turmoil that brought down Louis XVI's reign.[13]

DID THE ARISTOCRATS' VICTORY IN 1788
REPRESENT THE TRIUMPH OF LIBERAL IDEAS
OR OF TRADITIONAL PRIVILEGE?

From February 1787 to August 1788, the Crown, under Calonne and then Brienne, tried in vain to force structural reforms on the notables and then on the *parlements*. Its ultimate failure, on top of the government's bankruptcy, forced it to convene the Estates-General the following year and to back down before the opposition. Dominated by a liberal aristocracy eager to avenge itself for the despotism attempted earlier under Maupeou, the opposition enjoyed mixed success. Historians have long considered it a reactionary obstruction, orchestrated by the nobles of the robe and aimed against the efforts of an enlightened, progressive monarchy that had been rendered powerless by the privileged. This consensus was shattered only by Jean Egret, near the end of his life, who considered the magistrates of the royal court the political tutors of the prerevolutionary nation, defenders of the law and the subjects' rights against the authoritarian tendencies of the Crown. Their weakening under Maupeou, far from facilitating basic reforms, of which the government was incapable, instead further hampered the government just when it was coming into conflict with the businessmen and capitalists on whom it depended and who no longer had faith in it.[1]

The nature of the aristocratic opposition to absolute monarchy at the end of the *ancien régime* is thus problematic. Without an Estates-General, suddenly clamored for by certain *parlements* under Maupeou as a means of saving the state from despotism, and remaining thereafter a possible solution to political difficulties, and given the inability of other agents (provincial estates, municipalities, popular rebellions) to play this role, the monarchical government could be checked only by institutions that were closely integrated into the functioning of the state itself. The church, for example, which was dependent on it, remained an autonomous body, governed by its own organizational rules and protected from potential royal infringements by its enormous fortune in land. The clergy was thus able to fend off efforts by Controller General Machault, in the middle of the century and again in 1785, to tax it. An incomparably cohesive lobby, the church had never hesitated to use all possible means of agitating against the Crown.

The *parlementaires*, confident of their authority, did likewise in times of royal weakness. They dominated the king during the 1750s and 1760s, before Maupeou reduced them to silence. More than ever after their recall, the power they ultimately acquired was primarily an outgrowth of the inertia and vacillation of the ministers who, working within the well-known constraints of their authority, were sensitive to public opinion. It is clear that the 1770s saw the development of a crisis of confidence with regard to a government that was incapable of creating a coherent economic policy, keeping its commitments to creditors, or lightening the burden of its taxpayers. It was quickly accused of despotism when it rid itself, along with the *parlements*, of the intermediary bodies that were supposed to protect French political life from arbitrary rule. Maupeou's coup d'état, which was more a simple court intrigue than a grand project for reform, effectively silenced the opposition. But it also stripped the public of its illusions about guarantees against absolutism. For the first time since the beginning of the century there was talk again of the Estates-General.

At the same time that the status of the reinstated *parlements* was in decline, the young Louis XVI, unsure of himself and suffering from the unpopularity of his wife, was hardly in a position to exercise the absolute authority that he enjoyed in theory. His whole reign was thus marked, along with the frivolity of the court and the weakness of the Crown, by impassioned debates among the educated public as to how the country could be governed more responsibly and in ways that would further the public interest. Finally, by 1770, according to William Doyle, a patriotic party had sprung up to counter Maupeou and the Jesuits. The *parlements* justifiably took credit for creating this party, having proclaimed, in their *rémonstrances*, the idea of the primacy of the nation over the king. Opposition to the last initiatives undertaken by Louis XV had contributed as much as the writings of the *philosophes* to elite challenges to the notion of sovereignty.

Whence the importance, from then on, of the establishment of representative institutions that had long been sought at the local level by the physiocrats. Certain *parlementaires* in the early 1770s broadened these demands to include regular sessions of the Estates-General. Acting on Turgot's idea, Necker established the first provincial assemblies in 1778. They were unsatisfactory to the public in that they were neither elected nor representative and seemed directed, above all, against the *parlements*. There was, moreover, no agreement in the country or among the elite on a desirable form of representative government. The crisis of 1787 occurred in this feverish but uncertain atmosphere.[2]

The reforms proposed by Calonne extended the system of provincial assemblies by linking it to a new property tax. Joined with an ambitious program of economic development that provided for the absorption of the deficit by means of loans, these reforms nevertheless failed to win over the handpicked notables to whom they were at first proposed. Determined opposition by the clergy, in the name of its most exclusive privileges, and by the numerous personal enemies or rivals of the minister capitalized on the public's lack of confidence in him. Accused of concealing the exact condition of the nation's accounts, this clumsy reformer was consigned by certain elements to reappear during the future Estates-General. The notables' indignation at his behavior and his increasing isolation, despite his attempts to win over the public, led to Calonne's dismissal by Louis XVI in April 1787.

His successor, Brienne, worked under the threat of the convocation of the Estates-General. This last potential savior of the *ancien régime* monarchy was, like his predecessors, a determined reformer. But he had to dismiss certain notables who were now talking about assuming permanent financial control over the king, since there was no Estates-General to express the will "of the nation." Brienne's later reforms were the absolute monarchy's last attempts to resolve its problems without an elected assembly. The notables had raised the spectre of such an assembly because they justifiably doubted the competence of the government. Lacking the confidence of the king's most eminent subjects, and having revealed to all the disarray of its finances, the monarchy was, by the summer of 1787, irreparably compromised in the eyes of the public.

Its reformist programs did nothing to change this. The *parlements* could only go along with the general consensus that new taxes could be approved by the Estates-General alone. With the backing of the most influential of the old notables, the Paris *parlement* resumed leadership of the opposition. Its struggle against the ministry was backed by the people of the capital. Brienne tried in vain to placate them by announcing that the Estates-General would convene in 1792. Isolated and accused of despotism, he attempted to return to Maupeou's methods in the spring of 1788. These measures were greeted with general indignation, along with a deluge of tracts demanding a meeting of the Estates-General for the purpose of giving France a new constitution. Faced with the open refusal by the country's elite to cooperate with him, Brienne responded with an appeal to the public for help in setting up the Estates-General. The sudden financial crisis of the government, unable to obtain credit because of the intransigence of the businessmen, who were concerned about the economic and political problems, disabused him of his illusions. In August, in quick succession, the Estates-General was convoked for May 1789, payments drawn on the empty treasury were suspended, and Brienne, at last, was replaced, at his request, by Necker. Out of money and inspiration, the old monarchy was finished.[3]

This view of the prerevolutionary crisis contradicts the notion of a clear-cut victory by a privileged aristocracy over an enlightened monarchy. The notables and the magistrates were not merely trying to protect their selfish interests. They were also speaking out on behalf of a public that was dissatisfied with a worn-out system that had lost its prestige. According to Pasquier's *Mémoires*, the youngest members in particular, in their generous idealism, feared that the public interest had been compromised by ministerial tyranny. Their revolutionary demand for the convocation of the Estates-General reflected this concern, and was popular because it coincided with an ideological movement that had been developing for several decades.[4]

Historians have therefore been focusing increasingly on the remote origins of the new political ideology whose triumph brought an end to the *ancien régime*. Along with Eberhard Schmitt, they are tracing the evolution of the modern notion of national representation from one that, since Fénelon's time, associated the Crown with the idea of the "common good," to one that gradually transformed the *parlementaires* into the representatives of the nation. Along with the clergy, which had long been using a primarily representative system, certain members of the provincial estates were chosen by the different orders, and many rural and urban communities had political councils elected according to a tax-based system that was at times very loose. Jacques Godechot has observed that the revolutionary municipal councils were often composed of the same men as those that had preceded them.[5]

Considering the wide currency of the notion of representation, it is clear that the concept of a "national assembly" or a "legislative body" associated, by September 1788, with the future Estates-General, did not spring from an institutional or theoretical vacuum. On the contrary, by the sixteenth century, all of modern France was familiar with the idea of national representation, while the absolutist edifice was being built on the opposite concept. At the time of the Catholic League, the urban petty bourgeoisie, rising up against either the hereditary nobles or those who had acquired their nobility by purchasing royal offices, were making demands that were untenable under an absolutist system. Eighteenth-century liberalism harked back, beyond the breach marked by Louis XIV's reign, to an "aristo-democratic" tradition that was very much alive in Louis XIII's day. Under Louis XV it was to foster the constitutionalism of a small noble elite that was soon reinforced, after 1760, by an entire philosophical and political trend. There was thus a continuous line that led to the turmoil that preceded and laid down the foundations of the Revolution.[6]

In this regard, Keith Baker has stressed the theory advanced by Mably, in the late 1780s, according to which a conflict between the *parlement* of Paris and the Crown, such as the one that was then occurring over ecclesiastical issues, could lead to a revolution that would save France from the despotism in which it was sunk. The *philosophe* could envision no constitutional system worthy of the name in the absence of a clearly defined national will. Opposed to the so-called enlightened administrative reforms, he saw political crises and the accompanying "fermentation of spirits" as a way of bringing about the convocation of the Estates-General, which would ultimately set off the desired revolutionary process. It would lead to a national system of representation that would guarantee freedom. Though Mably died disappointed, without reaching the Promised Land, his classic republican language was one of the pre-1788 forerunners of the future revolutionary discourse.[7]

Analyzing the religious and ideological crisis that led to Mably's audacious theories, Dale Van Kley sees in the France of the 1760s the roots of the conservative and liberal parties that were to divide the country in the first half of the nineteenth century. The former he identifies with the Jesuits' ultramontane supporters and the adversaries of Jansenist-type Gallicanism, whereas the constitutionalism of the *parlementaires* associated with the latter foreshadowed the work of the Constituent Assembly. The flood of *political* literature that poured out of the ultimate theological conflict of the eighteenth century starkly pitted the ecclesiastical justification of absolutism against its critique in the name of the nascent concept of national sovereignty, so dear to the "patriots" who rose up against "tyranny" and "despotism." Among both the friends and the enemies of the devout, this secularization of public law corresponded to an indisputable desacralization of the monarchy that had been so poorly incarnated in Louis XV.[8]

Keith Baker stresses another aspect of this fundamental rift in French political thought early in Louis XVI's reign. The crowning of the king at Reims in 1775 was no doubt accompanied by the general enthusiasm that customarily surrounded these august traditional ceremonies. Whereas the patriots fumed because there was no mention of the people's consent to the election of the king, various pamphlets seized upon this occasion to contrast the old adulatory formulas with the new language of the social contract and national rights. Criticism of Maupeou and his "revolution" in pamphlets like *Ami des lois* ("The Friend of Laws") and *Catéchisme du citoyen* ("The Citizen's Catechism") foreshadowed the rhetoric of the enemies of "despotism." It reflected contemporary tensions between traditional absolutism and the new centralizing orientation of the government, between the old system of justice and the new adminstration, between the old style of royal authority and the new conditions for the exercise of power, between the public's demands on authority and its criticisms of its responses. Innumerable publicists voiced these discontents. They echoed enlightened public figures like Malesherbes, who, in the name of the *cour des aides* (sovereign tax courts), presented a list of grievances, the *rémontrances*, in which he sought the restoration of the right of representation at all levels and tried to make public the workings of the government. The former director of the *Librairie* here proclaimed to the king that it was the unanimous will of the nation to convoke the Estates-General. In a different spirit,

Turgot, as we have seen, was also attempting to reform the governmental structure by means of a hierarchy of representative assemblies. As for Bordeaux's Saige, author of the *Catéchisme*, he affirmed the right of the nation—which he identified with the Third Estate—to hold legislative powers. In the ideological constellation of ideas in the 1770s, new theories about the nature of royal authority thus coexisted with the ancient, immutable, sacred rites surrounding it. What was sought, beyond the restoration of cooperation between the king and the members of the sovereign courts, was some affirmation of either the enlightened and rational character of absolutism or the principles of national sovereignty that would be proclaimed in 1789. The whole question of the "rights of men and citizens" had been anticipated, early in Louis XVI's reign by reformers eager for administrative justice, by traditionalists who preferred to leave this task to the *parlements*, and by theoreticians, already disposed to revolution, who first put forth the political concept of the nation.[9]

Having inherited these conflicts and aspirations that fueled the struggles of the prerevolutionary period, the notables who had been called into session by Calonne must not be viewed merely as a privileged elite whose only thought was to protect their own interests. Outraged by the minister's attempts to portray them as such to the public, they saw their opposition as rooted in national and patriotic concerns that reflected the new aspirations of the political culture of the elite. As landowners determined to participate in the power structure, they were intent on wrestling from a bureaucracy they mistrusted the authority to approve and supervise taxation. Promoters of provincial autonomy, they saw the development of local institutions as an essential component of the kind of government they envisioned, in keeping with evolving trends in public opinion.[10]

Contrary to an old theory that was still being put forth in 1962 by Egret, the aristocratic revolt of 1787–88 did not constitute what Marcel Reinhard has called "a counterrevolution before the fact," born of the "refusal by the privileged majority to make sacrifices," which was to lay the foundations for revolution by preventing reforms and by forcing the government to convoke the Estates-General. The opposition, seizing upon the financial crisis at the end of Louis XVI's reign, expressed ideas that had already been fully formed at its inception. They had been formed before Maupeou's *coup d'état*, which, in 1771, had shattered the traditional equilibrium of the *ancien régime*. It had, indeed, unmasked the true nature of absolutism, in which royal power was above the law. The reestablishment of the *parlements* in 1774 in no way changed this situation, which was disturbing, most of all, to the king's creditors. It was only exacerbated, in the eyes of the adversaries of ministerial despotism, by Brienne's final initiative.[11]

DID THE MONARCHY ABDICATE ALL RESPONSIBILITY JUST BEFORE AND DURING THE EARLY STAGES OF THE REVOLUTION?

It is widely acknowledged that the government's collapse in August 1788 left a total vacuum at the center of the power structure, which was to last five years. Necker confined his efforts to preparing for the convocation of the Estates-General, which was given sole responsibility for solving the country's problems. The monarchy seems almost to have handed over to that body the task of re-creating the nation. It made no attempt to supervise its work or to use Necker's popularity and the trust he enjoyed among financiers to advance some political program. The minister even seemed to share the French people's mystical faith in the future accomplishments of the Estates.

He could no longer dictate the conditions of their election, which had been hotly debated in the fall of 1788. In a highly volatile atmosphere charged with hostility toward anything that smacked of despotism, Necker again consulted the notables on this issue. Against their advice, he decided at the end of the year that the Third Estate would have the same number of representatives as the privileged orders.

The question of voting by head, however, remained unresolved, and the monarchy had not chosen among the opposing parties on this point. During March and April of 1789, it did not nominate its own candidates to the elections. The government, in a state of total paralysis, was awaiting action by the future Estates. Elected largely on the basis of local issues, the deputies were to bring about changes that were totally alien to the old power structure, which was by now completely impotent.

It had fostered the revolutionary character of the electoral assemblies of the clergy by favoring the parish clergy that had until then been underrepresented in the Gallican church. When the Estates convened at Versailles in May the government had nothing to offer them, to their great disappointment, but pious wishes. It seemed opposed to any excessive innovation, and still failed to come out in favor of voting by head. This timidity and reticence, dismaying to everyone, was particularly irksome to the deputies of the Third Estate, who were thereby forced either to repudiate their mission or to revolt.

They began to complain to their constituents about the inactivity and obstructiveness of a government incapable, after a month, of putting the long-awaited Estates into action. This situation compromised Necker's position at the court, where his reputation was foundering. The troops around Versailles were reinforced without his knowledge. Word of this influx of foreign regiments spread, and rumors about an aristocratic plot to dissolve the Estates began to circulate. In an atmosphere of riots and upheaval, the government was, as usual, held responsible, along with the privileged classes, for the turmoil.

The Third Estate's decision on June 10 to begin verifying credentials without their participation challenged the legitimacy of the government for the first time, and attempted to dictate the conditions of its operation. Proclaiming themselves, on the seventeenth, a National Assembly, the revolutionary deputies were clearly laying claim to political sovereignty, although shouting all the while "Long live the king!"

His authority thus challenged, the monarch was finally jolted into action. In view of the urgency of the situation, and the risk of completely forfeiting control, he announced that a *Séance royale* would be held on the twenty-third, at which time he would reveal his program. His petty attempt at preventing his rivals from meeting before then only strengthened their unity and determination.

Necker had conceived the idea of the *Séance* on the twenty-third as a means of disarming the opposition with an onslaught of generous reforms, including the acceptance of a vote in common on important issues, the guarantee of regular sessions of the Estates, its approval of taxes, the establishment of provincial estates, etc. At the last minute, the queen and the king's brothers insisted on such extensive changes in the plan that Necker turned in his resignation.

The king retained most of his minister's measures, but denounced the resolutions of June 10 and 17, and proclaimed that the separation of the orders was inviolable. They could deliberate in common, but the nobility and the clergy retained the right to veto any proposals concerning them. The king concluded, moreover, with the implicit threat to carry out his reforms alone if he did not receive the cooperation of all.

The deputies of the Third Estate gave a chilly reception to these proposals that should have been set forth in early May, and that were now accompanied by a condemnation of all they had just accomplished. This last attempt by the crown to lead the nation came too late and was too limited. When the king left, ordering the deputies to disperse, he was disobeyed. Preoccupied as he was with his attempts to persuade Necker to retract his resignation, he hardly noticed.

His ineffectual display of authority ended at the first sign of resistance.

This failure showed the deputies of the clergy and the nobility that they could not count on Louis XVI's support. Moreover, the crowds that packed the Estates applauded Necker and threatened those who did not support the Assembly. The king's only hope for regaining control was to call in the army. It was decided, on the twenty-sixth, to double the number of troops stationed around Paris. But it would be some time before they could be assembled and ready for deployment, particularly since the regiments in the capital had begun to show signs of unrest. To counter the risk of a mass demonstration in favor of the uniting of the orders, and to gain time while awaiting reinforcements, Louis XVI advised the recalcitrant deputies to carry on with their work. All Versailles applauded, but perceptive observers doubted the sincerity of this capitulation.[1]

The troop reinforcements ordered on the twenty-sixth were, indeed, increased yet again in early July, and it was clear that the king remained firm in his determination to counter the Revolution with force. On the eighth, the Assembly requested in vain that Louis XVI withdraw all his troops from the Paris area. Immersed in their counterrevolutionary activities, the king and his aristocratic advisers decided, on the same day, to dismiss Necker, who was given notice on the eleventh and ordered to leave the country immediately. A conservative ministry was set up, with Breteuil and Marshal de Broglie at its head.

Despite his obvious political deficiencies, Necker was at the height of his popularity. He was seen as the people's protector within the power structure, and the king should have realized that his dismissal would prompt a major challenge. It unquestionably set off the definitive revolt by the people of Paris, before whom, by the evening of the twelfth, the troops were in retreat. On the sixteenth, Broglie notified Louis XVI that he could not count on his army. Totally unable from this point on to enforce his will, the king, after announcing the withdrawal of the troops and the recall of Necker, went to Paris to announce his capitulation.

The Revolution was thus saved early on from the monarchy, which, along with the courtiers, remained fundamentally opposed to it. The king tried again in late September to regain control over events by the use of force. It was only his return to the capital, in early October, that assured the innovators that the change they had sought had indeed been won. Forced to convoke the Estates-General, then unable to dominate it, the king had thrown all his weight in with those who opposed progress. The government's inability to crush the Revolution by force was the only guaranty, in 1789, that change was indeed forthcoming.[2]

The recall of Necker allows us to qualify the assertion that, starting in the summer of 1788, the king totally abdicated responsibility. His vacillations and inertia, up to mid-June 1789, certainly made him incapable of influencing the composition and early orientation of the Estates-General. This irreparable loss of time cost him a historic opportunity that was never again to arise, and left center stage to the rival parties. But when forced to choose among them, while retaining some of the reforms proposed by Necker, the king clearly sided with those opposing the nationwide transformation of state and society envisioned by the patriots. He even made futile attempts to prevent it by force. His later capitulations, poorly disguised by his well-known hypocrisy, never concealed his role as one of the leaders of the counterrevolution.

In his last free act as monarch in the old style, he gave a speech on June 23, calling for a constitutional monarchy, a departure from traditional absolutism. But, on the social level, he sided with the privileged orders that were trying to preserve their rights and prerogatives. The military strike ordered after the failure of the royal session aimed at safeguarding these. It would no doubt have been accompanied, as was customary under the old monarchy, by a crackdown on opponents. The twenty thousand men who were to be concentrated, around mid-July, in the Paris region would see to this. Supported by this formidable security buildup, Louis XVI, for so long indecisive and compliant, but now won over by the conniving coterie that surrounded him, gave in to the Revolution only because he was unable to crush it by force. His authority had collapsed throughout the country. But during the summer that followed, the king persisted in his refusal to ratify the early documents aimed at reorganizing the state and society. He thus exacerbated a political situation that was rapidly degenerating. His supporters elaborated plans aimed at protecting him from Paris and the Assembly. Only another *journée populaire* on October 6 forced him into a second, and definitive, surrender, which he never accepted wholeheartedly. He began then to plan the escape that he had until then considered dishonorable.[3]

This deep-seated hostility between the new nation and the old monarchy was all the more serious in that the latter retained great prestige in 1789. The March and April *cahiers de doléances*, written in the name of all the people of France, offer abundant evidence of this. They are filled with "outpourings of enthusiasm and love" from all the orders for a monarch from whom they had expected the regeneration of the people and its reconciliation with the government. With quasireligious fervor, the inhabitants of the poorest parishes revered him as a savior and a father who would bring them peace and happiness at last. They counted on his wisdom, equal to Henry IV's, to bring about a social and political transformation that would strengthen, not undermine, the monarchy. In an atmosphere of millennial optimism, which entended to Necker as well as his king, people from all regions of France and of all conditions offered the latter the "impassioned homage" of humble admirers, certain that he would solve even the most private problems of his subjects.[4]

This astonishing popularity, which contrasts with the accusation of arbitrary rule directed against the administration and the privileged classes, reduced the impact of the trivial rumors that circulated in Paris, such as the affair of the queen's necklace. The king enjoyed an immense stock of public confidence that even his behavior between the summers of 1789 and 1792 did not completely deplete. In spite of everything, under the first republic and until Bonaparte, the majority of the French remained promonarchist. The country's tragedy was that the initial choices made by Louis XVI turned this sentiment into a tool of the counterrevoltion.[5]

3. A VICTORY
FOR THE BOURGEOISIE?

Few historians still believe that the French Revolution originated in a hypothetical class struggle between the nobility and the bourgeoisie. Labeled a myth by Alfred Cobban in 1955, the idea that the events of 1789 were a decisive stage in the transition from feudalism to capitalism has, since then, run up against a series of insurmountable objections. Moreover, it is no longer possible to qualify as "bourgeois" or "capitalist" a revolution that was welcomed by the greater part of the enlightened elite and supported by peasants and fiercely anticapitalistic workers. For all these reasons, the difficult task of reconstructing the causes and social ramifications of 1789 is more pressing than ever.

WAS THERE A CLASS STRUGGLE BETWEEN THE NOBILITY AND THE BOURGEOISIE BEFORE 1789?

The traditional interpretation of the origins of the Revolution had the virtue of simplicity. Reacting against Louis XIV–style absolutism, the aristocracy had eventually weakened the power of the Crown, thereby provoking the resentment of an alienated and frustrated bourgeoisie. They, in turn, seized upon the crisis of the late 1780s to overthrow the political and social *ancien régime*, before clashing with the counterrevolution and, in the following century, the working class.

Clinging to traditional Marxist theories, historians continue to view the eighteenth century in terms of a class struggle between a decadent nobility and a rising bourgeoisie. They label the seignorial regime and, by extension, French society as a whole as "feudal," dominated by the aristocracy and challenged by the rest of the population. They see the bourgeoisie, bearer of a new ideology, as the natural vehicle of this dissent. According to this interpretation the Revolution of 1789 accomplished the goals sought by the bourgeoisie. In a thesis on Savoie, Jean

Nicolas offers evidence of this development. But the point remains to be proven for France, which, as a whole, suffered a revolution.[1]

The challenge to this dogma dates back to two ground-breaking articles, published in 1967 and 1973 by George Taylor and Colin Lucas, respectively. The first supported Alfred Cobban's findings that most prerevolutionary fortunes were noncapitalist in origin. The landed aristocracy and the property-owning bourgeoisie formed a single socioeconomic group. For this reason, the Revolution of 1789 must have had other causes, *i.e.*, political ones.[2]

Six years later, Colin Lucas underlined the impossibility of distinguishing clearly, in the French elite of the eighteenth century, two antagonistic classes of nobles and bourgeois. He showed, on the contrary, that they had a common interest distinct from that of the popular classes, and that there was no line separating them from each other within the so-called "feudal" regime. Little moved by the "capitalist" spirit, the tradesmen were themselves trying to join the system. A landed seignorial class, made up of nobles and nonnobles, dominated society. There was no class-conscious bourgeoisie to rise up against them or provoke a revolutionary crisis, which originated within the elite. The nobles constituted the purest example of social superiority and often possessed great wealth. Gaining entrance to this group was thus the standard form of upward mobility. It was often the most direct and the most coveted result of the acquisition of wealth. These various forms of competition within the body of the elite never took on the dimensions of a crisis before 1788. Political problems and the struggle against absolutism were much greater sources of turmoil in this group, within which the principle of noble privileges was never called into question. The revolt of the Third Estate was simply a demand for increased status by the lower elements of the elite. This revolutionary bourgeoisie struck out against the old order, in 1789, only with the greatest prudence. It adhered to a socioeconomic concept of a land-owning elite that pointed in a new direction without confuting the old order. The myth of an early conflict between the nobility and the bourgeoisie stems from the political opposition of the majority of the nobles to the Revolution. In the new legal framework that grew out of 1789, the elite, however, took on some new characteristics. In this sense, it was not the bourgeoisie that created the Revolution, but the other way around.[3]

French "revisionists" took up this interpretation in the *Annales*. Guy Chaussinand-Nogaret, defining the nobility as "the bourgeoisie that had arrived," observed that in the eighteenth century the former was more imbued with "bourgeois" ideology than the latter. He noted its new-found concern with merit and its absorption, after 1760, of the new values of economic and cultural modernism, which gradually produced a new elite based on ability. This tendency of the elite to adopt a bourgeois mentality, confirmed in 1789 by their *cahiers*, made it in many ways more liberal than the Third Estate. They were split by no fundamental ideological disagreement. This is understandable when we recall that the nobility was at the forefront of capitalist development. United by deep bonds of solidarity, the French elite suffered only superficial division. Temporarily reinforced by the events of the Revolution, these were rapidly healed within the new social order that was in many ways similar to the old one.[4]

This notion of a nobility that was in large part progressive and fully imbued with the "bourgeois" spirit has gained currency. Often composed of rational administrators, this class was no more privileged than many other segments of French society. It was, on the other hand, as involved as they in economic activity, and its upper ranks were part of the propertied elite. Any antagonism it bore toward a bourgeoisie that was, moreover, very divided was imaginary, like its so-called closed-caste status. The nobility was, moreover, totally fragmented, and it was only the convocation of the Estates-General that imposed an artificial semblance of unity upon it.

William Doyle's recent study, which takes these factors into account, presents the nobility as the dominant order in late-eighteenth-century France. Its privileges, as enviable as those of the church, as well as its way of life, attracted the upwardly mobile. Indispensable in service to the king, the nobility formed an elite that was open and unrivaled. Those who attacked it—or would soon—dreamed of joining it. The government naturally respected it, and the gravest danger it faced was no doubt to be found in its internal divisions. They explain in large part the measures of the so-called aristocratic reaction, by which the old nobles, who were often impoverished, tried to protect themselves from the ennobled rich. Alongside these social and political contrasts, a wide cultural gap separated the majority of the local squires from the liberal *grands seigneurs* who naturally headed the revolutionary movement.[5]

The amorphous bourgeoisie was even less unified and lacking in well-defined class-consciousness. It did not view itself as a distinct social group whose values were better than those of the others. Hostile to the populace, it aspired to nobility. The great heterogeneity of this class and the narrowness of its ambitions precluded any other concept of upward mobility. Scornful of manual laborers, it sought the quickest way out of trade. Buying offices and land, and hungry for respectability, it feared that access to the latter was shrinking during the 1780s. But its *rentier* mentality remained conservative, anticapitalist, and paranoble. The bourgeoisie could be concerned only by the blockage from above of social mobility, which in the *ancien régime* came from the purchase of ennobling offices. Its boldest members were thus envious of those richer than they who had taken other paths into the aristocracy. Eager for admission, bourgeois officeholders and lawyers were only beginning to feel these frustrations when the Estates-General was convened. The political crisis allowed them to express them to the extent that this group was more cultivated than before, though far from entirely won over by Enlightenment thought. But the educated bourgeoisie, like the corresponding segments of the nobility, shared the widespread new desire for a transformation of society and the nation. Until the summer of 1788 it supported the aristocratic opposition fully. Only during preparations for the Estates-General did it begin to be aware of itself as a class. Having broadened its horizons, it stopped viewing itself as a passive member of the community and political maneuverings as the exclusive domain of the nobles. It was, indeed, only the conservatism of the aristocracy that made the members of the French bourgeoisie aware, for the first time in their history, that they had common interests.[6]

This new view of the French aristocracy of the eighteenth century regards it as an open class, of recent origin, and linked to wealth. It was only the shock of the revolutionary struggle that forced it to define and preserve itself by privilege. Before that, it is misleading to label the declining *ancien régime* as insurmountably rigid. Its leaders were getting richer, not poorer. It was the nobles who engaged in maritime commerce and the slave trade, they who headed the iron industry. In addition to mines and metallurgy, they dominated the textile industries and the shareholding corporations, and were becoming involved in new developments in chemicals. Set against these realities, the "court society" so dear to Norbert Elias seems to be sheer fantasy, as does the traditional image of "feudalism." We are indebted to Guy Chaussinand-Nogaret for a thought-provoking insight into an order that was no doubt diverse, but in which plutocrats carried more weight than indigents, and where culture and capitalism were more often united than among the bourgeois. The true inspiration for putting an end to the *ancien régime* came from the aristocracy.[7]

These views have been greeted with skepticism by those who continue to explain the prerevolutionary nobility in terms of the one that followed it and who consider this "conception of the elite" "too much influenced by American psychology" and its supposed idealism. They remain convinced of the irreducible conflict, starting in the prerevolutionary period, "between bourgeois notables and gentlemen," and attribute the constitution of the future "property-owning class" to the inevitable eradication of aristocratic superiority.[8]

If this was indeed the case, the wholehearted endorsement of the ideology of merit in the nobles' 1789 *cahiers* is totally incomprehensible. It corresponds to a continuous trend in French aristocratic thought in the eighteenth century. The Comte d'Entraigues, who was to become a disciple of the counterrevolution, was at first, in 1788, a firm supporter of these ideas, friend of the people, and enemy of despotism.[9]

William Doyle has recently shown that the decline in the price of officers' appointments was far from universal in the eighteenth century. Those that conferred nobility or provided access thereto continued, on the contrary, to be highly coveted and were eagerly invested in. This tendency demonstrates the continuing strength, within the bourgeoisie, not of capitalistic aspirations, but of the traditional ambition to become part of the ruling social class. It was not as a result of their frustrations, but rather as the outcome of a sudden overturning of values, contrary to their previous interests, that the deputies of the Third Estate—who were, for the most part, officeholders—abolished, in 1789, a system of which they had until then hoped to become part. Revolutionary idealism, by radicalizing their outlook, made them abruptly abandon the conception of the world that had characterized their class.[10]

Doyle has helped challenge the myth of the aristocratic reaction peculiar to prerevolutionary France. In his view, the eighteenth century in no way changed the recruitment methods of a government that was already made up of nobles under Louis XIV. As for Ségur's famous 1781 ordinance, which limited entry into the corps of army officers to those who were four-quarters noble, it was intended to protect the less wealthy aristocrats against the nepotism of the courtiers and the newly ennobled. The strengthening of the seignorial regime on the eve of the Revolution, similarly, was neither universal nor unprecedented, and it involved property owners as much as nobles.[11]

David Bien maintains that during Louis XVI's reign there was no decisive campaign by the nobility to consolidate the traditional hierarchy and thus guarantee its preeminence over the commoners. This imaginary cause of the Revolution is no more than a retrospective projection onto the past, based on the events of 1789. It attributes to the army and the society of the eighteenth century problems that did not face them and ignores those that did. Among these last was the matter of ennoblement by the purchase of office, which Necker and many others considered too rapid and easy. Ségur's decree was a reaction in the name of the old nobility to the opening of military positions to this freshly minted aristocracy. The new aristocracy that dominated so many of the sovereign courts and often held top positions in government and society was particularly hard hit by this measure. Produced by technicians rather than ideologists, it was aimed at limiting the professional recruitment of army officers to families with a military heritage. The clash with the bourgeoisie was of less concern than the struggle against the court and wealth within the nobility, where divisions cut more deeply than in other segments of French society.[12]

In no way united by privilege, the aristocratic elite did not even consider consolidating its forces against its adversaries in 1789, so unaccustomed was it to acting in concert. The richest bourgeois had been trying for centuries to attain aristocratic status, which could now be obtained by the purchase of offices, a practice which was justified on the grounds that it stimulated the economy. This continuous line from merchant and wholesaler to officer to noble was the standard path to social mobility still accepted by the majority of French families on the eve of the Revolution.[13]

WAS THE POLITICAL REVOLUTION OF 1789 CAUSED BY THE BOURGEOISIE?

From Alfred Cobban on, it has been justifiably stressed that the "officeholding bourgeoisie" and not the capitalist class was at the forefront of revolutionary activity. Lawyers, notaries, solicitors, public prosecutors, and judges of local courts played a decisive role in the electoral campaigns for the Estates-General, just as they constituted the majority of the deputies of the Third Estate. Never had this group rallied behind a local or national political program as they did at this crucial moment. Georges Lefebvre has consequently concluded that, starting in September 1788, they interpreted and embodied the will of the bourgeoisie as a whole to shape the nascent revolution. Elizabeth Eisenstein, in 1965, disagreed, pointing out the overwhelmingly aristocratic character of the leaders of the patriotic party, who made up the core of the famous Society of Thirty which orchestrated this movement. In her opinion, the Revolution was set in motion by a heterogeneous alliance of equally enlightened aristocrats and bourgeois. To reduce it to a purely bourgeois movement is to make an unfounded theoretical deduction and to discount the consistently liberal character of aristocratic opposition to the monarchy of the *ancien régime* from at least early 1787. Far from being confined to such individuals as Sieyès, Mirabeau, and La Fayette, the *collective* participation of politicians and intellectuals of the privileged class in instigating the Revolution was, on the contrary, considerable, and precludes limiting its initial dimensions to those of a bourgeois enterprise.[1]

This outgrowth of Alfred Cobbans's ideas, though it clashed with the most conservative views, has finally prevailed, at least among historiographers of the English-speaking world, who have been more aware than their French colleagues of how abstract concepts of class are as applied to the dynamic interplay of political forces, particularly those of revolutionary periods. Nothing shakes this dogma more effectively than concrete observation, as Lynn Hunt's study of the elite of the principal towns of Champagne in the late eighteenth century demonstrates. Hunt's work confirms that despite numerous divisions society was jointly dominated by a motley array of capitalists and property owners, both noble and bourgeois. This group's cohesion and strength if anything increased, despite gains in civic awareness, until the summer of 1789. In Reims such domination even survived the events of the Revolution. An amalgam of a multiplicity of local circumstances, the social and political life of the urban notables reflects a surprising capacity for integration. Though temporarily thrown off-balance by the Revolution, it was able to survive it.[2]

On September 25, 1788, the *parlement* of Paris declared that the Estates-General were to be reconvened along the lines of the session of 1614. This was unacceptable to those who favored the recent Dauphiné model, in which the orders met jointly and the Third Estate had twice as many deputies as the others. We know that the campaign to sway public opinion toward this latter model was led not by the bourgeois but by the Society of Thirty, a political club which consisted primarily of nobles and met at the home of Duport, a member of the *parlement* of Paris. This microcosm of the Parisian elite, hungry for national regeneration, naturally hoped that wealth and talent would be accorded their rightful place. The Estates would accordingly have to be more representative of the better part of the country than the *parlement* wished. Mirabeau, moreover, called this project, which flooded the bourgeoisie with tracts and agitation, a "conspiracy of gentlemen." It profoundly shook French political consciousness by circulating model petitions that were to be sent to the government through official channels. This appeal to public opinion snowballed. By December, it was out of the control of its authors, and had succeeded only in arousing resentment against the privileged classes. Even the most moderate among them became more intransigent, and a strategy aimed at promoting social unity backfired. The ideal of a fusion of the orders, put forth by the

Vizille assembly in July and taken up by the Society of Thirty, became a minority goal.

The majority of notables reconvened by Necker came out against him, as did five of the seven princes of the blood. The majority of pamphlets and petitions, on the other hand, continued to support him, often on the basis of local initiatives. The *parlement* of Paris in the end partially supported this position, and as we know was followed in this by the government. This triumph of the campaign launched by the Thirty did not put an end to denunciations of the privileged elements that might hold out for vote by order. It was against this backdrop that Sieyès's famous pamphlet of January 1789 appeared, calling for the nobility and the clergy to be excluded from the nation unless they renounced their special privileges. Antagonism among the orders had increased, furthermore, because of the controversy surrounding the eventual reestablishment of the provincial estates. At the end of July, law students supporting reform of these estates squared off against servants of the conservative aristocracy in street clashes in Rennes. The question of the aristocracy's privileges polarized public opinion more and more. Its electoral assemblies were marked by bitter divisions; nobles of Brittany, for example, refused to be represented in the Estates-General. Few nobles of the robe were elected compared with those representing the silent majority of the order, who were poorer and had no experience in politics. Nevertheless, nearly a third of those elected were liberals, younger and closer to the urban mentality.

The order's *cahiers*, furthermore, reflected their influence. Only 41 percent reveal determined opposition to vote by head; 89 percent state a willingness to relinquish the nobility's tax privileges. Less than 10 percent of the order's demands aimed at a reactionary exclusivism. Far from being absolutely opposed to the Revolution to come, the noble deputies were prepared to make important concessions to it. They had numerous points of agreement with the Third Estate on constitutional issues. Their later clash, at the beginning of the meeting of the Estates, resulted more from procedural problems and the general political atmosphere than from disagreement on fundamental principles. As for the elections within the Third Estate, which were much more harmonious, they reflected the tendency of peasants and craftsmen to send to Versailles bourgeois representatives chosen in the main from among those legal professionals and officeholders who had always been the natural spokesmen of the commoners. Well-trained, particularly in legal matters, they were elected by wide margins. But the *cahiers* they brought with them expressed no especially virulent resentment, for example with regard to the eradication of the seignorial regime or even more strikingly, to the eventual confiscation of church properties. They were reformers, not revolutionaries, and the radicalization of the deputies of the Third Estate resulted not from their experience of the *ancien régime*, but rather from the events of May to July 1789. Only the question of vote by head separated the two upper orders from the rest of the nation. More striking is the agreement of the *cahiers* on most other issues. This liberal consensus was to serve as a basis for the National Assembly's work starting in July. But first, the negative effects of suspicion, resentment, and antagonism did their work, as did a level of popular engagement unforeseen even by the idealism of the *cahiers*. While this popular intervention saved the Revolution, it forced its leaders, who were distrustful of the people, to grant them concessions that went well beyond the intentions of the electorate of 1789.[3]

At the opening of the session of the Estates-General, Third Estate deputies who, like those from Dauphiné and Brittany, were used to working together challenging the government, and knowing exactly what they wanted induced the order as a whole to refuse to constitute itself as a separate body before the two other orders responded to its proposal that credentials be verified in common. This demand was rejected by the nobility on May 7. Its liberal minority, however, hoped that this view would change in time. The clergy was much more amenable from the outset to the proposals of the Third Estate, but talks held among delegates of the orders remained fruitless in the face of opposition by the majority of the nobles. This first month of inactivity hardened attitudes on all sides, and on June 10 this resulted in a revolutionary seizure of power, by the representatives of the bourgeoisie. Having shaken up the other deputies, they firmly resolved, as is known, to withstand pressure by the Crown. A National Assembly, voting by head without distinction by order, was finally constituted.[4]

This was the great goal of the liberal opposition, *both* aristocratic and bourgeois, whose presence had been felt since September 1788. The majority of the courtiers and young member magistrates who made up the Society of Thirty, for example, belonged to the oldest nobility. The reform program of the great patriotic *seigneurs*, who had the means to promote it, was approved in the provinces, most often by the bourgeois, and sometimes, as in Dauphiné, by the privileged classes. Furthermore, the majority of deputies elected (Third Estate lawyers, parish priests liberal nobles) were part of the new generation coming from the cultivated urban milieu of northern France. These homogeneous cultural groups, which transcended orders and classes, were to prove a source of support for the future activists of the Constituent Assembly. They reflected a wide, well-established, proconstitutional, antiabsolutist consensus mobilized in the service of a regenerated nation. There remained, however, certain differences of opinion over the ways these principles were to be applied. The nobility, for example, was much less receptive than the bourgeoisie to the idea of equality of opportunity or even the eradication of the practice of purchasing offices. The aristocracy that was represented in the Estates was basically divided between those who feared losing their institutional monopolies and those who accepted this risk, trusting in the social bases of their power. The Third Estate, for its part, sought change, not subversion, and new individual rights, not the eradication of old privileges. It spoke little of national sovereignty, and conservatism on this point was no doubt even greater among the electors than among the deputies.

Everything changed, as we have seen, with the fruitless polarization of May and June that weakened and discouraged the moderates while radicalizing the militants. The outlook of the latter took hold of an Assembly that had become much more amenable to the ideas advanced by Sieyès since January. Rescued by the people, the Revolution was radicalized by these lawyers. The French bourgeoisie as a whole had followed the events with fervent support for the Third Estate. Provincial towns often preceded Paris in rising up to impose a new order. This was particularly the case, as in the northern half of the country, where patriots were denied their share of power by conservatives. But almost everywhere new permanent committees sprang up, taking charge of the armed forces and simultaneously challenging both the aristocratic counterrevolution and popular unrest. Traditional royal authority was giving way before an urban revolution, for which, this time, the bourgeoisie was certainly responsible.[5]

Paradoxically, it was reaping the benefits of actions initiated by some of the best-pedigreed members of the court nobility. They were motivated in many cases by factional spirit and hostility to the type of patronage imposed by the coterie surrounding Marie-Antoinette. They were also resentful of the royal bureaucracy of the *maîtres des requêtes* who were instrumental in shutting them out of power. Disgruntled dukes and peers who had led the struggle against Calonne and Brienne shaped the one headed by the Society of Thirty. They included heroes of the American Revolution, such as La Fayette, who were opposed to the Crown's military policies. These aristocratic leaders of the patriotic party were to occupy prominent positions until the end of the Constituent Assembly, not to mention the liberal opposition at the time of the Restoration. The "bourgeois" Revolution was initiated and led, in part, by *grands seigneurs* whose titles went back to the Middle Ages.[6]

An examination of the political machine of the Duc d'Orléans, who played an important role in the events of 1788 and 1789, leaves a similar impression of liberalism and relative aristocratic irresponsibility. This rich and influential prince, who owned the equivalent of three or four of today's departments, headed the French Freemasons and ruled Paris from the Palais Royal, saw the revolutionary turmoil as an occasion to display his rebel spirit. This fanatical Anglophile, frustrated by social conventions, thought only of freedom, and raised his son, the future king Louis-Philippe, as a staunch republican. A member of the opposition to Maupeou, Calonne, and Brienne, he resolutely seized the reins of the struggle for reform. Starting in September 1788, he used his fortune to sway public opinion. Numerous advisers, under Laclos, aided him in this effort, laying the foundations for the Estates-General. One hundred thousand copies of his model *cahiers*, for example, were distributed. Elected to the Estates-General by the nobles of Ile-de-France, he did not play an important part there, but his earlier contributions to the political unrest confirm that this agitation was not confined to the bourgeoisie.[7]

The bourgeois had no difficulty imposing their will on the peasants, who were accustomed to being dominated by lawyers from the royal bureaucracy, themselves owners of manors and burning to acquire the nobility's lands.[8] But for a long time the provincial bourgeoisie left the leadership of the revolutionary struggle to the most traditional aristocrats, who were often more extremist than they. This most politicized segment of the aristocracy was the most open to ideological arguments and, in the context of the modern world of the city and the Englightenment, it was of capital importance to the Revolution.[9] A strange "bourgeois" revolution this, whose most illustrious participants were people like Sieyès, about whom Georges Lefebvre has maintained that, if only he had been made a bishop, he would doubtless not have become a revolutionary; Mirabeau, a libertine squire in revolt and in a hurry to achieve his ambitions; and La Fayette, who was to become the most powerful man in France for a short time *after* the 1789 schism, and who symbolized, until his death in 1834, the hope for a reconciliation of the Revolution and the ruling class as a whole.[10] This hope would no doubt have been realized if, starting with the Estates-General, the Third Estate had been able to win over not only the enlightened clergy, but also an aristocracy dominated by liberals rather than conservatives. But the Constituent Assembly did, indeed, represent the will of the monarchy's most prominent citizens, and reflected the fact that the aristocratic grave diggers of the *ancien régime* had contributed more to its disintegration than others. Men of continuity, the deputies of 1789 were epitomized by Démeunier, the reformist representative of the Parisian Third Estate. A former royal censor and secretary to Monsieur, son of an illiterate tradesman, but uplifted by the ideas of the Enlightenment, he became a senator of the empire. In the early phases of the revolutionary crisis he had undergone the ideological radicalization to which the majority of the elite had succumbed with no feelings of betrayal or conflict.[11]

WAS THE SOCIAL REVOLUTION OF 1789
A BOURGEOIS PHENOMENON?

Whereas the revolutionary bourgeoisie and its allies were able to control and direct the popular uprisings in the cities during the summer of 1789, this was not the case in the countryside. The chaos they created, for which the bourgeois and the aristocrats blamed each other, seemed to foreshadow a catastrophic threat to all property. The eradication of the feudal system proclaimed on August 4 was aimed at preventing this. It was not at all the product of a general mandate by the *cahiers*, nor was it of great interest to the Third Estate. Its deputies had no intention at first of eliminating seignorial rights. Faced with the general chaos toward which the country seemed headed, and the inability of the new authorities to remedy it, the idea of abolishing, with compensation, the "feudal dues" that weighed so heavily on the peasants seemed necessary. This manifestation of political and social radicalization was to be proposed to the assembly, moreover, by a member of the nobility.

During the famous night session that ensued this moderate proposal soon snowballed, and all privileges, tithes, venal offices, etc., were swept away by its momentum. This "moment of patriotic intoxication" symbolized more than anything the nation's new found unity. It was a maneuver intended to accelerate the desired changes, but there was certainly an element of "magic" in the overall exhilaration. It culminated, by morning, in the eradication of a large part of the country's social institutions, which were from then on consigned to history.

This act made the Revolution irreversible and meant that, barring a prolonged civil war, the *ancien régime* was doomed, all the more so since the new notables now had at their disposal the means to maintain order. Their principles were spelled out by the Decree of August 11 on the abolition of feudalism and by the Declaration of the Rights of Man and Citizen, passed on the twenty-sixth. This decree gave legal force to the political and constitutional struggle that had been raging, *since early 1787*, against despotism and the arbitrary power of the former monarchy. In this sense it voiced the liberal consensus that could be inferred from the *cahiers*. This consensus was hardest to obtain among the clergy.

But this document certainly expressed the will of the landowners, *bourgeois and nobles alike*, who had fought this revolution not in order to transform society, but to protect themselves from an irresponsible government.

Unlike the Declaration, which focused on the causes of 1789, the Decree of August 11 concentrated on its results. This codification of the decisions made on the fourth, undertaken with a view to settling with the peasantry and thus preventing the spread of disorder, permanently changed France's property system by mandating the reimbursement of the majority of the feudal dues that had been eliminated. Such was not the case for the church's revenues, which were eliminated without compensation. As for regional and local privileges, their eradication, the logical corollary of the elimination of the others, was just the opposite of what the majority of the French had seemed to want up until the end of 1788.

The elimination of the purchase of office constituted another fundamental social reform, this one more sought after by the *cahiers*, though for contradictory reasons. Those issued by the Third Estate denounced this system as an obstacle to the abilities of the poor, whereas those issued by the nobles saw it as a means of adulterating the purity of their ranks by giving access to parvenus. Even with compensation, what was at stake was the old society's most powerful mechanism of social mobility. The new order would never be the same. Instead of acquiring office to gain status, it would be necessary first to have the appropriate status in order to gain office.

Defining social status in terms of property was not a novel concept. What was new, however, was the political monopoly the Revolution was to grant property owners within the framework of representative institutions. Their creation was an outgrowth of the sudden protest against the old monopoly of the privileged. It resulted less from demands by bourgeois landowners than from the key sociopolitical decision to organize elections. The declining *ancien régime* thus created an elite of notables, composed only in part of aristocrats, which was to control the country for the greater part of the nineteenth century.

The struggles of the summer of 1789 centered mainly on the attempt to define this elite more precisely. In this process, the principle of equality of rights was offset by that of the inviolability of property, which meant that the nobles would in practice retain their privileges. The formation of the new elite, reinforced by the co-opting of talents, would result from a subtle alliance of wealth and ability. We know that the nobility was already willing to concede civil and fiscal equality. It was no less enthusiastic in its apparent support of the eradication of feudalism. Was not the fostering of merit in accordance with its principles and its whole history? The majority of the nobles accepted these changes with no thought of resisting them. Only a minority remained irreconcilable, choosing either to concede or to emigrate, and thereby creating an unresolvable conflict between the Revolution and what was henceforth referred to as the aristocracy.

The principles of 1789, therefore, do not strictly correspond to the aspirations of any of the groups that made up prerevolutionary society. They had no clear expression at the time of the meeting of the Estates-General and did not stem from a mandate by the *cahiers*. They were formulated in a largely haphazard manner, in keeping with the nature of the origins of the Revolution. The demise of the *ancien régime* was no doubt inevitable because of its financial debacle and its inability to adapt to new circumstances. The convocation of the Estates-General was forced on it after eighteen months of crisis. Its adversaries did not at first know what should replace it and confined their efforts to the definition of a liberal, constitutional consensus.

They then had to find a way to integrate the bourgeoisie politically into the nation. These onlookers who were becoming more and more knowledgeable about public affairs, did not seem eager to become active participants until 1788. The summoning, preparing, and organizing of the Estates-General drew them into the action. Their accession to a level of power previously limited to the nobility was little contested by most of its members, but was unfortunately accompanied by a new resentment of the noblest social dominance, and thus gave rise to mutual suspicion and misunderstanding. These antagonisms, accentuated by the drawing up of the *cahiers*, pitted the nobility against the bourgeoisie in a power struggle within the Estates-General, although both groups were basically in agreement over the way it should function. The eradication of aristocratic privilege thus became the indispensable condition for the constitution of a new elite that was not limited to the bourgeoisie. It was only the intervention of the people that overcame obstructionist efforts by the aristocracy and the government on this point. The abolition of feudalism soon thereafter resulted not from any clear-cut initial desire for it but rather as an improvised response to revolt in the countryside. The winners of this immensely significant social and political battle naturally claimed they had been seeking this outcome from the beginning. No one, in fact, had foreseen it two years before. Far from having created the Revolution, the revolutionaries, their attitudes, and their achievements were its products.[1]

This clarification by William Doyle can be disputed only on certain details. In particular, his interpretation of the night of August 4 may slight the deputies' financial concerns. It is also worth noting that the maneuver aimed at turning popular violence against the privileged classes appears to have been led by the Duc d'Aiguillon, one of the richest patriotic nobles, a former member of the Society of Thirty. His properties in the southwest brought him considerable income from seignorial dues, and his proposal for their compensation, which he set at a rate of 7 percent of their value for a period of thirty years, was very high. Like his associate Noailles, D'Aiguillon was a member of the court nobility who was less dependent on feudalism than many provincial landowners. But it is clear that idealism, as well as personal interest, was at the heart of most of the actions taken during this memorable session.

Perhaps its goal was also not so much to respond to the social crisis as it was to overcome a vexing obstacle to solving the problem of a constitution. Having abolished *all* privileges, the assembly could proceed vigorously in this direction. The concessions gained by the peasants, furthermore, were not negligible. As for the abolition of the tithe, achieved by the Duke of Chatelet in response to a bishop's motion which had eliminated hunting monopolies, it showed that there was already a movement to use church holdings to pay state debts. The eradication of provincial privileges, finally, resulted from the newly acquired political experience of the majority of the deputies, which dictated that privilege in any form was to be opposed.

This was La Fayette's proposal, in preparation since January and heavily influenced by the American Revolution, which served as a model for the Declaration of Rights. This last dealt with issues that were specifically French by suppressing the privileges of the aristocracy, limiting the power of the monarchy, and eliminating monopolies held by the church. Beyond this denunciation of the *ancien régime*, the document outlined a new society dominated by landowners. It was issued by an assembly that condoned the hanging of insurgent peasants who had been convicted by special courts (and who received nary a word of support from the revolutionary press). The work of city dwellers, the Revolution was from the beginning scornful of the rural popular classes. It was at once forced to come to terms, however, with the violence of urban artisans antagonistic to its notions of economic freedom. The new autonomy of the cities, which lasted until the Terror, led at first to a consolidation of the elite. Some vestiges of the *ancien régime* even remained in the administrations of Aix, Grenoble, and Toulouse. Nobles and priests retained some of their power in the province of Berry and in Lyons, while in Marseilles the local revolution, which had preceded the one in Paris, was quashed by a bloody military reprisal that lasted until the end of the year. The provincial nobility was thus rarely ousted from public affairs as abruptly as it was in Rennes or Montauban. In Rennes, moreover, officers of the national guard were even recruited from its ranks. The fear of brigands in the aftermath of the Revolution of 1789 tended to tighten the ranks of an elite that set aside its differences for the time being in the face of its fear of the popular classes.[2]

Going beyond any vague general speculations about the ideological fervor of the period and the radical character of its achievements, Jean-Pierre Hirsch's judicious depiction of the night of August 4 suggests its social significance. The participants did, indeed, view August 4 as a metaphysical and institutional rebirth of the world that ushered in a new era and put an end to the clash between the principles of the *ancien régime* and those, gradually emerging, of the new one. But the Marquis de Ferrières, deputy to the Constituent Assembly, cynically reminded his wife a year later that after all no one could ever help being "his father's son." Faced with the dual risk of bankruptcy and subversion, he had viewed the eradication of feudalism as a necessary sacrifice and compromise. So did most of his colleagues, both liberal aristocrats and bourgeois landowners. In addition to the solidarity that had just been demonstrated between the latter and the people of Paris, another link had been forged, this time between the nobility and a bourgeoisie committed to order and repression in the face of the peasants' threat to their property. The solution proposed by this two-pronged, apparently contradictory alliance was not to stop the Revolution, but on the contrary to broaden it at the expense of all privilege. Born of fear on the part of the rich, this "verbal and institutional use of the universal heir" was in fact a device for protecting property.* Satisfying all the interests represented in the assembly, it quieted those voices the members did not wish to hear. Capped by the abolition without compensation of the tithes, the night of August 4 was a triumph for the richest of the landowners, the nobles. They had, first of all, preserved the very basis of their order, honorific rights and seniority. Retaining all their properties and the greater part of their income, in addition to the main statutory bases of their superiority, they had little to lose, for the moment, from a change that undermined neither the social authority nor the real power of owners of fiefs. It was only on their own estates that they had occasionally been forced to bow their heads and stand by as their chateaux were burned down. But they now had at their disposal the weapons of the new order in their fight against the insurgent peasantry. Despite the abolition of feudalism, which soon became definitive, the former masters

---

* The universal heir was the offspring designated in a will to inherit the property, while the others were paid a sum of money.

of the land were able to hang onto it in a large part of postrevolutionary France, which was long marked by noble property-holding.[3]

The assembly that produced the August decrees was for the most part presided over by aristocrats. Nobles were at all times active participants in the formulation of laws. Defeated on the issue of compensation for a portion of feudal dues, they won one of their oldest and most persistent demands, the suppression of their payment of tithes to the clergy. This boon to landowners was of no use to small farmers, who in many cases found themselves worse off than before. Sieyès was therefore not wrong to view the night of August 4 as an aristocratic initiative whose goal was to reach a compromise with the revolutionary bourgeoisie on land reform, in exchange for moderation—which, moreover, did not occur—in government reform. But the abbé was himself so firmly rooted in the social practices of the *ancien régime* that he gave uncritical support to church holdings. He also relentlessly defended a social order paralyzed in maintaining acquired wealth. Harbinger of a noncapitalistic, purely political revolution, he linked his cause with the defense of *all* property. It was in the name of this principle that the Comte d'Entraigues, at this point, recalled the old merits of feudalism and argued that it was necessary to offer compensation for seignorial dues. Surprisingly cautious in this area, the economic and social ideology of the Revolution was, from the first, not forward looking but conservative. Obsessed with the threat of subversion and the need to repress it, it could not envision true liberty without "legitimate property" to "guarantee independence."[4]

4. A PEOPLE'S
REVOLUTION?

I*t is generally acknowledged that it was the involvement of the common people of the cities and the countryside during the summer of 1789 that brought about the defeat of the conservative minority in the Estates-General that sided with the monarchy, and then, after the defeat of absolutism, brought about the downfall of feudalism and the majority of the ancien régime's institutions. This phenomenon was not foreseen by the political leaders of the Revolution, who early in the year still believed, like Sieyès, that the mob always sided with the aristocracy. It transformed events permanently by forcing the rival elites to take the lower classes into consideration and by encouraging them to mobilize the people in their favor. But the people showed themselves to be untamable by revolutionaries and counterrevolutionaries alike. Before as well as after 1789, they were concerned above all with defending their own interests, which often were far removed from those of highly placed politicians. And the uniqueness of the sociocultural past of the popular classes no doubt explains, more than anything else, the complexity of their activities during the French Revolution.*[1]

WAS THE POPULAR INTERVENTION OF 1789 AN
UNPRECEDENTED UPRISING BY THE POOR?

Starting with Ernest Labrousse, much has been made of the economic causes of the Revolution. These had, until the spring of 1789, escaped its leaders, who perceived no social crisis in the country other than the one brought on by the collapse of the government. Budgetary and financial difficulties were, however, of little import compared with the consequences of the bad harvest of 1788, which profoundly altered the course of the Revolution.

French agriculture, which at that point was supposed to be feeding a population of over 26 million, had been able to accomplish this without any great difficulty throughout most of the eighteenth century. The government, moreover, viewed the distribution of grain among the people as one of its major priorities. This relative prosperity began to be replaced by serious fluctuations starting in 1770; these reached catastrophic proportions in 1788. The unreliability of harvests resulted in major reductions in income in rural areas throughout the country. The majority of inhabitants were small farmers with insufficient margins of security.

The economic crisis also affected industry, particularly textiles, since reduced incomes led to a drop in demand and a high level of urban unemployment, doubling the rate of rural pauperization. This general disaster exacerbated a long-standing erosion of the standard of living caused by inflation, which brought a growing depreciation of real earnings. The soaring bread prices, especially, had a catastrophic impact on the popular classes, who were already allotting 50 percent of their daily expenditures to its purchase. This proportion was to reach close to 90 percent among Parisian workers in the worst days of the spring of 1789. These workers had moreover just struggled through a particularly cold winter, which had further aggravated the situation.

The only prosperous sector of the country's economy remained maritime trade, linked with the reexport of colonial products to northern Europe. Bordeaux, which in 1789 handled 40 percent of this trade, was, along with Nantes, at its economic zenith, and was only affected after 1791 by slave revolts in Santo Domingo and then by the war with England. But this spectacular upsurge was a marginal phenomenon. All the rest of the French economy was suffering at the time the *cahiers* were drafted. This source of tension increased France's political difficulties as well as the general unrest focused on the government. The liberal commercial treaty the Crown made with London in 1786 was resented, as it put French industry at a disadvantage. Another experiment, backed by the physiocrats and repeated in the final months of the *ancien régime*, had consisted in deregulating the grain trade. This initiative, which had already caused problems under Turgot, was abandoned by Necker when he returned to office in 1788.

Underfed, poor, resentful of the duties and taxes they had to pay, the people of France found themselves, in the spring of 1789, in a state of latent upheaval. Their first concern, as usual, was to control the marketing of grain and fix the price of bread. From January to May, riots broke out in bakeries and granaries throughout the country before reaching Paris. Peace had long since been restored, however, when the Parisian manufacturer Réveillon imprudently spoke, on April 23, of cutting salaries. His factory was looted on the twenty-eighth and the repressive measures that followed left many dead. In the capital and the provinces, the problem of maintaining order thus became a pressing issue that the government was at a loss to solve. It could fall back only on the army, which was increasingly demoralized by the duties that had been imposed on it. It was against this backdrop of disorder and widespread anxiety among the people that the Estates-General convened. Preoccupied with its own concerns, which were totally divorced from those of the people, it viewed popular action only in terms of the need to repress it in order to defend the property of the rich. Bourgeois authority was thus established, first in Marseilles and then in other cities, starting in March, in order to rectify this chaotic situation.[2]

This standard interpretation is confirmed by analyses that stress the seriousness of the crisis affecting the everyday life of the popular classes. They still lived a very narrow existence, with no clear sense of national unity, which remained a chimera because of the diversity of dialects. Economic practices reinforced this social traditionalism. Recent changes in the rural world had had little effect on the distribution of land among the peasantry, the nobility, the bourgeoisie, and the clergy. Although it varied greatly by region, the overall inequality, whereby 50 percent of the land was owned by 10 percent of the population, was more marked in the north and the Midi than in the west. Highly stratified, the rural communities were made up of an elite which was diverse but firmly in control, along with a considerable mass of peasant families of insufficient means. They were not always able to make ends meet by working in industry or by emigrating, and 40 percent of the French population in 1789 depended on charity. The prevalence of pauperism and begging had long contributed to crime, and more or less organized gangs of brigands scoured the Paris region for the entire second half of the eighteenth century, both before and after the Revolution. From Dauphiné to Brittany, the outlaw was everywhere a popular hero, because the man of the people was often a potential outlaw.

The poor, however, did not in themselves play an important role in 1789 or afterward. They were simply regarded with fear, and many of them participated in the upsurge of banditry that followed the economic collapse of 1794. During the entire revolutionary period they continued to be preoccupied primarily with their own situation. But the overall decline in the French standard of living facilitated the outbreak of the Revolution within the context of an economy that was unable to keep pace with a demographic explosion that was throwing society off balance in the cities and the countryside. The population of France increased, in fact, by several million in the eighteenth century, with no parallel increase in basic food production. No agricultural revolution corresponded to the country's demographic expansion. Moreover, as we have seen, the rise in food prices made workers' lives even more difficult, and their increasing rate of pauperization reached crisis proportions on the eve of the Revolution. People were all the more vulnerable to the succession of bad crops, as well as to its impact on rural and urban employment and the general conditions of life.

Unlike later historians, the people of the time attributed this situation not to meteorological accidents, but to grain speculation, and they reacted, as we know, with spontaneous revolts. These hundreds of incidents, starting in 1770, revealed precapitalistic aspirations by the masses to a minimal level of community subsistence. When the government did not fulfill these aspirations through recourse to traditional controls, it was accused of betraying its paternal duties in the name of free trade. In the early 1760s the people of Paris came increasingly to believe in a hunger conspiracy, orchestrated by the ministries or perhaps even the king and aimed at absorbing the budget deficit by raising the price of grain. This myth, more than anything else, helped undermine the government's reputation in the capital at the end of Louis XV's reign. It persisted with regard to the ministers and the majority of officials on the eve of the Revolution. In the provinces, the wine-growers' debacle, the increase in peasants' dues, and the conjunction of constitutional crisis and economic calamities could only make 1789 a terrible year, marked by unemployment, famine, and poverty. Keeping order by traditional means thus became impossible, and beginning in March bourgeois militias, as we have seen, began to take this task into their own hands, anticipating the powers of the future National Guard. At the same time that it was caving in at the top, the *ancien régime's* foundations were crumbling, *before* the meeting of the Estates-General.

Invited to participate at a time when governmental authority was disintegrating, the popular classes for the first time had hopes of finding political solutions to their problems. Their sufferings, according to a certain millenarian perspective, would be alleviated by miraculous intervention from above. This did not spur them to become much involved in elections, which in the countryside were still dominated by the rural elite. The urban *cahiers* were therefore more hostile than the others to seignorial privileges. They were, furthermore, often drawn up, as in Paris, amid severe unrest among the workers. To their old notion of a hunger plot the people now added that of sinister manipulations of the future Estates-General by the aristocracy. This explosive psychological mix was not confined to Paris and was reinforced by the fear of brigands. Increasingly uncontrolled, the brigands were naturally lumped together with agents of the aristocratic conspiracy that opposed national regeneration. Were not these gangs planning to destroy crops, abetting the work of a foreign invasion favorable to the privileged classes? This multifaceted mythology, compounding fear of hunger, the machinations of the powerful, organized crime, and foreigners, continued to characterize the popular mentality in times of crisis until 1815.[3]

Recent research has tended to integrate this analysis, derived from Georges Lefebvre's work, into the long-term history of the country. The Revolution, in this sense, by no means represents a disjuncture. The intensity of popular movements as a form of social protest against the public order and its political and cultural norms constitutes one of the laws of the evolution of France from at least the sixteenth century on. Jean Nicolas has drawn up a juicy narrative of such uprisings in Savoie, and it is clear that the majority of French provinces, if approached in the same methodical manner, would yield similar results. Sporadic but persistent insubordination, made up of diverse emotions, rumors, and seditions, mobilized against abusive authority the conservative, restorative defenses of the traditional collectivity, opposed to any disruption of the equilibrium that ensured the survival of the group. Far from marginal, these movements were the expression of the collective unconscious arising from widespread poverty and the kinds of sensitivities that it engendered.[4]

Charles Tilly has attempted to outline the typology of this age-old revolt of the French heartland against capitalism and the state over the long term. All areas of the cities and the countryside alike were to experience it in more or less analogous forms. In 1775, Dijon, for example, like Paris, had its own grain war, whose goal was the maintenance of a system for feeding the poor. During the Revolution, Burgundy pursued its ancestral struggle against the authorities in the country and cities. The same impression of continuity, which lasted until at least 1848, is to be found elsewhere and can be explained by the necessity of struggle everywhere against the building of the modern state and the economic policies accompanying it. Toulouse thus fought, like Dijon and Paris, to assure its subsistence throughout the 1770s. In all the towns of Languedoc there were seizures of grain and other uprisings, such as those associated with the property system. The food crisis that sank the *ancien régime* did not set off any revolutionary break with the past. It marked a victory against the progress of capitalism and the state by the spontaneous, *traditional* response of popular revolt, which coincided this time, *by chance*, with a profound political upheaval. The Revolution that grew out of this accidental conjuncture could not solve the economic and social problems that had helped to bring it about.[5]

This is nowhere better demonstrated than by the grain riots, the major—though masked—form of political conflict in France from the late seventeenth to the mid-nineteenth century. Faced with this threat, the government's traditional policy on subsistence crops sought to regulate the market and control trade. The inadequacy or relaxation of these interventionist measures could only be resented by the popular classes as long as an insufficiently developed national market left consumers at the mercy of crises. Keeping bread prices low, by taxation if necessary, establishing grain reserves to be requisitioned or sold by force if necessary, prohibiting the export of grains from regions where needs were not being met in an acceptable manner: these three measures still constituted in 1789 the economic and social program of the people, and had long framed the orientation of the Crown. The growing rift, which appeared during the eighteenth century, between the government's views in this area and the people's wishes was the main bone of contention that cropped up in 1789 as it had in 1775. The government's new economic policy, an outgrowth of market expansion and administrative centralization, conflicted with the political demands of the masses, who considered the battle against hunger, wherever it occurred, using all appropriate means of control, to be the first duty of the authorities. Revolutionary violence simply was incorporated into this age-old attitude.[6]

Sensitive, above all, to the political dimensions of grain distribution, the popular classes revolted, starting late in the reign of Louis XV, against measures instituted under the influence of a liberal pressure group backed by the physiocrats. They suspected it of engaging in a hunger conspiracy and were joined in these sinister beliefs by opponents of economic liberalism, who were often close to *parlement* circles. Wavering between traditional paternalism and a modernist ideology that challenged its sacred nature, the Crown's food policy foreshadowed hesitations that would be those of the revolutionary period. It, too, would be torn between the people's demand for the right to subsistence and the new exigencies of capitalism and the state. But the new politics of subsistence had been inaugurated by the specter of a starvation pact, derived from a mentality of conspiracy that could not fathom how a country that was thought to be rich could be plagued with food shortages. This psychological obsession reflected the traditional importance of the problem of subsistence and the equally traditional difficulty of solving it. Seen from below as the government of a baker-King, the monarchy of the *ancien régime* was to succumb because of its inability to supply bread, a deficiency that had already fueled many rumors about profiteering by people in high places, and which caused many revolts. These grew out of a visceral conservatism that was to send former Controller General Laverdy to the guillotine after Louis XVI. A paranoid pamphleteer, who afterward suffered a long prison term in the Bastille, had accused Laverdy in 1768 of having plotted a famine, just as his successors would be accused in 1789.[7]

WHY DID PARIS RISE UP IN 1789?

Popular uprisings thus spread throughout all of France from the spring to the early summer of 1789. The members of the Estates-General were aware of the risk of generalized anarchy and agreed upon the absolute necessity for reestablishing public order. This anguished atmosphere even explains the bitterness expressed by many of them during the procrastination of the months of May and June. But it is not clear that the troops could not have maintained order until the harvest, nor that the unrest would have had such decisive political consequences, if it had not spread to the capital. The provincial cities, fearing the people's reactions to food shortages, were still awaiting orders from Paris in mid-July. This city of over seven hundred thousand, an enormous population for the time, indisputably dominated the country. In Paris, there were considerable social contrasts between the richest segment of the French population, along with government leaders, and the masses that were growing poorer and being pushed to the eastern part of the city. These humble folk caught glimpses of the ruling classes only when they drove their carriages through the narrow streets, causing accidents that increased class resentment. A drifting population of immigrant laborers came looking for work, and increased in times of economic crisis. As potential beggars and criminals, they were feared by the authorities, who saw them as a source of disorder.

In fact, with nothing to fear and little to protect, they rarely participated in riots. These potential criminals had neither the desire to organize nor the strong common interests necessary for collective action. These qualities were to be found rather among well-established Parisians, who owned some property, knew their neighbors, shared their concerns, and were used to getting together in guilds and confraternities. The majority of crafts enterprises employed no more than twenty people and were controlled by privileged organizations. The authorities responsible for keeping the peace indiscriminately branded all workers the enemies of order, savage beasts whose animalistic instincts had to be suppressed. Increased surveillance of the workplace characterized the eighteenth century and culminated in the institution in 1781 of the *livret*, the passbook which was indispensable for obtaining work. Unrest nevertheless remained on the upswing, causing more and more frequent strikes. These were a response to the economic difficulties of the time, but the first concern of the Parisian workers was to put pressure on the government to lower the prices of staple items.

Maintaining a reliable supply of bread was the real means of maintaining public order. The authorities were aware of this and their first priority was to maintain a constant supply of subsistence items for the capital at prices that they themselves set. Price increases, which were at times inevitable, brought on unrest, particularly on market days, while consumers awaited their turn. It was often the women who forced merchants and bakers to lower their prices. There was also great resentment over the customs duties on merchandise, which were symbolized, at the gates of Paris, by a wall and fences that had recently been mandated and were still under construction in 1789. It was not believed, however, that a popular uprising could succeed in the capital, and few police were stationed there. Keeping order was the responsibility of the permanent regiment of the French Guards, which held off riots until April 1789.

The people of Paris had played little role in the governmental collapse of the preceding year, backing, as they traditionally did, the *parlement*. But in this protracted period of political unrest and considerable economic problems there was increasing fear of their repeated intervention in public life. Were not the people once more going to take to the streets? Certain patriotic leaders began to hope that this would work in their favor. These were the most radical elements, who frequented the new cafés of the Palais Royal. This assembly of swindlers, deserters, and prostitutes, protected from police intervention by the Duc d'Orléans, became a hotbed of discussion and dissemination of rumors. In early June violent diatribes against the government were heard and applauded. The Réveillon affair had just cast the shadow of popular unrest and of the risk of its exploding on the Parisian and national political scenes. The French Guards, who had resolved this affair, were beginning to disintegrate because of a lack of attention to discipline and morale.

In this tense atmosphere, the exorbitant rise in bread prices, which attained their highest level since 1770 on July 14, led to a special reinforcement of the troops that had surrounded the capital since mid-April. This was seen as proof of a conspiracy against the Estates-General. Several companies of French Guards announced in late June that they would no longer put down demonstrations by the people, who proclaimed them heroes. The imprisoned leaders of the mutiny were liberated by the crowd and supported by the patriots of the Palais Royal. Order nevertheless continued to be maintained. It was shattered by the announcement of Necker's dismissal on Sunday the twelfth. The people

of Paris, convinced that this was an attempt to starve them out, felt that
they had been driven to legitimate self-defense, and the uprising that
was to culminate in the fall of the Bastille began. Marked by a frenzied
search for available arms, it logically led to this formidable depot. There
was also a food riot, in which the newly erected customs barriers were
burned. The armed populace was attempting to keep attention fixed on
the concrete problem of the food supply, which remained, in their eyes,
the most important issue. This movement alarmed the landowners, who,
as a result, called for the formation of a bourgeois militia that was from
then on to be in charge of Paris. Designed to contain the violence of the
people, it had to begin by drawing strength from it. Imitated throughout
the rest of France, this conduct by the local notables who formed the
basis of the National Guard hardly concealed the fact that the people's
intervention, which had salvaged the Revolution, would continue to
shape it.[1]

This communal action was a triumph for the politically aroused populace, which had succeeded in undermining the military bases of monarchical power by appealing to refractory soldiers and civilians.
Consisting at times of looting and anarchy, it posed grave dangers for
the future. The crowd had meted out its own brand of justice, parading
the heads of its enemies through the streets. It was to resume its involvement again, in early October, under the pressure of economic difficulties and the food crisis. Thousands of women descended on
Versailles to find the baker-King, and wound up bringing him back to
Paris. This offensive was another step in the disintegration of authority.
For a long time it placed the state under pressure from the masses in
the capital. Several months of continual turmoil had given them a political education and a taste of their power within the Revolution and
its institutions, which they had molded as much as, if not more than,
the bourgeoisie.[2]

After Georges Lefebvre we owe to George Rudé the broad outlines
of this view of the revolutionary crowds stirred up by the events of 1789.
The majority of their members were tradesmen, small shopkeepers, and
guildsmen from the outlying working-class neighborhoods, contrary to
the reactionary myth that labeled them shady characters and criminals.
They were motivated not by the idea of looting, nor by the political
catchwords of the moment, but chiefly by the fundamental social and
political demand of the humble folk of the *ancien régime*, namely, af-
fordable bread. This was to mobilize the future *sans-culottes* in support
of the leaders of the Revolution. A major source of agitation by the
people, it accounted for unrest among them until 1795. The political
crisis that coincided with it no doubt made it more explosive. But it was

always for the purpose of defending "traditional rights and supporting the enforcement of controls they felt were being threatened by the machinations of ministers, capitalists" and other reformers and speculators that the Parisians rose up during the Revolution. Their radicalization thus grew out of traditional consumer resistance to the new principles of the market. These upheavals, which inaugurated the modern age, were an echo of the most distant past.[3]

We now have a better understanding of the living conditions and the psychology of the popular classes of the capital in the eighteenth century. An examination of their material conditions confirms that two-thirds of all wage-earners lived in poverty and debt. Their housing was costly and of poor quality, and the growth of their consumption, particularly with regard to clothing, was slight. Largely literate, but deriving little benefit from this, they would charge food on credit at a tavern when there was nothing left to eat at home. Under surveillance and observation, their first concern was to scratch out a meager subsistence.[4]

There was a whole subcategory of marginal characters, delinquents, and outlaws even more deeply sunk in poverty—the beggars and vagrants. These poor people, documented to some degree by police records of arrests for begging, were often boys and young men who came mainly from the countryside surrounding Paris. They shuttled between unemployment and the difficult search for a new occupation, and remained, naturally, uneducated. Their biggest problem was to find lodging. They slept on the streets or stayed in furnished rooms either in the center of the city or outside its walls. They begged, preferably, in the good neighborhoods of the northwest. This group, dependent on charity or crime, was considered a menace to the city. The equivalent of such pauperism was to be found in the working-class cities of the country, where, as in Amiens, poverty was highly visible. Living in cramped quarters, indigent and sick, close to a third of the city's inhabitants were in need of aid. The result of large families and inadequate earnings, this poverty led to resignation, escape into the army, or emigration. Such were the social consequences of the economic difficulties of 1789. There was fear of "the war of the poor against the rich" with the former demanding bread and the latter taking up arms to keep it away from them.[5]

Around 1780, an upper-level administrator like Montyon and an opposition journalist like Mercier were alike in considering poverty an essential factor in criminality. They were scandalized and worried by a situation that incited so many of the needy to destructive passions stirred by hunger. In his hatred of inequality, Mercier went so far as to write that "the unfortunate who is sent to the scaffold" always seemed to him "to be accusing a rich man." But these two observers agreed in their

belief that in Paris the deprivation suffered by the popular classes multiplied the number of potential criminals. They attributed this danger to
the invasion of the capital by a young, unstable, jobless population that
was quick to resort to violence. Mobile, hard to control, and poorly
integrated, it disturbed public opinion and contributed significantly to
social tension and fear on the eve of the Revolution.[6] This was the
backdrop of the problem of maintaining social order. A matter of state
in Paris, where a riot could degenerate into a revolution, it led the
authorities to broaden their repressive activities, using the issue of public
security as an excuse. Charged with keeping tabs on the dangerous
drifters of the center city, the police in the capital became more and
more militarized, whereas the French Guard was transformed into a
police force. The city militia was in fact considered unsuited to the task
of maintaining order, which fell to the Parisian Guard and the army.
The former in 1789 numbered only fifteen hundred men, under the
jurisdiction of the secretary of state in the royal household. The French
Guard, originally simply an emergency force, thus became responsible
for day-to-day security. Often, moreover, in order to combat the discipline problems of its members, this regiment fell under the supervision
of the police system. It earned a reputation among the public for arbitrariness and excessive severity, while lacking the upper hand in developing an overall strategy for maintaining order. The increasing tendency
toward lodging the Guard in barracks led to recruitment difficulties,
which were compounded by the rigors of service. In view of this risk of
disintegration, there was even some talk, in 1788, of dissolving the
regiment. Its association with insurgent elements did not derive from
some imagined affinity with the poor, but from deficiencies in its own
system and its sequestration in barracks that facilitated collective reactions. Another factor contributing to the downfall of the *ancien régime*
was, thus, that the ministers in Paris, obsessed with matters of security,
fragmented the police on the pretext of maintaining order.[7]

This was necessary, in their eyes, to combat violent outbreaks by the
people, which seem, on the contrary, to have been on the decline. Admired throughout Europe, a masterpiece of modernity, the Parisian police force itself provoked disorder by its brutality and arbitrariness. Thus
confronted, the people often sided with its victims, whether they were
honest folk or vagrants. The conflicts the police were called upon to put
down or arbitrate were less the expression of the workers' need for a
psychological outlet than the blind revolt of the capital's new arrivals,
who were poorly housed, ill fed, and often scorned by those who exploited their cheap labor. These "savages" knew and believed only in

the language of brute force, of which they made a religion. They had brought with them to the big city where they landed their taste for fighting and handling weapons, their propensity for emotional outbursts, and their capacity to endure pain. Adding to the tensions surrounding the grain laws and workers' coalitions, they were standing by in the shadows, ready to transform popular frustration into revolutionary violence. Their future *journées* were to constitute, indeed, the brutal intrusion of the language of day-to-day violence into the sociopolitical arena that had until then been shielded from it.[8]

Arlette Farge, to whom we owe this insight, has just completed a fine study of the relationships among "violence, power, and coalitions" in eighteenth-century Paris. In it we find evidence from police archives of the psychological consequences of fundamental social instability and economic precariousness. In the first six months of 1750, there were fifteen demonstrations against child kidnappings attributed to the political authorities. Insecurity and instability in the capital thus shaped a "collective mental horizon" consisting above all of fear of a wide range of dangers and risks. This generalized tension, expressed in exaggerated outbursts of passion, was hardly offset by associations formed in the workplace. Violence broke out as often there as in the neighborhoods, and even more so among the population of drifters we have already mentioned, which sometimes included well-organized criminal gangs. For this world of marginal characters had its own networks. The mobs were made up of all these elements. They were regularly dispatched to public festivities, such as the birth of the dauphin in 1781. They participated in the pageantry of public executions, a familiar and fascinating scene. The celebration of the marriage of the future Louis XVI in 1770 was ruined by a stampede in which hundreds of craftsmen and small wage-earners were injured. The authorities were accused of negligence. Gullible and sensation-seeking, the people of Paris were perhaps matched in this by their leaders. Rife with rumors, the city was certainly prone to sudden collective upheavals. These crowds, at once a necessary outgrowth of urban society, an ingredient in monarchical ritual, and a burden for the government, represented a permanent source of worry. The streets of the capital were never quiet because the disorder constituted a demand for order in the face of an uncertain future. Disorderly behavior was thus identified as one of the "traditional forms of existence of the population." Unable to decipher this confused sea of revolts and turmoil, the police confined themselves to containing it blindly. The Revolution that was to come appeared to be nothing more than a larger version of the preceding upheavals.[9]

DID THE RURAL UPHEAVALS OF 1789 CONSTITUTE AN
ORIGINAL AND AUTONOMOUS PEASANT REVOLUTION?

Eighty percent of all the French at the time of the Revolution were
peasants, but they played no role in the events that preceded the fall of
the *ancien régime*. During the prerevolutionary crisis, in fact, and until
the spring of 1789, they merely observed what was happening, just
as the politicians engaged in the struggle gave little thought to them.
The peasants became important because of the bad harvest of 1788,
which threatened public order in the countryside as it did in the cities.
The drafting of the *cahiers*, moreover, raised great hopes in them. Their
subsequent dissatisfaction shortly thereafter led them to force their views
on the National Assembly.

The diversity of the rural world, in which four million peasants owned
perhaps a quarter of the country's land, was considerable. At the top
was a small group of wealthy farmers, whose lands were principally in
the north and the northeast. Beneath this elite of fewer than six hundred
thousand people, who profited from the absenteeism of nobles and bourgeois, came another minority of laborers, those who had enough land
to be self-sufficient or even have a surplus. Envied and respected by the
rest of the community, they had benefitted, like the wealthier peasant
farmers, from certain favorable circumstances in the eighteenth century.

The overwhelming majority was forced to find other means of survival
besides the cultivation of their land, if they had any. This precarious
economic situation was hardest on the large category of the poorest rural
inhabitants. This group included large numbers of beggars, vagrants,
and petty criminals, and was also the major source of itinerant unskilled
labor in the countryside and the cities. Rootless and difficult to control,
it frightened the more sedentary peasants.

Beyond the regional diversity that complicated these social contrasts,
this rural world was fundamentally marked by a demographic explosion
that caused overpopulation in relation to the available means of subsistence. The need for land was increased by the division of inheritances,
and led to fierce competition for use of collectively held rights. The
numbers of poor people, migrant workers, and beggars naturally swelled
in times of economic crisis, such as 1789, particularly since the peasantry
also suffered from the reduction in real earnings. On top of this, after
1770, there was the slump in wine production, in the textile industry,
and in employment possibilities in the city. Hard hit as producers, consumers, and taxpayers, the peasants were also hard hit, finally, by the
seignorial system.

This medieval inheritance remained much in force. It entailed numerous dues and other obligations that the country people owed to their many superiors, symbolizing the latter's honorific, legal, and above all economic power. Linked in the peasants' minds with the nobility, these dues and obligations represented a highly variable burden, bringing large profits to the nobility, the church, and many bourgeois as well. The increase of this burden as the century wore on was the logical outcome of new investment strategies adopted by the richest landowners, who sought more efficient management of the dues owed them. The *cahiers* submitted in 1789 by the peasants, however, complained little about this, aside from the most egregious examples of "feudalism." This was not the case in the cities, which were quite responsive to the economic attacks directed against the seignorial system. These attacks were soon followed by an assault on the related issue of the privileges of the nobility. Nevertheless, the struggle against the feudal system was not uppermost in the public consciousness either among the popular classes or the bourgeoisie on the eve of the Revolution. It was the crisis of spring 1789 that pushed it to the forefront.

In the countryside the components of this crisis, were hunger, hope, and fear. Economic difficulties account for the first, which brought on unrest starting in January. Grain convoys, mills, and bakeries were attacked and authorities threatened. On top of this, the electoral campaign raised hopes that things would soon be better. The peasants thought all the demands expressed in their grievances were going to be granted and consequently stopped paying what they owed. This national tax strike extended to the seignorial system. Starting in February, the inhabitants of Dauphiné refused to pay their dues. Unrest spread, especially to Provence. Impatience at the stalled opening of the Estates-General was increased in the provinces by rumors of an "aristocratic plot" to sabotage efforts at national regeneration. The execution of this sinister plot was attributed to "brigands" whose description matched the tramps drifting throughout the countryside. Tensions were only exacerbated by the summer's promise of a good harvest. Panic stemming from an understandable credulity took hold of the rural world at the thought that criminal machinations might sabotage it.

The political crisis of June 23 to July 16 heightened this anxiety and seemed to justify the peasants' worst fears. The news of the Parisian uprising was the final spark, and for three weeks order seems to have disappeared from the countryside. The attacks that had begun the preceding spring became widespread, and this time, a large number of chateaux were destroyed in the search for feudal titles. These sustained attacks on the seignorial system in the countryside were only strengthened by the Crown's capitulation, which, as a response to acts that had involved very little bloodshed, was interpreted by the peasants as authorization to step up their pressure on the aristocracy. This movement, moreover, frightened all the landowners and even a good number of the country people who were not involved in it. In an atmosphere tinged with hysteria, the people were convinced that the razing of the chateaux was the work of despicable thieves who had come to kill, pillage, and destroy crops. Amid such chaos, the peasants of Dauphiné, for example, took up arms against these imaginary brigands before setting upon the chateaux. We have seen how this generalized fear finally spread, for good reason, to the deputies themselves, who were unable to perceive the autonomy of the rural world and remained convinced that this gigantic revolt was the result of diabolical plots.[1]

This peasant revolt has intrigued historians, who have long explained it by reference to a seignorial reaction that occurred in the eighteenth century. According to this interpretation, the revision of seignorial land registers led to increases in dues, particularly in backward areas of the country. The people's resentment of this trend then culminated in the upheaval of 1789, and beyond that, in a struggle that lasted until the total eradication of the feudal regime in 1793. Countering this argument is the fact that the changes in question were neither new, nor generalized, nor frequent. They did not always result in an increase in dues, as they did in Brittany. In regions such as Flanders and Burgundy, peasants could always refuse to pay. In Normandy and Auvergne, they prevailed over *seigneurs* or their agents when they made exorbitant demands. Frequently armed, the country people had intimidated their masters well before 1789. And it sometimes happened that certain well-established communities in wealthy areas won lawsuits against an abusive *seigneur*.

Although it is impossible to prove that the "feudal" regime became more oppressive on the eve of the Revolution, it is clear that it became intolerable in such areas as Berry, Lorraine, and particularly, Franche-Comté, regions of virtual serfdom. The burden was often less oppressive than this, and no doubt amounted in most areas to the appropriation of 5 to 10 percent of agricultural production. It came down hardest on the richest peasants, who were most involved in commercial networks. They paid on behalf of their poorest neighbors, and under the reign of Louis XVI dissatisfaction with the seignorial system in Burgundy was most prevalent among the well-off villagers. A similar situation prevailed with regard to fiscal pressures, for the impoverishment of the countryside placed the tax burden more and more on rural notables. As they were also unhappy about increases in their obligations to the *seigneurs*, their hostility toward the privileged classes only grew.

These privileged classes, particularly in areas of unenclosed fields, aggressively exploited their economic superiority at the expense of collective rights, and the poor in the community suffered alongside the rich. A powerful antiseignorial coalition took shape in the villages and was directed against the traditional activities of large estates as a whole, whether owned by nobles or bourgeois. The economic crisis of 1789 aggravated these problems, as these large properties, whether in lay or church hands, monopolized the grain supplies to be sent to the cities. It was only natural to view their owners as enemies to be combated. This struggle, which began in the spring as a desperate resistance, was transformed into an overt offensive after the victory of the Third Estate and the capitulation of the king.

Taking matters into their own hands, the peasants thus rose up in a number of regions until early August. Their revolt took various forms appropriate to the different conditions of the seignorial regime. This uprising was thus by no means an explosion of blind rage. A settling of age-old accounts, it claimed official sanction almost everywhere, and was often led by the rural rich. A summary, if not violent, application of popular justice, the revolts pursued in new ways traditional procedures, which in some places had been suspended. In the Macon region citizens had set the tone by attacking grain merchants on July 20; the peasants, confident that they would not be punished, staged an elaborate *charivari* against the chateaux and those associated with them as a celebration of hope rewarded. Having cavalierly pillaged and eaten and drunk their fill, twenty-six of them were later sentenced by bourgeois courts to be hanged as rioters and looters. Gangs in Dauphiné carried out similar actions against their *seigneurs*, allegedly enemies of the Third Estate and suppliers of brigands, before being put down by the National Guard of Lyons. To the general turmoil over taxes, food, and the seignorial system, the events of the Great Fear, itself mixed with rumors of aristocratic and foreign conspiracies, merely added an irrational element. This latter obsession, which above all poisoned relations with the aristocracy, in the end reinforced the cohesion of the elite, particularly in the cities that opposed the countryside.[2]

The explanation for these events is to be found in the mental and social structures of the rural world under the *ancien régime*. Like the urban areas, it had an inclination toward delinquency that seems to have grown during the eighteenth century when, in Languedoc, for example, latent anxieties were more and more openly expressed toward those on the fringes of society, the vagrants and highway robbers who escaped the normal modes of justice. According to Nicole Castan, repressive measures by the *parlement* of Toulouse were directed at a "crime-

spawning society" caused by demographic expansion that led to an
increase in begging among the landless as well as in the vulnerability of
women and young people to crisis conditions. The judicial system could
hope to eliminate only the most dangerous elements by executing them
or sending them to the galleys. This turmoil in the rural areas of the
south, like that in the capital, was caused by the poverty of the most
dependent segments of the population. Without the least bit of security,
the poorest peasants, such as the sharecroppers from the Castres region
whose abjection was described by their subdelegate in 1777, could barely
eke out a living from day to day. As in the cities, they wound up as
vagrants and beggars hunted down by the authorities. The form of
criminal activity most typical of these hard-hit classes was rural banditry,
which was endemic from the Pyrenees to the Rhône around 1780. The
clutch of poverty was as much responsible for this as the price riots.
The situation culminated in 1783 in the revolt of the "Masked Ones,"
an outcry of despair in the Vivarais countryside that was being milked
by rings of usurers. The insurgents announced an imminent "time of
vengeance." The inability of the constabulary to maintain an emergency
police corps in rural areas left the countryside infested with gangs of
thieves.[3]

Criminality among the peasants of the eighteenth century, a topic
increasingly studied by historians, did not only involve marginal characters, vagrants, and drifters caught begging or stealing. It also involved
communities waging a determined struggle against their *seigneurs*, who
were subjected to insults, scorn, and assaults. The military governor of
Languedoc was besieged with complaints about groups of young people
attacking officials. There, the economic disarray of the end of the *ancien
régime* brought with it an upsurge in such violent outbreaks, which had
become impossible to control within the framework of traditional institutions. In Auvergne, where conditions were even harsher, villagers
directly challenged or ignored the law and the courts. Even north of the
Loire, the rural populace often preferred to settle accounts by brute
force. In any case, the number of crimes brought before the lower court,
which dealt with matters related to vagrancy, increased by 300 percent
in the second half of the century. This phenomenon was most widespread
in the large agricultural areas in the region surrounding Paris, where
gangs of brigands sometimes numbered in the hundreds and became a
source of terror. Sustained by the complicity of the people, indifferent
to the suffering of their victims, and hostile to military repression, some
of these bands survived until the very end of the Revolution. The rural
community basically disliked the police and often protected from them
harmless beggars and poachers sought by the *seigneurs*. The police were

viewed as intruders. In Brittany even priests were reluctant to help them. The opposite attitude, south of the Loire, was thought to have been responsible for the destruction of crops. The villagers were capable, in cases like these, of forbidding the parish priests to cooperate with the authorities. They considered themselves the sole natural enforcers of the law, and the occurrences of 1789—the fear of brigands and the spread of destruction in a context of economic difficulties—were above all manifestations of a "crisis in justice." The people of the rural areas wanted justice to come cheap, and thought they could always maintain order themselves. They could scarcely understand a revolution that would establish this justice by expanding the bureaucracy.[4]

The new hostility of the peasantry to the "feudal" regime dates back to the mid-eighteenth century, according to certain commentators, and can be traced through litigation that pitted peasants against *seigneurs*. The more sophisticated language of this new form of collective resistance often foreshadowed that of 1789: Having failed, for the most part, by means of recourse to the law, the peasants would avenge themselves by means of violence. This campaign for legal reform, backed at times by representatives of the Crown, for the first time took on the principle of the seignorial system itself. Such was the case in Burgundy after 1750, where it was the attitude of the peasantry and not the feudal reaction that was new and revolutionary. This strategy of the rural population testified to their refusal to pay even the traditional dues. Their communities were able to give them financial backing and they gained the support of lawyers and administrators. The former would forge in this fire some elements of future revolutionary discourse, and the latter were not always sympathetic to the feudal regime. Feudalism was thus plunged into the revolutionary ordeal in a weakened condition, for the country people felt that it was no longer supported by the state.[5]

The indisputably moderate nature of the eighteenth-century peasant revolts by no means signified an end to strife in the countryside. On the contrary, in 1750 the struggle against the seignorial system was ripening in the east central portion of France, and in 1780 it broke out in full force. A true demand for power by country people who were better equipped because they were better informed and more politically aware, it was the rural expression of the type of development of public opinion often associated with urban growth. Lawyers were appointed to defend a case that had been brought up-to-date ideologically, socially, and politically—a case against an agrarian capitalism that was at the heart of the new-style "feudalism." In the most backward areas of the Massif Central and Occitani similar developments were much less widespread. The woodlands of the west likewise remained more peaceful. Nonetheless, the groundwork for 1789 was laid in other areas by this conflict between a seignorial class trying to keep pace with economic developments and a more knowledgeable peasantry refusing to be sacrificed to them. In the *cahiers* of the Chartres region, a similar development of this novel aim has been noted.[6]

In a recent study of people's movements in rural areas during the French Revolution, Jean Nicolas detected without difficulty an extraordinary sociopolitical or regional complexity stemming from the conditions of rural life itself. Alongside antiseignorial activities and food riots, protests against taxes, collective poaching that took on an insurrectional character, repossession or sharing of communal properties, and rejection of the traditional authority of the local notables appeared after 1789. At the time of the Great Fear, the peasants of Dauphiné announced in this way the end of the domination of the "powerful of the earth" who possessed "immense wealth." These diverse motivations, which reinforced each other and shook the country profoundly in the first year of the Revolution, never totally disappeared. Analyses of these peasant revolts have increasingly stressed their passéist aspect, the fact that they were rooted in a long history of traditional protest. Independent of the activities of the elites, varied and contradictory, they were above all the manifestation of a heritage hostile to the cities and to authority. They were thus to resurface later, before rural France rallied to the cause of democracy in the nineteenth century, in the counterrevolutionary movements that began to appear in 1792. Yves-Marie Bercé, chronicling peasant upheavals in the seventeenth century, saw the peasants of 1789, despite changes that had occurred in their relations with their *seigneurs* or the state, as the inheritors of community upheavals of earlier times. He also pointed out the sequel of this continuous antiurban violence in the 1793 uprising in which, having helped topple the *ancien régime*, the rural regions of the west rose up against the Revolution.[7]

A LOGICAL COURSE OF EVENTS?

5. AN AVOIDABLE
DERAILMENT?

Fançois Furet and Denis Richet maintained, over twenty years ago, that in 1791 the French Revolution veered off course by failing to set up a constitutional monarchy and by becoming radicalized in an atmosphere of civil and foreign war. Weighing the elements for and against this theory on the eve of the king's flight to Varennes is difficult. Donald Sutherland suggests a different position on the subject. He notes that the climate created by the events of 1789 created its own revolutionary dynamic. This was the year in which the French invented the modern meaning of the word "revolution," no longer signifying a mere coup d'état, like Maupeou's, but a mass upheaval that transformed society. This heightened political consciousness was accompanied in many cases by the millenial dream of a regime that would, at long last, be perfect. Confronted with the realities of the day, particularly financial ones, the deputies could not maintain this illusion. By the end of 1790, blood had been shed over agrarian issues and religion, and economic and fiscal discontent persisted. This did not mean that a significant proportion of the people supported the aristocrats' counterrevolution, but it did provide openings for the armed émigrés stationed at the borders and the internal conspirators who were in contact with them. At the same time, however, the ideas of the Revolution were supported by institutions like the revolutionary clubs and the National Guard. Those who favored democratization of the nation were gaining ground and, with such widespread dissension and strife, the outbreak of civil war seemed probable.[1]

This historian tends to minimize, however, the significance in the spring of 1791 of opposition to the solutions adopted by the Constituent Assembly. He observes that its majority could count on the disunity of its adversaries, and he stresses the loyalty of most of the army and the National Guard to the new regime. The deputies adhered, for the most part, to the common ideals of 1789, opposing violence by the people and aspiring to change within the framework of parliamentary order. Even though the reorganization of the Catholic church had just shaken this basic harmony, the assembly still had faith in the king, and it was *only his flight that shattered the unity of the upper echelons of the elite in their conception of the Revolution.*[2]

*These ambiguities force us to reexamine how well the Constituent Assembly was carrying out its reorganizing mission.**

WAS A CONSTITUTIONAL MONARCHY VIABLE IN 1790?

The institutional structure established by the new regime had unified the country within the workable framework of departments. Their definition provoked some protest in cities such as Marseilles that were not at first designated as prefectures. Successors of Brienne's provincial assemblies, these districts headed the hierarchy of local government. Although the former shared responsibility with the central apparatus of the state, they in fact enjoyed a considerable degree of freedom. Independent of the royal bureaucracy, its leaders could defy the Crown with impunity.

This system was to work quite well insofar as it was in the hands of administrators who had already acquired a certain amount of political experience under the *ancien régime*. The electoral system, with its division based on economic factors among passive citizens, electors, and those eligible to be elected, explains the smooth operation of the system. The electoral qualifications represented moreover a fairly limited violation of the declaration of rights, as there were still over four million qualified electors. Based on the tax structure of the *ancien régime*, the system favored the rural areas over the cities. In Paris, for example, at least half of the adult males were denied the right to vote. Those eligible for election, the richest elements, were, on the other hand, mostly city dwellers. Bourgeois or aristocrats, they had succeeded in barring the peasants and artisans from power. Naturally, it was the bourgeoisie that gained the most. Local government fell into the hands of lawyers from the provinces, who had been involved in political life since 1787 and were often very different from the members of the permanent committees of 1789, who were considered too revolutionary. These moderates, concerned with maintaining order, nevertheless contributed to the radicalization of the Revolution when it was threatened in 1791 and 1792. Maintaining this decentralization of power, which had been the ideal of the early stages of the Revolution, would depend on how well other reforms enacted by the Constituent Assembly fared.[3]

The Constituent Assembly's solution to the always crucial and increasingly critical financial problem was the seizure of church property as of November 2, 1789. Having had little support in the spring, this measure was resorted to in response to the gravity of the situation, but did not remedy it, since the

* The exceptional quality of Donald Sutherland's *France 1789–1815: Revolution and Counter-Revolution* (Fontana, 1985; Oxford University Press, 1986), particularly with regard to the course of events between 1790 and 1799, leads us, for the reader's convenience, to divide our discussions in Part Two into (a) a summary, in smaller print, of this authoritative interpretation, which constitutes, in our opinion, the best synthesis of our knowledge on this subject; (b) and a more personal consideration of issues raised by other historians, which shed additional light.

deficit announced by Necker the following March was far greater than the one submitted earlier by Calonne. Whence the decision to sell church lands to the public and to issue *assignats* (interest-bearing bonds) guaranteed by this transaction. Their number was doubled in September, when paper currency was authorized. The total of *assignats* in circulation remained below the value of the *biens nationaux* (nationalized church property). But their appearance coincided with a monetary shortage and a balance of payments deficit. Local issues of *billets de confiance* (fiduciary notes), intended to head off the collapse of the economy, took control of the money supply away from the state, which exacerbated the situation by issuing quantities of small denominations, causing an inflationary spiral that culminated in 1791 in the beginning of the depreciation of the *assignats*. This triggered a decline in the standard of living of the poor, which only added to the general discontent and endangered the new political order.[4]

The eradication of fiscal privileges provided no more relief to the people. The new tax system remained based on the old tax assessments, and therefore maintained the considerable regional disparities. Capital income was relatively undertaxed because of insufficient documentation of private wealth. It would seem that, as a whole, the French paid more taxes after the Revolution than before, especially after 1792. The revolutionaries claimed the opposite, but it is clear that in certain cases the tax burden rose by 20 percent. As the new system was not progressive, the rich gained more than the poor. Taxes thus rose by 50 percent in the Nord in 1792, as compared with their levels under the *ancien régime*; the direct tax doubled in Haute Bretagne; the majority of cantons of Puy-de-Dôme did not change in this respect. As the abolition of privileges had not eased the tax burden, the taxpayers proved as recalcitrant as before. Their resistance was facilitated by the disarray of tax-collecting mechanisms, which prolonged the fiscal crisis.

The peasants were especially hard hit by the measures passed by the assembly on December 2, 1790, which allowed property owners to add to the duties owed them the equivalent of the former tithe. In all regions where the seignorial system had been relatively unburdensome with regard to taxes and tithes, this represented an overall loss of income for farmers. Tenants farming the Duke of Cossé-Brissac's domain in the Deux-Sèvres department thus had to pay him 25 percent more starting in 1791. Many rural inhabitants concluded from this that the Revolution was directed against their interests. The sale of *biens nationaux* no doubt attracted many buyers to the new regime. But they came above all from the urban bourgeoisie. Former officeholders who had received *assignats* in compensation used them for this purpose. The main outcome of the Revolution, in this sphere, was a reorganization of the forms of investment of the old landholding bourgeoisie. Its agrarian reforms, by favoring them, strengthened the influence of the richest city-dwellers over the countryside.

The main beneficiaries of the Constituent Assembly's labors were to be found among a large number of landowners, ranging from the richest bourgeois to small independent farmers. A certain number of city dwellers and the majority of the poor benefited from the elimination of numerous indirect taxes. But along with the church and many nobles of the regions in which seignorial income had been significant (Brittany, Burgundy, Auvergne, upper Languedoc), many rural dependents had no reason to back a regime that increased their expenses. This gave the counterrevolution an undeniable advantage, particularly if it could win over the poor and if the discontents of the masses were to be further stirred by religious, economic, or military pressures.[5]

These considerations outweigh the machinations of politicians who, like Mirabeau, were preoccupied with secretly passing themselves off as saviors of the monarchy (which, moreover, wanted nothing to do with them) while spouting demogogical speeches in the various public forums of Paris.[6] Samuel Scott chides historians who see 1790 as a "happy year" marked by universal fraternity and national consensus aside from conflicts of the *parlements*. As is often the case, Paris was taken to represent France as a whole, and the relative calm of the capital masked the disorder in the provinces. The future rifts in the Revolution were in fact born in its second year of existence. Along with the traditional violence associated with brigandage and hunger, new types of conflict sprang up at that time. They often revolved around the issue of legitimacy of power: The new fragmentation of authority encouraged disputes and confrontations about its exercise, making the problem of maintaining order a sensitive one. This task was assigned to the army and the National Guard, and the conditions of their deployment were bitterly disputed. Local officials fought the national authorities, while different groups among the former competed against one another. There were also rivalries between these two national organizations and within each, with soldiers opposing officers in the army and various factions vying for control of the National Guard. As a result, authority was paralyzed and disorder reigned. The latter took two main forms. The Revolution revived long-standing antagonisms while transforming and creating others linked to the struggle for power. In all cases, confrontations hinged on the benefits to be gained from the legitimate exercise of authority. Samuel Scott distinguishes three essential sources of violence that rocked 1790. Within the army, soldiers who were unhappy with the regime forced upon them earlier by their officers took advantage of the revolutionary atmosphere to break with traditional discipline. At the same time, the old hostility between Catholics and Protestants resurfaced, while the peasants' animosity toward the remains of the feudal system did not subside. This new politicization of old conflicts accompanied those brought on by the Revolution, involving elections, control of public forces, and the extent of local autonomy. The main issue in France came down to pinpointing legitimate authority and defining its powers.[7]

For the army, 1790 was a time of disintegration linked to an unprecedented level of insubordination, which took the form, above all, of open revolt against officers' authority. This movement came to a head late in August, in the great mutiny in Nancy, and it cast doubt on the government's ability to defend the country and to maintain order within it. Military insubordination also grew out of contacts between soldiers and civilians. Backed by patriotic citizens and members of the National Guard, regiments mutinied, like the one at Hesdin which was led by a renegade officer, the future Marshal Davout. After fraternizing with representatives of the new regime, soldiers refused to obey passively. The Federation movement increased such contacts and the mutual suspicions between officers and soldiers, as illustrated by the events at Nancy, which culminated in twenty-three death sentences, hundreds of imprisonments, and political repression that took on counterrevolutionary overtones. Their association with the patriots had provided the soldiers with an ideological justification for a revolt against aristocratic officers. This participation by civilians in military disorders only increased the difficulty of reestablishing order. Born of a common revolt against injustice and privilege, a desire for reform, and day-to-day contacts, it was able to paralyze the forces of order, especially when it had the backing of the National Guard. These military conflicts increased those among civilians by pitting the various members of local government against each other. Bitter recriminations among radical and moderate factions followed. Power that was so widely dispersed could no longer be defined. Who could rebut mutineers who claimed to be backed by the assembly or by local elected officials, citizens' approval, or the principles of the Revolution? Under these conditions, order was difficult to establish or maintain. In contrast to the fraternal illusions of the great Parisian *fête* of July 14, 1790, many regions were suffering from an incipient form of civil war.[8]

What else could have been expected of an army in which, among the twenty-two reformers who had survived 1781, only one chose the revolutionary side, while fifteen left the country and five fought against it? The politicization of the soldiers' old grievances, furthered by the Revolution, was to multiply the number of desertions and rebellions. The disintegration of the military merely reflected the crisis that permeated all of society.[9]

Added to this breakdown of a key element of public order was the intensification, in the Languedoc, of the old conflict between Catholics and Protestants. A segment of the former resented the latter for deriving excessive benefits from the Revolution. Starting in April 1790, a wave of violent incidents broke out in Uzès. A similar situation prevailed in Montauban, where the National Guard clashed with the conservative municipality. The most serious events of this type occurred in Nîmes in the spring, when Catholics and Calvinists settled old accounts. Protestant merchants and Papist peasants were on bad terms in the region and the

Nîmes oligarchy feared that the Revolution would drive it from power. As in Montauban, the oligarchy clashed with a Protestant National Guard. François Froment, leader of the local Catholics, assembled a plebeian militia to fight for his cause. Its provocations led to a regional civil war that left more than three hundred dead. The Revolution and the problems of authority and legitimacy that it created had thus exacerbated old conflicts that the country was unable to settle. The main result of this violence in the Midi was to develop a counterrevolutionary movement with populist leanings.[10]

James Hood and Gwynne Lewis have been studying its makeup for fifteen years. They have shown the religious, socioeconomic, and political roots of the confrontations in Nîmes, linked to a heritage of fear and hatred stemming from the *ancien régime*. Traditions of intolerance were more deeply ingrained than the leaders of the two communities had realized, and the Revolution, with its threat of disequilibrium, exacerbated them. Whence the birth of factions polarized for and against the changes that were taking place. The conflicts that had always characterized the Guard were multiplied by the Revolution, which exacerbated the class struggle between the Protestant bourgeoisie and the common people who had been won over to the royalist cause by their hatred of the bourgeoisie. Although the counterrevolutionary militia was unable to eradicate the patriots as it was to do later on in the West, it nevertheless revealed the possible double face, revolutionary *or* reactionary, of the French people during the Revolution. The political choices, in Languedoc as elsewhere, often derived from ongoing traditional conflicts and old local rivalries. The Revolution, reinterpreting but not erasing them, reactivated these divisions everywhere. Thus it was that in Nîmes, as in the sixteenth century, between October 1789 and June 1790, the Catholic oligarchy tried to oust the Protestant tyranny. The new labels, royalists and patriots, were a mere permutation of old rifts. This continuity was to last until the beginning of the nineteenth century, when the massacres of 1815 responded to those of 1790. As in the Gard, the Revolution often created a new *political* universe, made up of personal animosities and ongoing vengeance. Family rivalries and motivations played a decisive role in the commitments of local leaders.[11]

Historians are thus increasingly interested in a counterrevolution whose origins and outlines are still ill defined. It was not only the result of the plottings of groups of émigrés who had been congregating, since July 1789, around the Comte d'Artois and his associates. Unappreciated by the monarchy, which preferred paying off revolutionary leaders while hoping in vain for intervention by foreign powers, they had limited resources, even though the nobility began to turn away from the Revolution when it abolished hereditary titles in June 1790. The commoners assembled by Froment proved more useful, and were able, as we have seen, to stir up the Languedoc that year. After their defeat at Nîmes, twenty thousand Catholic National Guardsmen assembled at Jalès, in the Ardèche, and started a campaign of protest against the Assembly. This was echoed in Lyons, where a conspiracy was hatched, and failed, and similarly in Provence, where three imprisoned counterrevolution-aries were massacred in December. This unrest created a lasting threat in the southeast. It planted the seeds of an insurrectional strategy, tied to outside help, which was to endure. It found strong allies among the former privileged classes, the bourgeoisie associated with the institutions of the *ancien régime*, and artisans and Catholic peasants unhappy with measures directed against the church. These adherents to a traditional stratified society dominated by religion were also to be found in the world of manual laborers. As in Avignon, soon to be scarred by the Glacière massacres of 1791 in which sixty-five counterrevolutionaries perished, members of the popular classes, unlike the bourgeoisie, were to be found on both sides. It all depended on local circumstances, and the goals of the masses were often different from those of the leaders. In Jalès in 1791, members of the popular classes seized upon the occasion to wreak vengeance against the petty bourgeois of the patriots' faction, who had already been exploiting them under the *ancien régime*, and everywhere a segment of the rural population clashed in more or less confused fashion with the beneficiaries of a revolution that had not been kind enough to it.[12]

Violent incidents were a constant in the Midi beginning in 1789. The revolutionary elites that had assumed power during that year soon had to confront the victims of change and those who were distrustful of it. These violent tendencies, varying in strength and scope, deepened within the nobility as of late 1790. In many regions they rested on "a specific political line adopted by the masses of poor peasants and part of the rural elites . . . challenging the urban bourgeoisie's assumption of local power in the countryside." (Roger Dupuy) A backlash in favor of the *ancien régime* and popular dissatisfaction with certain aspects of the Revolution were inextricably mixed in this movement.[13]

It originated at a time of continuing peasant uprisings against the payment of feudal dues. These revolts left their stamp on 1790, from Quercy to Brittany and from the Bourbonnais to the Gâtinais. Their spread, associated with ambiguities in the Constituent Assembly's agrar-ian policies, illustrates the collapse of concepts of law and order at the beginning of the Revolution. This phenomenon was to be found in numerous cities of Alsace and Berry, in Belfort and Provence, Marseilles and Lyons. Martial law was proclaimed in this last city, in July 1790, but disorder persisted. The problem of deciding which public forces to deploy, the regular army or the National Guard, for maintaining order was a major source of conflict. The idyllic Parisian image of a fraternal revolution did not remotely correspond to the reality of the country. The year 1789 had not only introduced modern political jockeying and power plays among rival factions, it had also helped politicize conflicting local interests and even the authorities entrusted with law enforcement. In this extraordinary fragmentation, the concepts of consensus and legitimacy were replaced by those of competition and brute force. Violence in this climate became a normal phenomenon and centered on the control of the armed forces. As divided as the rest of society, they were no more capable than it was of defusing conflicts and stabilizing the state.[14]

Rural protest over the unenforceable redemption of a portion of seignorial dues must be viewed against this backdrop. Refusal to pay them became widespread in 1790, all the more so as seignorial courts were definitively abolished in August. Dozens of incidents in over a third of the departments give evidence of this protest in the countryside. It took a particularly dramatic form in upper Brittany, lower Limousin, and especially in Périgord, where uprisings reflected the villages' centuries-old dream of freeing themselves of a hated regime. These peaceful bands of peasants resented the bourgeois as much as the nobles. They soon used armed force to prevent the authorities from cutting down the "May trees" that symbolized their hope for regeneration. When the nobles resisted, their chateaux were attacked. This movement was especially active in areas with isolated farms and in the wooded areas of the west, where the new communes did not constitute an appropriate framework for the struggle against the dying feudal regime.[15]

Antifiscal revolts, attacks on forest guards, demonstrations against the machinations of large-scale buyers of biens nationaux, and demands for increases in agricultural salaries accompanied these disorders. They made this period a time of overall agrarian tension. The people continued to organize for revolt after the Revolution just as they had before. Struggles over basic subsistence commodities in areas of large-scale agriculture and the fight against feudalism elsewhere continued to go hand in hand. This resistance by the peasantry was directed as much against the "bourgeois" assembly and its allies as against the aristocracy. The frontal assault on the seigneurs and the demonstration of village power was aimed at all the notables. Whereas the hopes of 1789 and the political crisis they provoked favored this movement, in Périgord it was directed even more against the rural bourgeoisie than against the seigneurs. Artisans and day laborers, for the most part young, had taken up the traditional ritual of revolt against these profiteers. On their home territory, within the narrow framework of their parishes, they were attacking an enemy they knew well and against whom they could achieve maximum cohesion. The scope of this revolt is evidence of the pervasiveness in the countryside of an egalitarian spirit that alarmed the bourgeoisie as much as it did the nobility. The specter of "agrarian law" that was to dominate the Revolution echoed this, and the forced redistribution of communal properties appropriated by *seigneurs* was linked with it. It was at this time that, in a total power vacuum, thousands of Parisian followers of Abbé Fauchet, orator of the radical club of the *Cercle social,* learned from him that all men had the right to own land. In a similar vein, Sylvain Maréchal, future associate of Babeuf, in the immensely popular newspaper *Révolutions de Paris,* called on the rich to give a portion of their properties to the impoverished, and sought a share for farmers of the immense holdings that made up the *biens nationaux.*[16]

DID THE REVOLUTIONARY MOVEMENT BECOME RADICALIZED BEFORE THE FLIGHT TO VARENNES?

The example of Paris has been cited to support this claim, a theory linked to François Furet's recent findings concerning the role of ideology in dictating the course taken by the Revolution up to 1794. In the political vacuum left by the traditional authorities' abdication of responsibility, power would supposedly have been taken up by a symbolic system of mental representations and signs that dominated daily activity. This ideological dynamism, transcending classes and parties, would have obliterated the divisions and conflicts of civil society. In its abstract single-mindedness, on a par with the Marxist emphasis on economics, this "semiotic despotism" ignores the realities and constraints of class struggle, international relations, internal alliances, and the business of building a state. If there was a radicalization of the Revolution before Thermidor, its explanation is to be found *simultaneously* in the necessities of political evolution and the very structure of revolutionary ideology. This discourse, moreover, was never homogeneous. It allowed for the coexistence, before Varennes, of differing concepts of constitutional monarchy.[1]

These coexisted within revolutionary institutions that optimistically underestimated the amount of opposition to the reforms of the Constituent Assembly. It was thought, in mid-1791, that with their superior awareness and organization, the patriots would be able to rein in the excesses of the opposition. Less well known than the Jacobins, the National Guard was a key agent of repression. Its expeditions into the Midi and its actions in the west confirmed the local militants' devotion to the cause of the Revolution. They came from the lower and middle levels of the urban bourgeoisie, and remained a tiny minority of the population. They were often members of the Jacobin clubs, which were content, at this point, to remain on the sidelines of events but which constituted a rather tight-knit network. If the Parisian center functioned above all as a meeting place for radical deputies, the provincial societies provided former members of lodges and academies a place for discussions. Intense correspondence allowed them to increase their influence and convey their wishes to Paris. Although membership there was less expensive than in the capital, their recruitment policies were more elitist than populist. Frequent meetings provided a forum for the formation of future leaders. However, their influence on legislation and local life should not be overestimated. They were simply a forum for the radical movement, particularly in departments where the hostility of the rural population to the Revolution was most pronounced.

Although the Jacobins always included artisans and shopkeepers, there were also, in the biggest cities, popular societies that sprang up in response to aristocratic propaganda and agitation by the clergy. Membership was inexpensive, and they were highly successful. For example, there was one in each of Lyons's thirty-two sections by August 1790. Their delegates to a central club participated in revolutionary agitation. Their three thousand members soon outnumbered the atrophied Jacobin club and attracted the attention of the most ambitious politicians. Though Bordeaux and some other cities also had similar societies, on a smaller scale, it was in Paris, above all, that they flourished. They drew on the network of forty-eight sectional assemblies, established since July 1790, and the ring of fraternal societies that were often associated with professional activities. Some were affiliated with the famous *Cordelier Club* founded in the spring. Alongside radical journalists such as Marat, they criticized municipal authority, La Fayette's excessive power, and the distinction between active and passive citizens. In the prevailing atmosphere of institutional change, jurisdictional conflicts had quickly broken out between the commune and the sections, and between La Fayette's headquarters and the battalions of volunteers who were, in the final analysis, the last bastion of authority.

On an idealogical level, these struggles set the theory of representative government against the doctrine of representative democracy. The latter was in part elaborated and promulgated by the leaders of the Cordelier, who thus laid out the main points of the future ideology of year II: sectional sovereignty, the recall of deputies, the solidarity of sections, the right of insurrection, the right to hold referendums, the accountability of representatives to ensure that they not usurp popular sovereignty, and the symbolism of the watchful eye inscribed within the masonic triangle. These ideas, though certainly well received by the craftsmen and workers of Paris—because they expressed aspirations born of their everyday experience—were not created by men who belonged, themselves, to the popular classes. Unlike, for example, the Faubourg Saint-Antoine, the left-bank section where the Cordeliers lived had a high proportion of journalists, printers, and bookstore owners. The leaders of the club, which met at the Café Procope, were not manual laborers, but lawyers with neither clients nor work, or intellectuals rising from the sorry business of clandestine publications to new careers opened up by freedom of the press. Along with their incontestable idealism, Danton and Desmoulins among the former, and Hébert, Brissot, and Marat among the latter, shared a violent and personal hatred of the power, privileges, and authority of the rich and famous.

The origins of the members of the other popular societies and of the sectional militants were similar. They included members of the liberal professions and the administration together with craftsmen and shopkeepers who were to some degree skilled and well off. These democratic organizations included very few workers or poor people, who were insufficiently politicized. Though sympathetic to them, the most radical revolutionary leaders remained distrustful of the poor, who could too easily be corrupted by the aristocrats. The ideal citizen remained, for them, the independent worker, head of a family. Although their literature, by 1790, included generous proposals on fiscal and economic issues and denunciations of the moral and social evils of wealth, it devoted relatively little space to issues of this sort. It would be the extension of its hatred of oppression that would carry it further.[2]

This analysis by Donald Sutherland, supported by the most recent research, depicts a democratic movement in Paris largely backed by members of the lower and middle levels of the bourgeoisie connected with crafts and trade but led by intellectuals and lawyers. The movement's unity lay in its aspirations toward direct democracy in the capital. This ideal had its first trial in the sixty districts created in April 1789. Opposed by moderates, who saw in it the seeds of anarchy, it was taken up by the sections, whose frequent meetings gave them a de facto permanence. Jealously guarding their autonomy, they attempted to limit the powers of the municipality for their own benefit, all the while seeking to play a national role. Desirous of freedom, they nevertheless tolerated the inequities of tax qualifications for voting, while massive abstentions by active citizens "gave free reign to a militant minority, a veritable revolutionary vanguard," which did not even have to fight to win its way. This minority identified its idea of political order with a society of small independent property owners.[3]

The Jacobin clubs, descended in large part from the Masonic lodges, Mesmerist clubs, philanthropic societies, and literary circles of the prerevolutionary period, reflected the politicization of France. They quickly adopted an aggressive stance with regard to the aristocracy and affiliated themselves, throughout the country, with the parent organization in Paris. This contagion spread to most of the large cities in mid-1790, and the network only grew after that. Though there were often marked social contrasts in the makeup of the various clubs, their development, in general, followed lines of increasing membership and democratization.[4]

They were very involved in the spread of the revolutionary press. This powerful propaganda tool helped further reinforce the capital's predom-

inance over the nation. Devoted to freedom, the militant Jacobins nevertheless burned the odious aristocratic gazettes with great ceremony. But
they were no more tolerant of any traces of the extreme left, and none
of their societies subscribed to Marat's newspaper. They accused the
Cercle social's journal of backing agrarian laws, and were long suspicious
of Hébert's excesses. Desmoulins's weekly was more successful, but the
Abbé Cerutti's *Feuille villageoise* (*Village Paper*), which reached close
to three hundred thousand Frenchmen, was perhaps the Jacobins' preferred propaganda instrument after September 1790. Delegates were sent
into the countryside to read it to the peasants. This exceptional method
of rural political participation was an attempt to transform the villagers
into citizens. But it still smacked of the domineering and paternalistic
spirit of the urban elite, which only seemed to justify the country people's
distrust of the new regime. Otherwise, Carra's *Annales* was the major
shaper of political awareness among the Jacobins in the provinces. Its
internal and external radicalism, heedless though it was of social con-
troversies, both stirred and reassured them.[5]

The ultrarevolutionary press of the capital, associated in large part
with the leaders of the Cordeliers, worked more openly to advance the
theory of popular sovereignty. These supporters of direct democracy,
distrustful on principle of any government, forged the future ideology
of year II in the early years of the Revolution. More original still, Marat
showed evidence of a surprising flair for journalism and pamphleteering,
and his frustrated intellectual's personality adapted itself beautifully to
a novel situation that he exploited to perfection. Criticizing all institutions and denouncing all conspiracies, he styled himself the enemy of
the rich and champion of the oppressed. Apostle of legitimate violence
and necessary dictatorship, he joined the fight for direct democracy in
the guise of an enlightened teacher guiding the child populace. Distrustful
of the armed forces and their leader La Fayette, he ceaselessly called for
the people to unite in the face of treason. Condoning riots, he regretted
that "five hundred to six hundred heads" had not rolled "since the day
the Bastille fell." Confident of the virtue of beggars, but sensitive to their
poverty, he dreamed of social protections and a redistribution of property that would put an end to misery. If not, he announced to his readers
on October 27, 1790, "the progress of the Enlightenment" would soon
lead "three quarters of the nation" to demand "the division of the land."[6]

We know that Fanchot soon afterward evoked Rousseau's thought
in the same spirit at the Palais-Royal, thereby earning himself a bad
reputation. But six months later, when La Harpe fought Maréchal and
his agrarian law proposals in the name of conservative wisdom, the
Révolutions de Paris responded that, in the inevitable progress of the

Revolution, the people, having regained their rights, would win back their lands. A professor at the Collège de France, for his part, published a detailed plan under which inheritances would be abolished and four to five acres of land would be distributed to each person, with the rest to be rented out by the state, thus eliminating the need for taxes. Nicolas de Bonneville, a close friend of Fauchet's and an enlightened Freemason, was at that point defending the agrarian law, which he ascribed to the ancestral wisdom of the French nation. This was the time when Babeuf, having formulated his doctrine in the districts of Paris, was trying to apply it to the countryside of Picardy. Village priests supported his patriotic efforts on behalf of a populace crushed by taxes, and one of them pronounced himself openly in favor of the massacre of tax collectors and the lynching of recalcitrant authorities.[7]

What made these excesses serious, and accounted for them, was the profound state of anarchy in which the country found itself. The inhabitants of insurgent Périgord had both declared and deplored this early in 1790. The suspension of justice in a time of crisis, the total disappearance of authority during the transfer of power, the disorders resulting from the delay in the establishment of the new regime, the futile wait for guidance from above, and the resulting powerlessness of creditors and victims of violence—such were the characteristics of the transition period, and the rebellious peasants were well pleased with them. Freed of the constraints of law and justice, they felt they were entering a period of liberty for all. The satisfaction of their grievances from then on took precedence over everything else and became the guiding principle of action of the government and its agents. This frenzy accounts, above all, for the radicalization of the revolutionary movement that took place between 1789 and 1791. It stemmed less from the supposed virtues of its ideological discourse than from an exceptional political situation, marked by a crisis of all bases of authority, the interruption of legitimate power, and the bitterness of rivalries over assuming and sharing control of it.[8]

DID THE REVOLUTION'S REORGANIZATION OF THE CATHOLIC CHURCH INCREASE THE RISK OF CIVIL WAR?

Many historians feel that the Civil Constitution of the Clergy, passed by the assembly in 1790, and put into effect the next year, represented a decisive turning point and a major error in the course of the Revolution. Setting themselves against the majority of bishops and at least half of the priests and the faithful, its leaders offended the beliefs of a good portion of their compatriots, laying the ground for a schism and paving the way for the outbreak of civil war. Obvious as this may seem, it is not so easy to explain.

We could fall back on the convenient theory of an anti-Christian conspiracy concocted by the *philosophes* of the eighteenth century and carried out by their descendants in 1789. This simplistic theory, based on the battle waged by Voltaire and his friends against the Catholic church, is still being trumpeted by works that are to one degree or another the farfetched, latterday successors of a clerical literature that was once plentiful. More seriously, a similar error is committed by other analyses that no doubt overstate the influence of anti-Christian attacks on even well-informed opinion.[1]

Most specialists today agree on the relative solidity of the Church of France on the eve of the Revolution. Shortly before its tragic demise, seminaries were turning out impeccable parish priests, and the church was led by "prelates who diligently administered and served the dioceses." We do not even know whether members of the religious orders were really lapsing into decadence. It is clear, however, that alongside the parish framework formed by its priests and preachers, the church still played a prominent social role in the areas of culture and public assistance. Such was the body that with one blow was to lose all its authority and prestige amid the revolutionary turmoil. The suddenness of this change is striking when one considers, for example, the career of a Talleyrand, who stubbornly defended the material interests of his order throughout the 1780s before digging their grave at the Constituent Assembly and then assuming the dubious role of godfather to the new Constitutional Church. Many other more honest bishops were to be torn by this divorce between their long-term commitment to Enlightenment thought and freedom and their fidelity to a faith suddenly threatened by the Revolution.[2]

One possible explanation for this might be the divisions between the lower and higher clergy. The former, who were more bourgeois, if not more plebeian, supposedly fueled "anxiety, insecurity, and dissatisfaction" over the "unjust distribution of wealth in the church." According to this view, its esprit de corps and its demands led, at the end of the *ancien régime*, to a "revolt by the parish priests," who were attempting, moreover, to maintain their leadership role within society and therefore often came into conflict with lay notables. From this rift and from the deep gulf thus established between the bishops' caste and the dissident priests was born the desire among the latter for egalitarian reform and an insubordination fueled by the electoral triumph of 1789. In the majority among the order's representatives in the Estates-General, the parish priests little by little forced it to support the Third Estate and gained overwhelming popularity in that order.[3]

Missing from this outline is a thorough study of the eighteenth-century church in relation to the society of which it was a part. Still omnipresent and quite powerful, closely linked with the state, it took on a new aspect, more in keeping with the Catholic reform that had begun at the end of the sixteenth century. Better educated, its priests were admired by all for their sense of moral and social responsibility. Their pastorate, at once active and austere, contributed to a Christianization of the masses seemingly well suited to the bourgeois and popular-class values of the time. We know that there was no dearth of religious fervor in France at the time of the Enlightenment. Jean Quéniart has investigated whether this did not, in the final analysis, lead to a certain number of conflicts between its evolving tendencies and the state of the Gallican church. With individuals tending often to become freer with regard to its teachings, and thought becoming secularized, the clergy were becoming dangerously isolated, at least from a new kind of urban society. For all that, at the end of the eighteenth century the poor people of Paris remained committed to the old forms of practice and belief. Long-standing admirers of Jansenist miracles, they had not yet become de-Christianizing militants.[4]

Bernard Plongeron even maintains that religious thought squared with the spirit of the Revolution. Rejecting a manichean type of historiography that set the good priests, the future refractory ones, against the bad ones, who had been led astray by the Enlightenment, he has shown that the latter influenced Christians who supported reforms in government. The revolutionary phase fitted into a Catholic Enlightenment that was attuned to all the major intellectual currents of the day. The history of the church in this period, therefore, is not merely the story of a simple external attack against its saints and its old principles. The religious factor should be considered less as a framework of political conflicts than as the object of an ongoing cultural development. This was a time when the Revolution often viewed itself as a religion, and religion considered itself revolutionary. Theology and politics continued to be intimately, if not happily, linked. Whence this historian's interest in a constitutional church that had the merit, in difficult times, of accepting all the consequences of this situation. Sixteen bishops sat in the Convention, of whom ten were still priests at their death. Ecclesiastical leaders of a new type, they were guided as much by the fraternity taught by Jesus as by the ideas of the *philosophes*. They were more committed to religion than to the Enlightenment, abhorred Voltaire's anti-

Christianism, and sometimes criticized Rousseau. Only four of them were regicides, and shortly before he was assassinated by Breton royalists during an episcopal visit Audrein reaffirmed his opposition to Enlightened thought that did not accept the idea of revelation.[5]

The gravity of the misunderstanding surrounding the Constituent Assembly's religious policies is evident. Impressed by the commitment to the Revolution of its members who were of the low clergy, it misjudged how deeply unified the church of 1789 still was. Indeed, if its *cahiers* are to be believed, the church wanted Catholicism to remain the established religion and to retain control of the school system. It was distrustful of tolerance toward Protestants and remained in favor of censoring impious publications. Though it was ready to give up its fiscal privileges, its lesser members had come to the Estates driven above all by professional grievances relating to the betterment of their own lot. They had no intention of questioning the central role of their institution in public life, but rather sought to reinforce it. By a tragic but understandable irony, their lay colleagues were unable to understand this ambiguity. To borrow Louis Trénard's term, they thought they could absorb the church into a secularized state and "bureaucratize" its priests. Their only excuse is that this politicization of religion and this complete transfer were not without precedent in the long Christian history that preceded this period.[6]

Their reorganization of the church was motivated, first of all, by financial considerations. Left without resources, the clergy had to be salaried, and therefore controlled. On October 28, 1789, religious vows were eradicated and the contemplative orders dissolved. Fifty-two dioceses were soon eliminated. Although the declaration of rights, by guaranteeing freedom of thought, had undermined the existence of the church as a privileged body, the Constituent Assembly, like Voltaire, did not believe that the state would remain uninterested in organizing it. The assembly even tried to deepen this dependency in the interest of order, property, and the Revolution. Moreover, many, especially among the parish priests, had dreams of a return to the pure church of earlier centuries. This idealism explains, in particular, the ease with which the profitable but debatable nationalization of the clergy's property was passed.

The Civil Constitution was controversial above all because it assigned the election of the new leaders of the church to the active citizens as a whole, including non-Catholics. This disciplinary and doctrinal innovation was inevitable, given the assembly's theories and the political circumstances. The former required that the new government have at least as much control over the church as the old one. In response to this evocation of precedent, the proposal's adversaries demanded that the church be consulted, and consent. Ignoring their protests and wishing to replace the aristocrats with elected functionaries, the assembly adopted the Civil Constitution on July 12, 1790, just when counterrevolutionary insurgents in the Midi were brandishing the flag of the Catholic religion. Whence the refusal by the Constituent Assembly to call a national council along the lines of the meetings that, in the recent past, had dared to defy the Crown. Compromise, in these circumstances, was exceedingly difficult. Called on at last by a minority of the clergy, the pope temporized, and with agitation spreading at the end of the year, the assembly decided to require that all candidates for positions in the ecclesiastical system sign an oath of loyalty to the Constitution.

This oath marked a turning point in the history of the Revolution in that it brought wide popular support to its adversaries. We must distinguish between the motives for the priests' rejection of it and the reasons for the support they received. There were, indeed, many reasons to approve a program that endorsed certain demands of the *cahiers*, notably on the subject of the bishops' residency, reductions of injustices concerning their status and that of the village priests, etc. But the clergy had hoped for more. In many cases they had not envisioned national rebirth without some kind of theocracy, and now they had to contemplate being linked to the dissolution of the traditional church. If the constitutional clergy accepted this situation, the refractories viewed it, along with other measures enacted by the Constituent Assembly, as a deliberate attempt to secularize the state and society.

By mid-1791 60 percent of the village priests and only seven bishops had taken this oath. This rift had its sources not only in ideology or earlier attitudes. Some condemnations of the pope's in early spring had resulted in a few retractions. Various official and unofficial pressures, from family, friends, and the church, were brought to bear on the village priests. There was thus no simple explanation for taking the oath, although a correlation may be noted in Brittany between refusal and the presence of several priests in one parish. Pressure by the laity was no doubt a major factor. A large central zone, stretching from Picardy to Berry, and from Maine to Burgundy, took the oath. This was likewise the case in the southeast. On the other hand, the southern part of the Massif Central, Alsace, and the north were areas of massive refusal. There was another, even larger one, to the west of a line passing through Caen, Le Mans, and Poitiers. These boundaries roughly corresponded to the map of the people's future attitudes toward the Revolution, as well as the basic outlines of the future elections under the republics of the nineteenth and twentieth centuries.

The revolutionaries attributed the people's support for refractory priests to ignorance, and their later repressive legislation attempted to counter this hostility. Attempts have since been made to establish finer correlations between the taking of the oath and the cultural and religious situation, as if to imply that the constitutionals were less Catholic or less devout than the others. Donald Sutherland does not believe that a specifically religious element was the source of these differences. He observes that the Civil Constitution had nothing to do with the liturgy, which was much more important to the people than belief. The constitutional priests were just as able as the others to conduct these rites of passage and protection to which they were so attached. If, for this purpose, the people preferred the refractories in some places and in others not, it was because the Civil Constitution also represented a referendum for or against a church associated with a revolution that it was called upon to promote and serve. Siding with religious refusal meant rejecting the new political and social regime imposed by the patriots of 1790.[7]

The formulation of this choice came about late in 1790 and early in 1791 just when dissatisfaction with the work of the Constituent Assembly was mounting. Though not necessarily linked to it, religious conflict often affected regions in which peasants were unhappy with the little they had gained from the Revolution. They attempted, in the north and west in particular, to influence the decision of the village priests in this direction, and then made life miserable for the constitutional priests, who no longer had any support. These unfortunates, symbols of a purely urban revolution, could now rely only on a handful of administrators, Jacobins, and the National Guardsmen who had come from the cities. In many areas the country people supported the refractory priests in order to show their hostility to the Revolution. The presence and the rights of these priests, moreover, multiplied these conflicts, which rendered ecclesiastical rules unenforceable. Their denunciations of the constitutional clergy and its supporters as heretical and schismatic brought these regions one step closer to the brink of civil war. But public opinion frequently had no need of them to pronounce itself, en masse, against the Revolution. Following the lead of their counterparts in Aubenas, the women of Strasbourg revolted against the authorities over this issue in early 1791. Many Alsatian Catholics, like them, defended their religion against the municipalities. This popular resistance was particularly evident in the west. Silent protest processionals were held there, while stories of miraculous apparitions and prophecies spread. Investigating these disturbances in Anjou, La Révellière-Lépeaux, in a first act of de-Christianization, had a chapel of the Virgin destroyed. More serious instances of violence erupted in Vannes, in support of a refractory bishop; in Maulévrier, to defend religion against the authorities; in the Vendée, where a siege pitted bourgeois Jacobins against peasants who were barricaded inside a church; near Nantes, where patriotic women and their armed husbands invaded a convent of refractory Carmelites, and so forth.[8]

New light has just been shed on the origins of this dissidence by Timothy Tackett's research. Convinced that the key was to be found in the ecclesiastical structure and the clerical geography of France on the eve of the Revolution, he first noticed, with Claude Langlois, that certain of the refractory regions (in the west, the north, the southern part of the Massif Central, the southwest) had a higher proportion of native-born priests, notably in rural areas. They were a greater presence there than elsewhere. Whereas the future centers of the Constitutional Church, such as the Parisian basin and the central portion of the Loire, often recruited priests from outside, these other areas had a large circle of priests who came from the area and were deeply integrated into local life.[9]

Timothy Tackett's study of the 1791 oath broadens and expands on these observations. In it he spells out the sociology of clerical refusal (which was very pronounced in the cities, except for Paris), as well as its geographical distribution (which includes, in fact, an additional region in the southwest). After thorough investigation, the main explanation again is tied to the presence, in the west in particular, of a massive homogeneous clerical society, rural in origin (unlike in the center or the southeast), which shaped and gave vitality to the religion of the people.

Tackett observes also that it was often in future refractory regions that the *cahiers* of the Third Estate, issued by the urban bourgeoisie, were infused with a violent anticlericalism. Thus the seeds of the conflict between the religious countryside and the "enlightened" cities, which was to be at the heart of the Civil Constitution's crisis and, perhaps, the whole revolution, were already being planted.[10]

This reemergence of the religious, or at least the socioreligious factor, as the origin of the divisions in the west during the Revolution has just been confirmed by Jean-Louis Ormières in a study of the political situation in Mayenne and Maine-et-Loire in 1790 and 1791. In it he notes the seriousness of the disturbances, in the city as well as the country, linked to the application of the Civil Constitution. This was a religious conflict that naturally overflowed onto political territory, since the revolutionary authorities supported the Constitutional Church. Its formation gave exceptional reinforcement to the counterrevolution in the west, where the refractory parish priests had long had a symbiotic relationship with the rural community.[11]

Ordered to do so, half of France, through the intermediary of the priests it supported, had just rejected the civic oath that was to have been public testimony of adherence to the new social contract. This political disaster, which was to become a permanent source of turmoil, clearly indicated the opposition of very large numbers of regions, religious groups, and social categories in the country to the revolutionary ideology.[12]

6. AN IDEOLOGICAL WAR?

From the summer of 1791 to the summer of 1793, the course of the Revolution picked up speed, seemingly sweeping everything along in its path: Amid all this turmoil, it declared war on Europe, overthrew the monarchy, executed the king, and fomented civil war. In this whirlwind of upheaval, three points may be distinguished. The first involves the origins and significance of the conflict between France and Europe that was to continue for over twenty years. The second has to do with the exact nature of the mobilization of the people, which was to work both for and against the Revolution. Finally, the divisions among the revolutionary leaders, which were symbolized by the clash between the Girondins and the Montagnards and which, in the spring of 1793, added a civil war to so many others, invite the question: Did these rifts stem from absolute oppositions, of social origin, for example, or were they simple rivalries over the exercise of power?

WAS REVOLUTIONARY FRANCE RESPONSIBLE
FOR ITS CONFLICT WITH EUROPE?

The king's flight in June 1791, and its pathetic failure had significant consequences. Having left in order to regain his authority, Louis XVI destroyed the unity of the patriots and impelled some of them to fall back on the popular movement. Others, like Brissot, looked to war as a solution to political difficulties. The local authorities' distrust of the Parisians grew, and the Constituent Assembly's prestige declined. So did the king's, in the provinces as well as in the capital. Divisions within the country only deepened after this debacle. Although the assembly calmly set about taking charge of the situation, Paris was frightened and there were rumors of a prison conspiracy. Permanent committees on the border were put into a state of alert for fear of an invasion. The repression of dissidents increased, and a few aristocrats were murdered. Confidence in local administrators, however, prevented legitimate fears of a counterrevolution from intensifying. But in Paris, the radicals' agitation against the king aggravated the opposition between the democrats and the assembly, which did not want to depose him. It was accompanied by a social struggle between the workers and the bourgeois legislators. A protest with twenty thousand participants took place on July 4. On the seventeenth, the National Guard fired on a crowd of petitioners assembled on the Champ-de-Mars, killing perhaps fifty people and injuring many others. A crackdown directed mainly against the far left followed, but the Parisian radical movement emerged from these events, if anything, stronger than before. It had nonetheless failed, for the moment, to force the Republic on the assembly and the country. The Feuillants, who split off from the less moderate Jacobins at this point, succeeded in winning over neither the provincial patriots, nor the king, nor the assembly. Their attempts at constitutional revision failed.

The new deputies to the Legislative Assembly, which opened on October 1 and was to start the war with Europe seven months later, were local administrators, independent of factions, but seeking a solution to the problems posed by the counterrevolution, both internal and external. Barely a quarter of the active citizens had elected them, and only ten percent in Paris: They thus represented the minority of the politically active population of the nation, moderate but committed to the gains achieved in 1789. The second sentiment soon won out over their moderate inclinations, in the same way that, in the provinces, the authorities stepped up repression of dissidents. They labeled them as being in a latent state of insurrection and constituting a danger to the safety of the people and honest citizens. These declarations, which placed the defense of the Revolution above the law, foreshadowed the mentality of the Terror. They were given some credence, as in Ille-et-Vilaine, where patriots closed churches and the homes of their adversaries. Similar disputes occurred in the north, in Ardèche, in the Sarthe; they pitted the villagers, supporters of the traditional priests, against the National Guard, the only supporters of the regime's church. Violent outbreaks by the people over this issue escalated, as did repression by the authorities. Whereas these city dwellers' attempts to set up outsider priests were regarded by the rural populace as criminal acts, the city patriots considered their rural adversaries ignorant and superstitious.

The problem of religion was soon compounded by that of the émigrés. Armed and assembled around Coblenz, they hardly posed a threat, but the desertion of six thousand officers after Varennes was alarming. Other émigrés were believed to be concocting plots of vengeance, in the hope of a future victorious war. These conspiracies were particularly widespread in the southeast and the west. At Pillnitz, moreover, the emperor and the king of Prussia had announced their eventual support of the reestablishment of the rights of Louis XVI. Even though this did not signify the launching of an antirevolutionary crusade, the patriots of Paris felt the threat of an imminent clash. Whence the idea of a preventive war that would solve the nation's problems while meeting this challenge. After Varennes, France was in constant dread of war, and more and more Frenchmen began to see some advantages in it. Thus, bearing in mind the American example, Brissot thought that a free people would always win out against despots. The opportunity presented by the assemblages of émigrés that the German princes refused to disperse would make it possible to purify and uplift the French by means of armed struggle. This romantic idea of a revolutionary crusade, which was also advanced by Madame Roland, was touted extravagantly by their friends, demagogical deputies or journalists.

The movement toward war thus sprang from errors of judgment stemming from traditional diplomatic practices and liberation-minded ideologies. Until his death in March 1792, Leopold II held this movement in check, but a number of his actions were misinterpreted. In France, the royal couple, La Fayette's followers, and other politicians were all hoping for a war, for contradictory reasons. Their pressure led to a definitive decline in the influence of the Feuillants. Because of his opposition to the laws that had been passed against émigrés and refactory priests, Louis XVI was accused of undermining the interests of the Revolution, but he did not prevent close to fifty departments, by spring 1792, from exiling or imprisoning, on the grounds of public safety, priests who had not taken the oath. Paris's radical movement was revived in the midst of this political crisis. It denounced the refractories and their associates as agents of the counterrevolution. The desire to go to war in the interests of the Revolution was thus linked, from the start, to resistance against internal enemies and defiance of the king. A number of clubs and National Guardsmen made this known to the assembly, and, if the outbreak of war was favored by financial and commercial interests in cooperation with the followers of Brissot, it also carried overtones, in the revolutionary milieu, of a liberating crusade. At issue, however, was a new type of conflict, destined to transform Europe's future. The few Jacobins such as Marat and Robespierre who came out against it, out of skepticism and prudence, were ignored. The struggle against Brissot, however, contained the germ of the future rift between the Montagnards and the Girondins, who recklessly led the country into a war that soon became less popular than they had thought.[1]

T. C. W. Blanning has just begun a thorough study of its origins, linking them to traditional patterns of international relations in eighteenth-century Europe. He observes, in particular, that revolutionary France's warmongering tendencies were a carryover of the Anglophobia and the antagonism toward Austria that characterized many officials of the *ancien régime*. He recalls, furthermore, the basic incompatibility between the diplomatic traditions of secrecy and egotism retained by representatives of the old regime outside France, and the new style of revolutionary foreign policy founded on the principles of national sovereignty and self-determination. Reactionaries believed that the Revolution had put France into a position of total powerlessness, as evidenced by its behavior during the Anglo-Spanish crisis of 1790. The Austro-Prussian rapprochement of 1791 was a blow to the Legislative Assembly, where the Brissotin party stepped up its campaign in favor of war. Blanning notes the enthusiasm it was able to drum up early in 1792. Playing simultaneously on the sentiments, ideals, and interests of the deputies, it convinced them of an easy victory in a truly pathological atmosphere where "great betrayals" were eagerly anticipated as a way of unmasking and rooting out the enemies of the Revolution. For the French who started it, this war was thus a total ideological conflict, fostered on the Austro-Prussian side by an equally unfortunate attitude. This attitude was soon displayed in the famous manifesto, signed by

Brunswick, which hoped to scare off the revolutionary forces by threatening them with total destruction.[2]

In this climate of feverish nationalism, France broke with almost all of Europe in 1793. Having conquered Belgium and threatened the United Provinces, its leaders were sure that London would soon collapse in the face of a general insurrection. They also scornfully declared war on Spain. Brissot and his followers, who envisioned peace for France only at the cost of a universal conflagration of the rest of the world, divided the map of Europe into territory conquered by France and republics protected by it. Prussia, it is true, had already had designs on France in 1790, and in 1793 the strategy of the counterrevolutionary coalition sought to dismember its enemy and return it, at least, to its pre–Louis XIV borders.[3]

The presumed weakness of revolutionary France tempted its adversaries all the more in that they were not at all intimidated by its attempts at subversion. The expansion of its territorial power disturbed them more than spread of its ideology: To their great consternation, the Revolution had once again made France a great power. As for the revolutionaries, their naive faith in the invincibility of their cause was the mark of an analogous presumption. These errors in judgment, by the conservatives as much as by the radicals, helped, above all, set off a conflict that was to ravage Europe for over twenty years. It sprang from the revolutionaries' illusions about the decadence of their enemy, and their certainty of victory, as well as from their rivals' mistaken belief in the irremediable powerlessness of the new France.[4]

After going to war in April 1792, the Revolution could never be quite the same. This conflict, which "revolutionized" it all the more, also affected the course of a movement that was to spread to a large part of Europe. Its external aspects were, from then on, as important as its internal ones, and one of the rare weaknesses of Donald Sutherland's recent study is to have underestimated the impact of international issues on its development. Both in itself and by its expansion, the French Revolution shaped the modern world.[5]

These different factors are disentangled in Jacques Godechot's book on the history of the *Grande Nation*. He traces its roots to the strength and influence of France among countries of European culture at the end of the eighteenth century. After an initial declaration of world peace and a solemn proclamation of the right of self-determination by all peoples, the war that had been started so heedlessly in 1792 shifted to the more realistic idea of territorial acquisition and the creation of sister republics. This mixture of imperialism and ideology was helped by some sympathizers who had taken refuge in France and by certain Frenchmen living abroad. It made use of propaganda in the press and the theater, as well as the means provided by the army and diplomacy. The ideological expansion of revolutionary France little by little touched all countries of European culture, from America to Russia. Its armed forces spread its ideas along with their conquests. Along all its borders, from Holland to Italy, patriots answered the call of their French counterparts, furthering the cause of national unity within their own countries. Their clubs, political newspapers, constitutions, governments, administrative institutions, and also, unfortunately, their religious problems often reflected those of the *Grande Nation*. In the course of the economic exploitation of a French Europe, France extracted from them various contributions and requisitions while giving them, at times, social progress in return. This progress naturally affected the bourgeoisie more than the popular classes in their quest for liberty and equality. Built upon legions of patriots, the national armies of the countries occupied by France sometimes became the symbol of new aspirations. The cultural expansion of the *Grande Nation* benefited from its military and political gains, but at the cost of numerous abuses. Discontent and resistance thus created as many uprisings against the Revolution from outside its borders as from within. For starting in 1792, France presented two indissolubly linked faces to Europe, one of liberation and one of exploitation.[6]

A French society of popular origins thus flourished in Charleston, South Carolina, starting in early 1792. It considered affiliating itself with the Jacobin clubs of France and organized numerous patriotic demonstrations against the aristocracy during public ceremonies. The following year its leaders won the support of the new republic's ambassador to the United States, the young Girondin Genet, who had just been trying, during a three-year stay in Russia which began in 1789, to promote the universal democratic revolution. He informed the convention of his intentions two days before Louis XVI was executed. These dreams stand in contrast to the isolation of the revolutionaries in Brussels, faced with traditionalists supported by the popular classes, or of the German Jacobins who, like their French protectors, were unable to enact sufficiently wide-ranging social reforms to win over the peasantry. These intellectuals welcomed the revolutionary army of occupation, the very instrument that prevented the liberation of their country. For a people whose standard of living was often higher than that of their conquerors, the French conquest was a catastrophe. The poor had to pay the price, which was high, and economic collapse was the result. Ravaged by French bureaucrats and outraged at their religious profanations, the Rhineland identified its national struggle with the defense of Catholicism. Its radical leaders, Kantians who believed in the triumph of reason and were backed by foreign soldiers, took refuge in the disillusionment born of failure. Although there was no upheaval of the Vendéan type, as there was in Calabria, brigandage was soon added to passive resistance and sabotage. The "missionaries in army boots" hailed by Robespierre had tainted the notion of liberation and discredited the idea of cosmopolitanism. Weighed against the harsh realities of revolutionary imperialism, what good was the authentic idealism of intellectuals like the Swiss César-Frédéric de la Harpe, who had supported the ill-fated adventure of the sister republics?[7]

Despite widespread desertions and resistance to mandatory military service, the main legacy of the revolutionary war was, no doubt, the lasting reconciliation of France with its army, which had become, for the first time, a national one. Jean-Pierre Bertaud recently pointed out the essential characteristics of this key revolution. Planned before 1789, it had to overcome resistance by career military men concerned with maintaining the quality of the army, by prominent citizens "worried about losing a young labor force," and by peasants opposed to this arduous obligation. The patriotic fervor that had accounted for the success of voluntary recruitment in 1791 and 1792 certainly had its limits, and there were still deserters and rebellious elements stirring up serious revolts. But civic awareness and coercion took care of these matters. The revolutionary bourgeoisie thus absorbed certain aristocratic values, and the society it created came to be dominated by the theme of military glory. The nobles, moreover, retained numerous positions in the high command until 1793 and even later. The new men who replaced them were often excellent technicians and the hierarchy they headed was only very slightly affected by the promotion of officers of popular origins. The Revolution was particularly careful about military training and, with its *ancien régime* heritage, passed on to Napoleon an excellent combat instrument, despite its traditional weaknesses in logistics and medical services. These wars, which by 1799 had cost France just under five hundred thousand men, created at its borders an antiaristocratic school of Jacobinism that was dedicated to the principles of 1789.[8]

The revolutionary bourgeoisie's participation in the military put the traditional esprit de corps at the service of the new patriotism and overcame opposition to requisitions. This resulted in a regeneration of the military, apparent by 1791, that made the French army at the end of 1792 much stronger than it had been in 1789. More representative of the nation, it forced a massive war on an astounded Europe. This was also an ideological war, soon to be pressed into faithful service of the Republic and the homeland. Although based on the tactical organization handed down from the *ancien régime*, it was infused with a revolutionary spirit and a system of offense that was ready to be handed over to Napoleon. Until 1789, ten percent of the infantry were "officers of fortune," recruited on the basis of class, but never from the poorest segments of the population. Masséna was the nephew of one of these, and the generals of the Revolution were of the same bourgeois origins. These wars opened up wide career possibilities to new talents. Their esprit de corps, passed down from military tradition, was to lead them to try to impose their views on a government that, while victorious, little by little became a hostage of its army.[9]

WAS THE MOBILIZATION OF THE PEOPLE IN 1792–93 FAVORABLE TO THE REVOLUTION OR THE COUNTERREVOLUTION?

The poor harvest of 1791 was followed by bad weather conditions, the interruption of colonial trade, a drop in the value of the *assignat*, and the collapse of industry. Grain imports in Marseilles were seriously disrupted, so that grain prices rose in the area. Speculators everywhere were taking advantage of the situation, while the peasants refused to sell their products for worthless currency, which was reserved for the poor people of the cities. The system of trade and production deteriorated. A wave of riots followed in autumn. In the Nord they were aimed at securing the people's right to set grain prices, and grain convoys were seized. In Paris in early 1792 throngs of women forced down the price of sugar. The disruption of market mechanisms struck the poorest regions and the most marginal elements of rural society hardest. In late winter and early spring, gangs of poor people marched from market to market, behind their mayors, setting prices, stopping convoys, looking for food. This movement also affected the popular classes of the cities. Led in many cases by constitutional priests, they reverted to old apocalyptic ideas of a revitalizing bloodbath that would precede the coming of paradise on earth. On a more prosaic level, these mobs were seeking restitution of their communal properties or an equitable distribution of resources. Whence their egalitarian demands for salary increases and their protests against the rich farmers, who were returning to the theory of a hunger plot.

Mobilization of the people was even more widespread in the Midi, where the Jacobins were roused by the stirrings of a counterrevolution. They turned to the rural areas, which shared with the agricultural villages an extremely active collective life. The clubs' activities burgeoned throughout all the villages, from the Ardèche to the Gard, and from the Drôme to the Var. In Marseilles, from spring to summer 1792 attendance at section meetings quadrupled, and patriots marched on Arles in March to disarm their adversaries. The citizens felt that the government's impotence justified taking matters into their own hands, and rural mobilization launched a series of peasant revolts that in April and May spread from Provence to Charente and the Haute-Garonne. Homes of counterrevolutionaries, especially *seigneurs*, were demolished, along with the deeds of title inside. Prices in these regions were fixed, and properties judged to belong to the community repossessed. This new unrest, stemming from the seriousness of the economic situation, spread to the National Guard and municipal authorities. It was directed not only against aristocrats and priests, but also against rich landowners, even when they were local administrators. Its egalitarian demands were aimed equally against a revolution that had done very little for the peasants, who, in the Midi, pursued an autonomous movement that sometimes seemed to correspond to that of the elites, but which never overlapped entirely with their concerns.

The riots in the Nord and the disturbances in the Midi were viewed rather as annoyances at the national level. Despite Robespierre's sympathy for the rebellious northerners, their demands were ignored by the Jacobins, who, as a whole, remained opposed to their aims and agreed to repressive measures of which the victims were not free until September. The leaders of wartime France were thus confronted with deep-rooted dissatisfaction over agrarian problems and food supplies.[1]

Brissot's supporters had entered the government in April, and led a campaign that fell short of their hopes. Their first defeats were seen as evidence of treason, which alarmed the *sans-culottes* of Paris. In response to the dismissal of the Girondin ministers by Louis XVI, who refused to sign popular laws (such as those against the refractory priests, for example), an armed protest took place on June 20. It had no effect on the king and did nothing but aggravate the divisions in the country. La Fayette tried in vain to turn it against the Jacobins, while highly politicized National Guardsmen from the provinces marched on the capital to defend the Revolution. By declaring the "fatherland in danger" on July 11, and by authorizing the sections to remain in permanent attendance on the twenty-fifth, the assembly increased this mobilization. This reflected the new role assigned to the poor in the service of the armed nation.

Militants in the provinces who, particularly in the west, were more affected by the counterrevolutionary threat, added to this pressure. Hence on June 19 the popular societies of Lyons proclaimed the king a traitor; the municipality of Marseilles shortly thereafter declared itself opposed to the hereditary monarchy; a petition in Anjou on July 18 demanded that Louis be deposed. Originating in the departments, this movement spread. The *fédérés* (citizen soldiers) of Marseilles arrived in Paris spoiling for a fight. Nevertheless, although on August 3 the capital's sections demanded the elimination of the dynasty and the convocation of a National Convention, their ranks were far from united, with political divisions not always corresponding to social ones.

The rift that occurred at this point between the Girondins and the popular movement was all the more unfortunate in that it came at just the time of the publication of Brunswick's manifesto threatening Paris with total destruction in case of resistance. This only spurred the most radical sections to demand that the king be deposed by an insurrection. The assembly declined, and the committee which led it in conjunction with the *fédérés* then had to contend with the reticence of the National Guardsmen and with the defenders of the Tuileries. Their capitulation on August 10 led to a radicalization of the Revolution marked, in particular, by the deportation of the refractory priests. Forty percent of the clergy of the *ancien régime* thus found itself scattered throughout Europe and America. The secularization of the *état civil* (civil registry), which passed into the hands of the communes, followed. Popular among local authorities, who had in some cases enacted them in advance, these measures did not stop the refractories from conducting their activities clandestinely.

Hostility to this secularization, along with opposition to the Revolution, led to royalist uprisings in the west at the end of August. Gangs of peasants refusing to do their military service had to be dispersed. In the capital, and soon throughout the whole country, power struggles between the Assembly and the commune added a new element of paralysis to a general atmosphere of defeat and anarchy. Fear of treason exacerbated repressive measures and accounts, in large part, for the massacres that took place in Paris in early September. The belief in a prison conspiracy was a throwback to the *ancien régime*. The revolutionary mentality compounded this traditional fear, analogous to the panic over brigands in 1789, with an obsession about a royalist conspiracy whose agents were prisoners preparing to massacre the patriots. A countermassacre thus seemed to many to be a way of eradicating this plot. Over the summer such a preventive measure, founded on similar kinds of rumors, had already been tried in the countryside against priests, suspect administrators, and counterrevolutionaries. Panic over the invasion and its internal allies, who were accused of attacking defenseless civilians, the inertia of the authorities and the belief in the necessity for a punitive reaction: These were the ingredients of a massacre, worsened by official inducements to the murderers. The people's revenge consisted of the methodical liquidation of over a thousand prisoners in the capital, half the total then incarcerated, three quarters of whom were not political detainees. Its agents no doubt considered themselves to be as worthy patriots as the conquerors of the Tuileries and Valmy, who, on September 20, saved the Revolution. The next day the Convention abolished the monarchy and proclaimed the Republic.[2]

Had the first revolution, which had just ended, moved from bourgeois monarchy to *sans-culotte* democracy? Sentiment in the first two assemblies, as in the local administrators, had been favorable to the rich. They had attempted to limit promotion on the basis of merit to families able to finance their sons' careers. August 10 seems to represent the end of this practice of limiting power to the elites. This *journée* passed the power on to radical democrats who believed in universal male suffrage and the direct sovereignty of the people. Despite certain limitations in the application of this principle, a third of the new Paris commune, for example, was composed of shopkeepers and artisans along with militants from the popular societies. But these advances by the *sans-culottes* were accompanied by a radicalization of the social groups already participating in the political system. The leaders of the local administrations, which were so hostile to the dissidents, as well as of the Jacobins and the National Guard continued to be drawn from the bourgeoisie. The radicalization of the second revolution thus did not mean that the popular classes were stepping into the roles formerly occupied by the notables. There was indeed a certain democratization of the militant factions as a by-product of the war, as in the case of Strasbourg, but the role of the bourgeois intellectuals remained predominant. The political crisis, which was mobilizing more and more people on both the left and the right, did not perceptibly change the internal balance of the revolutionary group, which had been led from 1789 on by members of the legal profession. The young people who enrolled in the National Guard were still commanded by officers of bourgeois origins, and the battalions of 1791, recruited in theory among the active citizenry, were the authors, the following year, of petitions, expeditions, and massacres.

Appearances notwithstanding, mobilization was not universal. Only on rare occasions did more than 50 percent of the voters participate in elections to the Convention, and in the west, where this percentage fell to 10, it was the sacred cause of the counterrevolution that stirred young people. The year 1792 was less one of revolutionary enthusiasm than of a deep national division caused, above all, by the religious policies of the Revolution. Unwilling to challenge property, the Revolution responded no better to the people's economic demands. The laws aimed at facilitating the abolition of the seignorial regime that were passed in July and August reveal no link in the assembly between political divisions and a socially-based opposition. The first revolution, which had been fundamentally conservative, had neither reduced taxes nor destroyed the feudal system. It had, however, coincided with the increased impoverishment of the masses and a pointless religious schism. The group that was to dominate the Convention, monopolizing power there, was faced not only with the exigencies of the war, but also with discontent stemming from the insufficient progress achieved since 1789.[3]

The crisis of February and March 1793 revealed the deputies' inability to deal with such a critical situation. At the beginning of that winter, the counterrevolution seemed to have disappeared as an external or internal threat. The country seemed never in the past two years to have been as "calm," and religious incidents in particular had diminished considerably. It was the events stemming from war that gave new life to the counterrevolution and brought it new support. On February 24 the Convention, anticipating the new campaign that was just beginning and the spread of conflict, decreed that three hundred thousand men would be drafted. This initial appeal for sacrifice by the Republic provoked a wave of upheavals that were more significant than those of the preceding year. They pushed the authorities down the path of centralization and systematic repression. Some of these disturbances were directed only at the draft, but fueled by religious discontent in the rural areas of the west, they sometimes involved entire communities. Liberty trees were destroyed there, official registers burned, National Guardsmen and constitutional priests were harassed, and royalist cockades were brandished. Armed gangs carrying white flags marched on the cities demanding the abolition of the districts. In Brittany they seized control of their principal town and asked local nobles to lead them. Order was reestablished in early April, but south of the Loire, in four departments which were to constitute "military Vendée," where fewer troops were available and communications were more difficult, the government collapsed. By the end of March the rebels had taken all the towns and massacred republicans. They were threatening Nantes, Angers, and Saumur, and their leaders announced the formation of a royal Catholic army under the emblem of the cross and the Sacred Heart and sent emissaries out to seek English aid.

The uprisings on the northen border coincided with the defeat and treason of Dumouriez. An undisciplined and poorly maintained army had alienated the Belgians, who were already dissatisfied with the introduction of the *assignat* and the religious reforms. The disorganization of the civil and military authorities also contributed to the squandering of this victory. Unable to take charge of his defeated army in order to restore the monarchy in Paris, Dumouriez shamelessly fled to the enemy. The economic crisis, meanwhile, continued. Having exhausted all its resources, the government could finance the war only by pumping out notes that were depreciating daily. External trade collapsed along with confidence in the regime. Prices continued to rise and food supply problems became acute.

The people's movement of Paris began to concentrate once more on the issue of subsistence. In February it denounced the principle of free trade so dear to the Convention and demanded that a national maximum grain price be set. These grievances, a carryover from the mentality of the *ancien régime,* were proclaimed by the group of *enragés* led by Roux and Varlet. They encouraged riots by the poor, who looted stores. The National Guard was able to stop them, but the commune shared, in part, the concerns of the rioters. Like many Jacobins, it hoped to satisfy the poor in order to win them over to the Revolution.

The patriots attributed their problems on the whole to sinister plots. They had always had this tendency, but the exceptional scope of the crisis of 1793 led them to justify the Terror. They thus attributed the food riots to the counterrevolution or to Marat and blamed the disturbances in the west on émigré conspiracies. They linked them with Dumouriez's treason and extended this theory to include machinations originating in London. These myths colored the people's response to the crisis. They thought that the economic difficulties were entirely the fault of speculators, while the politicians attributed popular unrest to dangerous manipulation. The conspiracy theory also accounts for the measures taken to head off defeat. The purpose of the revolutionary tribunal, set up in response to the setbacks suffered in Belgium, was to mete out summary justice on issues concerning national security. Similarly, the belief in the omnipresence of traitors led to the creation in March of revolutionary committees in every section and commune. At first their only function was to detain foreigners and suspects without papers, but their police powers were extended during the summer. Similar suspicions led to the creation in April of the Committee of Public Safety, which was initially responsible for surveillance of the executive council, but was quickly transformed into an extralegal regime.

In the guise of defending the Revolution, the Convention strayed further and further onto the path of extremism. On March 19, in response to uprisings in the west, it decided that the rebel armies could be summarily executed within twenty-four hours. Confronted with massive internal resistance and lacking confidence in the generals, it conferred increased powers on its representatives on mission. Eighty-two of them had been sent out in early March to aid in the recruitment of the three hundred thousand men. They were given full powers in military and administrative matters. They had already begun to respond to the crisis by instituting and coordinating repressive measures in the civil war zones. These extraordinary decisions, which wound up restoring the authority of the central government, rested on the idea of the primacy of public safety, which was not new. It had often been used against dissidents. But 1793 added to it a rejection of moderation as the supreme danger to the Republic. The radicalization of large numbers of deputies and militants stemmed from this attribution of the failures of the convention to a tolerance of evil.[4]

This view, as outlined by Donald Sutherland, seems to be confirmed by recent studies of the popular movements of 1792 and 1793. They stress the persistence of a multifaceted agrarian revolt that would finally be turned against the Revolution's religious and military recruitment policies. The French countryside's rejection of the Jacobins was from then on a continuing source of support for the counterrevolution. Antiseignorial Brittany thus became the home of the Chouans, the red Midi turned white, and the forest-tax assessors of the Perche became royalist outlaws. The peasant's discontent, totally ignored by the new urban authorities, had challenged the principles of the liberal economy and property. Their subsistence riots and their tax proposals echoed those of the humble people of the cities. In this revolutionary atmosphere *ancien régime* consumers found a spokesman for their demands in the person of Pierre Dolivier, a parish priest from near Étampes who supported grain price controls for the common good. In the eyes of the bourgeois authorities he thus raised once again the specter of agrarian reform.[5]

These officials had to deal with a Parisian movement animated by the same ideas and responsible for the *journées* that had brought them to power. Growing more and more egalitarian, the sections of the capital were more attentive to the concerns of the *sans-culottes* who had created the Republic but were also small producers and independent workers, hostile to the merchants and the "powerful." They had lent a hand in the September massacres, that outpouring of the anguish of the honest people faced with "wrongdoers of all stripes." (Frédéric Bluche.) Their pressure continued to weigh on the authorities until the Jacobin dictatorship was established. It could also be a tool for moderates who made use of the poverty of the masses to turn them toward the counterrevolution. Preoccupied above all with the issue of subsistence, they believed in the capital that the application of direct democracy would solve this problem. Some members of Robespierre's circle began to challenge economic liberalism. The anticapitalism of the militants, on the other hand, had its roots in the mentality of the *ancien régime*. It was this throwback to earlier expectations that rocked Paris in early 1793 and forced the Revolution finally to organize a government capable of both maintaining order and engaging in war. Far from homogeneous, revolutionary sentiment was more confused and disparate than ever at the moment when, thanks to the mixed support of the *sans-culottes*, the Jacobins succeeded in imposing their dictatorship. Marat detested Jacques Roux and was distrustful of the *enragés*. He soon became concerned with limiting freedom of expression, for he knew that "to bring about a rapid return of the *ancien régime*" all that was needed was "for some clever mischief-maker . . . to compare food costs under despotism and under the Republic."[6]

Clashes in the provinces echoed these contradictions, but in the Midi the remoteness of the threat of invasion worked against the *sans-culottes* and to the advantage of the established classes, which had benefited from the Revolution and dominated its administrations. The upsurge of Jacobinism was thus by no means homogeneous throughout the departments. While it was able to impose on Strasbourg the domination of an activist minority that was in many cases from outside the city, it had different consequences in the southeast despite its exceptionally strong foothold there. The radicalization of the National Guardsmen and the clubs did spur a significant revolutionary movement in 1792, but it was much less pronounced in the Var and the Gard than in the Bouches-du-Rhône. In Marseilles itself in the spring of 1793 the moderates were to reclaim power, as they did in the rest of the Midi. In Lyons, the *sans-culottes*, grouped around Chalier, were in power for only a short time in March. The silk workers, ever attentive to maintaining their standard of living, never considered overthrowing the supremacy of the merchants. Their mobilization, since 1789, had brought these workers important gains, and they were the spearhead of the anticapitalist Jacobin movement. But this movement, with its obsessive hatred of "those who have carriages, servants, silk clothes, and go to the theater," alarmed many of the poor, for it disrupted the economy and increased unemployment among them.[7]

In their way, the workers of Lyons, who were to help the bourgeois oligarchy overturn the despotism of the patriots, participated in an impressive popular counterrevolution. The rural west, with its large peasant population, was naturally the primary theater of activity. Historians have long observed that the uprising in the Vendée was the result of *both* social and religious factors and was too violent a reaction to have been caused by the recruitment of 1793 alone. Numerous studies have connected it to a fundamental opposition between the rural areas, which had gained little from the Revolution, and the dominant cities, which they were to identify from then on as the source of their exploitation. This observation needs to be qualified, insofar as there were rural patriots in Brittany and agrarian unrest was directed as much against the seignorial regime as against the dominant role of the cities. But the social makeup of the Vendéan armies of Anjou, studied by Claude Petit-frère, corresponds exactly to the nonbourgeois population of the region. These rural folk, for the most part illiterate, clashed with republicans who were better off and better educated. In this class struggle, as in Italy in 1799, the proletariat rose up against the Revolution. Their revolt, which was quickly taken over by the gentry, was not the product of any manipulation. Nor was it the spontaneous uprising of an "angelic society" serving God and king. This armed populace, from old men to women and children, was one of peasants in their parishes who felt betrayed by the patriotic cities. They were protesting in their way against an incomplete revolution and wreaking fierce revenge on the bourgeois, those new *seigneurs* who were trying to send them out to die in their place. The February 24 decree exempted civil servants from military service and granted the rich the opportunity to buy replacements for themselves. Whence the rage of the rural young, who, in *May-sur-Evre*, tried to "raze Cholet, destroy the district and cut off the heads of all the patriots." Under the cumulative weight of their social frustrations, their hatred of the city and all authorities became identified with rejection of the Revolution.[8]

This sentiment alone is not enough to explain an insurrection that was not isolated, for there were "unfinished Vendées," to use Jean-Clément Martin's expression, in the Midi and elsewhere during this whole period. The clash of cultures that caused them was not simply the product of class conflicts. The religious fervor of the Vendéan soldiers was linked to their ties to the refractory priests, with whom they proclaimed their solidarity within a community symbolized by its church tower. They viewed the Revolution and its church as breaking this sacred, traditional tie. Evoking those meetings in the chapels and moors of Brittany where "from time immemorial, the populations of several outlying cantons would come together," Roger Dupuy notes that "far from the National Guardsmen and the police, a whole counterrevolutionary litany was proclaimed, and the *assignat* was decried." These meetings were forbidden by the authorities early in 1793. Popular resistance to the Revolution in western France was the result of divisions that arose, when the Civil Constitution of the Clergy was put in force, between a cultivated urban elite and a rural mentality that remained hostile to it. The rural population was plunged into anxiety by the disruption of their religious traditions and the intrusion of newcomers. Their revolt was a desperate response to a political affront that had lasted long enough. It sprang up above all among a peasantry accustomed to a strong clerical presence with solid ties to the local population. In these regions, furthermore, a bourgeoisie critical of the organization of the church had just begun to take root. This contrast contributed to the outbreak of a tragic civil war. In her *Mémoires*, the Marquise de la Rochejaquelein described the way cities were taken over, with insurgents running to the churches and ringing the bells before rushing out to burn liberty trees and municipal documents.[9]

WAS THE ANTAGONISM BETWEEN THE GIRONDINS
AND THE MONTAGNARDS INSURMOUNTABLE?

The significance of the Convention lies not so much in the legendary status it acquired in the nineteenth century as in the fact that its members for all practical purposes governed France from 1792 to 1799. Until 1795, faced with the most serious crises of the revolutionary period, they were able to contain the internal counterrevolution and to lay down the bases of French expansion in Europe by dividing the foreign coalition. These achievements were gained at the expense of violent methods, economic and financial failure, and a break with the popular movement that was to cause insurmountable problems.

Of the 730 officials elected in September 1792, over six hundred already had some political experience. Younger than the deputies of the Third Estate to the Constituent Assembly (two thirds, rather than half, were under forty-four years old), they were of similar urban origins, with a quarter coming from cities numbering over fifteen hundred inhabitants, which represented at the time, only ten percent of the population. Over fifty percent were men of the legal professions. But these were no longer the malleable officials of the *ancien régime*. Half of this new world of local activists still came from lawyers' families. There were also fifty-five ecclesiastics and some ex-nobles, including the Duc d'Orléans and other leftist deputies.

The history of the Convention was dominated until June 2, 1793, by the struggle between the Girondins, successors of the Brissotins, and the Montagnards, who were organized around the Paris contingent and occupied the highest ranks of the Assembly. These were not disciplined parties united in support of a particular program. The spirit of the era, with its condemnations of factionalism and its exaltation of individual independence, precluded this. It is thus difficult to classify the deputies in groups. The fluidity of the situation makes this even more difficult. The Parisian revolutionaries, pitted against the Girondins, grew up constantly changing lists of their enemies. They were often based on a vote in favor of an appeal to the people over the fate of the king, hardly a definitive criterion. Each deputy took a highly individual course, with extremists ending up at times as moderates and vice versa, and with fluctuations in between. The Girondins and the Montagnards, who did not make up the majority, were simply two groups vying for influence over the remaining group, known as the Plain. Their leaders were not unified. Even among the Montagnards, who were somewhat more cohesive because of their dominant position among the Jacobins, there were major differences of opinion, and they were far from unanimous in following Robespierre or, even more so, Marat. The Girondins, who preferred discussion to concerted action, were even less homogeneous. The majority of the deputies shared a certain number of convictions: They favored an aggressive foreign policy, marked by the extension of a war intended to bring down the *ancien régime* in all of Europe; backed economic policies favorable to private property and to free trade in grain; were opposed to subsistence riots and agrarian disturbances. No member of the Convention, even from the extreme left, ever identified with the people's aspirations on this point.

Violent and hasty conflicts grew out of deep mutual suspicions. The Montagnards thought the Girondins were royalists and counterrevolutionaries, whereas the Girondins considered their opponents ready to organize massacres or insurrections in order to establish a dictatorship or Paris's hegemony over the provinces. Many debates amounted to narrow factional quarrels, and it is difficult to deduce from them any information on the respective strengths of the parties. Such was the case with the trial of the king, which began in late 1792. There was almost unanimous agreement over his treason and the need to condemn it. The proposal by several Girondins to submit the verdict to a referendum was rejected for fear that a vote favorable to the king would produce chaos. The idea of granting a reprieve in the hope of placating foreign opinion was no more successful. The execution of Louis XVI, on February 21, 1793, which symbolized a definitive break with the *ancien régime*, left the factions irreconcilable. It represented a triumph for the Montagnards, who had forced the assembly to refuse any compromise and thereby gained a lasting advantage. This trial had divided the Girondins, who increasingly left the leadership of the Convention's committees to the Montagnards. The latter consolidated their political base in Paris and the provinces by labeling their adversaries cryptoroyalists. But their victory was not total and relied on a centrist bloc that potentially constituted a majority. Later crises were to aggravate the dangers of this situation and led to the expulsion of the Girondins under pressure from the capital's radicals.[1]

The Girondins' position had been weakened since the beginning of the year by their increasing moderation. Though they at times supported extra-legal measures, they feared that these might be used by their enemies. Robespierre, for example, demanded on April 14 that Brissot be tried before the Revolutionary Tribunal. The Girondins' opposition to according increased powers to representatives on mission stemmed from the fact that these were mostly Montagnards. This mutual distrust turned the creation of a government for the public good into an object of partisan struggles. The Girondins proved less favorable than their adversaries to a policy of popular mobilization in the service of the Republic. This reversal of the position they had held the preceding year contrasted with their enemies' strategy of granting economic and social concessions in an attempt to save the Revolution.

Its defense by exceptional means was not unique to any one faction and was part of a complex process. On April 5, Parisian militants were able to force through a tax on the rich, the goal of which was to subsidize bread for the poor. The demonetization of gold and silver followed on the eleventh. On May 5, faced with difficulties in supplying provisions, the Convention set a maximum price for grains, accompanied by authorizations for requisitions. This return to *ancien régime* practices was hardly a nuisance to speculators, and by discouraging production, it risked disappointing the *sans-culottes*.

The body of measures adopted *as of spring 1793* constituted an essential element of the future Terror. They appeared amid a general atmosphere of disorder in which everyone was attempting to respond to the crisis that had arisen in March. These decisions thus did not amount to a system and they were applied without enthusiasm outside of the zones of civil war. But their image in the provinces and their promulgation by the Jacobins accelerated the process of disintegration they had hoped to remedy.

Public opinion in the various regions had until then been rather neutral with regard to the struggles within the assembly. The clubs, which deplored them, devoted themselves above all to national defense, and their concerns rarely coincided with those of the capital. Federalism, as the revolt against the terrorist legislation of the Convention was known, varied according to local political conditions. It was a rebellion that was marked by intense rivalries and Paris maintained several sources of support within it.

The federalist movement was neither counterrevolutionary nor in favor of decentralization. Its manifestos were republican, and if some of its leaders were sometimes royalists, they did not encourage emigration. They supported constitutional monarchy, not the reestablishment of the *ancien régime*, a project dear to the Comte de Provence, who had proclaimed himself regent. This revolt was an expression of fear of the Jacobins, who were believed to favor murdering and pillaging the rich. This sentiment was at the heart of the movement in the large towns of the Midi. The Maximum (price limit) was very poorly received there, for the region's people were dependent upon precarious outside sources of food. Unlike the rural folk of the Nord, who were often landless, those of the Midi, where small peasant properties were more widespread, rose up against a measure that reduced incomes already seriously compromised. It was regarded as a plot emanating from the capital. Southern extremism, rooted in long previous struggles, alienated many social groups. The humble people of Toulon initiated the toppling of the Jacobin municipality in July. Similarly, in Lyons, the policies of intimidation so dear to Chalier's friends led to the division of the popular movement and provided an opportunity for the moderates, who resumed power in an uprising on the twenty-ninth of May. They immediately called for the solidarity of the "wealthy folk" of Bordeaux and Marseilles, where similar developments had taken place. In this last city, economic difficulties and political unrest had at first caused a very crude form of radicalization. The persecution of the rich and the irresponsible despotism of local agents of the Terror, supported, as in Lyons, by the government's representatives on mission, led to a general uprising against "anarchists" in May. The popularity of federalism was due to in large part to the unpopularity of those it was overthrowing, who were often regarded as fanatics increasing the unemployment of the unfortunate. Most of the time they were patriots hardened by the presence of the counterrevolution. Their tragedy presaged the one that Jacobinism was to experience a year later, on a national scale, when an overwhelming majority of the country tried to rid itself of them.

The Montagnards were mistaken in identifying the privileged classes as their adversaries. In Marseilles, three quarters of the federalists' victims were of the common people, but so were more than half of their executioners. Led by the rich, federalism enjoyed widespread support among the people. In Lyons, over a third of its army officers were artisans. This resulted in a realignment of the sociopolitical coalition that had, until then, led the Revolution.

This crisis resulted in the assembly's purge of the Girondins, in the belief that they constituted the enemy within and were responsible for treason. In March and April, the Jacobins called for the recall of the *appelants*, as the deputies who had supported a referendum on the question of executing the king were known, and to the removal of conspirators from positions where they might cause harm. It was hoped at first that this could be accomplished without the use of force, but the Girondins' counterattacks, first on Marat and then on the commune of Paris, led to the May 31 and June 2 uprisings, which resulted in the arrest of twenty-nine deputies and two ministers. These *journées*, which could have provoked a break with the countryside, were unneccessary, as the Montagnards controlled the Convention, except during exceptional votes. Since January, the Girondins had been either in the minority or in agreement with them, particularly with regard to the laws of exception. They were paying for their turnabout of the preceding summer, when they had declared themselves opposed to the insurrection and criticized the capital. Their support of a referendum on the fate of the king strengthened suspicions about them, and they became the victims of a mentality, pervasive since 1789, which sought to account for all the nation's problems by a sinister conspiracy. In the face of defeats, the sections thus pressed for the elimination of the Girondins and the establishment of a revolutionary tribunal. The spread of civil war spurred the Jacobins and the commune to join this movement.

The Girondins did not represent the interests of a conservative bourgeoisie opposed to a people's government, as shown by the limited social consequences of their eradication. The Parisian movement gained only a few perfunctory concessions from the Montagnards. It was decided that suspects could be arrested without specific charges. The principle of a revolutionary army was voted on and passed, but not put into practice. Local authorities were asked to sell émigrés' property in small lots, but this was not done. The authorization granted to the villages to share their *biens communaux* had been discussed, without opposition, before the Girondins were purged. In the interest of the Republic, everyone agreed upon the maximal distribution of property. The law of July 17, which definitively abolished feudalism, simply legitimized an existing practice. For the Jacobins, the peasants and the *sans-culottes* mattered less than the federalist rebellion.[2]

The administrations of many departments had long expressed their distrust of Paris. They had grown used to resorting to independent actions and extra-legal measures. The future federalists of Calvados had approved the measures taken by the Convention. The anti-Montagnard revolt preceded the fall of the Girondins, which lent it unforeseen national dimensions. Although sixty departments protested against it, their movement was never coordinated and often crumbled in the face of hostility or indifference. Such was the case in Caen in July, and in the Jura in August. The federalist leaders of the west did not enjoy any real support. Their partisan attitude ruffled public opinion and their incompetence allowed the Convention to regain the upper hand by means of a constitution, published in June, whose goal was to disarm its adversaries. The assembly intimidated them by demanding their surrender and proceeding with a reasonable pacification plan. The rebellion continued in Lyon, Marseille, and Toulon, where there were executions and negotiations with the enemy. Accelerated by the food crisis, these talks led to the intervention of the English and the Spanish in Toulon at the end of August. The situation was marked, furthermore, by a general deterioration in the military situation. The Vendéans had won some impressive victories against bitterly divided republican forces. A royalist uprising took place in the Ariège at the end of August; there had been another in Lozere in May. Defeats on all the borders coincided with them. The expulsion of the Girondins had not helped the war effort. It needed reinforcement. This was the significance of Robespierre's joining the Committee of Public Safety on July 27. He brought with him a program of redoubled national energy, hostility to the "bourgeois," and heavy repression. Carrying it out in the country's divided atmosphere was going to be difficult. Police measures were no longer sufficient to combat the federalists and the Vendéans. The Jacobins were now convinced that "the people" alone could save the Revolution against the "rich." Thus was born their alliance with the *sans-culottes*. But many elements of the popular classes had already joined the counterrevolution. Marat's murder, on July 13, only confirmed the omnipresence of treason, hostility to moderation, and the patriotic value of generalized suspicion.[3]

This analysis of Donald Sutherland's characterizes the opposition between Girondins and Montagnards in terms that are above all social. The former, in what Marc Bouloiseau calls this "divorce between bourgeoisies," might embody the liberalism of the propertied classes, whereas the latter would represent the support given by later democrats to the economic interventionism sought by the popular classes. This seems less clear in light of recent research. Jacqueline Chaumié has pointed out the strength of the Girondins' "republican" convictions. Since 1969, Alison Patrick has added a great deal to our knowledge of the early stages of the Convention, which was divided into three blocs: slightly fewer than two hundred deputies of Girondin leanings; slightly more than three hundred who were more or less allied with the Montagnards; and the rest, referred to as the Plain, who were split into two halves, one which participated in the Jacobin regime and another which held off commitment to either and was to come into its glory after 9 thermidor. Alison Patrick has shown the cohesion of the Montagnards as compared with the wavering loyalties of the other groups, including the Girondins, in the midst of increasing abstentionism. Although they did not constitute the majority, the Montagnards, numbering over forty percent of the deputies, quickly became a particularly influential group within the Assembly.[4]

The Girondins were weakened, in 1793, by their growing opposition to certain revolutionary measures whose necessity they did not question, but which they feared would be turned to account by their adversaries. This position became more and more untenable as the crisis deepened. This interpretation, which minimized the importance of the *journées* of May 31 and June 2, has been criticized by those who have pointed out that the deputies were under pressure from the popular movement. But this pressure had already brought about a significant radicalization of the ruling bourgeoisie and, after the coup d'état, the rift between *enragés* and Montagnards only deepened. The Convention followed its own logic, born of the complex relations among men who were sometimes undecided and groups that were often divided, and power never strayed from this hall, in which deliberations were dominated by the clash between the Revolution and counterrevolution.[5]

Patrice Higonnet has recently redefined the opposition between Montagnards and Girondins in the context of the discontinuities that characterized the history of the Revolution up to the Terror. He notes the underlying unity of the Convention members and accounts for their rifts by the "schizophrenic" state of a French bourgeoisie abruptly thrust into power, without advance preparation by a general process of evolution. During this period, when new roles and ambiguities among these roles were developing, the Revolution's leaders were unsteady, squeezed between the nobility and the people and vacillating between the defense and the condemnation of capitalism or of violence. The majority of the assembly, aside from those at the center of power, was composed of ordinary revolutionaries, doomed to misunderstanding by their inadequate grasp of the sources of the political and ideological drifting that had occurred since 1789 and that they were trying desperately to save themselves from. Their partisan antagonisms, stemming from moral outrage at an unforeseen and exceptionally dangerous situation, impelled them toward irreconcilable rifts that some of them regretted at the time and that many hastened, later on, to forget. This interpretation seems confirmed by a recent study of the *Cercle social*, the best known of the Girondins' attempts to reach out to the nation, whose radical roots are undisputed. Bonneville and Fauchet began their careers there as agitators on behalf of the capital's sections, before becoming moderate intellectuals aligned with Brissot and his circle. They shared in the period's contradictions between bourgeois individualism and the dream of a communal republic. Tensions springing from pressure exerted by the people and the counterrevolution increasingly turned the struggle for power into a chaotic rush, with people striking out at friends as well as enemies.[6]

The problems associated with the federalist revolt illustrated the complexities of the situation in the summer of 1793. While the Paris movement continued to rise up against a nascent revolutionary government, peasants continued to pursue their egalitarian goals. Other rural populations had risen up, in the west, against the Republic. The same contrast was to be seen in a city like Lyons, where textile workers were divided into supporters and opponents of the bourgeois insurrection. More than a drive toward decentralization, federalism was the expression of the reality of local independence that, for the past four years, had been at the heart of the Revolution. In contrast with the royalists, the rebels of Rennes, for example, considered themselves to be just as good republicans as the Montagnards they were fighting. Amid the overall confusion, stemming from the incoherence of the movement and the variable nature of popular support, federalism was an extension of the old search for legitimate authority begun in 1789. Three centers of resistance to the Convention's authority persisted: one in Marseilles until August, one in Lyons until October, and one in Toulon until December. They had nothing to do with any maneuvering by the upper bourgeoisie or any counterrevolutionary conspiracy. This revolt was the expression of provincial discontent, which exploded in places where moderate authorities were no longer able to contain it. The violence of social conflicts made it possible to exploit the hatred and fear of many segments of the population toward a Jacobin dictatorship supported by the Montagnards. There was thus a spontaneous people's federalism, neither reactionary nor particularist. The fall of the Girondins provided it with justification after the fact and its virulence confirmed a profound political instability. The only departments to escape it were those that were able to keep to the safe path of waiting to see what happened.[7]

7. A LOGIC
TO THE TERROR?

I t is difficult to attribute the regime of 1793 solely to the pressures of external circumstances or to the pure evolution of revolutionary ideology. According to Augustin Cochin, the logic of bourgeois individualism led inevitably to an egalitarian reign of Virtue supported by denunciations, fixed trials, and institutionalized envy. This sociologist thereby accounts for a system of progressive exclusion, in which the pure were constantly purging the impure, and in which radicalized moderates, for moralistic reasons, became agents of the Terror. Their barbarism, according to this view, was the product of the Enlightenment.

Patrice Higonnet challenges this traditional view of totalitarian democracy, attributing it instead to the ideological fluctuations of the ruling bourgeoisie, destabilized by its political situation and its relations with the popular movement that had surged uncontrollably since 1791. The Terror, in this scheme of things, was an attempt to unite the bourgeoisie and the people under the Revolution. It was the work not of exceptional personalities but of ordinary lawyers. It attempted to fuse the simultaneously individualistic and communal aspirations handed down by the philosophes and only partially understood by a class that was undergoing its political apprenticeship. The French bourgeoisie, at once particularist and universal, came to its basic liberalism only after being momentarily betrayed by the experiment of the Terror. The bourgeoisie had been led there by the gap between the immensity of its objectives and the poverty of its resources. The lesson it learned was that the ancient concepts of freedom were meaningless in the modern world.[1]

The gravity of the crisis that rocked France at this time cannot be overstated. Its inhabitants were not ideology-spouting automata. Their concerns were down-to-earth. As John Talmon has remarked, the ideological violence that Jacobinism created was something of an "improvisation." Examining these gropings is all the more necessary in that the sans-culottes and the Montagnards who acted together did not have the same concept of the "aristocratic conspiracy" or how to solve it.[2]

WHO WERE THE INSTIGATORS OF THE TERROR, WHAT WAS THEIR PROGRAM, AND HOW WAS IT CARRIED OUT?

The *sans-culottes*, from whose ranks came a large portion of the agents of the Terror, believed more in the direct practice of popular sovereignty than in the value of representative institutions. Sectional militants pitted against these the principles of popular initiative, of the referendum, the recall of deputies, and the right to bear arms. The goal of their petitions and protests was to impose their will on the officials they had elected. Their ideas of popular justice, and the punishments that went along with it, were simply improvised responses to necessity. Experience had taught the *sans-culottes* to be wary of their leaders and to rise up against traitors. They realized that they could be duped and were aware of how much they had to learn. Their anticlericalism grew out of the conviction that the priests, for centuries, had been teaching them to obey the aristocracy and the rich. Their struggle against oppression stemmed from an awareness of their rights and a desire to exercise them, and their idea of the Revolution was above all a moral one. But their egalitarianism was that of men attached to a society of small landowners. They were fighting against economic dependency and aspired to a decent life. This ideal might lead to the forced requisition of food that was headed to the cities, revolutionary taxes on the rich, the organization of a system of public assistance, the reduction of inequities, and the institution of a system of social security. All this could be attained only within the framework of permanent struggle.

This outlook did not always originate with manual laborers. The authors of a *sans-culotte* manifesto in Lyons, considered typical by Albert Soboul, were mostly intellectuals, lawyers, ex-ecclesiastics, and administrators. When the majority were craftsmen, as in Toulouse, they were above all small-scale employers. Like three quarters of the local Jacobin leaders, these landowners were sometimes rather well off. The agents of the Terror of Montbrison belonged to the middle classes and were led by the richest among them. The post-1792 Jacobins continued to be more heavily taxed than the rest of the population and this proportion increased the higher one went in their hierarchy. Although the *sans-culottes* were often urban workers, as in Paris, where they made up two thirds of the revolutionary committees, their movement was socially diverse and frequently bourgeois. Their literacy rate was higher than that of the average population. This heterogeneous group constituted a neighborhood and professional elite. Even in Paris, it continued to draw its membership from the active citizens in 1791. In the provinces this dual phenomenon of a more plebeian membership always led by the better established was even more pronounced. The agents of the Terror of year II were politicians who had been active for several years.

This minority was very unevenly distributed among the communes, with about one club for every ten of them. There were many more of them in the southeast, the plains, and on the coasts than in mountainous or highly religious regions. Even in the large cities, there were rarely more than a hundred members per club. Over three quarters of Parisians did not move to ratify the constitution of 1793; in June, only nine thousand of them, as against six thousand opposed, confirmed the appointment of the revolutionary Henriot as the head of the National Guard. The elimination of the moderates further reduced participation in the life of the sections, which rarely exceeded 10 percent.

The militants devoted a good part of their time to attempting to mobilize others. Their insurrections depended on a handful of leaders recruited, as in Faubourg Saint-Antoine, from the circles of master craftsmen of average means and mature age, long established in the capital and with close contacts with other workers of the neighborhood. Their visceral hatred of "big shots" was linked to egalitarian ideas that were confined to the limitation of "excessive" wealth and to activities against speculators. Their political horizon was as limited as their social outlook. Their power, resulting from the traditional hierarchy of professional association, was limited to their own sections. It brought no mass support to Jacques Roux. The Parisian *sans-culottes* had no coordinating organization aside from the commune, and the Convention still retained its authority over them.[3]

We are indebted to Richard Cobb and his students for this useful corrective to Albert Soboul's ideas. They have stressed the minority nature of the popular movement and have linked it to a moral stance that was sometimes threatening to the Revolution. In rejecting the full-scale application of the *sans-culottes*'s program, the ruling bourgeois, who were trying to manage a rural country at war, were bowing to necessity. The mentality of the "average" participant in the Terror, according to Richard Cobb, was characterized by a poor sense of humor and immense political gullibility, stemming from a profound ignorance of reality. Elevating denunciation to the height of civic virtue, the *sans-culottes* sanctified repression out of their concern for national regeneration. These patriots, hungry for cohesion and often xenophobic, were above all proud to be French. They naively awaited the conversion to the Revolution of enslaved peoples from Madrid to Saint Petersburg, and the evaporation of this dream often led them to lassitude and indifference. In the minds of these artisans who worshiped small-property ownership, revolutionary ideology was identified with extremely "nationalistic" fervor. Born of an atmosphere of struggle and crisis, their generosity needed this tension in order to endure, and died without it. Their militancy, which was momentary and exceptional, soon wore out.[4]

Richard Cobb returned to this scenario in 1970 in his study of popular protest during the revolutionary period. Although it paved the way for the triumph of the Terror's spirit of orthodoxy and inquisition, it expressed above all, in the service of a minority whose rise to power was purely accidental, the desperate violence of the humble urban folk faced with the threat of invasion and the more pressing danger of a shortage of "bread in the house." Its strategies and institutions were dominated by the issue of subsistence and the "fear for tomorrow" that went along with it. The events of year II resulted from the confluence of this traditional obsession with food shortages, the already old but worsening ravages of civil war, and the sudden need to mobilize a million men. Demands for equality and the myth of a hunger plot were intensified by all this. So, too, was the gap between the cities and the countryside, which was further accentuated by de-Christianizing efforts. This widening rift transformed the requisition of food and the provisioning of the army into a direct assault on the rural world. Rigid and lacking the dynamism of the *sans-culottes*, the impoverished country people viewed the Terror as some sort of urban hallucination. Reduced to the austerity born of rationing, their horizons extended no further than the need for daily provisions. The psychological tyranny of this problem of subsistence permeated the constellation of fears and solutions handed down from the *ancien régime*.[5]

Such was the backdrop for the activities of the militant Jacobins. As Marie-Thérèse Lagasquié has observed in the case of Toulouse, few were concerned with the "truly disinherited classes of society" whose struggle against hunger had nevertheless brought them to power. Fifty-five of the 293 "bloodthirsty men" counted in Toulouse were members of the upper bourgeoisie, including 21 wholesale merchants. There were also 133 craftsmen, it is true, but there was not a poor person among them. These southern agents of the Terror were under the control of the rich and prominent, whose major concern was to use the Revolution to grow even richer. In this former *parlement* city the militancy of all sides had been confined to the settling of old accounts, which culminated in over eighty executions (in Toulouse and Paris) and eight hundred arrests. Seeking a common thread leading to such repression in the personalities of those involved, Martyn Lyons has hit upon desire for upward mobility on the part of men who came from outside the cities in which they were active. The political upheaval improved their material situation. It also gave them the opportunity to avenge themselves for humiliations that sometimes dated back to the *ancien régime*. On the local level, the Terror may be explained as the vengeance of groups or individuals who had formerly felt excluded: soldiers in Lille, domestics in Versailles, shopkeepers in Bordeaux.

Everywhere these militants thought and acted like bourgeois, former or future, great or petty, not proletarians. In Lyons, the master silk workers, small employers becoming proletarianized, had had great hopes for the retaking of the city by the revolutionary government. Had they not provided a good number of the victims of the federalist uprising? They were bittery disappointed in the new regime, whose representatives were leery of their aspirations toward autonomy; they treated them like colonial subjects and refused to carry out their program of confiscating the property of the rich and providing aid for the poor. The Jacobins of Lyons, an exceptionally high proportion of whom were artisans, tried to find a role in the revolutionary administration. But the latter was unable to work out a plan for revitalizing the silk industry. One of the leaders of the workers' movement of Lyons was even executed under the Terror. Hurt as much as they were helped by the repression, and still unemployed, these *sans-culottes* could find work only in demolishing the fallen city or guarding the houses of suspects. Their participation in the administration of the Terror served only to give them a bad reputation. Victims of the economic crisis, they found no relief in the somersaults of the Revolution.[6]

A similar misapprehension characterizes the realization of the planned economy, which ill-suited the desires of the militants and was limited by the profoundly rural character of society. Although the first Maximum had been a temporary measure, circumstances forced the Convention down the path of economic controls. The law had been poorly conceived, for it set one department against another and was unpopular in the countryside, upon which everything depended. Civil war, coming on top of all this, did not help. Official measures against speculators were finally taken on July 26, when commissioners to control hoarding were introduced. But these quickly turned out to be unworkable if not disastrous, for they increased shortages. Before the state stepped in, cities such as Toulouse, beginning in August 1792, started to fill this gap by creating "subsistence bureaux" to meet the most urgent needs. This also occurred in Bordeaux, where the federalists and then the Montagnards set up systems of requisitions and inspections. As in Marseilles, panicky municipalities everywhere warmly welcomed the September 1793 Maximum, which put an end to their provisioning difficulties.

This decision was an outgrowth of the people's deep-rooted antagonism, in the name of equality and the Republic, to the laws of the market. Siding with urban consumers, the poorest of the country people felt the same way, in opposition to the interests of the farmer. But the result was an economic federalism that was as dangerous as its political counterpart. Pressure from the streets of Paris pushed the government to institute further controls. A protest campaign culminated on June 25 in Roux's presentation to the Convention of grievances against hoarders. Food supply problems and the inflation from which the capital was suffering led to disturbances there. Although Roux was repudiated by most of the revolutionary leaders, the problem he had brought up remained unsolved. The distribution of ration cards began, in view of the poor prospects for the upcoming harvests. Militants from the sections and the clubs added further proposals for price controls and requisitions. This was a concrete response to a grievance that we know had been voiced at least as far back as 1790. The Convention gave in only when forced. The representatives of the people's movement stressed the struggle against speculation more than the Maximum. It was only the exigencies of war that brought about the nationalization of the economy. Repeated defeats led to a new radicalization in the middle of the summer, resulting in a clampdown on the Girondins, federalists, Vendéans, and royalists. The assembly at first did not give in to all the demands made on it against right-wing deputies, nobles, priests, and the rich. It did accept, however, the famous measure of mass conscription of *levée en masse* still popular among the *sans-culottes*. Demanded on August 16 by the Parisian sections as a means of achieving the wholesale extermination of enemies, it was channeled by the Committee of Public Safety into the equally energetic but more military framework of "war of the masses": Carnot, who had been put in charge of operations on the fourteenth, pushed through a successful version of this proposal on the twenty-third. This universal mobilization greatly increased the authority of the government charged with its execution and forced it to establish the Maximum. Representatives on mission complained about food shortages caused by the peasants' unwillingness to comply with price controls and requisitions. The return to a free market, amid uncontrolled inflation, would have been a fatal blow to the Revolution at a time when it needed to provision cities and armies. Instituting increased controls seemed to be a way to avoid bankruptcy and win the war while at the same time mollifying the *sans-culottes*. This line of thinking led the Convention to adopt the General Maximum on September 29. This authoritarian limiting of the prices of thirty-nine essential commodities was accompanied by an analogous measure regarding salaries, which was not to be enforced in the capital until ten months later.

This effort to reduce the cost of living stemmed less from basic pressures than from military necessities. In this highly decentralized economy and in the absence of adequate administrative mechanisms it was an extremely ambitious operation requiring the cooperation of large numbers of officials. Conflicts were inevitable. The Subsistence Commission, created on October 22 and saddled with a bureaucracy of over five hundred people, attempted to resolve them by coordinating distribution, investigating production, and stimulating productivity. The goals of this fine-tuning of *ancien régime* methods were first of all military. Everyone complained, but the system worked fairly well despite a certain deterioration in the quality of products and widespread corruption that angered the people. This led to an increase in controls to avoid shortages. Most of the cities introduced rationing and public bakeries. Militants added to these measures threats against speculators. The urban population, in the meantime, was fed.

The rural areas paid the price, even outside the war zones. Agricultural prices had been pegged lower than production costs, and paper currency began to lose its value in January. This interfered with the observance of Maximum by poorly remunerated sellers. Military call-ups had reduced the rural work force, driving up salaries in spite of the law. Government representatives viewed this as a new economic crime, prosecuted in vain by the law. Prices were forced upwards, in favor of the producers, in February. The *sans-culottes* would have preferred "broad measures" against the countryside, but these proved impossible to enforce. The structure of French society put the authorities at the mercy of the rich peasants, who controlled the crops and were indispensable to the regime. They often were the pool from which municipal councilors, tax collectors, controllers, and distributors essential to government operations were recruited. The maintenance of their egalitarian policies forced the leaders of the Terror, who did not want to disturb private property, to strike bargains with the richest country people. This concrete form of "peasant power" reflected the primacy of the issue of food shortages in the eyes of the ordinary people of the cities.[7]

It was not, however, the question of subsistence but the de-Christianizing campaign that brought on the initial conflict between the politicians and the popular movement. This complex phenomenon is difficult to explain. It began at the lowest level with the material and economic despoiling of the churches for the benefit of the war machine. This process, begun in 1792, reappeared strengthened in the fall of 1793, and this time was overlaid with iconoclasm and anticlericalism. Churches were transformed into barracks and arsenals, but the ceremonial destruction of sacred objects went beyond military need. The culmination of the process was the resignation, forced or not, of the priests, the eventual repudiation of their vows, or their marriage. This suppression of the old religious order was accompanied by efforts to create a new one, in the form of various revolutionary cults and the radical desacralization of everyday life. Names of streets and cities, first names, and the calendar were stripped of all references to the Christian past. Sundays and holidays were replaced by *decadis*, the tenth day of each ten-day period, a practice which eliminated one or two days of rest per month.

How could this have happened, only three years after the new regime had allied itself so closely with the church? The Civil Constitution of the Clergy as well as various patriotic masses had symbolized this early association. An old Catholic tradition traces de-Christianization to the *philosophes* of the Enlightenment, but they had not envisioned such a destructive process. We have seen that there was no preliminary "de-Christianization" under the *ancien régime* that might have constituted a prelude to that of year II. A certain growth of indifference did not erase the traces of Catholic religiosity present in the revolutionary cults. The wealthy authors of laicized testaments were a class apart from the practicing, devout members of the popular classes who were transformed, under the Revolution, into de-Christianizers. The most that can be guessed is that their misogyny had its roots in an age-old male resentment of the preachers' influence on women. It is clear, on the other hand, that right from the start the Revolution had many of the trappings of religion, with its mystical vocabulary, its symbols, and its missionary zeal, all of which were compatible with the Constitutional Church. Until 1793, attending it was a sign of revolutionary sentiments, and it remained Christian and Catholic despite its opposition to the pope. The break represented by de-Christianization stemmed at first from the failure of this remodeled church. As part of the regime, it was expected to proselytize, and many of its priests did so with enthusiasm. The authorities supported them in their struggle against the people's counterrevolution. But the success of the popular movement, which apparently came close to triumphing, particularly in the west, spelled the doom of the Constitutional Church. Joseph Fouché, the main spokesman of de-Christianization, had spoken in 1792 of the "necessity" for religious sentiments. His tour of duty against the Vendéans in Nantes the following March led him to denounce the clergy as a group as preaching ignorance and fanaticism in order to aid in the aristocrats' fight against the cities; the deputy of the lower Loire now spoke of spreading the teachings of the revolutionary spirit, which would dissipate the "odious influence of religion." The Rousseauist Couthon, despite his anticlerical deism, did not become a de-Christianizer until after observing the participation of many constitutional priests in the rebellion in Lyon. The fact that religion was blamed for the aristocratic manipulation of popular credulity led to de-Christianization. As a contributor to counterrevolutionary unrest, Catholicism, *in all its forms*, was to be destroyed. In terms of political strategy, de-Christianization worked hand in hand with the persecution and deportation of refractory priests.

It was also linked with egalitarianism. In the Nièvre and the Allier, for example, Fouché applied the principles of the one to the other. Other deputies did likewise, without, naturally, going so far as to assert agrarian law. But they linked their de-Christianizing efforts to forming a new republican man, stripped of vices and perfectly virtuous. The representatives on mission spearheaded the movement, which was much less vigorously pursued by local authorities after their departure. But many segments of the revolutionary coalition were involved, often in very different ways, in de-Christianization. When the signal was given in Paris in early November, the activists surrounding the deputies forced many priests to resign. Some of them suddenly became violent adversaries of the church they had long served. After having believed that religion and the Revolution were inseparable, they transferred their enthusiasm for the former to the latter, which they sometimes joined as dutiful bureaucrats. The revolutionary army of Paris thus played a large part in the destruction of churches on its way to Lyon. Other departmental armies, conscripts from the *levée en masse* or, in the Vendée, soldiers from the regular army, all behaved similarly. The involvement of the clubs and the organizating of civic festivals around this phenomenon, attest, finally, to the popularity of de-Christianization. Although Paris may not have originated it, and even had to be pushed into it, the sections took up the cause with gusto. Bishop Gobel resigned there on November 7 and three days later, in Notre-Dame, which had been transformed into a temple of Reason, an opera singer officiated as the personification of Liberty. This wholesale renunciation of Catholicism was definitely greeted with enthusiasm, and the majority of supporters of the Terror participated in the de-Christianizing effort. It encouraged atheists in certain villages to step forward. It permitted spectacular outings by more or less eccentric activists. Resignations by priests took place mainly in the civil war zones where they were supported by representatives on mission. This was the case in the departments surrounding Lyons and in Normandy immediately after the Vendéan invasion. De-Christianization was thus very representative of the Terror and like the Terror, it fed on fear of the counterrevolution.[8]

In France, de-Christianization has always been a favored area of historical research, and recent studies seem to confirm these conclusions by Donald Sutherland. They stress the extent of participation by revolutionary militants (from the bourgeois elite and popular classes alike) in the movement. In Puy-de-Dôme and the district of Compiègne, patriotism was defined very early on by opposition to the church and even to Christianity. From 1793 to prairial year II, the western departments delivered 375 de-Christianizing proposals to the Convention. In their efforts to snuff out the priests, the Jacobins of Toulouse set off veritable witch-hunts in the neighboring villages. The red priests enthusiastically resigned, in proportions which Michel Vovelle estimates as 10 percent of the total. They were to be found at all levels in the administration of *départements*, perfectly integrated into the popular societies and eagerly promoting the persecution of their brothers.[9]

This de-Christianization was nevertheless, at the same time, a superficial phenomenon. Despite some momentary successes, the substitute cults that it created and the practices it led to did not last long. Above all, it caused the ruin of the Constitutional Church. Although the overwhelming majority of resignations were forced, after late 1792 a tenth of its priests got married. Three quarters of them never returned to the church after the torment was over. The refractory priests, on the other hand, were either hidden or saved by emigration. In this way de-Christianization accomplished exactly the opposite of what it had set out to do. It contributed, certainly, to a decline in the French clergy, which was sometimes dramatic in numerical terms. From 1791 on, and in many cases for over fifteen years, many regions of the country lived without priests.

But de-Christianization also encountered resistance that broadened the struggle against the Civil Constitution of the Clergy. In the countryside of the Paris region, men and women opposed the removal of church bells and demanded the reopening of the churches according to the terms of the unenforced law of December 16, 1793. This attitude on the part of country folk was also apparent in the Nièvre, the center of de-Christianization and future cradle of a Chouan uprising. It cropped up as well in the Val de Loire; in the Manche, where night meetings attracted the faithful to miraculous masses in June 1794; in Brittany, where apparitions foretold the end of the world and God's vengeance. People walked great distances to reach local sanctuaries; they demanded a return to the religion of the old days, in Hérault, for example, in May. Lay people sometimes took over the duties of priests even in some nondevout regions. This source of unrest was accompanied at the height of the Terror by the continuing activities of refractory priests, some of whom were martyred.

At this point, most of the French were affected by de-Christianization. Many people remained untouched by repressive measures, economic regulations, and even conscription. But all were touched by de-Christianization and many suffered from it. The goal of popular religion was the control of a supernatural world that was omnipresent and dangerous, and its disappearance was viewed as a threat. Peasants in Burgundy attributed the disaster that blighted their grapes to the disappearance of their priests and the statues of their saints.[10]

These observations by Donald Sutherland echo the current debate among French historians over revolutionary de-Christianization. This debate has become part of the analysis, always difficult, of an ambiguous concept, corresponding less to a state than to a movement, linked more to a type of mentality than to a type of behavior. The downfall of the church that had at first been protected by the revolutionary state occurred in a climate of persecutory violence and passion that stemmed from basic problems and cannot be attributed solely to the counterrevolution. Its prime movers were attempting to replace the old religion with a new conception of society and culture. Gérard Cholvy has noted, however, that the chroniclers of their exploits overstated their significance while underestimating the people's attachment to traditional faith. He has uncovered numerous signs of this resistance in the midst of the torment unleashed by the Terror. The testimony of the humble faithful is certainly worth that of the refractory priests. It also undermines the theory of a continuous process of de-Christianization since the Enlightenment. On the contrary, we have noted the profound entrenchment of religious France at the end of the eighteenth century. The Revolution's assault on it was driven by circumstance and political motives. Its de-Christianizing effort was a risky operation carried out by a segment of the militants in opposition to the intentions of the government, deserving of Richard Cobb's 1964 characterization of it as "uneven" and "fragile."[11]

Its unfortunate leaders everywhere resembled Pierre Bastey, a national representative in Seine-Inférieure during the year II who was recently studied by Philippe Goujard. Claiming to act and speak on behalf of the masses, they were in reality cut off from them. Their cultural scorn for the little people of the country brought on their ruin.[12]

Like the controlled economy, de-Christianization helped weaken the regime of the Terror, which could end this crisis only by increasing repression, which, far from leading to military victories, was preceded by them. In the first place, federalism was eradicated as of the summer of 1793, except in Lyons and Toulon for a brief period. The northern border was cleared during September and October and the eastern one at the end of the year. Defeated at Granville in mid-November, the Vendéans collapsed in Savenay on December 23. The Terror, which was beginning to take on its full dimensions at the time, was not a new phenomenon in the history of the Revolution. Instinctual fear and the desire to punish its adversaries had been a part of the latter from the first. Furthermore, their aftereffects persisted, more or less episodically, until the beginning of the Consulate, in the form of exceptional courts set up to order the spontaneous repression. The workings of the revolutionary tribunals of Year II paralleled fairly closely those of the regular courts until June 10, 1794. Military or civil commissions simply handed over to judges the role that had been assigned to juries under *ancien régime* procedure. As for the majority of the executions, notably those of thousands of Vendéans, they were the result of the law of March 19, 1793, aimed against assemblies of armed counter-revolutionaries and proposed by the Girondin Lanjuinais, whom Louis XVIII later made a peer of France.

The legal powers of the revolutionary tribunals did not, of course, define the whole of their activity. Their goal was to terrorize the enemy and they served a system of political justice whose responsibility it was to mould public opinion in favor of the government. Famous or not, all of its victims were thus designated in advance. Its magistrates, in interpreting these exceptional laws, were little concerned with evidence. There were exceptions, even in the civil war zones, as in the Loire or in Marseilles, where professional judges were able to slow these excesses. This no doubt explains why a mere thirteen departments were responsible for 90 percent of all death sentences. They were located in the west, the Midi and Paris. The first two of these regions was also the scene of worst atrocities of official repression, such as the march of Turreau's "infernal columns" across the Vendée and the executions without trial that occurred near Angers and in Toulon. Examination of the cases of Lyons and Nantes confirms, finally, that Terror of the Year II was part of a continuing cycle of repression and counterrepression. The period of the revolutionary government only amplified it.

Two special courts in Lyons sentenced over two hundred people to death before December 1. The Parisian rulers cracked down especially hard on this counterrevolutionary center, which was to be partially destroyed and renamed. Upon being dispatched to this city, Collot d'Herbois and Fouché first enacted a de-Christianizing ceremony with blasphematory overtones. Then, in the name of the power of the people, a "temporary commission" composed exclusively of people not from Lyons proceeded, over the next 130 days, to execute close to two thousand people. The main outcome of this revolutionary justice, accompanied by ineffective social measures, was to spur the creation of a center of intense counterrevolutionary activity without advancing in any way the cause of the local militants. This was one of the many disillusionments that Jacobin dictatorship was to bring to *sans-culottes* everywhere. In Nantes, organized drownings in which two thousand people died, along with even bloodier executions by firing squad, are attributed to representative Carrier. This deputy seems to have intended the drownings for the execution of Vendéan prisoners who had already been convicted, but his subordinates included other prisoners, priests, and common-law criminals. The city was reeling under the Vendéan atrocities and its prisons were bursting with convict soldiers who inspired considerable dread. The threat of Charette or the English was still real, and the fear of a conspiracy, which had accounted for the 1792 massacres in Paris, was still a factor here. Carrier was recalled in February 1794, because the local extremists found him too lenient, and the Jacobins of the capital gave him a hero's welcome.

The agents of the Terror were thus often swept along by their own institutions. During the winter, the government itself seems to have lost control of the repression. It spoke of the Terror as if its mission were the purification of society, whereas it was directed above all against the counterrevolution. Although it struck harder, proportionally, against the members of the clergy and the nobility, a regional study of its activities reveals that in the Vendée, for example, the social distribution of its victims corresponded precisely to that of the insurgents. The Terror was thus not a class war, but an operation directed against individuals. In the west, it marked the apogee of a permanent struggle that extended from the beginning of the Revolution to 1832. In Lyons, while half of the victims of repression belonged to the city's former ruling elite, a large number were also workers from outside the silk industry, as opposed to workers from within it. The Lyons Terror's selectivity makes it a mere magnification of a very particular social struggle that had begun in the middle of the eighteenth century.

Although much has been made of the role of the representatives on mission and the special tribunals, none of what happened would have been possible without the more modest efforts of the committees and the revolutionary armies. The former were by far the most efficient. Organized in the spring of 1793, they were inactive during the summer. It was the September 17 law concerning suspects that provided them with their mission. It stipulated that supporters of tyranny or federalism and enemies of freedom were to be imprisoned or kept under surveillance by the committees. This terrible power gave them new life, under the direction of energetic government representatives. The committees thus set about purging the administration, collecting funds, hunting down deserters, censoring mail, issuing passports, enforcing price controls, issuing the *certificats de civisme* that were indispensable for obtaining official positions, closing churches, making sure that the *décadi*, was respected, and enforcing the regulations of the local police. They supplemented or replaced the regular government organizations. Their contacts with the clubs filled them with zealous militants, who were essential to the functioning of the system. These committees were, however, relatively few in number, except in certain important centers. They were not very active in the countryside, and very unevenly so in the cities. Their zeal depended largely on that of the various representatives on mission, and the large number of suspects released throughout the whole period makes it very difficult to estimate their number. The most likely estimate is something on the order of seventy thousand people, or less than 0.5 percent of the population.

The arbitrariness of the committees and the absence of any appeals were the main sources of their effectiveness. They sometimes covered 85 percent of the communes of a district, starting with the capital city. The preferred instrument of Jacobin dictatorship and urban control over the countryside, the committees were in charge of de-Christianization and the enforcement of price controls. Like the National Guard before them, they also represented a solution to the difficult problem of surveillance of the peasants. But their concerns remained above all local. Didn't some of them request a confessor for the soldiers, or demand the expulsion of Jews? They were concerned first of all with arresting the *local* representatives of the counterrevolution. Suspects of clerical or noble origins were overrepresented in Toulouse and Dijon. In the west, they were more likely to be artisans or peasants. Far from the civil war zones, complicity with refractory priests was an essential cause of suspicion. The committees were thus less the instrument of a class war than institutions that extended the local struggle against the counterrevolution. In this respect, the opponents of the Civil Constitution of the Clergy remained, throughout the entire revolution, a preferred target.

The *sans-culottes* had a legendary image of the revolutionary armies, the quintessence of their purest aspirations. The reality of these sixty-some formations, which attracted many young conscripts with motives of their own, was very different. The majority of their members, city dwellers of humble origins, were far from zealous militants. They confined themselves to backing up the local authorities in the most trivial aspects of the hunt for suspects. The army of Paris set about provisioning the capital by acting against the interests and aspirations of large numbers of the rural rebels of 1792. The civil commissioners of these armies, rarely of plebeian origins, did not support authentic egalitarianism either. As for the majority of their officers, they saw this episode as nothing more than another stage in their military careers.[13]

Recent research, much of it by Anglo-Saxon historians, has allowed us to study the regional diversity of the repression which existed under the Terror. Although most of France was spared its bloodiest consequences, it was nevertheless one of the revolutionary government's essential weapons everywhere. Its architects, from the top down, were attempting simultaneously to respond to the counterrevolution and prepare the ground for the advent of pure Virtue. Were the deification of the guillotine and the institution of a perfunctory system of justice necessary means to these ends? Michel Pertué has shown that, despite some apparent precedents under the *ancien régime*, these procedures were, indeed, aspects of exceptional conditions that existed during the Revolution. The Revolution's tribunals and "infernal columns" put the great goal of "killing all enemies" within reach. The pursuit of this dream of unity set the Revolution apart from the modern Republic as well as from the cities of antiquity that the Jacobin dictorship claimed as models. Our times are perhaps less sensitive to the nobility of this ambition than to the individual fates of its unfortunate victims: Alongside conspirators and speculators were to be found Catholic peasants, devout nuns, and dissidents thrown together by a mechanism that was more absurd than rational. Although this infernal machine may have saved the Revolution, and this remains to be seen, it is doubtful that it gained it many followers.[14]

WHY DID THE TERROR BECOME BUREAUCRATIZED?

Relations between the Jacobin leaders and the *sans-culottes* were marked by constant conflicts, since the former, in order to govern, had to accommodate other social groups whose interests were opposed to those of the *sans-culottes*. The *journées* of September 4 and 5, 1793, which brought the Terror into its own, illustrate this divergence within the ranks of the revolutionary forces. Demonstrators in Paris were expressing an anxiety that was already well rooted. It was caused by the delay in the establishment of the revolutionary system of justice, by the slowness with which the struggle against the aristocrats proceeded, by the problem of subsistence, and by the demand for the creation of a revolutionary army. The announcement of the fall of Toulon, after the Mayence, further aroused this zeal. The initiative came from the Jacobins, many of whom shared these sentiments. They demanded that the sections join their movement, and twenty-nine of them did, in accordance with the collective petition of the fifth. The commune lent its support to this *journée* at the last minute. Indeed, on the fourth, demonstrators demanding bread and salary increases invaded the Hôtel de Ville. They were referred to the Convention the next day. This swelled the ranks of the supporters of the Jacobin petition. It led to the proclamation, by the Convention, of a revolutionary army, of the new policy on arrests of suspects, and of the Terror.

The Terror was thus launched under pressure from a peaceful demonstration that had been in preparation for a long time. But it was caused by the initiative of the Jacobins and not the popular movement. Although the Jacobins shared the fears and grievances of the people, they had no intention of being governed by them. At this time Billaud-Varenne and Collot d'Herbois were made members of the Committee of Public Safety, but demands that all aristocrats be arrested or barred from army service were resisted. The revolutionary army's responsibility was confined to the issue of subsistence, whereas the militants had envisioned it as a cohort that would terrorize hoarders in the countryside and exercise summary justice against internal enemies. The revolutionary committees remained, moreover, under the control of the authorities, instead of being totally subsumed by the sections. This was the beginning of the bureaucratization of the popular movement. Before the end of the year, for example, the committees were completely under the control of the Convention's Committee of General Security. It does not seem, moreover, that the deputies had been surprised by a demonstration that had been talked about for over two weeks. Danton seized upon this necessary channeling of revolutionary energy to limit the section meetings to two per week, while compensating those who participated in them. This was an attempt to undercut the influence of the militants among the poorest elements. On this occasion, Barère denounced counterrevolutionaries who were encouraging women to demonstrate over the subsistence issue, and Jacques Roux was arrested that very evening. Varlet followed two weeks later, and Leclerc, having gotten wind of what was happening, disappeared. This day thus marked the beginning of the end for the popular movement, which, by choosing the Jacobins and the municipality as its spokesmen, had made them its masters. The profusion of revolutionary rhetoric barely concealed the deep rift between the Convention's wish for control and the *sans-culottes'* conception of direct democracy. This became clear during the de-Christianizing campaign, and this breach created a further problem for the leaders.[1]

They may well have believed, at the end of the year, that they had saved the Republic, even though the war, the counterrevolution, and the economic difficulties were not over. Some of them began to think of relaxing the Terror, but since those who advanced this notion were often considered suspicious characters, the resulting debate merely served to reinforce the dictatorship. So did the necessity of streamlining a regime that was fragmented among a multitude of local efforts. They were controlled by a process of bureaucratization present in the revolutionary movement ever since the mass military call-up. This tendency had stripped the surveillance committees of their control of the police, and had only been accelerated by resistance to government policies. In becoming more systematic, the Terror risked becoming more repressive, thereby deepening divisions among the Montagnards.

At the end of the winter of 1794, it was relatively easy to reform the controlled economy by loosening price controls and attempting to align interests more closely with those of the state. Although it stirred up much discontent in Paris, this concession to producers and sellers at the expense of consumers created few problems for the Convention. Handling the issue of de-Christianization was more difficult. It was linked to mutual denunciations by Danton's associates with regard to corrupt practices in the liquidation of the *Compagnie des Indes.* Cosmopolitan revolutionaries and the counterrevolutionary Baron de Batz were implicated in this scandal, which planted the idea of a plot concocted abroad, a vast international conspiracy whose goal was to destroy the Revolution. Combining elements of fiction and reality, it offered Robespierre a new way to combat extremism, since large numbers of de-Christianizers were denounced as conspirators. Robespierre was against the atheism of this movement, in which he saw a danger at once social, moral, and political. The idea of a foreign plot provided him with a reason to confront it, starting on November 21, by labeling de-Christianization a counterrevolutionary enterprise. The confirmation of religious freedom by the Convention on December 8 did not undo all that the anti-Catholic campaign had accomplished; nor did it put an end to it. It was a weapon of use to the government but of no significance to the faithful. It was linked, moreover, with a substitute civic religion—a theistic one as evidenced by the Festival of the Supreme Being the following June 8, that inaugurated a series honoring Reason and Virtue. The first was fairly successful, at least in Paris, but not among the deputies, who saw it as proof of Robespierre's aspirations toward personal dictatorship.

This suspicion also grew out of the two-fold debate that had just taken place over repression and corruption. It is difficult to shed much light on the latter, and Danton's dubious morality does not diminish the validity of his demand for an easing of the Terror in the fall of 1793. For him, in any case, it had never been anything other than an expedient. But discussion over whether or not to carry on a relentless struggle until the last enemy of the Revolution had been eradicated was complicated by the usual involvement of private capitalists in financing the war and its equally traditional corrupting consequences in political circles. Deputies, particularly those on the Committee of General Security, were implicated; they were pressured, and Robespierre was informed. Like his colleagues, he was reluctant to take action in view of the risk involved in prosecuting a man like Hébert, who was so influential among the *sans-culottes*. These accusations meanwhile further envenomed an atmosphere that was still permeated, among the Montagnards, by the tendency toward generalized defiance.

The Indulgents, as those who advocated clemency were known, brought matters to a head on November 10 by launching a campaign against the tyranny of the committees and the incompetence of the *sans-culotte* generals. Extremism was thus being called to account, and on December 15 in his *Vieux Cordelier* Desmoulins compared the present state of the Terror to the situation under the Roman emperors. His opponents, grouped around Collot and Hébert, took up the challenge. On the twenty-fifth, Robespierre attempted to rise above all factions by elevating the revolutionary government's struggle into a battle of Virtue against Vice, which, from all evidence, was far from its initiators' intent. This speech did not put an end to internal discord, and the Hébertists, eager for revenge, called for an insurrection. The capital's economic difficulties and the attitudes of its militants added to the perils of the situation. The Committee of Public Safety was forced to act against these "conspirators" without military support. Their imprudent outbursts had left them open to accusations of involvement in a sinister conspiracy, and this led to their execution on March 24. The downfall of the Hébertists led to that of the Dantonists, who continued their attacks on the government. Although their leader remained silent, the committee viewed him as a rallying point for those who favored more lenient policies. He was executed with his followers, after a travesty of a trial, on April 5.

Large numbers of politicians still remained who were associated to one degree or another with these erstwhile factions. Their existence continued to be a source of hostility toward the dictatorship of the committees. The trials, above all, had a decisive effect on the popular movement. The Hébertists had been mistaken in accusing the revolutionary government of moderation, when it was still preoccupied, like Carnot, with the everyday conduct of the war. This concern for bureaucratic organization had been reflected in the law of

December 4, 1793, which by subordinating local activities as a whole to the Convention signalled a fundamental change. National sovereignty was thus identified, once and for all, with the center of power. The freedom of action of all other authorities was tightly constricted. The laws of ventôse (February and March 1794) transformed the bureaucratization of the Terror into a dictatorship of the committees. This proposal to sequester the property of suspects and use it as compensation for poor patriots has been interpreted as a gesture toward the *sans-culottes* during the struggle against the Hébertists or as rather clumsy attempt to solve social problems in the countryside. Speeches by Saint-Just in defense of this program show that it was aimed, above all, at an internal enemy. And it was carried out in the Puy-de-Dôme, for example, in the spirit of partisan politics, not economic justice. The main result of these laws was to transform an extralegal regime into a permanent dictatorship. Although on the preceding October 10 the government had declared itself to be in a state of revolution until the advent of peace, expropriations and the perpetual banishment of suspects now cast it in an entirely different light. This was no longer a transitional regime but rather the institutionalization of a system of detention and punishment. By early May, the Committee of General Security, responsible for the revision of lists of suspects, had already received files on half of them, a telling display of the efficiency of the bureaucracy of the Terror.

Starting from the top, the Jacobin dictatorship little by little eliminated all resistance, and the people's movement was its principal victim. The power of the sections was gradually weakened. The mass conscription absorbed twenty-three thousand Parisians, while many older militants entered the ever-expanding new, and increasingly overstaffed, bureaucracy. The revolutionary committees themselves were integrated into the police bureaucracy. Sansculottism either found a place for itself in the Jacobin bureaucracy or lost all momentum. The popular societies, which were the lifeblood of the sections, had been regarded with distrust by the government ever since the denunciation of the foreign conspiracy. There followed a series of purges that set the militants against one another and moved them even further away from the people. There had been, in any case, a gradual parting of the ways, as the commune of Paris, for example, either handpicked its members or left vacant positions empty. It also conferred on itself the right to control the membership of sectional committees. Their meetings were of less and less interest and were limited to paramilitary activities. Even before the fall of the Hébertists, political life had thus lost its basic spontaneity, and many militants had become mere agents of the power structure, with the commune becoming a branch of the government and the revolutionary committees an arm of the Committee of General Security. This situation no doubt explains the failure of the "Hébertist" insurrectionary plan. The liquidation of the factions increased divisions among the militants and their distrust of the people's politicians, even though they maintained their faith in the Convention. The government took advantage of the situation in Paris and the provinces to undermine the prestige of the *sans-culotte* movement. The fall of the Hébertists marked the first retreat from extremism since 1791. The government further consolidated its power by dissolving the revolutionary army in the capital, suppressing the hoarding commissioners, dismantling the Ministry of War, which had been riddled with *sans-culottes*, scattering them throughout the administration, and appointing Jacobin loyalists to head the commune. Under these pressures, the popular

societies began to disband. Well underway by the end of May, this dispersion
signified the death of the *sans-culotte* movement as an autonomous force.[2]

Following Michelet, Albert Mathiez, and Daniel Guérin, Albert Soboul had admirably analyzed the workings of this unequal struggle between the bureaucratic dictatorship of the committees and the
spontaneity of the militants. This matter is of greater interest today than
the minutiae of parliamentary corruption among the Montagnard ranks
where, despite appearances, moral accusations were less important than
the rift between supporters of the revolutionary goverment and its opponents. Starting in the summer of 1793, Robespierre, Marat, and their
friends had done their best to undermine Jacques Roux's influence among
the Parisian popular classes: This calumny hounded and led to the death
of this apostle of the poor, defender of the masses, theologist of a revolution whose leaders killed him. Along with him, Jean Varlet and Théo-
phile Leclerc advocated the concept of direct democracy so mistrusted
by the "statesmen" who were the architects of the Jacobin dictatorship.
We have just shown the difference between these two types of revolutionary discourse, revealed especially during the *journées* of September
when the Terror was gaining its foothold. The *sans-culottes* were preoccupied with mass mobilization and the arrest of all suspects in the name
of their day-to-day revolution, symbolized by their demand for a revolutionary army: The Montagnards set up a legal framework to contain
popular pressure "in the continuity of the laws" and in the sole service
of public safety.[3]

The revolutionary government spent all the latter part of 1793 muf-
fling the spirit of independence and autonomy in the popular societies
of the provinces, even though they had helped rescue the state during
the federalist crisis of the summer. The leaders of the Terror in Paris
were in fact distrustful on principle of the democratic spontaneity of the
local *sans-culottes*, preferring their bureaucratic hierarchy of national
agents, who no doubt had regional roots but were hardly representative
of the dynamics of the popular revolution.[4]

The culmination of this trend came the following spring in the capital,
where, in less than two months 77 percent of the popular societies were
liquidated by the committees of public safety and general security.[5]

WHY DID THE JACOBIN DICTATORSHIP
DESTROY ITSELF ON 9 THERMIDOR?

It was was not his break with the *sans-culottes* that brought on Robespierre's downfall. The Jacobin dictatorship had become largely independent of the popular movement that had contributed to its establishment. The Subsistence Commission superseded the revolutionary armies; the national agents representing the government in the departments crowded out the revolutionary committees, and so forth. The still unfinished process of bureaucratization might have been more solid with time. The fact that this evolution did not take place resulted not from the alienation of the people but from internal quarrels among the Montagnards. The Committee of Public Safety had imposed its views on the Convention, but there was no consensus. Many of the Indulgents had a hero to avenge and some extremist deputies had particular reason to be afraid. Carrier, who had been compromised in the Hébertist affair, had been criticized by one of Robespierre's agents for having oppressed "patriots," i.e., the murderers of Nantes and Morbihan. Many Jacobins from Lyons were still denouncing Fouché's abuses of power in Paris. Barras and Freron had likewise committed some offenses in the Midi, where, as Collot had said of the workers of Lyons, the laborers in the port of Toulon were as counterrevolutionary as the merchants. These representatives had even managed to alienate the Jacobins of Marseilles, whom they considered too moderate. This was not a conflict between a committee that wished to relax the Terror and deputies who opposed it, but rather, as was the case in Lyons, a conflict between the more lenient delegates and local Jacobins, who were fiercely independent but supported by Robespierre. His agent Jullien criticized Tallien, in Bordeaux, for pursuing policies that were not egalitarian enough. The recall of these representatives aggravated the disputes that raged in Paris over the dimensions and the orientation of the Terror, but not over its principles.

Convincing evidence of this is to be found on examination of the Terror's policies toward the Vendée. It approved the plan for general destruction that Turreau began to execute in January 1794. It sent deputies out to coordinate these measures of extermination. It decided in February that after the patriots of the region had been evacuated all the remaining inhabitants could be killed. Turreau was relieved of his command in May only because the savagery of his troops, of which the government was well aware, was inciting the population to resist. Some of his subordinates nevertheless carried on these looting expeditions unsupervised and unreprimanded. Jullien even denounced them to Robespierre as royalists, because they were unable to win the war. This destructive phase of the repression in Vendée came to an end only because some of the troops needed to be withdrawn from there for the summer campaign. The committee even then offered no amnesty and continued to hand unarmed rebels over to the military commissions. This foolish policy of eradicating internal enemies had in some cases exterminated a third of the population of the communes and constituted a true economic catastrophe for the region.

The government was concerned above all with maintaining control of the apparatus of repression, which it often preferred to assign to local extremists rather than to representatives. This naturally did not make for a policy of moderation. On May 8 the provincial revolutionary tribunals were suppressed in favor of the Paris tribunal. On June 10 the law of 22 prairial stripped the accused of all means of defense and allowed juries to deliver verdicts on the basis of moral arguments alone. Beyond the creation of this killing machine, the plan was that a good portion of the accused would be sent to six special commissions charged by the laws of ventôse with examining the files of suspects, who were now at ever-increasing risk of death in this universe of administrative repression. This was the case in June and July of victims of imaginary conspiracies in Paris. The law that condemned them was the result of assassination attempts on Robespierre and Collot. The choice of this response, rather than, for example, providing committee members with increased protection testifies to the political atmosphere of the times. No deputy could feel safe, particularly after Danton's death. Many members of the Convention began to carry arms and change addresses.

This discontent in the Convention could have been checked if the government had not been so divided. The Committee of General Security regarded the Committee of Public Safety's creation of a police bureau, rumored to be under Robespierre's control, as a usurpation of power. The leaders of the same committee saw the Festival of the Supreme Being as prefiguring the appeasement of the Catholics. Supported by de-Christianizers and the anti-clericals of the Midi and the west, they associated Robespierre with religion and thus the counterrevolution. Harmony was no more in evidence in the other committee. Its administrators, Lindet, Carnot, and Prieur de la Côte-d'Or, were becoming less and less tolerant of the ideologues Robespierre, Couthon, and Saint-Just. Billaud and Collot were moving closer and closer to the Committee of General Security. Both Robespierre and Saint-Just were profoundly affected by this situation.

Their position was undermined by Fleurus's victory, on June 26, which made the Terror less indispensable as means of exceptional government. But on February 5 Robespierre had assigned to the Republic a mission of moral regeneration that went well beyond the military goals of the legislation of the spring of 1793. He himself stopped working with his colleagues in mid-June because he no longer got along with them. Poring over files in his office, he only attracted more suspicion. He was no doubt planning to purge some deputies, including Fouché, whom he had expelled from the Jacobins and who began to plot against him. A return to harmony within the government nevertheless remained possible until the end, and on 4 and 5 thermidor (July 22 and 23), the two committees agreed to reduce the powers of the police bureau while speeding up the examination of lists of suspects. Doubting his colleagues' sincerity, Robespierre broke this truce. On the eighth he threatened them in a long speech that attacked the Indulgents, denounced a "criminal coalition" within the Convention, and demanded that the government be purged. Billaud and Collot were expelled that night from the Jacobin club to cries of "To the guillotine." The next day at the Convention, Billaud attacked Robespierre, who prevented him from speaking and arrested him with his friends.

The commune defended them but received little backing from the sections. This has been explained by the proclamation of a wage maximum four days earlier. This measure was certainly unpopular and had been accompanied since April by official repression of strikes. But the *sans-culottes* were not wage earners. Those who espoused this social policy and supported Robespierre were artisans, small employers, bureaucrats, and intellectuals. The outcome of this *journée* was the result not of economic considerations, but of leadership and organizational ability. The Convention acted quickly to notify the sections. Nineteen not particularly moderate ones refused to follow the commune, which, at the instigation of the Committee of General Security, received equally little support from the revolutionary committees. The police forces remained loyal to the government and carried with them the majority of the *sans-culottes*. Four of the six commanding officers of the National Guard did likewise. With so few resources, and caught off guard by this unprecedented crisis, the commune could not act expeditiously. Many of the militants of the sections failed to grasp what was happening or turned against each other. The Convention declared the deputies who had been freed from prison outlaws, along with the commune. This measure, which had earlier been demanded by Saint-Just against the Girondins, led to the disbanding of the armed forces assembled in front of the Hôtel de Ville. The Convention had triumphed because its collective prestige remained, as always, more powerful than that of any of its members. This prestige was subsequently expressed through a hierarchy of institutions that controlled the popular movement more than either the Jacobins or the commune could. In this sense, 9 thermidor was a victory for revolutionary power, even though it destroyed some of its staunchest militants. Companies from the sections put down the pitiful attempt at a Robespierrist insurrection before its leaders in the committee were executed on the afternoon of the tenth. And nobody yet suspected that their death marked the end of the Terror.[1]

Martyn Lyons has correctly observed that the fall of Robespierre and his associates was instigated, above all, by members of the Committee of General Security, who had until then played an essential role in the government's police apparatus. Their action, on this day, had political as well as personal motives and they felt, not without justification, that they had acted in the interests of the Revolution. At once bureaucratic and parliamentary, their coup d'état was precisely the image of what the Montagnard regime had become. As Albert Mathiez has noted, it remained suspended in a vacuum between the apathy or unthinking discontent of the masses and the unanimous facade of the Convention. Although military victories were making the dictatorship less and less necessary, Robespierre's followers seemed to cling to it. Many of the deputies feared them, and this tension preceded and laid the groundwork for 9 thermidor. It accounts for the secret maneuverings and the precautionary and surveillance measures concocted in the back rooms of the leaders of the Terror who became, in turn, its victims. The crisis erupted, finally, to dissipate an intolerable atmosphere in which the threat of death seemed to hover over so many heads. Thus, *on the Montagnards' side*, hatred and self-defense on the part of government members driven to desperation were the main cause of 9 thermidor. They viewed the law of 22 prairial as an attempt to justify their future elimination. These rumors of condemnation were not without foundation, particularly with regard to former representatives on mission.

They were thus among the architects of Robespierre's downfall, along with the Dantonists and especially the members of the two government committees. Excluding the center and the rightist portions of the Assembly, this was thus a mixture of *leftist* deputies, both Indulgents and extremists. Among the latter especially, aside from committee members, were to be found victims of the centralization of the Terror and de-Christianizers. This gave Robespierre two reasons to despise them, but they were protected by the leaders of the Committee of General Security. Grouped around Vadier, Amar, and Voulland, these officials increasingly clashed with the Robespierrists over the exercise of their common power. They blamed them for the Committee of Public Safety's tendency to monopolize the police dictatorship and saw the establishment of a special bureau under one of Robespierre's agents as both a tool for personal influence and a gesture of defiance. Control of the network of government informers was a particularly central issue in these disputes. They were intensified by the opposition of the majority of the Committee of General Security, which was violently anticlerical, to Robespierre's religious policies, which it suspected of favoring Catholicism. On this point, Vadier succeeded in gravely compromising the Incorruptible by linking him with counterrevolutionary conspiracies in the Catherine Théot affair. Many Montagnards shared his view of Robespierre as a friend of superstition and fanaticism.

Lastly, it is known that within the Committee of Public Safety itself, Billaud, Collot, and Carnot were distancing themselves more and more from the followers of Robespierre. But it was he who launched the final battle by breaking a compromise that was still believed to be firm on 8 thermidor. The speech given that day by Robespierre clearly represented an indictment of the revolutionary government by a part of its membership. It suddenly pitted this group against virtually the entire left wing of the Convention. The events of 9 thermidor represented the victory of the most extreme agents of the Terror over a group that it wrongfully denounced as moderate. They had no idea that in return for its support the Plain would demand an end to the policies of repression. Their error in judgment was compounded by their underestimation of the consequences of the bureaucratization of the Revolution in which they themselves had participated. But they were driven to action by Robespierre's threats and sincerely believed, each in his own way, that by destroying him they were saving the Republic.[2]

Far from questioning the social orientation of the government or suggesting a loosening of the Terror, this coup d'état was above all the result of rifts that had opened up within the ranks of its leaders. In this political struggle, for example, Carnot was pitted against the Robespierrists, whose downfall he orchestrated as artfully as he had their victories. His *Soirée du camp*, a newspaper intended for armies that first appeared on 2 thermidor, announced first the imminent event and then its significance. Historians are also reconsidering the law of 22 prairial, which Henri Calvet already described in 1949 as part of the "logical evolution of the Terror." Georges Lefebvre connected it more with external circumstances that unnerved the members of the committees. Michel Eude has recently observed that this repressive clampdown was a direct continuation of the actions of the revolutionary government. Although this bill, introduced by Couthon and defended by Robespierre, was not worked out in conjunction with the Committee of General Security, its leaders certainly approved its spirit. The rivalry among these leaders of the Terror thus did not revolve around the principle of the Terror itself. Responsible, in different capacities, for the political administration of the regime, they knew that repression was its very soul, and the bureaucratic organization of this killing machine, methodically built up since September 1793, was at once their main claim to glory and their common creation. The fundamental conflict that in the end divided them sprang not from administrative differences but from the emergent rift in the heart of the government between Robespierre's followers and the rest. Whether Michel Eude is correct in attributing this division above all to personality clashes, unlike Martyn Lyons, is open to question. Equally debatable is the inevitability of the end of the Terror, considering that both of the camps that clashed on 9 thermidor wished to intensify it. Is it certain that the violent tensions imposed by an iron regime would not have continued if the regime had not destroyed itself?[3]

Vadier was one of Robespierre's staunchest defenders but also one of the principal causes of his downfall. He is now better known to us for his brutal vengeance against his old rivals from the Ariège, whom he sent to the guillotine for fanaticism and counterrevolution. A large landowner and influential notable, he made use of his new revolutionary power to liquidate his personal enemies. Martyn Lyons has closely studied this curious specimen of the Jacobin mentality, who was already fifty-three years old in 1789. More Voltairian than Rousseauist, he came from a region known for violence and what he saw as "fanaticism." He himself had reacted against the prevailing clericalism even though it had been responsible for the rise of his family and his own education. In this milieu, this well-off bourgeois who had pretensions to being a *seigneur* was considered a parvenu; he did not forget these insults, which were to send their authors to the guillotine. Having become a provincial magistrate, he used the Revolution to avenge his frustrations and settle his local political scores. This obsession dictated his behavior at the time of the Constituent Assembly, where he took care to oppose his rivals in his district. A family vendetta thus marked life in the Ariège until the time of the Directory. The opportunistic Vadier made use of his mandate as deputy and his Jacobin connections. This allowed him to label his inherited adversaries "aristocrats." Rooted though they were in these obsessions, his anticlericalism and radicalism were nonetheless sincere, though the latter sometimes fluctuated. Fully won over to the cause of the Montagnards and having become an important figure in the government, Vadier still did not neglect to settle his personal quarrels and proceeded with the liquidation of his rivals. Toward this end, he made use of his position within the Committee of General Security. Private vengeance was at the root of the public conduct of this architect of the Terror. In his political activities, he favored methods of patronage and clannishness. Likewise, it was out of personal hatred that he opposed Danton and, in part, Robespierre. But above all he criticized the latter, as we have seen, for his religious ideas. Despite the Thermidorean reaction, from which he was to suffer, Vadier never regretted having destroyed the Incorruptible one. He remained, until the end of his life in 1828, a Jacobin, a republican, and a partisan of the Terror. Like many revolutionary leaders, he had passed from the verbal violence of the frustrated provincial to the personal use of bureaucratic and police power. His old hostility toward the nobles and the church was the sole but powerful ideological justification of his attitude.[4]

It is, indeed, no longer possible to study the Terror without considering its manipulators' appetite for permanent power. Under the pretext of combatting a sinister myth, commentators following Albert Mathiez's lead have for too long portrayed them as saints worthy of a glorious legend. As Georges Lefebvre observed of Robespierre, they were certainly the authors of the revolutionary resistance, which was never as great as in the second half of 1793. But these idealists, often poorly equipped to understand their time on an economic or intellectual level, were unable to tear themselves away from the utopian and bloody dream of the modern resurrection of a republic like those of antiquity. Norman Hampson's original and penetrating biography of Robespierre portrays him, in his last months, as Michelet always saw him: at once tragic and ridiculous, pathetic, and grotesque. Caught in the web of his paranoia, he became more and more obsessed by death, his own and that of others. His disappearance was, for all concerned, a deliverance. An absurd romanticism has too often made supermen of these politicians who were unable to control a situation that they had in large part helped to create. Saint-Just, for example, has been transformed by many into a sort of archangel of the guillotine, whereas his personality was poorly developed, his ideas unoriginal, and his actions prosaically Machiavellian.[5]

The sacred halo surrounding these apostles of the Terror is itself derived from the obvious religious sources of the concept by which the Revolution politicized long-standing existential or metaphysical sources of trouble. In the eyes of *ancien régime* liberals, this concept was a sign of arbitrary despotism; the Jacobin leaders who applied it in the name of the legitimate violence of popular vengeance were unable to extricate themselves from the compelling universe they were trying to escape. Like their religious vocabulary, their politics of death was a throwback to the ideology and practices of the absolutist past. Their aesthetic alliance with the impossible, correctly noted by Tocqueville and Quinet, led them to rationalize and discipline the revolutionary reactions to the moral contagion of fear. But, in so doing, they subjected their activity to the hallucinatory logic by which the Terror, which could end only with the elimination of the last enemy, was doomed not only to permanence, but to constant expansion. Four days after the fall of Robespierre, Carnot was still speaking of turning the "brigands" and "monsters" of the Vendée over to the "avenging sword," and begging the representatives to set "revolutionary justice" back "on course." Two months later he saw no way out of this civil war other than by destroying the countryside. Historians agree that this insanity cost the lives of one hundred fifty thousand victims, not to mention the total economic devastation of the region. Without entering into excessive detail on this subject, we can only conclude that this disaster resulted above all from the unchecked paranoia of Terror that was rampant in Paris and the provinces from 1793 to 1794.[6]

8. AN INEVITABLE
DICTATORSHIP?

M*any historians following Michelet have closed the story of the Revolution with the fall of Robespierre, as if everything ended there. In fact, the period between 9 thermidor and 18 brumaire raises a series of key questions on the meaning of the chain of events that began in 1789. First of all, did the Thermidorean reaction represent the end of the Revolution or was it a continuation of it? And why did the regime it created fail to take hold? Was the self-destruction of the first "bourgeois" Republic inevitable?*[1]

DID THE THERMIDOREAN REACTION MARK
THE END OF THE REVOLUTION?

Historiographic tradition, represented by Albert Mathiez and Georges Lefebvre, viewed the Thermidorean period as the beginning of a bourgeois reaction that logically led to the exploits of Bonaparte. The succession of catastrophes that struck France between 1794 and 1801, however, was not totally rooted in the overturning of a system no longer supported even by the majority of the Montagnards. The passing of this dictatorship was welcomed with a general enthusiasm that subsided only six months later when the militants who had supported it began to be called to account. The new leaders of the Convention, no longer able to resort to the methods used by their predecessors, were faced with the old problems inherited from the Terror and with new circumstances that aggravated them. The sacrifices required to combat the counterrevolution were excessive. Discontent and resentments were fueled by a royalist opposition that was still armed. To destroy it totally would have required cutting the war short and staving off economic collapse. The new government was not up to these tasks, for it did not have sufficient political support. The result was the paralysis of authority and the administrative apparatus.

The renegade partisans of the Terror, the Indulgents or the moderates who replaced Robespierre and his followers, wanted above all to avoid a return to despotism. The dismantling of the committees and the revolutionary apparatus, however, did not for the most part undermine the legal bases of repression. But with smoother relations within the Convention, the bloodiest aspects of the Terror suddenly disappeared and suspects began gradually to be freed. The remaining revolutionary committees were driven to this by public opinion. Their former victims constituted a powerful pressure group against the agents of the Terror, while resistance to de-Christianization was growing in the countryside. The consequences of 9 thermidor marked a definite upsurge in the popular counterrevolution, based largely on religious foundations.

Opposition from this quarter was reinforced by the Convention's economic policies. The revolutionary government's legacy in this area was a relatively healthy one, but it was compromised by the poor harvest of 1794. Its damaging effects were magnified by an extremely cold winter, which disrupted transportation and food supplies. The controlled economy could not withstand these pressures, to which was added the peasants' usual unwillingness to deliver their goods. Speculation returned and markets emptied. On December 24 the Convention abolished price controls, cavalierly assuming that suppressing the economic bureaucracy would take care of matters. It did nothing but hasten the collapse of the *assignat*, raise prices, and create shortages. Poverty was more widespread than at any time since the beginning of the Revolution and in certain cities like Rouen the number of deaths doubled. This abnormal death toll among the elderly, the young, and the workers signaled France's return to a situation unparalleled since the beginning of the century. With it came an upsurge of crime caused by gangs of drifters wandering through the countryside. Faced with rampant inflation, poverty, and unchecked brigandage, the government was on the verge of collapse.[2]

This bolstered the counterrevolution, particularly in the countryside, where requisitions and rationing turned the communities as a whole against the government. In the Gers, rural discontent, already apparent under the Terror, was aggravated by the Convention's support of the landowners' interests, which only intensified the region's support of the cause of the refractory priests, deserters, and soon, royalists. These Midi sharecroppers were, however, offset by numbers of small landowners who were more favorable to the new regime. In the west, on the other hand, the majority of the peasants, dissatisfied with the results of a revolution whose legitimacy they did not recognize, provided an ideal base for the insurrectionary Chouan movement. This armed expression of rural solidarity was the embodiment of its revolt against the disruptions that had occurred since 1790 and of its nostalgia for an *ancien régime* more favorable than the new one to local autonomy. Ever since the Civil Constitution had been passed, the rural populace had been dreaming of the return of the traditional order and the removal of an illegitimate republic. For this reason they supported the émigrés, although they had to limit themselves to guerrilla tactics and ambushes that, starting in September 1794, put the government on the defensive in ten departments north of the Loire. As we have seen, the policies of the Terror in the Vendée had revived the resistance movement. Their backs against the wall, the Thermidoreans had no choice but to grant amnesty and then religious freedom on February 21, 1795. Temporary as it was, the resulting calm set the stage for the beginnings of a restoration of authority, which was, however, compromised by the divisions that split the Convention.

The Convention had tried, at first, to avoid emphasizing the past Terror. Carrier's execution on December 16, 1794, marked a change of focus insofar as he had come to symbolize the preceding period as a whole. Many democrats, such as Babeuf, clamored for his condemnation. The Jacobins' adversaries took advantage of it to eliminate the clubs from political life. Before the end of the year the Assembly, hounded by retrospective recriminations, particularly over the May 31 coup, voted to impeach Barère, Billaud, Collot, and Vadier. On March 8, 1795, it reinstated all the surviving Girondin deputies. Their return definitively shifted the balance of power within the Convention: Without seeking vengeance, they were intent on proving to Paris and the provinces just how staunchly opposed they were to the Terror. The spring uprisings in the capital gave them their opportunity. These were just one episode in the most significant wave of popular disturbances to arise in the preceding three years, particularly in the northwest, over grain shortages. Women, especially, protested against the difficulty of obtaining food supplies. Royalist or republican, their political slogans were intended to annoy the authorities. In Paris, where leadership of the sections had passed into the hands of the moderates, the *sans-culottes* had lost control of the streets to the gangs of the *jeunesse dorée* (armed young anti-Jacobins) composed of petty bureaucrats and deserters. Their anti-Jacobin pressure had made itself felt in the Convention and in public places since the preceding autumn. But the *journées* of germinal and prairial year III (April 1 and May 20, 1795) were not directed against these vandals, and revealed the profound depoliticization of the people of the capital. No longer concerned with speculators, they demanded bread, waxed nostalgic over both the king and the guillotine, and sometimes clamored for the constitution of 1793 out of a desire for direct democracy and municipal autonomy. The peaceful protest of germinal, similar to the one held in September 1793, disintegrated because of the confused invasion of the Convention by over ten thousand people. It provided the majority the opportunity to eliminate many Montagnards, declare Paris in a state of siege, and begin disarming the agents of the Terror.

The *journée* of prairial, initiated by housewives from the eastern neighborhoods, started off as a hunger riot but turned into a real attempt at armed subversion and a display of political strength, analogous to those of August 10 and June 2. One deputy was killed during the attack on the Convention, which convened for hours amid this tumult before being cleared by loyalist National Guardsmen. Another threatening demonstration was dispersed the next day. The government's counteroffensive, backed by the regular army, resulted in the definitive disarming and surrender of Faubourg Saint-Antoine. There were numerous arrests and sentencings, including of deputies (forty Montagnards were arrested, and six sentenced to death). This was the end of the *sans-culotte* movement, whose militants were henceforth confined to conspiratorial activities under close police surveillance. Thermidorean repression thus put an end to the cycle of Parisian uprisings that had begun the Revolution. This cycle ended in weakness and disorganization in popular agitation. But the regime was more than ever dependent on armed force. The deterioration of economic conditions, which was to become even more marked later, led to no new uprisings, for the hopes of the masses had died.[3]

Provincial militants suffered numerous setbacks starting in April 1795. Besides being disarmed, the regions that had formerly been ravaged by the antifederalist Terror were subjected to severe repression, often instigated by representatives on mission. This was particularly true in the Midi. There and in the Lyons region, Jacobin prisoners were massacred on the same scale as in 1792 and 1793. Incited to murder, and provided with numerous accomplices and facilitating conditions, the agents of this "White Terror" had practically free rein to avenge themselves on their onetime executioners and massacred them with impunity. Fear and a desire to punish also came into play, resulting in a hundred murders in Lyons, for example, in May. In Marseilles there were thirty, while in Toulon patriots marched on the city. They were driven back, and fifty-two of them were sentenced to death. A hundred Jacobins were killed in Marseilles in June, as well as twenty-three at Tarascon. Popular violence against the Terror, which had preceded these more or less organized massacres, continued to accompany and prolong them. It was directed, especially in the Midi, against former members of the revolutionary tribunals. Representatives on mission often looked favorably on these murderous gangs of young draft dodgers who took advantage of the weakness of the local authorities. The Jacobins were blamed for having disrupted the traditional order by trying to hand over responsibilities to people who should not have had them. While the royalist motivations of these assassinations may be doubtful, their premeditation is not. The fact that these anonymous atrocities could be carried out unimpeded in Lyons, for example, testifies to the total breakdown of the municipal administration. Official escorts were no guarantee against murder, and guilty parties, whose identities were well known, had nothing to fear from terrified witnesses. On the contrary, they boasted about their exploits, and drew their members from the social milieu that had supported federalism in 1793. Among them were large numbers of artisans, but also rich people, deserters, and former suspects of the Terror. Their victims might be workers, constitutional priests, Protestants, or Jews, along with agents of the Terror. In early fall these gangs were still in operation in about thirty cities scattered throughout ten departments of the southeast. Although responsibile for many fewer deaths than the Terror of year II, they had succeeded in bringing government there to a standstill.

This upsurge of "royalism" and the elimination of militant Jacobinism formed the basis of a political compromise within the ranks of the elites. It could have taken the form of a restored constitutional monarchy uniting monarchists, followers of La Fayette, and conservative Thermidoreans. But this solution, which would also have required a moratorium on counterrevolutionary violence, was precluded by the death of Louis XVI's son in June. In his outlandish Declaration of Verona the Comte de Provence, who had become "Louis XVIII," announced a return to the *ancien régime* that was totally out of touch with reality. He thus strengthened the position of the Convention and forced the royalists into a civil war, while eliminating the possibility of a conservative coalition. Despite its victories abroad, the Republic was widely thought to be on the verge of internal collapse. The English tried to hasten this demise by opening a new front in Brittany. This led only to the Quiberon disaster in July, at the end of which six hundred of the émigrés who had landed were executed by firing squad. Chouannerie, so foreign to their aristocratic temperament, did not die out, however. It continued its assassinations and ambushes that, in western France, pitted the countryside against cities and, in the eyes of Paris, transformed the area into an occupied country.

When some measure of peace was restored at last, the politicians were able to turn to the task of drafting the Constitution of the Year III. This revision of the 1793 constitution led to an entirely new project. Although it designated a larger number of active citizens than in 1791, it limited the pool of electors of deputies to thirty thousand people. In this way, the social groups that had led the Revolution since its beginning were preempted, and its fate was transferred to the hands of the richest segments of the bourgeoisie, the peasantry, and the former nobles, who became eligible to vote on condition that they had not emigrated. The majority of these men were against the Republic, as became apparent later under the Directory. Another element that contributed to the destabilization of the regime was the complex internal structure that stemmed from the Thermidorean fear of dictatorship. It called for the separation of powers, the division of the legislature into two chambers, and the assignment of executive authority to a five-member Directory that held important powers and controlled the government and administration. Its commissioners, in particular, went over the heads of elected authorities in the departments and cantons in their centralizing efforts. As these commissioners were often former Jacobins, the principle of coopting patriots continued. Thus equipped, the Directory could have survived a system of frequent elections by building up a national constituency. Lacking money and the means to influence public opinion, it risked colliding with a legislature dominated by opponents and impatient with an executive branch that was much slower to renew itself.

Aware of its unpopularity, the Convention decided, in August, that two thirds of its new deputies should be chosen from within its membership. This measure, which was also put to a referendum, was passed by a much slimmer margin. Massive abstentions and the domination of many primary assemblies by counterrevolutionaries were a bad omen for the future of representative government in France. Hoping for a return to peace, order, and prosperity, the electorate voted overwhelmingly for moderates, old members of the Convention or new ones, out of disgust with former policies. Protests against the two-thirds decree resulted, moreover, in the Paris uprising of 13 vendémiaire, year IV (October 5, 1795). This strange movement, led by constitutional monarchists, adopted the language of popular sovereignty, and the majority of its members were artisans. Born of the unhealthy conditions in which the referendum had been held in Paris and the country's refusal to recognize its outcome, it was linked to persistent agitation by the *jeunesse dorée* and the press opposed to the Terror. On October 3, seven sections declared themselves in favor of dissolving the Convention, which decided to rearm the agents of the Terror. The forces it finally put under Barras's command succeeded in dispersing the section's troops. Repression was minimal, and reserved mainly for clerks and deserters. It provided the opportunity for the National Guard to be placed under the new general of the army of the interior, Bonaparte.

The royalist offensive of year III thus ended in failure. It had, however, pointed up the unrealistic nature of Thermidorean hopes for national reconciliation in the wake of the Terror. The defenders of the work of the Constituent Assembly had been confronted with uprisings in the west, massacres in the Midi, and a Catholic revival. They saw in all this the hand of a Pretender vowing death to regicides and a return to the *ancien régime*. The Convention thus ended its term by reviving old measures against refractory priests and émigrés. In the majority in the new legislature, its members chose, as a guarantee, five regicides as Directors. Thus, despite 9 thermidor and the promulgation of a new constitution, the First Republic was to remain a revolutionary regime because the counterrevolution had not been disarmed.[4]

Donald Sutherland's analysis qualifies the usual interpretation of the Thermidorean period as a time of bourgeois reaction. It was more a time in which the threat of counterrevolution kept the Revolution from coming to a true close. Internal popular pressures were the most significant sources of this danger. The personal, psychological, and anecdotal aspects of members of the Convention are by comparison much less important. François Gendron has just conducted a new study of the *jeunesse dorée*, that gang of two to three thousand lower-level bourgeois youths that ruled the streets of the capital and its political life from thermidor to vendémiaire. It helped the moderate republicans crush food riots in germinal and prairial before vainly turning against them in October 1795. What was primarily merely the regime's unofficial militia, however, should not be blown up into a key cause of "reactionary dynamism" and the "Thermidorean phenomenon." These had many other sources, as is clear when we recall that Babeuf initially supported them, before being imprisoned like Varlet. As for the monarchist La Harpe, when the Convention was drawing to a close, he did not hesitate to label its leaders successors of Robespierre.[5]

The complexity of the Thermidoreans was matched by that of their adversaries, the last Montagnards. Françoise Brunel estimates that they numbered about a hundred deputies, who banded together in early 1795 when they realized the extent of what seemed to them to be a "reaction" to the Revolution. Against this step backward they held up the glories of a revolutionary heritage that they identified with the proclamation of equality. But they were slow to catch on to Thermidorean tactics and strategies, which moreover, were gradually refined. These were the outgrowth of a still fragile alliance between a small part of the revolutionary bourgeoisie and the upstanding citizens who formed the elite of the notables. The political acumen displayed by this new power proved highly effective in managing administrators and manipulating public opinion. More than simply a reactionary force, it resulted in the creation of an order based on electoral participation of those who were financially qualified. This marked a complete break with the austere and moral ideology inspired, until then, by Rousseau. By proclaiming the necessity of inequalities, the new order finally paved the way for the capitalism of the future. While retaining some of the aspirations of the preceding period, the liberalism of year III made that date a decisive one in French political history. Rejecting Jacobinism and its aspirations toward "happiness for all," Daunou's followers turned "national society" into a simple "business venture" on the mercantile model proposed by Adam Smith. The economy was elevated to the sacred status occupied in previous years by politics, and the old dream of forming a new man was relegated to the realm of utopian fantasy. In its place arose a belief in the primacy of competence. With Sieyès, the Thermidorean Convention proclaimed that the Republic would not be what Sieyès called a *Re-totale*, in other words, simultaneously despotic and leveling, like all the succeeding ones that were to take their inspiration from the experiment of year II.[6]

Clive Church has preferred to study the Constituent Assembly members of year III in terms of their approach to the thorny problem of the unwieldy bureaucracy created by the Revolution. Distrustful of it, but unable to get rid of it, they attempted to dilute the powers of the government apparatus. Momentarily united in this effort, a bloc of moderate republicans and royalists had difficulty maintaining a precarious balance between the threat of social subversion and that of a return to the *ancien régime*. The latter was voiced by the right-wing press made up of men whose disappointment with the Revolution had turned them into counterrevolutionaries. These journalists and their readers had roughly the same social background as the other camp, which shows how hard it is to establish direct links between class membership and political behavior. The Thermidoreans, moreover, were mistaken in their belief that an electorate chosen on the basis of financial qualifications would necessarily support their program. They were equally off the mark at the end of their mandate when they equated the bureaucracy they had inherited with the counterrevolution they feared. Following Max Weber's lead, Clive Church has shown that during the entire revolutionary period, changing circumstances did nothing to hamper the rise of the bureaucracy. The new administration, reinforced by the revolutionary government, alarmed its successors. They therefore eliminated price limits, but still failed to create the bureaucrat-free republic of their dreams. Having defeated the controlled economy, they were unable to control the hated bureaucracy, and had to limit themselves to purging it for reasons that were, in fact, illusory. Cleared of the suspicion of having fomented the vendémiaire coup, this administration born of the Revolution was rather favorable to the Republic. Its rise was not a function of politics, but of the unprecedented requirements of the government apparatus. It employed close to twelve thousand people in government service in Paris, while in the central ministries alone, the staff had grown from 420 in 1788 to 5,000 in 1795. It is clear that, Tocqueville notwithstanding, revolutionary centralization was on a scale different from that of the monarchy. The beneficiaries of this expansion had ridden out the changing policies of the new regime to become a mere professional interest group.[7]

The people, meanwhile, were dying of hunger. Richard Cobb stresses the ramifications of this food shortage that, on the contrary, accentuated, decentralizing tendencies: In this time of poverty, when people were fighting over food, local and social egotism had free reign. This was also a period of vengeance against former partisans of the Terror, isolated in their positions as revolutionary bureaucrats. The return to power of these despots was long dreaded. After five years of upheaval, in the midst of the agricultural crisis and the ruin of medical facilities, unequal food distribution aggravated the effects of epidemics. More than ever, France was divided into those who had enough to eat and those who did not. The result was an increased mortality rate that lasted over two years and overwhelmed the poor people of the cities and the countryside. Years III and IV were, above all, a period of food shortages for most of the French, in which workers crisscrossed the countryside from farm to farm and girls who went to Paris often wound up as prostitutes. Women sold themselves for bread or ham, and the suicide rate soared. Apathetic and discouraged, the common people were as broken by hunger and shame as by repression. In the Midi, where manhunts were common, the "blood-thirsty ones" were treated like "wild beasts." Village *sans-culottes* were often lynched in the main square, with their families, in full view of the public. In the countryside, the White Terror was a way of settling personal scores in which women's anger had free reign. Themidorean legality was thus marked by violence and anarchy in the face of official powerlessness. This was a time of private passions and communal poverty. With the revolutionary utopia at an end, 1795 revealed the egotism of the bourgeois republic.[8]

Opposition to the new regime mounted at the same time that the ranks of its militants were shrinking amid the radicalization of clan conflicts and the politicization of murder. All the poor could do was try to avoid dying of starvation, whether by prostitution, begging, or migrating. The omnipresent food problem thus weighed on a revolution that offered no improvements on *ancien régime* practices and attitudes: irregular production and consumption, contradictory governmental policies, anxiety and gullibility on the part of the populace, social inequities, regional antagonisms, and the schism between the cities and the countryside.[9]

The elimination of price limits rashly aggravated this situation. By restoring a liberal economy it unleashed forces that were not conducive to the maintenance of normal food supplies. Inflation, increasing poverty, and riots against high prices and shortages were the results of this imprudent lifting of necessary controls. Such was the case in the Nord, where the slide in living standards by comparison with 1790 was catastrophic. The Thermidorean Convention increased the number of indigents no longer benefiting from either the old paternalism or recent egalitarianism. Its policy of disengagement marked a definite regression in comparison with the situation before 1789.[10]

The political reaction sparked by this social regression was less drastic than the factors that had provoked it. The greater part of the country was spared its bloodiest consequences, as it had been spared those of the Terror, the memory of which it was struggling with. While in Toulouse, as in Paris and other departments, there was a hunt for Jacobins and a royalist offensive, Michèle Schlumberger has noted that these disturbances affected only a tiny minority and that, during year III, as during year II, the masses were interested in only two things: getting enough to eat and getting back their priests. In all other matters, apathy and indifference dominated the life of the Republic, with a 75 percent voter-abstention rate at the end of the period. There was more violence in other regions where local hatreds were more deeply rooted. Colin Lucas has offered an explanation of this violence in the Forez. In this area, beginning in the spring of 1795, political murders were part of the reaction. The throat slitters and thugs there were young people of good bourgeois stock, rich landowners whose families had suffered under the Terror. Avenging their past misfortunes in paramilitary gangs, they reflected the persistence of elements of the traditional society. These groups of armed youths were a part of the social organization of the south under the *ancien régime*. In their quasiritual parades, their raids, and their invasions of homes, they took up the ancient forms of the defiant exploits of their predecessors. Their deserters' solidarity led them to view group membership as a sort of initiation and group activities as a form of community organization. The humiliations they inflicted on the Jacobins were carried out according to tacit rules that were aimed at specific behavior. Above all, they hated the partisans of the Terror for having brought about changes, and their assassinations amounted to rites of exclusion. Most of all they hated the informers among them. Rooted in a youthful population that was soon to be urbanized, Thermidorean violence was first of all an expression of the resentment of a traditional milieu toward those who had disturbed it.[11]

WAS THE LIBERAL DIRECTORY A VIABLE EXPERIMENT?

The Directory was rooted in its founders' belief that social prominence would necessarily be translated into the political sphere. The regime would have the backing of landowners and would not be opposed by others. In fact, it had very few supporters among the prominent citizenry and many opponents among the people. Making it work would have required a level of participation and support from the electorate that simply did not exist. The French government of the time thus had all the appearances of a ruling clique whose only weapon was the coup d'état. Its victories against the Vendéans and the Austrians were of little help because they were not definitive. Persistent financial chaos, moreover, threatened the foundations of the dominance of the rich. All that was needed to clear the way for Bonaparte was for the Directory to alienate the greater part of the politically active class.

This pessimistic view recently expressed by Donald Sutherland seems justified by the government's powerlessness stemming, in large part, from the religious policies handed down from the Convention. As we have seen, the latter had granted freedom of conscience, but limited freedom of religious expression. The financial weakness of the church coincided with many restrictions on religious practice that originated in the iconoclastic traditions of year II. Such practices thus remained clandestine activities that received wide popular support. The laity continued to defy the law, particularly in isolated mountainous areas where the government was weak. This was the case in numerous regions in the Massif Central, where supporters of the refractory priests ignored the government and scorned the constitutional clergy. The forbidden ceremonies were much more popular than the official cults. In Languedoc and Alsace, anti-Jacobin processions and ardent demands for a Mass defied the authorities. In the Nord, armed peasants protected the activities of Belgian missionaries. To some extent, simple devout people, particularly women, filled in during services for the missing priests. The people's desire for religion was the basis of what is referred to as the religious "awakening" under the Directory. Women played an essential role in it by forcing the reopening of churches, helping refractory priests escape, and holding off the police. The reinstatement of the power of the priests went hand in hand, in their eyes, with the return of their own moral authority as mothers. The geographical incidence of this phenomenon largely coincides with the opposition that sprang up in 1791 to the Civil Constitution, and that also hastened the decline of the Constitutional Church.

Forced to seek refuge in the cities, the clergy of the west, like that of the north and center, had practically no parish bases. Even in other places it was demoralized by the indifference or the hostility of the faithful. Despite Grégoire's efforts to organize it, there were twenty-eight vacant episcopal seats in 1801, and only thirty-two of the bishops elected ten years earlier were still sitting. This failure was the result of the shameful abandonment of the Constitutional Church by a revolution that had at first exploited it. After thermidor, many parish priests made peace with the refractory clergy, which was responsible for the religious revival of the period and was slowly rebuilding its parish organization with the help of devout members of the laity. Vicars-general sent in by émigré bishops took charge of this process in many dioceses. This activity by the refractory priests, unlike that of other Parisian Catholics was completely royalist in orientation. The Republic was illegitimate in their eyes, and they sometimes advised monarchist insurgents from the west or the Midi. But their pastoral work was even more subversive in that it was directed against the impious elements that had abolished seignorial dues and church property. Refractory priests in Brittany were accused of promising that people who killed patriots would go to heaven; elsewhere they were charged with encouraging people not to pay taxes or do their military service and telling them to avoid like the plague any contact with republicans. Reconciliation between these men and a godless state seemed impossible.

The Republic, in addition, had no real control over the country, which added to its unpopularity. The war diminished the size of the armed forces it could use to put down royalist gangs. Left to fend for themselves, the departments depended on the National Guard, which was becoming less and less reliable, or the police, who were neither more numerous nor more efficient than they had been under the former constabulary. Their financial means were extremely limited and this hardly encouraged zealous commitment. The commissioners of the Directory had difficulty filling the ranks of the administration. At times it took months to staff these positions. Apathy had become the order of the day in republican France. Disappointment and disillusionment with politics were largely responsible, and citizens mainly seemed interested in distancing themselves from the whole business. Local power fell into the hands of the weak or the angry, who either disobeyed the state or encouraged its enemies. The religious resurgence in the countryside was greatly advanced by this state of affairs, as was the incidence of unpunished assassinations, tax evasion, and émigré plotting.

One outcome of this administrative collapse was an upsurge in brigandage. The forms it took under the Republic were similar to those found under the *ancien régime*. Born of poverty, brigandage was only aggravated by the terrible economic crisis of 1795–96. The unemployed and the hungry, who had already participated in subsistence riots and had nothing left, were driven to despair. Agricultural workers and impoverished artisans joined gangs of thugs that scoured the countryside between Rouen and Gand. Villagers and refractory priests often took their side against the agents of repression. This popular "royalism" turned the pure and simple looting of vehicles transporting government property into an act of political opposition. Chouans had picked up support against republican merchants and owners of nationalized church lands from as far away as Provence, where brigands could sleep soundly, believing themselves protected by Christ. A good part of the brigandage of the period thus was linked to the counterrevolution and was directed, as in the rural Midi, against Jacobins, Protestants, the Constitutional Church, and former agents of the Terror. These activities expressed the traditional community's revolt against those who had dared shake its time-tested order either by brute force or by illegitimate measures passed in the cities.

The popular royalism of the Midi was thus largely supported by the majority of the local people, who were hostile to the "liberty trees," tried to humiliate the local Jacobins, and among the women in particular, were nostalgic about the idealized past state that had been destroyed by the Revolution. These villagers, in sum, associated the idea of happiness with the old France. In their name, rather than serve in the armies of the Republic, the young people persecuted or killed those who defended them. The "royal brigands" were made up in large part of deserters, against whom the regime was as powerless as it was against the refractory priests. Its only choice was between leaving them alone and provoking a revolt. Whence the impunity long granted to the murderous Basque gangs. Their ideology sanctified their pillaging in the eyes of the people. Émigrés quickly joined their networks and in many regions of the Languedoc old tendencies toward antirevolutionary guerrilla activity were intensified under the Directory. With the momentum they gained over the religious schism they lasted in some cases until 1801.

Information about the conspiratorial activities of these clandestine gangs and the types of support they received is difficult to find. But they extended from the Rhône valley to the Pyrenees and the Maritime Alps. Their social makeup, with the exception of a few émigrés, was basically the same as that of the revolutionary committees of year II. The people convicted by special tribunals in the southeast were mostly peasants and artisans. The royal brigands in these areas were representative of the population, and only the leadership of the movement was composed of priests or nobles. Unlike the northern gangs, which were the products of poverty, those of the Midi had deep roots in the areas where they operated and were clearly linked to the refusal of conscription. The Directory interfered little with them, since they did not seriously hamper its military efforts. The west was more dangerous because of its proximity to England, which could arm the peasants. Thus in 1795 the government placed it under the control of General Hoche, who was soon to head an army of one hundred thousand men. His antiguerrilla tactics were totally successful against Stofflet and Charette. Unable to exploit this Vendéan involvement, the Chouan leaders surrendered in turn. But this pacification was only partial, as it brought neither religious freedom nor economic relief. The republican troops, moreover, were poorly disciplined and had to provision themselves in the countryside.[1]

Hoche's victory nonetheless helped stabilize the Republic, which also needed successes against Austria and England. Early victories were won by Napoleon in Italy, as we know, with only thirty thousand ill-equipped men who looked more like a horde of scavengers than a regular army. He was also able to take over the rich region of Lombardy, and then central Italy, which turned out to be extremely lucrative for the government as well as for the generals. This campaign, which ended victoriously in 1797, was the basis of the legend of Bonaparte, which he himself helped create. He seemed at last to be the republican hero who would put an end to the war. His victory also made him a major player on the French political scene.

The stabilizing mission of the Directory set it against the gradual reconstruction of the Jacobin movement. Babeuf's "Conspiracy of Equals" provided a convenient pretext for striking out at the entire leftist opposition. This marginal revolutionary had been a rural agitator before becoming, in 1795, an adversary of the principle of private property. This enemy of monopolies went so far as to propose the elimination of the market and its replacement, within a generation, by a communistic system of production and distribution that would put an end to poverty. This earnest democrat was thus able to accept an authoritarian and bureaucratic utopia. But his evolving political strategy brought him to believe that leadership should be entrusted to an advance-guard revolutionary minority. This stance stemmed largely from the Directory's attitude toward the clubs. Their postvendémiaire reconciliation was short-lived, for the government needed to prove to upstanding citizens that it opposed disorder. This was how it chose to interpret the democratic tendencies of the neo-Jacobin movement, despite its loyalist stance. In early 1796, the government closed the clubs in Paris and the provinces and purged the administration. Babeuf then set to work preparing a revolt whose motives were highly diverse, and which led only to his arrest on May 10. This affair gave the Directory an excuse to imprison hundreds of Jacobins for the sake of impressing the public. Aside from that, the repression was limited to the execution of Babeuf and an ally of his a year later. But by unleashing the indignation of a segment of the press, its effect was rather to reinforce the trend it had intended to stop.

The workers' poverty explains in part their support of the democratic movement. It was aggravated by a disastrous monetary policy that alienated the rich as well as the poor. The financial conditions the Directory inherited were no doubt deplorable because of the collapse of the *assignat* and price increases. This situation led to increased poverty for the masses, and the mortality rate in large cities between 1793 and 1796 was twice as high as it had been before the Revolution. The main result in urban areas was a drop in population. The government attempted to remedy this catastrophe by forced loans from the rich, which had to be abandoned in the summer of 1796, and the replacement of *assignats* by territorial notes that depreciated even faster and were demonetized early in 1797. In these dire straits, the Directory seemed easy prey for the counterrevolution.

It thus increasingly leaned toward a strategy of internal subversion, which as of 1794 was led from Berne by the English spy Wickham. It was limited at first to financing the murderous gangs of the White Terror and, in the autumn of 1795, buying off the timid general Pichegru, who was relieved of his command six months later. These efforts were redirected toward attaining a royalist victory in the upcoming legislative elections. The moderate monarchists of the philanthropic institutes, who had a clandestine military organization in the southwest and were in touch with royal brigands, refractory priests, and popular opinion, received more money from Wickham than the Directory had at its disposal for the electoral campaign. In the end they were represented in sixty departments. Among the conservative deputies of the Clichy Club were both republicans and a wide range of monarchists. It was difficult to bring them into accord, especially in view of the reactionary stubbornness of the pretender to the throne. The right-wing campaign was thus vague, and its cause was advanced mainly by the weakness of the Directory.

The electorate rejected the outgoing Convention delegates in 1797 as it had in 1795. Only 11 out of 216 were reelected, and after these March elections barely a fifth of the legislature was made up of regicides. Royalists won the majority of seats, amassing enough power to dominate the councils. Their victory was by no means the result of a decisive trend, for there were huge numbers of abstentions: The opinion of the rich, the only one to find expression, was above all hostile to seasoned revolutionary politicians and preferred to try out newcomers. The north and, generally speaking, the most populated and developed regions were the furthest to the right. These had been the most progressive areas in 1789, which meant that the regime had lost the support of the elites. It still was able, however, to beat its divided adversaries, even after the newly elected Barthélémy and Carnot formed a conservative minority in the Directory. While awaiting 1798, the royalists of the councils passed measures in favor of the émigrés and practiced obstructionism in financial matters. Faced with widespread internal subversion, Barras, Reubell, and La Révellière (who were to remain in top positions until the spring of 1799) decided to take action against their colleagues and the deputies. They brought troops into Paris in violation of the constitution and reorganized the ministry to suit their inclinations. Their opponents had clumsily attacked the armies and their generals (who became a bastion of the Republic) without taking sufficient precautions to ensure their safety.

The coup d'état of 18 fructidor (September 4, 1797) resulted from the divisions in the regime and marked the beginning of a turn to the left that lasted six months. Loyal troops stood by while 2 directors were purged, 53 deputies were deported, elections were cancelled in 49 departments, 32 journalists were arrested, and 42 newspapers were banned. The purge extended to the administration of the provinces, which had proven unable to prevent counterrevolutionary demonstrations. This purge was much more systematic than the one of year II. The Terror of year VI often brought Jacobins with a great deal of political experience back into local affairs. This was an attempt by the Directory to bureaucratize local authorities, a policy that was to be pursued by Bonaparte. The new regime also took aim at émigrés and refractory priests, but a law stripping ex-nobles of their citizenship went virtually unenforced. Having carried out only a few hundred executions, the revitalized administration was better able to manage the country. Given the continued incidence of brigandage, this return to order was of course relative, especially in the Midi and the west. But the government took advantage of it to consolidate its finances at the expense of its creditors. In 1798 it set up a system of conscription by lottery. The war with England continued, however, and a revival of the war on the continent threatened despite the treaty of Campoformio, which had been concluded with Austria in October 1797. How could a regime with so little support in the nation demand new sacrifices? This vacuum, at once social and political, was the main cause of the Directory's downfall.[2]

Donald Sutherland's analysis follows a historiographical tradition that is still being challenged by efforts to rehabilitate a constitutional republic doomed to a lamentable collapse. Attempts have been made to do justice to a directory that was slandered by Bonaparte, whose triumph was in part made possible by its work. But at just the time when this regime was barely hanging on through the use of illegal procedures before dying ignominiously, the United States was crowning its revolution with a republic that was to last without a break until our day. It is true that in the 1790s there were many violent clashes and fierce struggles, and that especially during national elections momentous decisions squeaked through by a very slim majority. Jacques Godechot has explained this contrast in terms of the force of circumstance, and in particular, the foreign war. We shall also see that historians of the English-speaking world stress France's inability to institutionalize a regime made up of parties, which was essential to democratic life, but condemned them in favor of myths of unity that have remained dominant ever since 1789. It is also possible, as Jean-René Suratteau has conjectured that the failure of the Directory experiment was simply caused by the continuing attachment of the majority of the French to the monarchy, particularly for religious reasons. Donald Sutherland does not suggest otherwise. The major accomplishment of the First Republic, according to Clive Church, was in the area of administration. Despite Necker's efforts, no real reforms had been achieved in this sphere since 1792. The early phases of the Revolution, while employing more administrators and eliminating the purchase of office, had led neither to the standardization of career opportunities, nor standardization of pay, nor parliamentary control of state employees. The revolutionary government departed from this state of affairs by increasing the bureaucracy and the degree of control exercised by the central power, and by sketching in a preliminary definition of positions. The Directory strengthened these tendencies by rationalizing, formalizing, and professionalizing the administrative structure, defining its hierarchy better, and by making it better organized, more closely linked to the service of the state, and easier to control. The great political innovation of the First Republic was the bureaucratization of this governing apparatus. An outgrowth of exceptional regimes, it was to outlive them despite opposition by numerous segments of society, becoming an integral part of the new elite.[3]

The Directory was unable to provide a stable constitutional regime for the country. Proclaiming the new reign of law and order, it tried to become its guarantor and protector against the rival groups into which public opinion was divided. But reconciling liberalism and efficiency proved difficult. Having inherited an era filled with turmoil and violence, it was unable to eliminate them. The countryside, overflowing with refractory priests and deserters, eluded its control. Lacking resources and reliable agents, the government was neither heard nor heeded in these areas. The powerlessness of its local administration paralyzed the early Directory when faced with royalist peasants rising up against the Jacobin cities. Revolutionary France offered the curious spectacle of a state that was in the process of conquering part of Europe while unable to check anarchy and opposition within its own borders. The majority of the country desired the return of neither the émigrés nor the agents of the Terror, but simply hoped for a restoration of peace and order. The Directory could not comply because, like the preceding regimes, it expressed only the views of the nation as a political entity, cut off from the masses. Even these views were fragmented by an infinity of legal situations that the government was unable to control. Its inability to impose an awareness of common interests sealed its fate despite the administrative progress made after fructidor. All Bonaparte had to do was show that he was at once the product of the Revolution and superior to it.[4]

In the west, resistance to the Revolution was even more the product of a rural culture that had remained untouched by the spirit of the Enlightenment. Hoche's victories there turned the Republic into an occupying colonial power, which the local population held responsible for its misfortunes. The peasants still did not favor a return to the monarchy, much to the consternation of the émigrés who understood them no better than the revolutionaries and found them as egalitarian as the Jacobins.

The peasants' spontaneous revolt had been the eruption of a people hostile to all the elites. They rejected the Revolution with its urban bureaucratic processes of modernization and centralization. Their anguish stemmed from the intrustion of abnormality into the traditional life of their communities. This was the basis of their total rejection of the constitutional clergy, whom they viewed as intruders, and their attachment in the countryside to the parish priests who were inseparable elements of their conception of order and reality.[5]

It is clear that the social origins of a movement that led so many of the French to revolt against the Republic ran deep. The religious resurgence that occurred under the Directory was its cultural analogue. It was centered not so much in the clergy as in a Catholic populace that was the animating spirit of resistance to de-Christianization. At its head were women, yearning for the sacraments and defending their ancestral rites. In the absence of priests, religion became once again a family phenomenon, and clandestine baptisms were sometimes performed by lay people. Masses were held in caves and basements, while pilgrims continued to flock to chapels. Open resistance led to the reappearance of crosses and support for the activities of refractory priests. During the entire period of the Directory, authorities from Marseilles to Lille came under intense popular pressure to reinstate public religion. In the cities and the country, from the west to the east, vast processions honored a Virgin that the Revolution had been unable to dethrone. The devout maintained their faith despite official persecution. They urged parish priests to return, or formed congregations. A miraculous fountain in Moselle could draw worshipers by the thousands. In many regions, the abiding image of the Revolution in the collective memory was that of the martyrs it had created. It was at this time that the notion of supernatural punishments to be visited on the guiltiest de-Christianizers gained currency. Under the Directory the religious fervor of the masses was perhaps the strongest national sentiment of all.[6]

The official political game was thus only played out on the surface of things. The press reflected this in its narrow clientele and its abstract ideology, even when it wrote for the military establishment. It also expressed what remained of republican militancy, which was *above all anticlerical.* Isser Woloch has studied the persistence of the Jacobin movement under the Directory in the patriotic circles of the urban petite bourgeoisie. He has followed the propaganda activity of its clubs, and especially its newspapers, which were unable to turn the regime in a democratic direction. They no doubt had little to do with Babeuf and represented the political stance of a vehemently antiroyalist minority. Their futile electoral successes in 1798 and 1799 show that they struck a responsive chord in public opinion. This had not been true of the Conspiracy of Equals, which has subsequently been seized upon as a harbinger of twentieth-century communism. Richard Andrews has traced its roots to Paris during the early period of the Directory, when police and conspirators alike were the common heirs of the period of the Terror. The memory of this tacit past complicity haunted the elaboration and repression of a clandestine movement sprung from a Jacobin bureaucracy that, as we have seen, was to remain in power by other means and in the name of another cause. Babeuf's followers reflected not so much aspirations toward a new world as the diminution of revolutionary militancy in Paris after the disappointments of year III. They failed, in particular, to attract the former revolutionary potentates of Faubourg Saint-Antoine, who by now had completely withdrawn from political affairs. After the time of struggle and glory, their survival instincts were no longer stirred by this appeal to a futile crusade. Lacking social bases and undermined by police infiltration, the conspiracy fell into the net like an overripe fruit. The usual amalgam of anarchy, royalism, and treason, this plot was concocted by a group of rootless people whose ideology was an aberrant carryover from the past. It was in no way connected with the socialism of the future. Born of despair at the collapse of the Revolution, it was equally impotent, as Buonarroti acknowledged in 1797, thirty years before he transformed this event into elemental myth.[7]

WAS THE BRUMAIRE COUP D'ÉTAT A FATAL BLOW?

The Republic could survive only by violating its constitution. After fructidor, the representative institutions could not function normally, since the electors had shown their preference for the counterrevolution. The Directory was thus left to solve the nation's problems alone, which it did to some extent, as we have seen, on the levels of internal order and external peace. But it was unable either to stabilize itself or to win over public opinion, which was increasingly turning away from the regime. With the resumption of the war in 1799, the government was forced to demand new sacrifices of the country, which refused to make them. Subversion and instability reappeared. Though it was firmly in control of its administration, the government did not have a good grasp on its army that, after having rescued the Thermidoreans on several occasions, helped topple a regime that no one defended.

These problems had been apparent since the elections of 1798, which, because of the Fructidor purges, involved over four hundred deputies. With the possibility of new royalist gains looming, it was decided that the departing legislators would validate the new ones. The specter of a Jacobin victory complicated the situation, despite the Directory's attempts to ensure a favorable outcome. It warned the electors in vain of the dual dangers posed by the left and the right, banned eleven Jacobin newspapers, shut down thirty clubs, and placed several cities and departments under a state of siege. This repression was only partial and the Jacobins often retained their important local role. In Paris, their newspapers continued to demand the democratization of the regime, while in the country their clubs were mistrustful of the counterrevolution. In this enterprise of defending republicanism, they parted ways with the Directory, whose oligarchical tendencies they criticized. The social makeup of the Jacobins recalled that of the former fraternal societies and their artisanal milieu, bringing together veterans of the revolutionary movement as a whole.

The elections were marked by a high level of abstention and the frequent splitting of electoral assemblies into antagonistic groups. Despite their gains, the Jacobins were unable to obtain more than a third of the seats. The Directory, moreover, annulled the elections of those candidates it viewed as hostile. It overstated the number of partisans of the Terror elected in order to cancel a hundred of these results. The only objective of this curious application of the parliamentary system was to consolidate power. The government took upon itself the task of cutting off any possibility of victory by the opposition. Public opinion interpreted this maneuver as an inducement to relax the anticlericalism instituted in fructidor. But the Directory was determined to strike at all its adversaries, both Jacobins and conservatives. It encouraged the ceremonies of its state-sponsored *culte décadaire*, the embodiment of de-Christianization, as an antidote to Catholicism. Its success was limited, and its social bases remained narrow.

The regime made the mistake of yielding to the temptation of exploiting its conquered territories, a policy encouraged by its suppliers, who were highly influential in official circles. This resulted in a disastrous resumption of the war, accompanied by a return to instability and institutional paralysis. The conflict between revolutionary France and Europe begun so recklessly, turned out to be interminable. The treaty of Campoformio did not end it, for the Directory, like its predecessors, tried to extract from the "liberated" peoples contributions and requisitions, notably for the upkeep of the army of occupation. Along with this policy, which was probably inevitable, came an attempt to establish the economic hegemony of France. Military victories and territorial expansion advanced it. Holland, Belgium, and the Rhineland were ruined by it, and Italy was turned into a protected market. This unfraternal pillage provoked many rebellions, for the Directory was unable to control its own staff. The occupations of Switzerland and Rome in the first half of 1798 illustrate this combination of strategy and greed. The former was an attempt to put pressure on the Austrians and to take hold of major treasures. Troops were therefore sent to support uprisings by Swiss patriots. Next came a rising in the Catholic cantons and wholesale exploitation in the guise of contributions to the war effort. A similar chain of events followed the proclamation of the Roman Republic. Bonaparte left during this time to fight the British in Egypt, where the destruction of his fleet left him stranded with his army. The second coalition was the result, and with it the downfall of the Directory. After Turkey and the Neapolitans captured Rome in November, Russia declared war on France in December. Hostilities with Austria were renewed at the beginning of 1799. The Directory at first took advantage of this to recapture Rome and then set up a new Republic in Naples. The Piedmont was captured (and annexed) in its turn, and then Tuscany. The pope, who had been taken prisoner, was to die in France. Under these conditions it became increasingly difficult for the government to control its generals and financiers. Its commissioners, who attempted to do so, ran up against an army that was attempting to profit from the war and whose leaders differed with the Directory over the control of the sister republics.[1]

These struggles made it impossible for Paris to rely on its generals at a time when the national crisis was deepening. Jacobins and more-or-less hidden reactionaries constituted a powerful opposition. The Directory could not count on an automatic majority in a legislature composed of bureaucrats who above all feared the return of the *ancien régime*. They objected to bad appointments and widespread corruption and demanded fiscal justice. Though less marked by governmental intervention, the elections of spring 1799 were characterized even more than usual by abstentions. The continued rejection of official candidates and seasoned politicians signified, above all, a rejection of the regime. Sieyès took Reubell's place, amid continuing questions about the Directory's financial dealings. The new member, like the rest, supported the revision of the constitution and the strengthening of the executive branch. The influence he and his allies acquired testifies to the government's loss of stature.

This was increased by military defeats in Italy, where disturbances broke out in the north. Dauphiné and Provence were threatened by a campaign whose aims had outstripped its means and whose generals had acted without discipline. Infighting among the Allies saved France while factional struggles raged in Paris. Defeats increased protests there against official corruption, to which they were, as usual, attributed. This Jacobin offensive in the councils and the press led to a partial purge of the Directory with the support of Sieyès's allies. This coincided with an increase in the army's influence on internal politics. In July the Jacobins pushed through the passage of a law on hostages according to which relatives of suspects could be deported or held financially responsible in the event of disturbances in certain departments. This measure had been preceded by the imposition on the rich of a forced loan aimed at financing the simultaneous call-up of five classes of conscripts. Forty percent of them deserted, thereby swelling the ranks of the brigands who were encouraged by the royalists. This resistance by young people was facilitated by the complicity or powerlessness of local authorities. Similar circumstances canceled out the effects of the law on hostages and the forced loan, which only increased the unpopularity of the government. As had been the case from 1791 to 1793, repressive measures touched off bloody reprisals in the western departments that were most affected. Adversaries of the Jacobins in Paris silenced them in August by shutting down their club and rejecting their accusations against the Directors. The latter's standing in the eyes of the public nevertheless was not enhanced by this.

Counterrevolutionary pressures threatened to provide new opportunities for a Jacobin offensive. It materialized in 1799 in the usual form of a combination of internal subversion and foreign invasion. The philanthropic institutes had been reorganized under leadership from Lyons but they were under strict surveillance. Throughout the Midi the vast royalist movement, with its gangs bolstered by deserters, raged out of control. Its leaders were hard-pressed to maintain contacts, arms, and coordination. During the summer an ill-prepared uprising broke out in the Toulouse region. Although it involved over thirty thousand rebels it was repelled by a republican counterattack that left four thousand dead. Many of these were humble peasants from the Garonne valley, hostile to Protestantism and frustrated by the bourgeois revolution.

The allied advance had given them great hopes, but the Austro-Russians were defeated near Zurich on September 25 and the Anglo-Russian landing in Holland ended in a pitiful retreat. Despite such victories, the political situation in France continued to deteriorate. While the Directory put the blame on opposition newspapers, the Jacobins tried in vain to have the fatherland declared in danger, as it had been in 1792. Their failure did not keep them from being a threatening presence. They celebrated Bonaparte's return on October 9 as a hero of the Republic. Not suspecting that he would become directly engaged in politics, the moderates hailed him also. As a victorious leader he enjoyed immense prestige, embodying the popularity still attached in certain sectors of public opinion to the spread of revolutionary ideas by armed force. He was naturally well liked by the military, which considered itself the last bastion of democracy and the guarantor of national regeneration. But Bonaparte had many contacts among the political and intellectual elite. His colleagues at the institute, in particular, dreamed of a government that would be both enlightened and efficient. Through them and his brothers the general linked himself with Sieyès's faction. This coalition was backed by moderate deputies and anti-Jacobin newcomers. It was animated by the desire to revise the constitution in ways that would strengthen executive power, and believed this could be accomplished with a veneer of legality. On 18 brumaire (November 9) the Council of the Elders was notified of a terrible Jacobin plot, and initial measures indispensable to the coup that was brewing were taken. But the next day at Saint-Cloud, where the deputies were meeting, the other council decided to defend the constitution, and treated Bonaparte as a tyrant. Fortunately for him, his brother Lucien, who was presiding, made the guards disperse the deputies under the "protection" of Murat's soldiers. That night, a rump session of Parliament appointed a temporary Consulate of three members, including Bonaparte and Sieyès, and two legislative commissions charged with drafting a new constitution.

The year III version crumbled, according to Donald Sutherland, because the ruling group that it had favored, and which had created it, was never accepted by the country. It was composed of convention members who had, since 1792, refused to give up power even when the electors tried to remove them. Their commitment to preserving the Revolution had always outweighed considerations of legality. This political elite had no support among the voting public, which in 1799 reelected only 12 percent of the Convention members and 5 percent of the regicides. The electorate, composed of the richest elements of France, rejected leaders it viewed as too adventurist or demanding. The high rate of abstentions grew out of their disgust with political maneuverings. This trend, apparent since year III, increased steadily in the following years. Young people chose desertion from the army over civic duty. The newly elected representatives, on the other hand, were truly new men on the national scene, coming out of local politics but independent of the government. Those who replaced the Convention members were of the same social class as their predecessors and shared their convictions. Their administrative experience, which often went back to 1790, had taken them through all the meanderings of the Revolution, except perhaps the exploits of year II. These former Third Estate militants or department heads wound up serving Bonaparte, who seemed to fulfill the dream that had guided their careers, the aspiration toward a government that would maintain order while respecting the principles of 1789. Their temporary rejection of a constitutional monarchy was based on the association of royalist principles with the counterrevolution. But they were

equally distrustful of aggressive Jacobinism and its hostility toward the rich.
Whence their choice in Brumaire.[2]

Recent work on the origins of this coup d'état revolve around three
themes: its external setting, the importance of the counterrevolutionary
threat, and the contradictions of government political dealings.

On the first point, T. C. W. Blanning has connected the resumption
of war in 1798 with deficiencies in the Campoformio agreement, which
Paris and Vienna saw as a mere truce. French expansionism confirmed
this view and, more than anything else, shook a fragile peace. In this
respect the Directory repeated the errors of the Brissotin party as ex-
emplified by the Egyptian expedition. Feeling threatened, Russia made
its first true foray into the war against the Revolution, pulling Austria
into the conflict. The Republic eventually had to pay for multiplying its
enemies and scattering its forces. But the war had become a normal
condition of its existence. The Directory needed it to keep its army busy
and maintain and justify its existence. Early in 1799 Reubell was pleased
to find himself at the head of a martial nation that thrived on war. It
was thus natural that before the end of the year the country should hand
control over to a general. After ten years, revolutionary expansionism
remained the main cause of political instability in Europe. It impelled
the Girondins' successors to attempt to push their way into India and
Russia. This resurgence of French power was the main external result
of the Revolution. It had given its defenders a feeling of invinciblity
derived from their belief in the absolute superiority of their principles.
In this heady atmosphere they often underestimated their opponents.[3]

The Directory's military strategy during the 1799 campaign at first
piled errors on errors, encouraging simultaneous attacks along an immense front on enemies who enjoyed numerical superiority. Serious
defeats resulted. This disaster, which left France under threat of invasion,
could not be corrected immediately because of tactical errors by the
generals. The first decisive victory against the coalition did not come
until early autumn, when the counteroffensive planned by the new minister of war, Bernadotte, was correctly executed by Masséna in Switzerland and Brune in Holland. This comeback, although belated, reveals
a certain strategic competence on the part of the Directory that is not
always recognized.[4]

Jacques Godechot first described this "great counterrevolutionary assault" of 1799 in 1961. He has recently focused on the situation in
Toulouse, where a royalist uprising, exploiting the existence of large
numbers of underground forces composed of deserters, nearly took over
the city in early August. This was not the only popular uprising to

challenge the Republic that year. From the Ionian islands to Brittany peasants rose up en masse against the Revolution. In Calabria, their hostility to the Neapolitan bourgeoisie, brought to power by a foreign army, sprang from the bitterness they harbored toward the feudalism the new regime was not quick enough to abolish. Their discontents were stirred up by the wily Cardinal Ruffo, who promised them lands and the chance to loot Jacobin property. This partisan movement was thus aimed against the rich in the name of the counterrevolution, as the seizure of Naples in June demonstrated. It ushered in a state of true agrarian anarchy and an atmosphere of lawlessness that were to last for years. It spread to central Italy as well, where peasants revolted in May and burned Jews alive in Siena in June. Their counterparts on the Ionian islands were to conduct similar massacres in October to help the Russians and the Turks expel the French. Revolts against French troops erupted once more in Switzerland, chiefly in the Grisons and the Valais; they were brutally repressed. The Rhineland and Holland had disturbances as well. In France itself, the west was even more seriously shaken than the southwest, with Chouans briefly taking Le Mans, Nantes, and Saint-Brieuc in October.[5]

This indicates the scope of the revolt that, within France, signified the rejection of the republican regime by many Catholic regions. In Italy, adopted homeland of the popular counterrevolution, the partisan movement, according to John Davis, was perhaps less a social conflict than a civil war in which countless rivalries among communities, classes, regions, and factions were revived by the French intervention and the revolutionary movement it had unleashed. Conflicting interests rooted in a long history of prior developments erupted violently at this time, making the Neapolitian counterrevolution part of the age-old pattern of unrest in the Mezzogiorno. In the French countryside, even in areas like Caux where there was no antirepublican revolt, Guy Lemarchand has noted the peasants' profound lack of interest in issues relative to national defense and official ideology. They turned massively away from the regime, as their electoral abstentions, their political indifference, and their attachment to Catholicism demonstrate. Alan Forrest has characterized the hostility of the rural areas of the west, with their striking incidence of draft dodging and religious dissidence, as resentment against a centralizing, interventionist state that disrupted the villagers' way of life and offended their sensitivities. Their autonomous spirit was distrustful of a power structure that was alien to their traditions and their mentality.[6]

This no doubt caused the failure of the liberal Republic forced on the

French heartland by the revolutionary bourgeoisie. Along with David Lansky and Paul Hamson, Lynn Hunt has attempted to clarify the significance of 18 brumaire. These historians have noted that Bonaparte did not seize power until the majority of deputies had abandoned the notion of parliamentary government. His dictatorship proceeded to use a good part of the bureaucratic structures and administrative staff it had inherited. Far from arising in a political vacuum, it was provoked by calls for intervention from revisionists who preferred the uncertainties of authoritarianism to the ambiguities of the regime. The regime did not strike back. The traditional explanation for this is the establishment's fear of a resurgence of Jacobinism. But we have seen that the Jacobin element had been defeated before Brumaire. Moreover, shouldn't political apathy have led to the unquestioned prolongation of the Republic? Lynn Hunt and her colleagues link its fall to its fundamental internal contradictions. This representative system, with its frequent elections, refused to allow the existence of organized parties that would have been essential to its survival. The republicans who led it thus set themselves against the very principle of political liberalism. Unwilling to recognize organized opposition, they were unable to establish a party, both anti-aristocratic and antipopulist, that would advance their interests. They remained fixated on the original revolutionary myth of a fraternal civic community, undivided by factions. This ideology had been perpetuated since 1789, despite the existence of parties that were not recognized as legitimate. They were thought to be working against the higher goals of the nation by selfishly mobilizing individual classes. Nevertheless, under the Directory, a left, a center, and a right did indeed exist with regard to the issues that came up. They were, however, never able to organize themselves in a clear and legally recognized manner. The Constitution of the Year III seemed to rule this out. Close study of the deputies under the Directory allows us to sketch the outlines of these groups. They certainly lacked internal coherence and support within the nation. The Jacobins of 1799 began, however, to present themselves to public opinion as an organized party. Their enemies who were victorious in Brumaire rejected this kind of system, which they identified with factional divisions. The Directory thus crumbled not because it was too weak, too isolated, or too divided, but because its leaders ultimately preferred the establishment of an authoritarian dictatorship to the creation of a party system like the one in the United States. The electoral and parliamentary schemes that grew out of this attitude undermined the regime by encouraging indifference and disengagement. They facilitated the rise to power of local administrators who, although dedicated revolutionaries, were not much concerned with republican principles and were easily won over, like the French elite as a whole, to the technocratic and apolitical orientation ushered in by Bonaparte.[7]

During this time, the last of the Parisian *sans-culottes*, artisans, or shopkeepers, were continuing their hopeless struggle. Raymonde Monnier has studied their democratic resistance to the bourgeois Republic despite the listlessness and repression of year III. Early in the Directory, these militant revolutionaries supported Babeuf's agitation, and afterward were able to maintain a conspiratorial spirit and to some extent gain a new lease on life. After fructidor, they backed the neo-Jacobin reorganization, which frightened off the moderates. Forced underground under the Consulate, these people were the relics of a large movement that was henceforth remote from the people.[8]

DECISIVE CHANGES?

9. A NEW STATE?

R*ather than the liberal regime of its leaders' dreams, the Revolution led to the establishment of Bonaparte's dictatorship. Historians have tried to trace the causes of this unhappy outcome, to discern whether they are to be found in the mentality of the Brumaireans or their social fears, or perhaps in the weight of circumstances and the conflicts they provoked, or in the overweening ambition of the future Napoleon I. They agree that he strengthened the administrative centralization he had inherited, but are divided over the extent to which this represented a legacy from the* ancien régime. *As for the new regime, did it succeed, as the architects of Brumaire hoped, in putting an end to the various rifts that divided the nation?*

WHY DID THE FRENCH REVOLUTION RESULT IN THE ESTABLISHMENT OF A PERSONAL DICTATORSHIP?

In his study of Bonaparte's domestic political achievements, Louis Bergeron has pointed out a fundamental ambiguity: The last of the enlightened despots, Napoleon was at the same time the founder of the rational, unified system that still governs France. From a national point of view, he brought France the order and stability that had been lacking since 1789. In one stroke, sovereignty fell entirely to him; freedom was the price of ending anarchy. His regime rejected informed public opinion in favor of omnipresent police activity. Without setting up either a military dictatorship or a traditional monarchy, Napoleon established a new kind of power that concentrated authority in the hands of a man dedicated to modernizing both state and society. This unexpected result of the Revolution grew out of the combined efforts of a large network of competent administrators. But this executive branch had neither direction nor power without its master. His rise to the monarchy, which grew out of a desire to combat the royalist threat while taking on its attributes, in no way affected the bases of a system whose artificial forms rested above all on the consent of the elites.[1]

Donald Sutherland has recently returned to the problem of the origins of this ambiguous political entity by linking it to the conditions in which they appeared. The Brumaireans, while proclaiming their desire to create a strong government, in fact presided for a long time over a weak state. Their restoration of internal order always depended on military victory. They also had to reach compromises with the popular counterrevolution as represented by the Catholic church. Whence the transformation into a personal dictatorship of a power that the authors of the coup d'état had hoped would be independent of the deputies and the nation and absolute master of administration and justice. By this account, Bonaparte's personal ambition was of secondary importance in this process. It was aimed more at posterity than at the throne. From the first, however, he was a consummate opportunist and born manipulator of the emotions of others. This skeptic made use of religion to suit his purposes; this man of the Enlightenment reintroduced arbitrary rule. He resorted to violence only when necessary. His contempt for humanity sprang as much from his gift for manipulating it as from his awareness of the immensity of his own gifts.

He sought to establish his government's authority in opposition to the factions. His first target was the Jacobins, whose measures were rescinded, while Bonaparte promised bankers order and social tranquillity. He prevented Sieyès from deporting inordinate numbers of leftists and took steps to ease the lot of relatives of émigrés. This conciliatory stance was accompanied by very strong authoritarianism, as reflected in the Constitution of the Year VIII. He retained Sieyès's idea of reducing the role of elections but opposed any restraints on the role of the executive. Named First Consul for ten years, Bonaparte became absolute master, freed of all supervision and assisted by the administrative specialists of the Council of State. The nation's reaction to this program, which was submitted to it for approval, shows the extent of the depoliticization that had occurred since 1793: There were four hundred thousand more abstentions than there had been before, and only 20 percent of the electors from Paris and Toulouse participated. To conceal this fact, the regime falsified the results by doubling the number of positive votes.

It began its work, however, by establishing harmonious relations between the executive and the legislative branches. The politicians were eager to cooperate in this reconstructive effort and sensed the need for unity in view of the dangers still facing the Republic. But the desire for stability and authority could easily give rise to the accusation of arbitrariness against a government that wanted to prove its strength. Having gone along with the antiroyalist military commissions and the deportation without trial of Jacobins, the opposition declared itself early in 1801, upon the passage of a law that set up special tribunals against brigandage. Bonaparte, who considered himself the sole representative of the nation, viewed the critical speeches by members of the Tribunate as pure subversion. He attributed their attitude to a partisan continuation of the spirit of factionalism and consequently reduced the number of authorized newspapers. Like many of his contemporaries, he had no concept of the way a liberal regime worked, nor did he view politics as the forging of enduring compromises. Following in the footsteps of the Montagnards and the directors, he had no solution for the problems of his era but to eliminate his adversaries in the name of unity. Above all he sought applause, not objections, from the legislators who were called upon to pronounce on his proposals or achievements.

In the absence of a Concordat with the church, a crisis erupted again at the end of the year with allusions to absolutism or the rejection of provisions of the Civil Code. Legislative elections soon gave Bonaparte the opportunity to get rid of his primary opponents. This done, in 1802 he was able to push through the Concordat, amnesty for émigrés (who were still under surveillance), the Legion of Honor, and soon his own appointment as consul for life, which was approved no more freely, but perhaps more enthusiastically, than the constitution. The electors were in fact paying lower taxes and above all were providing fewer conscripts than under the Directory. They had greater religious freedom, the liberty most cherished by the majority of the French. For many of them, especially in the west, the establishment of the dictatorship meant if anything a reduction in government interference.

The Constitution of the Year X, which laid out Bonaparte's new powers, gave him the authority to name his successor, as well as absolute control over the legislators and electoral colleges. Participation by the nation or its representatives in political life and decision making had become totally illusory. The Senate was well enough treated to keep its members, the new "feudal" class, docile. Bonaparte regarded any constitutional document as merely a piece of paper. He believed that the Revolution had proven that laws were subject to men and circumstances, dependent on the government and the kinds of force it had at its disposal. But his dictatorship was still not a military regime. Although it was dependent both internally and abroad on the success of the army, the military never held power. The army's personnel was not integrated into civil institutions and its leaders for a long time nurtured a Jacobin-style hostility to "tyranny." Bonaparte's declaration that he governed France not as a general but as a statesman was justified.

Although he had achieved a certain popularity in a nation that was tired of disorder, his power was based not on the approval of the people, but rather on their political apathy. Their indifference, more and more marked ever since the year II, prevented any sectors of public opinion from influencing the course of events. The return of the priests had the same effect among Catholics and royalists. The dual principle of repression and co-optation thus replaced the old forms of popular intervention and activity. This made for the most efficient government since the beginning of the Revolution.

The government scarcely needed to exercise its constitutional right to intervene in legislative matters. The purge of 1802 had been enough to put down any displays of opposition among the deputies. Bonaparte was not a usurper and his power was conferred upon him by a narrow political class which, properly speaking, represented no one, since it was self-appointed. Like the Directory and all the leaders of the Revolution since 1792, the Brumaireans were above all distrustful of the electoral system and the parliamentary regime. Thibaudeau was the only member of the Council of State to defend it, as did Lanjuinais in the Senate. Cambaceres felt that any assembly was in itself an obstacle to administration. This attitude stemmed from an awareness of the fragility of the Consulate. Its institutions had not yet taken root, and the people of the time realized how much depended on Bonaparte. In a country that had just returned to peace it might well have seemed necessary to turn over all power to a man whose talents and, eventually, brutality were well known. In proclaiming him Consul for Life, the Council of State expressed this sentiment, while vaunting the advantages of stability.[2]

These analyses perhaps neglect the personal aspects of Bonaparte's exploits, which have been studied by Harold Parker in an essay on the psychological makeup of the future dictator. His family background, which first shaped the young Napoleon, encouraged displays of aggressivity designed to impress his mother. His father, a clever pro-French schemer, introduced him to political maneuverings. Attending school in Brienne among enemies, the conquerors of his country, encouraged him to rely on himself and develop defense mechanisms that were to be useful later. It was there that he learned to control his impulses, and there that his Corsican identity was strengthened. Success in school reinforced his self-confidence and he already began to see himself as the liberator of his nation. The consolations of religion and sex did not interest him.

His aggressiveness was therefore turned toward his work, dreams, and projects. This pattern persisted at the *École militaire* in Paris. From 1785 to 1793 he led a double life. Outwardly very much the correct French officer, well regarded and even pleasant, he was at the same time, in his imagination, the author of grandiose, Rousseau-inspired plans for the liberation of Corsica. He had returned there after eight years' absence in 1786, and took up revolutionary activities three years later. But he opposed the nationalist leader Paoli, whom he had hitherto admired. His egotism and ambition brought him closer and closer to revolutionary France. The death of his adolescent dream freed him of the prejudices and sentiments that blocked the development of his personality.

His first conquest was a military one. With the help of Barras, he also married his mistress, the immoral Josephine, for whom he vowed to conquer Italy but who did not love him and was afraid of him. This disillusionment was the final blow that drove him to seek omnipotence. The Italian campaign provided him with the occasion to show off his new imperial style of command to French generals and Italian patriots. It was well suited to strong family traditions and authoritarian politics, and he used it to impose his will on others. This completed his transformation, and the public man devoured the private one. Politics increasingly subsumed his existence and turned him into a creature of pure calculation. He proved to have a genius for improvisation in this area and to be a master of strategies for the manipulation of people and groups. The Italian experience made him a national hero in France and gave him the idea of taking it over. People henceforth became for him no more than means of realizing this ambition. An astonished Madame de Staël viewed him as at once less and more than a man. He had lost all sense of humanity and become a simple chess player manipulating pawns. People became prey for his appetite for power. His desire for success, rooted in his early childhood but aggravated by difficulties, could in fact never be satisfied. The formation of his personality had also been determined by the circumstances of the Revolution. Along with the painful experiences of his childhood and adolescence, they led him to reject dreams of Corsican liberation and of sexual intimacy. All that was left to him was to pursue his career with energy and with contempt for all other human beings. His basic self-confidence, which had been instilled long before and reinforced by succeeding events, helped him to do so. Incapable of sincerely loving or being loved, he avenged himself by dominating others in work and politics. He cannot be understood apart from this psychology, which had made power and its attendant satisfactions a necessity.[3]

WAS THE ADMINISTRATIVE CENTRALIZATION
ACHIEVED BY THE REVOLUTION AND NAPOLEON
A CARRYOVER FROM THE *ANCIEN RÉGIME*?

Observing how France was brought under administrative control by
Napoleon, Louis Bergeron has explained it less as a result of his political
achievements than as a reflection of the legacy of both monarchical and
republican centralization, often carried out by the same men. The administration was headed by the prefects, who worked closely with the all-
powerful Ministry of the Interior. These administrators were the embodiment of authority within the departments. They were in charge of
maintaining order, enforcing laws handed down by the power structure,
and appointing those who were to serve it. They also were to stimulate
the economy and keep an eye on the provisions that were so closely
linked with security issues. Their communications with Paris provided
the government with valuable information about the state of affairs of
the country. However, they counted for little in comparison with the
central administration. Created in 1803, the post of entry-level civil
servants of the Council of State became their training ground.

Society was controlled, moreover, by a procedural system that had
been reorganized along revolutionary lines but with an emphasis on
repression. The establishment of a state-supervised educational system
by means of a university that had monopoly status was a step in this
direction. The Church of the Concordat was likewise supposed to aid
in the reestablishment of national unity, but obtained very mixed results.
It was in the financial realm that Napoleon was able to fashion an
effective administrative instrument based on the fiscal heritage of the
Revolution. His main concern was to increase indirect taxes on consumption. Opposed to loans, he stubbornly insisted on a metal monetary
system. But in order to solve the credit problems he had inherited, he
was forced to practice a disguised policy of issuing paper money. His
administrative rigor bureaucratized financial management without
unifying it into a cohesive whole.[1]

Following Jean Tulard, who recalled the relatively "reactionary" character of consular institutions, Michel Bruguière has recently conducted
an in-depth study of the matter in relation to the financial question. The
imprudence of the Constituent Assembly had dismantled *ancien régime*
structures just at the time when many of its agents were retiring. But a
dozen of them had survived the reforms and adapted themselves to the
new situation. The continuing presence of these experts maintained the
continuity of their administrative tradition through all the diverse re-

gimes. Their task was extremely difficult, but was facilitated by the creation of new bureaux. The management of the "mountains of paper" launched by the Revolution justified this and was the cradle of future bourgeois dynasties. It was above all the establishment of the National Treasury in the summer of 1791 that created a "hidden heart of power." Through it, the state's interests became more entangled than ever with those of private speculators. While the Treasury's officials were intimately involved in political struggles, many of their co-workers continued to work there just as they had under the *ancien régime*. It was in this sense the "twin of Loménie de Brienne's Treasury" and was the foundation of an administrative tradition that was to last until the Restoration. The Revolution, a taxpayers' revolt, had changed only the system of taxation. In all other respects, it transferred the spirit and the men of the old financial system to the *sans-culotte* Republic intact.[2]

Contrary to a myth dear to historians of Jacobinism, admirers and detractors both, the financial records of the Convention prove that it was, of necessity, heavily involved in banking and trade. Joseph Cambon, deputy from the Hérault and a leading member of the financial world of the Republic, was an important figure in the textile industry of Montpellier. State control of the economy, over which he presided, was by no means hostile to private property, which he represented well. Like Clavière and Ramel, who were also specialists in printed fabrics, he epitomized the central role of this leading industry in the Revolution. The latter did not put an end to the power of the bureaus. Starting in 1794, they were part of a Commission of National Revenues whose staff was recruited from the *ancien régime* administration. Duly provided with the requisite certificates of civic devotion (*certificats de civisme*), these traditional administrators brought to the new era the attitudes of earlier times. Besides them, specialists drawn from institutions that had been abolished far outnumbered patriots. These experienced officials were able to retain their positions under the Directory. The complex process of transferring fortunes, inaugurated under the Revolution, was thus handled, under the Republic, by bourgeois specialists who were either colonial traders or former associates of Louis XVI's *intendants*. This situation was symbolized by Barrême, the embodiment of a hereditary tradition, who was responsible for drawing up lists of émigrés. The management of nationalized lands was, moreover, often put into the hands of men from the north, the key area of external conflict since 1792. This was the region in which wheat and wood purchases were handled and which, with the conquest of Belgium, was left wide open to speculators. Their opportunistic connivings constantly hounded the Revolution in its attempts to impose a controlled economy. The Subsistence Commission, for example, was in the hands of men who were closely associated with wholesale trade. By means of its accredited official representatives, wholesale commerce also dominated foreign trade. The Maximum instituted by the Montagnards so closely resembled the *ancien régime*'s economic approach to shortages that the former cashier of one of Louis XV's major financiers became privy to all the dealings of the Committee of General Security.[3]

Their strategy was to deal with a small number of large speculators in order to circumvent the various schemes of the others. As for the National Treasury, it continued to function, undisturbed, *according to the powers granted by Louis XVI* from August 10 until 18 brumaire. Under the Convention, its position was decisively bolstered by Cambon, who gave it a free hand in the provisioning of armies and populations. On 8 thermidor, when Robespierre in all his virtuous paranoia lashed out against these transactions, he acted, as Michel Bruguière has commented, "too early or too late." The triumph of the Revolution had in fact just been ensured by the close cooperation of an administration that was independent of political vicissitudes and suppliers who had been able to hide their dealings under the guise of serving the public good.

The secrets of both remained "in the family" and have not been passed down to posterity. The Terror thus had as its controller of general accounts a man who had been involved since 1785 with the operations of the royal treasury. There are few new people within the treasury, which was shaped more by carryovers from the aristocracy than by changes brought about by democracy. The new administrators it hired confined themselves for the most part to covering up corrupt trade and supply transactions. For the majority of shady business operators, of course, escaped the guillotine thanks to the protection of bureaucrats who, within their own little domains, carried on the administrative traditions of the monarchy. From their offices, these *ancien régime* specialists easily rode the changing tides of the Terror. They had discovered the great law of public service in the France of their day, which was to set aside ideology and link "the well-being of an undying State with the preservation of their own personal safety."[4]

From Saint-Just to Sébastien Mercier, many observers have noted the all-powerful nature of this overgrown bureaucracy that remained invulnerable in the midst of upheaval. They have seen this as the main outcome of 1789. It stemmed in fact, as noted by Michel Bruguière, from a merciless war, which naturally encouraged the administrative system to return to an exaggerated form of *ancien régime* practices. When faced with a hostile Europe, France, having dismissed the state as a relic of the past, was forced to strengthen it in order to consolidate its financial bases. In this, the Revolution completed the work of the monarchy. The Convention merely passed down to the Directory the vexing question of the role of private fortunes in this system. But before the Republic, the monarchy had already been forced to negotiate a similar compromise with the moneyed classes. The unique contribution of the Revolution was the creation, by virtue of the kinds of speculation to which it had given rise, of a new kind of profiteer, who joined in the traditional division of economic power between those who had wealth and those who had political power.

Under the Directory, the government had a great deal of difficulty managing its finances. Its minister Ramel, who was on good terms with both capitalists and Thermidoreans, came from an important family in the clothing trade of the Languedoc and had become involved in maritime commerce and foreign banking. He tried to consolidate his department while retaining its original staff, and set up a general secretariat in order to concentrate technical documentation and command. Amid the various administrators, this expert, whose experience dated back to the time of Louis XV, stood out. The monetary drift and the treasury crisis were combatted with the help of the cooperation of foreign bankers and the pillage of conquered territory. In this morass, millionaire suppliers became collectors of public funds, while political operatives in the treasury crowded out the traditional technicians. The latter, however, carryovers from the *ancien régime*, were still in charge of fiscal reorganization, which was also characterized by the return of brutal tax-collecting procedures and the reestablishment of indirect taxes. The result was true bankruptcy and constant recourse to military suppliers, who dominated public finance from 1798 to 1806, particularly insofar as they paid the government bureaucracy's salaries. Bankers in credit institutions, likewise, were closely associated with the government. These speculators collected their income through local agents and made a point of liquidating past debts. In this respect, the financiers of the Directory were the direct descendants of the suppliers of year II.[5]

A similar continuity may be seen between the Directory and the Consulate from the administrative and financial points of view. Bonaparte added the intermingling of personal fortunes and public funds that was to remain the rule until the end of the Empire. Gaudin's appointment to the ministry epitomized both the return in force of men of the *ancien régime* and the necessity of accommodating both bankers and suppliers. In matters relating to the Treasury and tax collection, new institutions reflected this dual influence. This restoration returned France to many practices of the monarchy at the same time that it integrated and retained the best specialists of the revolutionary years. This represented a compromise, more political than technical, between those who served royalty and those who served the Republic. For the Consulate prolonged the financial acrobatics that it had inherited. On the other hand, it centralized the collection of direct taxes while initiating a return to the indirect taxes of the *ancien régime*. After the Revolution the French were thus paying 20 percent more in taxes under a system that retained the same directors but had a staff thirty times larger than the one established by the Constituent Assembly. Massive accounting logjams ensued, and if ever there was an area in which the principles of 1789 were reduced to meaningless words, it was certainly in the domain of public finance.[6]

During this tormented period it had remained in the hands of the same men and groups, continually adapting to institutional changes and political shifts. The bureaucracy that headed this system was henceforth less concerned with worldly triumphs than with simply perpetuating its existence by staying in the good graces of those in power. The vicissitudes of the Revolution had taught it the harsh reality that in politics the wisest course was to keep quiet and go along with the system. The French financial apparatus thus brought together elements of Louis XV's time and Napoleon's at the price of compromises that were highly profitable for those who knew how to subscribe to them. In this way the imperialism of the state apparatus achieved a stranglehold on the nation, a process that had begun under the *ancien régime*. With the passing of the old order, the tyranny of the bureaux was freed of all constraints. Although it had been able to adapt to changing political conditions, it came into full flower upon the return in 1799 of a vastly toughened version of royal centralization. With the obstacle of the monarchy and the sovereign courts out of the way, the government bureaucrats of France finally became an autonomous force. Bonaparte's rise to power signified the beginning of their golden age, that of anonymous management by the nation's officials who could now cover up their secret operations even more efficiently than before. In this respect the Revolution created an administrative authoritarianism infinitely harsher than the old one, while "most of the vices deplored before 1789 remained." Mollien partially ameliorated this situation in 1808 by instituting a system of ongoing reciprocal accounts between the treasury and the receivers general of the departments, an inspired maneuver which, had it been instituted earlier, would no doubt have saved Louis XVI's government from the treasury crisis into which it sank. Although these technical innovations gave the appearance of regularizing the system, the Revolution's financial fiasco was nonetheless total. It had paved the way for the solution of the future, which was characterized by the automatic omnipotence of the administration. Later than many contemporary states, France had made this slow march toward efficiency and coherence only through close association with the practices of international capitalism. In the last analysis, the Revolution amounted to a reconciliation among landowners, with the opportunists it had encouraged being quick to seize their share. Michael Bruguière has acknowledged the unity that sprang up between managers and profiteers in the service of a paralyzed state, that is, of national solidarity and social cohesiveness.[7]

Focusing less on these links with the *ancien régime*, historians of the English-speaking world have concentrated instead on the Revolution's creativity in the area of administration. Harold Parker and Clive Church, in particular, have focused on the period of the Directory, which marked a decisive turning point in this process. In his study of two bureaux of the Ministry of the Interior, Parker has determined the relative weight of inherited structures and structures stemming from innovations in the elaboration of official economic policy. He has done research in this area where science, industry, and administration overlapped in various ways between 1780 and 1800. Clive Church has focused on the intermingling of *ancien régime* insititutions with those of the Terror during the Thermidorean era, which he correctly identifies as the time when the foundations for Napoleonic structures were laid. His sociological analysis of the bureaucratic personnel of the Directory reveals the presence of experienced funtionaries, nearly a third of whom had already worked under the *ancien régime* and been in the administration during the Revolution. Their respectable social status had made them acceptable for government service before 1789, and their rank still corresponded to their birth. In this respect, the new ruling class was no more favorable than the old to upward mobility within the ranks. Stabilized at the top, this bureaucracy was extremely mobile at the lower levels. But it was very rare for a functionary who left one branch of the administration not to enter another. The bureaucratization brought on by the Revolution was not an end point but a point of departure. It created a national, structured professional corps that until then had had no equivalent. The exigencies of war and the Terror led to this basic transformation, which reached its definitive form under the Directory, when France saw the creation of a civil service that was truly uniform and controlled, hierarchical and qualified, salaried and impersonal. Bonaparte made judicious use of this weapon in the interest of his depoliticized state. Far from the paternalism of the *ancien régime*, a modern administration, prodded into existence by the Revolution, had consolidated with a logic of its own. It even spawned one of the most tenacious of national myths, that of the love-hate relationship of the French with their bureaucracy.[8]

Edward Whitcomb has recently reexamined the establishment of the prefectures and their personnel in Napoleon's time. This key administrative device was to be steadily improved. Thirty percent of the prefects were drawn from one of the revolutionary assemblies—indeed, the proportion at first was close to half. The number of nobles, originally a quarter of the total, later climbed to over 40 percent. Bonaparte's fusion of social strata was particularly successful here. But in terms of their professional background, the prefects were mainly drawn from the administration, followed by lawyers. Having long represented close to a third of the total, lawyers accounted for 20 percent after 1810, when those who had already been in the administration occupied twice as many positions, a development which marked a professionalization of the corps. These men in their prime had chosen a career that served as a refuge for many former politicians. Its gradual decline is no more than a myth, according to Edward Whitcomb, who, on the contrary, views the prefectoral organization as meeting Max Weber's critieria for bureaucratic excellence: experience, stability, hierarchical organization, internal promotion, and specialized training, all of which continued to increase. Napoleon's prefects, as essential element of the administrative legacy of the Revolution, confirm the importance of his contribution to institutional modernization and rationalization.[9]

In his analysis of this phenomenon, Donald Sutherland combines the two types of interpretation. He links Napoleon's attempts to centralize consular government to his desire for stricter control over local authorities. The upsurge in disturbances and the difficulties of law enforcement likewise pushed him in this direction. The creation of prefects in 1800 was substituted for the citizen participation dreamt of in 1790. The process was completed by the takeover of the municipal councils and the suspension of elections, which were replaced by consultation with handpicked prominent individuals. This was a radical departure from the whole revolutionary experience. The return of numerous nobles to administrative and diplomatic positions offered a final confirmation of this fact. These measures as a whole show how much Bonaparte valued the dual qualities of competence and social rank. We have seen how this applied in the fiscal realm, where, under Gaudin's authority, the modern bureaucracy assimilated many characteristics handed down from the *ancien régime*. This did not prevent the system from functioning correctly for the first time since the beginning of the Revolution. The organization of the Bank of France similarly mixed private interests and public service. In spite of official measures, moreover, average citizens for a long time remained untouched by the monetary system that had been set up. But at the level of administrative staffing, the new regime

had succeeded in bringing together men who had been fighting each
other since 1789. Putting aside their quarrels, they met within the Council of State where, as with the prefects, bureaucrats who had proved
their abilities under either the monarchy or the Republic were increasingly preferred to tested politicians. The victors of Brumaire sought
refuge especially in the ranks of the consular legislators. But there again,
recognized talent or social prestige were stronger credentials than a
political past, especially a Jacobin one.[10]

DID NAPOLEON'S REGIME ELIMINATE ALL OPPOSITION?

Louis Bergeron has shown that despite the apparent extinction of political life, dissent persisted. He finds it, first of all, within the government's own institutions, since liberals were present in the assemblies and
the Tribunate exploited all areas of conflict. These "ideologues" were
linked to intellectuals of the institute, the editors of *Décade*, and certain
senators. This potential conspiracy was the expression of an authentic
trend in philosophical thought, which presaged the future at the same
time that it inherited elements from the Enlightenment. But these major
cultural figures were simply unable to surmount the problems of political
organization handed down by the Revolution. In favor of progress and
the eventual advancement of the public good through the redistribution
of property, they viewed the dictatorship of the Terror as the incarnation
of the counterrevolution and therefore supported the idea of a conservative Republic. Bonaparte exploited their imprudent aspirations toward
a strong state and no one paid attention to their nostalgia for a representative regime. But the dictator was forced to get rid of these dissidents
who continued to exercise a strong intellectual influence even after they
withdrew from public life. It overlapped with that of Benjamin Constant
and Madame de Staël, who were further removed from the *philosophes*
of the eighteenth century and better able to reconcile religion and freedom. These political and social tutors of the nation and of public opinion
extolled the virtues of the parliamentary system and moral freedom
against authoritarianism and the abuse of personal power. They resolutely chose exile, internal or external.

Along with them, a whole range of plotters and conspirators was
arrayed against Napoleon. However, the absence of any serious participation in their efforts by the military deprived them of any real significance. Drawing on lessons learned in ten years of counterrevolutionary
struggles, royalists on the whole laid more ambitious plans of attacks

than republicans. Although their organizations were quickly dismantled, the west was not really secure until 1810. The apathy of the masses, meanwhile, continued to work to the advantage of the government and signaled the true end of the Revolution. This indifference, however, did not prevent a return to the forms of popular protest that sprang from economic difficulties. In 1801 as in 1811 the reappearance of subsistence problems immediately set off social conflicts. They were less widespread in the cities, which were better supplied thanks to a return to the policies of year II, than in the countryside, which was still prey to armies of drifters. Especially in the northwest, the crisis couldn't be contained by the surveillance of gangs of the unemployed, fueling a chronic, endemic state of disorder in which banditry was an option preferred to conscription. In certain regions, such as the Var as studied by Maurice Agulhon, Bonaparte inherited a country whose rural areas were ravaged by the insecurity brigandage had caused. Village revolts were echoed by military insubordination, while indirect taxation increased the unpopularity of this oppressive and repressive regime. It was propped up mainly by the public's reluctance to act and the backing of the propertied classes, both of which stemmed from a desire to have the Revolution over and done with. But the regime had no firm roots in the nation and never had the benefit of a stable power structure. Its final disintegration because of the war was already presaged in its latent rejection by the social body.[1]

Donald Sutherland, who criticizes this interpretation for granting too great a role to the opposition, nevertheless stresses France's profound disintegration upon the rise of the Consulate. It suffered all the growing pains of a fragile regime, including disobedience by local administrations and the continuation of political sabotage and brigandage, particularly in the southeast and the west. The leaders of 18 Brumaire took over a country in which the concepts of authority and order had become meaningless. Bonaparte quickly restored them against the Chouans who, as we have seen, revolted in October 1799. He then turned to disarming popular royalism by granting religious concessions. But it took him a year to gain control of the situation. His first conciliatory measures could have met with no more success than those of year III. The rural areas greeted them with joy as evidence of an imminent return to Catholicism and hence the destruction of the Republic. This was what the rural populace in many regions, rallying around the refractory priests, hoped for. As for the émigrés, their return in large numbers constituted a political risk.[2]

The Directory's victorious coalition was itself made up of divergent factions united by the need to liquidate internal and external subversion. Ever sensitive to the links between them, Bonaparte, before returning to war in 1800, first went about securing the Midi and the west. The declaration of martial law in the latter quickly put an end to the gangs of Chouans and, along with them, eight years of counterrevolutionary activity by the people. Victories over Austria and the subsequent declaration of peace had enormous consequences within France, where they put an end to Parisian intrigues against Bonaparte and heightened his stature. Troops and gendarmes were, furthermore, aided in their repressive activities by the new administrative system. Dispersed or arrested, several hundred brigands were sentenced to death by special commissions. This display of force, along with cooperation by the populace, helped restore order in the Midi.

This successful use of repression forced the government's adversaries into conspiracy and royalist organizations came close to killing Bonaparte. This assassination attempt reinforced the regime's evolution toward dictatorship by increasing its leader's authority against opponents. His associates supported him by using totally illegal methods against innocent Jacobins. The return to peace in 1802 brought a full consolidation of the prestige of Bonaparte, already the restorer of Catholicism by means of the Concordat. He did not hesitate, the following year, to enter again into war with England, a step which led to his proclaiming himself monarch. In this conflict he was helped by public opinion and the bad light he was able to cast on new conspirators who were arrested early in 1804. Their failure led to lawful assassination of the Duc d'Enghien among other measures of intimidation adopted by the regime. While the English from then on made the restoration of the Bourbons and the suppression of French conquests their main goals in the war, Bonaparte seized upon this opportunity to have himself proclaimed emperor with the general consent of his followers, who had already witnessed so many other violations of the principles of the Revolution. Carnot was the only exception. The arbitrary nature of the government was thus reinforced. Donald Sutherland is not unjustified in contrasting this lackluster conclusion to the revolutionary period with the hopes that had begun it. It created, in fact, a form of despotism that was infinitely harsher than that of the monarchy. The entire political and intellectual elite of the country participated in this perversion in the name of national stability. In so doing it ran the gravest of risks by conferring unlimited power on an irresponsible dictator in time of war.[3]

Though established by force, his regime did not rely on it to govern. The delicate problem of conscription, for example, was settled by intimidation and other measures. This was a key issue, as during the entire Revolution resistance to military service had been a powerful force joining popular royalism, brigandage, and simple disobedience. The Consulate at first used the usual coercive measures to control desertion. But it effectively combined them with the *communal system of* responsibility and diversification of demand by region. The west got off much more lightly than the east. Increased centralization and coordination, along with the execution of the Concordat, ensured greater compliance. Above all, Bonaparte's military victories allowed him to demand fewer men than his predecessors, and harmony between the state and the nation, so conspicuously lacking under the Revolution, was enchanced. The draft still did not spark enthusiasm, but under Napoleon it affected only 7 percent of the nation, or only a third of what it was to reach during World War I. It remained a problem for the empire in the mountainous regions, but the Midi and the west accepted it with much less resistance than before 1799, at least until the final defeats. The new government owned this success to the geographic and social inequities of its policies. Five to 10 percent of the conscripts bought substitutes at an extremely high price. This discriminatory policy was echoed by a tax system that hit consumers and poor people the hardest. In this respect the empire exacerbated the Directory's policies favoring indirect taxes. This made it unpopular but brought it favors from landowners, if not economic success. In any case, Napoleon was able to put down disturbances by judiciously manipulating his gendarmes, prefects, and priests.[4]

The guiding principles of his government were thus repression, the consolidation of the elites, the bureaucratization of the administration, the granting of favors to friends and the rich, the creation of hierachies within institutions and the militarization of the young. The increasing exigencies of the war made the regime more dictatorial. It was no longer in any way representative and all means of expressing opposition were suppressed. Along with manipulation of opinion came internment without trial. The 640 detainees of 1814, half of whom were political prisoners, were far more numerous than the victims of *lettres de cachet* (arbitrary warrants of imprisonment) in 1789. Donald Sutherland, who points this out, does not think that opposition to Napoleon, whether Catholic, royalist, popular, or military increased much under his reign. He survived his 1809 break with the pope very well. French Catholics remained for the most part loyal, whether out of fear or gratitude. The royalists, who had never disappeared, set up new clandestine organizations that posed little danger to the regime. The members of the *Petite Église*, which opposed the Concordat, were no more threatening in spite of the bravery of the religious leaders who directed it. They were often supported by public sentiment, with its taste for prophecy, but this well-established but scattered assemblage of poor people and women did not constitute a real danger. There remained then only the military, who

with Malet concocted the best-known of the conspiracies against Napoleon in 1812. The latter illustrates both the ideological inconsistency
of the opposition and the basic fragility of the regime. In terms of political
intelligence, the dictatorship had instilled even in its own bureaucracy
nothing but credulity and passive obedience.[5]

10. A NEW SOCIETY?

T*he Marxist myth that calls the Revolution of 1789 a decisive stage in the development of the capitalist economy and industrial society is easily belied by the stagnation of the French economy as a whole during the revolutionary period and beyond, as well as by the reconstitution under Bonaparte of a social hierarchy based on the landed power of the elite. While the acknowledgment of these characteristics is almost unanimous, the same cannot be said of historians' assessments of the damage done to the French economy by the Revolution. Those who speak of a "national catastrophe" in this domain are challenged by judgments that are more qualified, if not more positive.*

DID THE REVOLUTION RUIN THE FRENCH ECONOMY?

Most analyses agree with Alfred Cobban's conclusion that the events of the Revolution resulted in a decline in the economy.[1] Economists are not the last to say so. Among them, Florin Aftalion has recently warned against the "destructive cycle" leading from the crisis to the Terror by way of inflation and nationalizations. He views this process, tested in 1789, as the model for totalitarian regimes.[2] As for René Sédillot, his recent account of the ways various sectors of the French economy were affected by the Revolution emphasizes in turn the blocking of agricultural advances, the fragility of industrialization, the destruction of foreign trade, and an overall inferiority to England.[3] We are indebted to François Crouzet for the most thorough study of this interpretation.[4]

In 1962 he analyzed a memorandum written in 1802 by Francis d'Ivernois, a Genevan émigré in London, on the economic consequences of the Revolution from a counterrevolutionary perspective. This observer had already painted a negative picture of the results of the events of 1789. The attacks on large landholdings had led to the impoverishment of the country and, in particular, agricultural ruin. The crisis in industry, likewise hastened by inflation and confiscations, had been the result. Bonaparte had thus inherited a country that was drained, doomed to stagnation and deficits. It is clear that D'Ivernois had no understanding of the financial comeback realized under the Consulate. On the other hand, he only partially overstated the evidence of industrial stagnation, while underestimating the possibilities for recovery. Increases in prime costs and the shortage of capital constituted major obstacles to development, as did the loss of numerous foreign markets. But the productive capacities of the country remained untapped and often unused. Far from a factor in modernization, the Revolution had blocked growth for a generation by disorganizing the economy.[5]

In later studies François Crouzet showed that, on the contrary, it was England, at war with France and mistress of the sea and world trade, that developed a decisive industrial superiority over the continent during this period. More perspicacious than their rivals, its statesmen had a better grasp of the interests of their country. This phenomenon was all the more remarkable in that France's growth on the eve of the Revolution was comparable to England's. It was only the economic catastrophes that began in 1789 that made the gap between France and its rival irremediable. This judgment seems confirmed by the anti-industrial ideology of many of the counterrevolutionaries who returned to power after the storm had passed. They fought the rise of machines as much as the bureaucratic centralization of the modern state.[6]

The Revolution's economic failure seems strange when one thinks of the sudden enthusiasm for publications dealing with political economy that arose as of the 1750s. One explanation is to be found in the many longstanding obstacles to agricultural development in France. Emmanuel Le Roy Ladurie has recalled that two contrasting models were available in 1789. Rather than an English-style solution, characterized by an alliance of large landowners and farmers at the expense of small farmers and family farms, the Revolution at least momentarily opted for an alliance of farmers and peasants working small plots of land against the seigniorial regime and its vestiges. This was hardly favorable, to say the least, to advances in the rural economy.[7]

Large-scale maritime commerce, though superficial and peripheral, was the leading sector of the French economy in this period. The key to foreign trade, not without internal repercussions, particularly in the industrial areas, it remained tightly linked to the slave trade and the colonial system that were sorely tested by the Revolution and the wars it led to. This activity of the Atlantic ports, which was typical of the *ancien régime* and reached its apogee just before 1792, influenced the economic deliberations of the Constituent Assembly. The English-style liberalism of this assembly, moreover, was tested by its inability to solve the problem of poverty.[8]

These various considerations lead us to conclude, along with Jean-Claude Perrot, that the economic history of the period remains to be written. It was characterized by contrasting events and contradictory strategies. Geographically it was equally dispersed and varied. Transfers of capital and income reveal a return to archaic practices and weaknesses of trade. The dislocation of wealth by inflationary processes prevented capitalist growth in France, weakened competition, and increased the tax burden. In terms of the division of labor, on the other hand, economic modernization and individualism progressed. Competition was bolstered by this before suffering major setbacks from the effects of the war. In terms of advances in labor practices, the Revolution was a failure, with the exception of those rare individuals who promoted a technically oriented philosophy. In the name of administrative efficiency, however, it brought the country into the era of statistical knowledge.[9]

Far from these original views, Albert Soboul has maintained a traditional vision of economic development under the Revolution, according to which the Constituent Assembly's liberalism, which unified the national market and destroyed feudalism, favored agrarian individualism while unleashing inflation. The war and its aftermath pushed the right to exist and the controlled economy to the forefront, but the return in force of liberalism after thermidor set off a monetary catastrophe, an economic crisis, stagnation, and depression, which were to end only gradually in the period of the Consulate. Reacting against this interpretation, which was scarcely more optimistic than that of the "detractors" of the Revolution, Hubert Bonin maintains that the spirit of enterprise survived this upheaval and that nascent industry was not stifled. The birth of new industry was at first associated with the revolutionary process, even though the latter eventually turned against the entrepreneurs. Their recovery under the Directory was very slow, and the Revolution might seem at first glance to have undermined the capitalist spirit in favor of a land-based economy. This was not so, however, for the bourgeoisie of the business world was able to hang on to its power and resume its activities. The dynamism of the newly rich brought new vitality to banking, as Bergeron has demonstrated, and metallurgy, according to recent studies by Woronoff. This liberal capitalism was better equipped than before 1789 to adapt to the changes and reconversions brought about by the war. It led to an industrial resurgence fueled by an enormous military market and increased consumption among the upper levels of society. Their luxurious tastes stimulated an upswing in production and a renewed trend to mechanization under the Directory, particularly in the textile industry. This mobilization of energies was symbolized by the National Exposition in Paris organized in 1798 by François de Neufchâteau, the remarkable Minister of the Interior.

Despite the upheavals, traumas, and reversals brought about by the Revolution, it did not throw any lasting roadblocks in the way of an upsurge in French industry that brought it to a level that was 50 percent higher in 1810 than in 1789. The new opportunities for money making spawned by the war and bourgeois wealth had stimulated the spirit of enterprise.[10]

It remains to be seen, obviously, whether historians of the French economy between 1799 and 1815 share this optimistic view. In 1792 Louis Bergeron did not. Observing that the elimination of the orders had changed neither the social equilibrium nor traditional values, he accounted for this by the slow pace of economic transformations. Entrepreneurial dynamism seemed to him to be blocked not only by unfavorable circumstances but also by a set of attitudes toward consumption, education, and society. Disinclined to innovation, postrevolutionary France was, according to this interpretation, in a period of agricultural stagnation, unbalanced foreign trade, and an incomplete technical transformation. Juxtaposed with an immobile *ancien régime* agrarian system were ports that were suddenly suffocating after a century of expansion and an industrial system in which several leading sectors enjoyed a "brilliant but localized success" without pulling up the rest. This assessment stemmed from the difficulty of evaluating the Revolution's effects on the rural economy. Farming was not improved and attitudes remained unchanged. They were still characterized by greed for land and the spread of agricultural self-sufficiency. Advances in agronomy were either nonexistent or well below official exaggerations, and new crops did nothing to transform the traditional system. Along with the indisputable breakdown of large-scale maritime trade, there were, no doubt, the beginnings of industrialization. This was a novel phenomenon in that it grew out of new conditions in the makeup of the Continental market. It was characterized by the mechanization of the cotton industry, which sprang up largely spontaneously under the Directory. It also affected the chemical industry, following a largely prerevolutionary impetus. Tradition had a stronger hold in the metal industry. At the deepest level, the Revolution above all disturbed the geographic equilibrium of the French economy, turning it inward, toward its land borders and away from the sea and the English model. The beneficiaries of this change were the capitalists of Paris, quickly followed by those of Lyons and Strasbourg. Existing imbalances were thus accentuated, especially on an industrial level, between the north as supplier and the Midi as consumer less adapted to change.[11]

More recent studies have added little to this picture. Like Louis Bergeron, Jean Tulard sees as many elements of stagnation as of progress in the economy under Napoleon. Albert Soboul writes more optimistically of a recovery aided by monetary and banking reorganization and wartime mercantilism. He perceives the postrevolutionary movement of prices and profits as signs of a favorable turn. He acknowledges at most the unevenness of this prosperity and growth among the sectors, with industry having gained more, in his view, than agriculture or, especially, maritime commerce. Large-scale Continental trade, on the other hand, showed an indisputable upsurge. Donald Sutherland has recently confirmed this relative prosperity, particularly among sellers of agricultural products and large landowners. But he notes that this progress did nothing to boost the level of productivity, which still lagged well behind that of England. Far from reinvesting their gains, landowners did nothing to improve their properties. The eradication of feudalism did not lead to rural capitalism. The war economy and technical innovations even brought about a grave structural crisis that led to the deindustrialization of the countryside in the north and west. In the cities, the traditional textile industry also suffered, while the cotton industry operated in artificial and unhealthy conditions, marked by speculation and undercapitalization. The return to peace was a catastrophe for it. Parisian businesses remained on an artisanal scale, and their resurgence was due, above all, to government support. A similar situation prevailed in the provinces, and the marked upsurge in productivity had little effect on the lot of the workers, while conditions for rural artisans and the majority of peasants deteriorated even further. The unstable equilibrium between insufficient resources and a growing population changed little, for rather than solving agrarian problems, the Revolution accelerated France's historical tendency toward the bourgeois takeover of land. City dwellers increasingly monopolized the large farms while peasants worked small lots, and because of persistent demographic pressures poverty was as debilitating for the majority of the French in 1815 as it had been in 1789, if not more so.[12]

DID THE FRENCH REVOLUTION
RESULT IN A RENEWAL OF THE ELITES?

In 1964 Alfred Cobban observed that the new ruling class that emerged from the revolutionary upheavals was above all composed of large land-owners. With its contingent of former nobles, this group had no con-nection with the Marxist myth of the industrial bourgeoisie's rise to power. Its predominance under Napoleon confirmed, rather, that after much buffeting about, the landed elite that had launched the Revolution was finally profiting from it. The integration of the old aristocracy into the new one completed the process by which the French establishment took on the rural conservative tinge it was to retain throughout the entire nineteenth century.[1]

This view of the social outcome of the Revolution has been confirmed by recent research. It indicates, as in the case of Toulouse as studied by Jean Sentou, the preponderance of landed wealth throughout the whole period. The aristocrats' fortunes, though diminished, continued to dom-inate society in 1799. The various sectors of the bourgeoisie undoubtedly became richer, for they benefited massively from the sale of nationalized lands. But the nobles benefited eight times as much as the popular classes, and by confining all their investments to land the bourgeoisie confirmed its attachment to the *ancien régime* way of life.[2]

Under Napoleon, the Revolution finally acquired the landowning elite it had always wanted. It was not so much that high society became bourgeois, but rather that the upper strata of the bourgeoisie became the new aristocracy. In this triumph of the landowning class lies the social significance of the Revolution. The nobles' property in the west, in central France, and in the Midi was almost totally restored. In a very large number of departments, former aristocrats headed the list of the wealthiest taxpayers. Business capitalism in the Rhône valley and the Paris region played a negligible role in comparison with that of the former high nobility, which still had a monopoly on the largest land fortunes and therefore on wealth in general. The social clash between "feudalism" and the bourgeoisie under the Revolution is mythical. Dur-ing the entire period, the former nobility flocked to the civil and military careers open to them by countless paths. They laid the foundation for the integration achieved by Napoleon and ensured the consolidation of the aristocracy's position in the modernized state and future capitalism.[3]

In addition, the bourgeoisie made incontestable gains in France during this period. But after its initial break with the nobility, the bourgeoisie sought only to retain the economic, professional, and mental structures of the *ancien régime*. Its pursuit of upward mobility continued to be guided by its desire to be identified with the aristocracy. The model it imposed in the aftermath of the Revolution resembled the one so dear to the royal officeholders of the seventeenth century. In charge of a public service whose upper echelons were reserved for the elite, this ruling class saw matters from the perspective of landed wealth. In Marseille it easily slid into ennoblement and the aristocratic way of life. Among the French bourgeoisie, the true victors in the Revolution were those who were able to use it to increase their ground rents. The key word to arise from the upheavals that began in 1789 was "property owner" *(propriétaire)*, which applied to a large number of social and professional circumstances and became almost synonymous with entry into the new Establishment. Associated with the status of *rentier* and city dweller, it completed the transformation of postrevolutionary society into one in which the masters of city life were at the same time masters of the land worked by the peasants. They of course reinvested a part of their income in credit, so that the landed basis of their fortunes did not mean that their capital was frozen. But economic development and the modernization of the country were clearly not their primary concerns.[4]

Jean Nicolas has uncovered such a preponderance of landed wealth at the core of the new elite of Savoy, which was at that point temporarily part of France. Less than 10 percent of the nobles owned over 20 percent of the value of all property, and their political and material restoration was particularly noteworthy. This group played a key role among the prominent figures who came to power in the society that grew out of the Revolution. The state aristocracy Napoleon sought to create with his imperial nobility in no way changed this situation. Albert Soboul, while pointing out the setbacks suffered by the feudal aristocracy and the renewal of the bourgeoisie after 1789, has acknowledged the continued presence of the old nobility at the head of an establishment not totally molded by the bourgeoisie. The social structure of France at the beginning of the nineteenth century was thus not much different from what it had been before 1789. The Revolution merely added to the traditional aristocracy and bourgeoisie a newly enriched class derived from trade and manufacturing that was easily integrated into the world of social prominence in which all the elites were soon joined. Income-producing property and a government position were more important there than mercantile or industrial capitalism.[5]

The importance of the great noble estates was not precisely the same at the end of the Revolution as it had been at the beginning. The social power of these landholdings was to come under constant challenge from new forces appearing in the countryside. But the speed with which the

aristocracy recovered after the revolutionary turmoil was striking. Diminished, impoverished, and stripped of some of its stature, it was not
totally broken and was able to recover itself. Reconsolidated, its fortune
restored, it dominated the world of the local establishment of Franche-
Comté by 1808. Just as the Revolution did not originate in a class
struggle, neither did it end with the overthrow of one class by the other.
It concluded, rather, where it could have begun, with the establishment
of a compromise within the ranks of the elite.[6]

The French Revolution heightened inequities. Sebastien Mercier demonstrated at the time of the Directory that the new society bore little
resemblance to eighteenth-century utopias. The system teemed with nouveaux riches. The Parisian journalist was struck by the continuity of a
country in which the reign of privilege was simply replaced by the reign
of money. Only the names had changed, and social reality continued to
make popular sovereignty a mere chimera. From the perspective of the
hopes of the *philosophes*, the Revolution had done little to change the
state of affairs that had prevailed under the *ancien régime*. The division
between the men and women of the people and those of respectable
society was to persist throughout nearly the entire nineteenth century.[7]

Louis Trénard has studied one of the prominent men who survived
the Revolution and emerged more powerful than before. Pierre-
Toussaint Dechazelle was a silk designer from a wealthy family that had
originally come from Saint-Étienne. His flourishing business had pro-
cured for him the comfortable life available to certain people at the end
of the *ancien régime*. He had become caught up in the irrationalist vogue.
Compromised with the insurgents of 1793, this *grand bourgeois* owner
of extensive properties was hard hit by the Terror. Opposed to the
Republic, he returned, like de Maistre, to religion and resumed his activities with the help of the economic and technical resurgence. Encouraging innovations, he oversaw the reorganization of his factory and
recruited local talents to this fusion of art and industry. Early retirement
allowed him to see to the management of his property and write. Dead
at the age of eighty-two in 1833, this man of culture and mysticism was
the perfect embodiment of Lyons's ruling circles from Louis XV to the
July monarchy. For him as for them, the Revolution had been nothing
more than a painful and pointless interlude.[8]

Adrien Duquesnoy of Lorraine was thirty years old in 1789. The son
of a lower-level royal officeholder, he was an active member of the Third
Estate in the Constituent Assembly. Hostile to Rousseauian abstraction
and concerned with practical organization, he had opposed the radicalization of the Revolution despite his decided anticlericalism. Elected
mayor of Nancy in 1792 and then imprisoned by the Jacobins, he reap-

peared under the Directory in François de Neufchâteau's entourage. Under the Consulate he continued to work with the Ministry of the Interior in Chaptal's time. With his interest in economic development and social order, statistics and progress, utility and practical research, this man of immense culture and vast curiosity was greatly appreciated by the Bonapartes. He retired to Rouen, where he committed suicide in 1808 because of his cotton factory's financial difficulties. His personal ideological evolution had followed the typical path of revolutionary administrators who were more and more aware of the role of the state in building the nation. For them, knowledge, competence, authority, the importance of informed opinion as it reflected the social elite and the help that elite could give the government had become key concepts. In 1802 Duquesnoy complained about the inferior quality of the new general councils as compared with the provincial assemblies of 1788. In the eyes of this eminent technocrat, a destructive revolution had reduced the level of civic responsibility in the nation. Nostalgic for the regrouping of talents that had marked the final days of the *ancien régime*, in contrast with the situation in 1789, he saw the state as France's only hope. He ended his political career in sorrow over the split that had arisen between it and the provincial elite.[9]

It was at this point that Napoleon tried to erect some "blocks of granite" on the soil of a country that had been crushed by the Revolution. Like him, the Brumaireans had abandoned the liberal tendencies they had displayed at the time of the Constituent Assembly and embraced the new primacy of order and hierarchy. They wound up establishing the tyranny of wealth united with the celebration of military virtues. The bureaucratic edifice of this absolutism, more arbitrary than the monarchy's, could be destroyed only by foreign invasion. The Revolution led to the creation of a militarized society, as evidenced in 1802 by the establishment of the Legion of Honor, which was closer in spirit to the orders of the *ancien régime* than to the preceding awards for civic merit. The creation of an imperial nobility symbolized this rebirth of the aristocratic ideal according to which status determined fortune. This system of distributing bounty was limited, moreover, to increasing the wealth already amassed illicitly by the generals at the end of the revolutionary period. Thanks to the army, the Revolution had thus culminated in the rise to the top of the social elite of a handful of men who came from the lower or middle levels of the bourgeoisie. The military model was even extended to the molding of future generations by the *lycée* system.[10]

The socially prominent, favored at last by the upheavals, involved themselves once more, as we have seen, in landholdings and administration rather than industry and commerce. Reinforcing Louis Bergeron's conclusions, Donald Sutherland stresses the very limited scope of the renewal of the elite in this period. Few newcomers appeared and the positions of most of the formerly dominant were unaffected. In some cases the upper echelons of society may have suffered something of an economic setback by comparison to 1789. The wealthy business bourgeoisie of the Var region was less numerous in 1801 than it had been at the beginning of the Revolution. In the devastated ports of the west, merchant families went back to the land, which sometimes provided lucrative investment possibilities and which was still, as it had been during the *ancien régime*, the economic definition of the French elite. The old nobility remained as much a part of this elite after the Revolution as it had been before. This class ultimately suffered relatively little from the Revolution, having pursued a prudent course of noncommitment, like the vast majority of the population. Although this process of social restoration varied according to region, the Napoleonic era allowed the former aristocracy, which had been steadily declining since the seventeenth century, to recoup its losses. Despite the strengthened position of its rivals, it clung to the dominant positions at the top of the social scale for a long time. Of all the classes, it remained the wealthiest, after the Revolution as well as before. Although deprived of its fiscal privileges and professional monopolies, it maintained a level of influence within the ruling group well beyond its numerical strength. Its prominent members as a group did not govern the country like their counterparts in the English-speaking world. The withering of representative institutions prevented them from doing so. They served, rather, as a pool of talent for the government apparatus, dominating public life in part by virtue of their close links with government officials. In several regions virtual local dynasties that were to last for over a century were created thanks to the Revolution. The Revolution had created a ruling class made up of a combination of most of the former nobles, with a few new bourgeois elements. Inveterate counterrevolutionaries did not join, and the social advancement permitted by this process remained limited to a narrow elite. The increasing professionalization of the administrative bureaucracy accentuated the tendency to bar the great masses of the population from any true upward mobility.[11]

Historians all agree on the increasingly bourgeois but static character of the society handed down by a revolution that kept the French bound to the land. Modern capitalism had by no means triumphed against the great families of the *ancien régime* and traditional landowners. These lethargic propertied classes proceeded in some cases, as in the west, to deindustrialize their investments. The restored power of the bourgeoisie, along with economic liberalism, no doubt bolstered the confidence of entrepreneurs, bankers, and wholesalers. Fully rehabilitated (as though they needed to be) they returned to business as usual after the revolutionary interlude. Having observed without entering into a political upheaval that left them either angry or indifferent, they emerged from their hibernation with renewed zest for investing, with their capital intact, and in the company of the newly rich. But these future captains of the nation's industry were still far from setting the tone of the ruling class.[12]

DID THE FRENCH REVOLUTION CHANGE
THE CONDITION OF THE POPULAR CLASSES?

Was the world of the peasants, by far the majority in France during the Revolution, significantly affected by it? Ginguené, chief editor of *La Feuille villageoise*, was perhaps a bit hasty when in 1795 he proclaimed its overall enrichment. He was, in any case, expressing an ideal that was in vogue when he hoped that rural areas would remain unchanged, sheltered from the dangerous influences of the city and its vices. This commonplace was in tune with a social reality that remained extremely conservative amid political upheavals. It is difficult to claim that the changes occurring at that time in the countryside contributed to the capitalist modernization of the country. Peasants remained deeply rooted in their home regions. In 1800 in the Vendômois region two thirds of the men were in the same line of work as their fathers, and three quarters of them married within the same milieu, while nine out of every ten women married in the district of their birth and 70 percent of them lived no more than ten kilometers from their birthplace. This stability was epitomized in Artois by the fact that the *fermiers*, former seignorial agents, enjoyed continuing power in the villages throughout the Revolution. The new elections confirmed rather than weakened their position, and their reign, momentarily shaken under the Terror, reclaimed all its hegemony long after Thermidor. It sprang from the economic and familial strength and from the contacts of the large farmers whose dominance over the communities lasted from the *ancien régime* until the nineteenth century, largely unaffected by the Revolution.[1]

Maurice Agulhon does not attribute any new distribution of land to the Revolution. The richest peasants had been able to participate in the transfer of property among the wealthy classes, but the access others gained to a tiny bit of land, far from bringing them independence, had merely exacerbated the breaking up of property that was one of the basic problems of the rural world. Provence exemplifies the situation of two-tiered agrarian society. Doomed to dependency or reliance on make-shift resources, poor peasants clashed with farmers who were relatively well off in that they were economically autonomous and never dependent on wages. These rifts among the peasantry have been acknowledged by Albert Soboul. While the Revolution may have improved the overall lot of the rural populace, it had not offered the majority of them a solution to the agrarian problem by providing them with a way to live off their land. The Revolution's exacerbation of inequality in the countryside, according to this interpretation, powerfully accelerated the distintegration of the traditional community. The paths of large and small farmers and day laborers diverged increasingly. This analysis leads to the division of the peasant masses into three groups: small and medium-size independent producers; owners of small lots who were self-sufficient but often in debt; and those who were, or were becoming, wage earners. The conflict of interests among them was obvious and the Revolution generally favored the first group, all the while keeping up many communal practices but rejecting the egalitarian distribution of land. Given the dominance of the rural establishment, the contradictions in the existence of the divided peasantry increased, and for the majority of its members conditions deteriorated and economic conservatism became more entrenched. It was difficult to reach a compromise between, on the one hand, the new principle of freedom of cultivation that was dear to the hearts of landowners, and, on the other, guaranteeing the continuation of collective rights for the poor.[2]

During the Revolution, the "republic in the village" of the Southern Massif Central, as studied by Peter Jones, did not put an end to divisions inherited from the past. The politicization of the countryside often amounted simply to the translation of old quarrels into the terminology of modern factions. Isolated in the midst of the hostile masses, Jacobin militants were identified there with the intrusive bureaucratic ideology of an already dominant rural bourgeoisie. The veneer of revolutionary rhetoric hid bitter private struggles for local power, rooted in the customs of the *ancien régime*. The era of the Terror was a time when procedure-bound and greedy lawyers seized control of rural communities or consolidated their grip on them. Both before and after 1789, the use of nationalized lands in this region remained the major business and principal source of conflicts. These sometimes were extensions of old quarrels that dated back to well before the Revolution and were revived by it. Within a traditional society marked by structures of patronage, the ideal of citizens choosing freely among various principles was an absurdity. In communities divided between Catholics and Protestants, their antagonisms simply turned this era into the latest episode in the religious wars.

The words "monarchists" and "republicans" were empty, as reality still lay in old clan divisions to which militants affixed the labels of the day. After Thermidor their conflict revealed itself more openly as a bitter struggle for power. The opposing sides were divided less by their ideologies than by traditions rooted in their sociological and geographical situations. These colored the coteries, cliques, and cabals that marked the Directory's elections in this area in ways that had nothing to do with its hypothetical political modernization. Jacobins and royalists in the rural areas perpetuated existing tensions that had been exacerbated by the decentralization of the administrative and justice systems. Through the activities of minorities linked to some degree with Paris, authentic peasant reactions took precedence over revolutionary sloganeering.[3]

The problem of poverty was, as we know, the major social issue on the eve of the Revolution. It was inevitable that poverty should have accompanied the Revolution throughout its history. Its incidence among urban workers has been the most accessible to study. Daniel Roche has disputed its spread among the common people of Paris in the eighteenth century. It does not appear that the lot of groups such as apprentices and domestics improved with the passing of the *ancien régime*. The more general question is how the French Revolution dealt with the poverty it inherited.[4]

In his study of Bayeux, Olwen Hufton has done a detailed analysis of the third of the population that lived off Christian charity and was hard hit by the church's crisis under the Revolution. Their lot having deteriorated and their numbers having swelled at the very moment when their benefactor was destroyed, these people were the great victims of the Revolution. In 1795 a mob in this town in Normandy threw down a bust of Jean-Jacques Rousseau jeering "Down with you, whore! When God was here, we had bread." Olwen Hufton has since broadened the scope of his investigation to cover the immense mass of poor people who already existed under the *ancien régime* but whose numbers would be increased by the Revolution and its aftermath. She has shown that they were not a marginal phenomenon, but an integral part of a society marked by fear of shortages and vulnerability to crises. The ways they found to survive were in themselves a significant branch of the economy of the time.[5]

What became of them during the revolutionary period? The increase in poverty seems to have been a significant phenomenon, especially in the cities. Alan Forrest has provided a gripping description of the situation in Bordeaux. The incidence of begging and vagrancy far exceeded the meager resources of charitable agencies in this city that was hit head-on by economic difficulties. Women and workers in the poor neighborhoods were increasingly doomed to prostitution and indigence, which the activities of revolutionary militants were unable to curb. As men of the Enlightenment, they no doubt tried in good conscience to root out beggars. But in destroying the feudal system and the church, they had eradicated the only available means of assistance in French society. War further eroded the financial resources available for helping the poor while aggravating the difficulties of the working classes. Famine loomed in 1793, in Bordeaux and elsewhere, and it did nothing to bring the poor around to the cause of the Revolution.[6]

Alan Forrest has recently done a study reexamining the Revolution's policies on this problem. They grew out of the idea of social obligation that was central to elite thought in the eighteenth century, according to which the fight against poverty became a duty of humanity and a responsibility of the state. This program, very imperfectly applied by the *ancien régime*, was handed down to the Revolution. The Constituent Assembly's Committee on Begging attempted to set forth the methods and conditions of an aid policy. The succeeding period saw the total breakdown of public assistance systems, which had been turned over to the lay population, shattered by the turn of events, and fruitlessly centralized by the Jacobins. Their Thermidorean successors aggravated the situation by abandoning all true assistance to the poor, whose needs took second place to the exigencies of war. Public charity and household assistance could not check a general state of indigence that was exacerbated by unemployment and economic difficulties. In sharp contrast with the lofty words of the deputies, the victims of poverty were piled into dirty, punitive warehouses. At the beginning of the Revolution there had been an attempt to create jobs and set up public workshops. But these ambitious projects never got beyond the planning stage. The abandonment of children, often illegitimate, continued to plague the big cities, and the poor were unwilling to join a revolutionary army that was not going to alleviate their financial problems. They often chose to desert. This disheartening picture, in which impressive legislative gains contrasted with total disaster on the level of concrete reality, scarcely does honor to the French Revolution's social conscience. If its bureaucratic ambitions in this area were undeveloped, the resources it devoted to their realization were pitiful.[7]

Albert Soboul has observed this deterioration in the living conditions of urban populations after 1789 and followed the upsurge of indigence up to the Napoleonic era, which by no means put an end to it. As under the *ancien régime*, a third of the residents of the working-class neighborhoods of Paris depended on help from charitable agencies. The wretched fate of large numbers of wage earners was exacerbated by their subordination and their inferior legal status as well as by their very difficult work conditions, which remained inhuman for women and children. The material existence of the majority of the French, especially in the cities, continued to be precarious and fragile.[8]

Any other outcome of the period is no doubt inconceivable, but according to Louis Bergeron, "wage earners were the big losers in the French society of the early nineteenth century." Antiworker repression by employers and the police, backed by the law, increased. The surveillance and containment of the popular classes were more than ever the bases of political and social order. As for the workers' movement, its organization, methods of struggle, objectives, and mentality could at best be only a reprise of what they had been under the *ancien régime*. Within an immobile, plutocratic society, obsessed by equilibrium and resistant to change, the masses still constituted a France apart. They remained hounded by poverty, weighed down by inequality and dependency, and hostile to modernity. Their apparent enduring calm, at the end of such a storm, was no doubt as illusory as the unfulfilled promises of the Revolution.[9]

11. A CULTURAL
REVOLUTION?

For a long time it was customary to contrast the political and social *disruptions brought about by the Revolution with the cultural and religious continuity that characterized France during this period. This perspective has recently undergone a profound reevaluation. Greater emphasis is being placed on the changes in mentality that occurred at the time. Is it clear, however, that the Revolution succeeded in de-Christianizing France, in disrupting traditional ideas of the family and of moral order, or in creating a new man?*[1]

DID THE REVOLUTION DE-CHRISTIANIZE FRANCE?

Jean de Viguerie concludes that it did, in a penetrating study that demonstrates the efficacy of the Revolution's persecution of the church. According to this interpretation, in 1799 there remained only a few isolated pockets of religious practice, precarious refuges for the faithful. A significant proportion of the population had given up regular observance. In certain regions of northwest and central France, the number of Easter communicants was a third lower than it had been in 1789. Working on Sunday became customary, and churches, once reopened, were often deserted. In 1808 Lamennais proclaimed the breakdown of religion. Does this evidence justify "crediting" the Revolution with having succeeded in its de-Christianizing effort? Jean de Viguerie views the various stages of the religious history of the Revolution as the embodiment of a campaign to separate the faithful from the priests and keep them from turning to the sacraments. He sees in this campaign a coherent and efficient system of persecution.[2]

This interpretation understates Catholic resistance to the Revolution as expressed in revolts against antireligious measures, clandestine efforts by the church and its ministers, and the administering of sacraments. The proportion of unbaptized children was thus tiny, and extraordinarily ingenious efforts were made to celebrate mass in spite of circumstances. Lay people often took the place of the clergy in performing certain functions and their efforts show their attachment to Sunday meetings and a deep feeling for the church. The resistance of nuns and the sacrifice of priests, several thousand of whom were put to death for refusing to take an oath against their conscience, complete the picture. It confirms the spiritual power of a French Catholicism that answered its executioners with prayers and devoutness. It seems unfair to view the heroism of its martyrs as a purely peripheral phenomenon, since it was a manifestation of the massive rejection of the government's antireligious policies by the majority of the population. It was this collective attitude that led to the reestablishment of the church and the return of faith.[3]

To attribute large-scale success to de-Christianization is to overstate its effects. This bourgeois enterprise had scant support among the common people. Changes in the image of Jesus in eighteenth-century France gives evidence of the persistence of a religious vision of politics from the *ancien régime* to the Revolution. Imbued with the spirit of the Enlightenment, Christians were often receptive to the upheavals of 1789. Fauchet seized upon this occasion to recall that it was the aristocracy that had crucified the Son of God. Followers of the constitutional and retractory churches claimed allegiance to the same faith, and the Jacobins made a point of associating themselves with the principle of evangelical equality. Among the *sans-culottes*, devotion to Marat did not erase fidelity to the prophet from Nazareth. After Thermidor, respect for this divine lawgiver grew to such an extent that he was proposed as a model for all regimes. Although Chateaubriand was to epitomize this movement toward reconciliation, the patriarchal society of the late eighteenth century described by Restif de la Bretonne had already proclaimed Bible-reading the great initiation into life. Something of this spirit remained during a revolution characterized less by the success of de-Christianization than by the resurgence of millennialism and the propagation of moral teachings derived from the Scriptures. The rediscovery of the spirit of faith in the Western world constitutes one of the great achievements of the period.[4]

This point is missed if the church is viewed simply as an ideological organ of the state. Louis Trénard has shown how deeply the cultivated bourgeoisie of Lyons in 1789 was moved by a powerful upsurge of mystical religiosity avid for regeneration. Proclaiming the coming of the apocalypse that was to follow, Ballanche and Ampère adhered to a providentialist interpretation of events after failure and disappointment. Faith in the Revolution was replaced, in these circles, by faith in the counterrevolution. This new consciousness favored a reawakening of Catholicism, and the future ideology of the Restoration might be defined as the revenge of faith against Reason. The refractory church demonstrated this by proving itself often more adept at modern political maneuvering than the monarchy of the *ancien régime*. The spearhead of the counterrevolution was not royalty and its illusions, but Christianity and its truths. Its most authentic followers were championing not tradition, but eternity. Hence the key role, among French intellectuals in 1800, of the collective conversion movement, through which the reborn new man responded to the instability brought on by the Revolution. Just as this movement had sprung from a childish revolt against the teachings of the priests, the reaction that ended it was associated with a return to the religious practices of childhood. In the midst of an immense crisis in civilization, this aspiration toward original innocence signified the rejection of the reigning rationalism. As in the case of Chateaubriand, the new generation was receptive to visionary prophecy, which suited an era permeated by the power of religious thought. In 1802, *Le Génie du christianisme* proclaimed, like Hegel, the reconciliation between the modern world and faith. After a disappointing revolution informed opinion returned to a religion renewed by the spirit of the irrational.[5]

In this psychological atmosphere Bonaparte's reestablishment of the church takes on its full significance. Correctly judging the importance of settling the religious issue over and above merely reopening churches, he made this a political priority. He had in mind, no doubt, a bureaucratized church that would go along with the policies of the state and primarily serve a social function. But this latest avatar of philosophical thought, while recommending the integration and subordination of the clergy, allowed for the maintenance of Catholic unity and the resumption of pastoral activities. The clergy quickly resumed partial control of the schools and took advantage of its restoration to spread its influence. We have seen the depth of the spiritual renewal it expressed. Despite the unhappy situation of the priests, the negative consequences of the interruption of parish life, and incontestable manifestations of impiety in the city, the church hierarchy set out to reconquer the faithful. Its authority was bolstered by its missions, which were part of a powerful antirationalist reaction. After ten years of revolution, religion was rehabilitated. Louis Bergeron mistakenly views this as a sign of passionate convictions and a rejection of analytical thinking. Hostility to the *philosophes* and the exaltation of faith were instead the expression of the birth of the Romantic sensibility. Rousseauian sentimentality had culminated in the celebration of Christian piety, and musicians who had sung the praises of the Revolution were now composing liturgical hymns.

This was not simply a matter of opportunism. Faced with the disasters of the Revolution, a traditionalist, authoritarian mindset took hold, and its spread was to become one of the major characteristics of the nineteenth century. It was motivated in part by opposition to the Enlightenment, already evident before 1789.[6]

Donald Sutherland has recently sketched the outlines of this restoration of Catholicism. Facilitated by Bonaparte's view of religion as a useful tool, it was rooted above all in popular faith. Despite opposition by intellectuals, politicians, and Jacobin generals, the Consulate entered into the Concordat to avoid prolonging a war with the clergy that was disastrously interfering with the maintenance of order. This agreement gave the government control over both public opinion and the church. The latter's reconstruction, which turned out to be a long process, was led by former refractory elements. They were aided by the discrediting of the constitutional clergy and their disappearance in the course of events. The enforcement of the Concordat thus became a joint effort between the government that grew out of the Revolution and the segments of the population that had been its main adversaries. While the priests with the most royalist leanings still did not participate, the constitutional clergy was often forced into humiliating retractions. There were many ceremonies purifying churches that had been sullied by them and vast collective remarriages and rebaptisms. Religious holidays and orders were also restored. Public assistance institutions were re-Christianized, and the church as a whole regained some of its former influence. There were, no doubt, problems on the pastoral level, since the clergy had been cut off from its leadership by de-Christianization. Its new foundations were increasingly rural, and, for the first time, popular. Some of the strains of nineteenth-century French Catholicism, with its hostility to the cities and their culture, originated there. *Ancien régime* forms of observance were reinstated and brotherhoods quickly reconsolidated. In spite of the priests' efforts, religious sentiment among the rural populace continued to lean toward pilgrimages and local feasts, even though these had been banned. The cult of the dead, with its "pagan" overtones, continued to address itself to the souls of dead Breton sailors. Under an authoritarian regime, the faithful recovered a degree of freedom of expression in this long-lost area.[7]

Claude Langlois and Timothy Tackett have best depicted the ordeal the Revolution represented for French Catholics. These historians still grant too much importance to the theory of a definitive *prerevolutionary* religious crisis. Is it certain that key changes in social practices and in the collective mentality occurred at that time? As the authors themselves admit, more thorough knowledge of the period will doubtless make possible a more accurate assessment. The era was marked as much by mysticism as by rationalism, and the bourgeois *philosophes* could offer no substitute for the people's Catholicism. What was true for Angers was not true for Marseilles, and on the threshold of the Revolution France had many religious models. The main conflict that divided it was the antagonism between the elites and the masses, the cities and the countryside, and perhaps, men and women. Reactions to the events of the Revolution were dictated by this diversity, refracted across the various regions. It is known that close to forty thousand priests and members of religious orders were driven out, and that upon their return they preached reconciliation and devoted themselves to rebuilding the church. Amid the masquerades of profanation and the harsh realities of persecution, holidays were still celebrated and the fight for the observance of Sunday as a day of rest was carried on. By modeling itself on the programs of the *philosophes*, the Revolution cemented the alliance between Catholicism and popular culture. By reducing all religious activity to the level of superstition, the revolutionaries mobilized and consolidated the fervor of both the humble people *and* the clergy in opposition to them. Pilgrimage stations became churches for dissidents, and religious theater in Brittany assumed the role of a substitute liturgy. The populace took the liberty of canonizing martyrs of the Revolution, who entered the pantheon of healing saints and became the object of new cults. Refractory priests in exile, moreover, saw to the continuity of diocesan government, soon took over the training of missionaries, and found ways around the problems posed by the pastoral guidance of a country in disarray. Missions continued to create a climate favorable to Roman Catholicism. A spiritual life with neither organized religion, sacramental practices, nor clergy had sprung up within families and was another form of resistance by the rural populace to de-Christianization. Plans for spiritual reconquest were elaborated, penitential mysticism developed, and congregations were founded by the women who had been partly responsibile for safeguarding religion against the ravages of the Revolution. Upheavals in this domain culminated in Bonaparte's establishment of a Ministry of Religion headed by Portalis, which led to the slow reestablishment of the church. Although its social influence had declined, it had again become a political power.[8]

Focusing on certain carryovers from the *ancien régime*, historians of the English-speaking world have linked this development to traditional elements that persisted or reappeared under the Revolution. Its cults, in particular, had clerical precursors before 1789, such as the festivals of Virtue concocted by anti-Voltairian apologists. The practice of selecting *rosières*, young virgins who represented Virtue, was an attempt to base the survival of Catholicism on its moral utility. Created in the last days of the eighteenth century, these festivals crowned a rustic, Rousseauian Virgin, to the great joy of the defenders of Christianity. A celebration of common values, they linked traditional religion to the new trends in thought. The revolutionary cults developed largely along these primitively Christian lines. Their vindicatory theology was echoed by the virtuous orthodoxy of Robespierre, whose faith was equally steeped in sentimentality. As John McManners has observed, revolutionary religion did not develop until the break with Catholicism occurred in 1791. But it retained some Enlightenment influences that were not foreign to the spirit of Bonaparte's venture. This abiding need for a moralizing liturgy, which pervaded the entire period, seems a more salient characteristic of the era than the ambiguous concept of de-Christianization.[9]

Resistance to the Revolution in the rural communities, particularly in the forested areas and sparsely inhabited regions of western and central France, stemmed in large part from the key role played by the traditional parish in unifying the population. The dominant position maintained by the church was linked in these regions to this sociological base. The year 1789 was only a minor crisis in the Tridentine reform movement that was to continue into the early twentieth century. The close-knit clerical network in the villages was the cornerstone of spirituality among the populace. Religion was, moreover, peasant culture's only means of integration and self-expression. The people of the countryside rallied around their old cemeteries to oppose the suppression of the parishes that occurred in the revolutionary period. This reorganization unsettled a region that was very attached to its places of worship. These small autonomous collectivities regarded them as the symbols of their very existence. Their conception of the community was based on the notion of psychological and spiritual communion between the living and the dead. The church and its cemetery embodied this and formed the basis of the peasants' visceral attachment to religion. They respected the parish priest as the symbol of the collectivity, and in order to win their loyalty the clergy had to acquiesce in the practices of infanticide and sexual assault that were often rampant in the countryside. Good peasants that they themselves were, they yielded to this rule. Like the moral ambitions of Tridentine Catholicism, the Revolution foundered on this notion of collective identity, as expressed in the internal structures of the parish.[10]

DID THE FRENCH REVOLUTION UNDERMINE
THE TRADITIONAL FAMILY?

France began to show a demographic decline in the revolutionary period. War losses were, however, offset by a high birthrate, despite the tentative beginnings of contraception. The population continued to increase, as did the gross rate of reproduction. Year II registered a record number of births (over 1.2 million) and circumstances were conducive to marriage, which provided exemption from the army. Births were the result. Although the French population aged slightly and grew less quickly than that of neighboring countries, the Revolution did not represent a demographic catastrophe. Historians are divided as to whether it coincided with a decrease in the birthrate. The reduction in the number of children per family seems certain, but Jacques Dupâquier has pointed out that by raising the number of marriages and births, the Revolution increased the population by 1.3 million. He maintains that a Malthusian turn attributable to the progress of petit-bourgeois individualism occurred only at the end of the Directory. The leaders of the Revolution had all been supporters of the family and increasing population. The link between the decline in fertility and the social phenomena of the period (disruption of traditional religion, proclamation of the principle of equality, propagation of the bourgeois ethos) is only a probability. André Armengaud has observed that the economic difficulties of the late *ancien régime* sprang in part from the rapid growth of the population and that people at the time, even in the rural areas, were aware of this. Not conducive to urbanization, the Revolution left in its wake changing demographic patterns and a population that was still young.[1]

Donald Sutherland has recently concluded that the revolutionary period witnessed the large-scale adoption of birth control by young rural inhabitants. For a long time their only response to the problem of poverty had been to marry late. The average age of marriage, which had already begun to fall before the Revolution, dropped drastically after 1789. At the same time there was a spread of contraceptive techniques known until then only in a few areas of the northwest and the Languedoc. The economic catastrophes of the 1790s and the loosening of traditional family ties were the main causes of this behavior, which reduced the number of births per married woman, particularly in regions that supported the Civil Constitution of the Clergy. The dismantling of the Constitutional Church in 1793 and the later difficulties of the church that grew out of the Concordat loosened religious discipline and made the sexual attitudes of couples more independent of it. Demographic change thus resulted from the weakening of the Catholic church's hold on the institution of marriage. The old Lenten prohibitions were likewise no longer respected.[2]

From 1789 to Bonaparte's time there was no single, coherent family policy, but rather three totally contradictory periods, as Philippe Sagnac had already pointed out almost a hundred years ago. The Constituent Assembly became involved in this area only to the extent that it was forced to do so by its other reforms. The division of the clergy, in particular, obliged it to turn to the issue of civil status. It confined itself, however, to noting that in the eyes of the law marriage was nothing more than a civil contract. The Legislative Assembly was spurred to secularize civil status by the large number of refractory priests. Its law of September 20, 1792, changed the conditions of marriage and instituted divorce for the first time. As Jacques Godechot noted, this was not an assault on Catholicism, but a way of raising public morale by eliminating the scandals caused by separations. The Constituent Assembly, moreover, set up family courts to settle disputes by supplanting the absolute authority of the father. In addition, the Legislative Assembly deprived parents of the authority to have children who were minors, henceforth defined as those under twenty-one years of age, jailed for disciplinary purposes. Except in the case of the law on divorce, these changes were quite modest ones.[3]

On the other hand, the Convention made divorce even easier, without declaring itself in favor of the equality of husband and wife. In 1793 it dropped the legal differentiation between illegitimate and legitimate children and voted to adopt the principle of equal inheritance rights. But the Civil Code, which assumed its definitive form early in the Consulate, reorganized the family along authoritarian lines even though it retained the system of civil status, the secularization of marriage, and divorce. Unmarried women were no longer considered the equals of men, and married women were placed under the absolute authority of their husbands. With no legal rights, they were wards and subordinates, even if they earned a salary, had an income, or ran a business. The proclamation of their obedience to their husbands was without precedent in the revolutionary period. Women had to follow their spouses everywhere, were not permitted to participate in the management of their common property, and above all, were required to obtain authorization from their husbands in all matters. These measures extended throughout the whole of France legal handicaps hitherto unheard-of in regions governed according to common law. Illegitimate children were expelled from the family. Divorce, which had nearly been abolished, was no longer permitted for reasons of temperamental incompatibility. Divorce by mutual consent was restricted and became rare. All laws touching upon it elaborated on the principle of inequality of the sexes. The goal was to prevent women from introducing a stranger into the legitimate family. A husband could thus have his adulterous wife, a virtual slave, imprisoned. If he lived with a mistress in the conjugal home, on the other hand, he got off with a mere fine. He could be pardoned if he killed his wife *in flagrante delicto*, whereas she, in the opposite case, could not.[4]

Albert Soboul has observed that the Civil Code, despite these measures, which were regressive by comparison with revolutionary legislation, constituted a lesser evil. This symbol of the Revolution, which consecrated the monetary basis of political participation and was concerned only with property, expressed a traditional concept of the legitimate family, viewed from the perspective of inheritance and a man's authority over his wife and children. The freedom to dispose of property as one chose in one's will was restored, and the oldest child could enjoy half of the property. This code represented a system of constraints linked with a repressive morality. Though it presented itself as the legal expression of the rights of man, it acknowledged the inequality of individuals and was based on the inequality of property. Concerned above all with the conditions of transferring land, it laid down a set of prohibitions that limited the scope of the freedoms proclaimed in 1789. It retained the early revolutionary period's aspirations to achieve uniformity of the law, equality of rights, and protection of the individual. But its legislation concerning the family, obsessed with the necessity of defending property, reinforced the patriarchal character of society. Women who had been abandoned, for example, could no longer divorce. Bonaparte and his colleagues had succeeded in imposing on the family the same subordination and hierarchy they had imposed on the nation. As for the eradication of the practice of issuing arrest warrants at the request of families, it led to legal supervision of parental discipline of minors, for the good of society.[5]

Historians have recently turned their attention to the practical consequences of the divorce law of 1792. It had been known that divorce was extremely limited outside certain cities like Paris, and that this institution did not enter into the social mores of the French at the time. Marriage remained an economic transaction in which personal satisfaction was not an essential consideration. In his study of the situation in Rouen, Roderick Phillips has shown that there was an increase in conjugal separation just before the Revolution. He has noted that during the Revolution divorces were requested primarily by women. Urban working women were no longer accustomed to the traditional family structure that still prevailed in the countryside. They revolted against the shoddy treatment that stemmed from the application of marital power. The new law thus met their social and material needs, even though it was resisted by a religion to which they remained faithful. These conclusions seem confirmed by the cases of other cities like Metz, Toulouse, and Lyons. In the last of these, Dominique Dessertine has found signs of a new pattern of behavior characterized by women's aspiration to liberty and equality.[6]

Before its defeat by the Civil Code, this attitude had scarcely been encouraged by the Revolution, which, irrespective of the kind of community it championed, was at all times dominated by patriarchal ideology and its corollary, contempt for women. This was an outgrowth of Enlightenment philosophy, which was unanimous on this point. Feminism, in the form of true and complete equality of the sexes, had no place in it. The inability of women to perform certain essential functions was always considered part of their lot in life. The Revolution did little to upgrade their legal status, despite the fact that women were often its most active participants. Some of them demanded their rights and outlined proposals for the improvement of their condition. Their grievances went unheeded, and in November 1793, the government barred them from political life. Female citizens were to be nothing more than procreators. For them, the new regime brought only very limited advances over the old one, and the Revolution was, above all, a time of lost illusions. Dominated by a well-entrenched antifeminism, it reduced women to old stereotypes of evil and hysteria.[7]

This defeat represented a triumph of the spirit of sexual discrimination. It had been expressed by Sieyès in 1789 when he ruled out participation by women as well as children in public affairs. The right to vote, which they had at times enjoyed under the *ancien régime*, was withdrawn. It is true that the vast majority of French women accepted the prevailing contemptuous definition of femininity. The Revolution played out its upheavals against an unchanging background of profound social and familial conservatism. In referring to the natural inferiority and obedience of women, the Civil Code was simply echoing Rousseau's *Emile*. At the end of a period marked by the affirmation of the feminist movement and women's participation in the Revolution, this tumultuous upheaval led only to the continuation of their subjection.[8]

Olwen Hufton has studied this phenomenon in the context of the concrete conditions of the economic life of the majority of the populace. The main concern of young girls was to escape poverty by creating a new family unit. To accomplish this they needed to amass a modest amount of capital, which they often earned by doing housework, either in the country or in the city, where it was often linked with industry.

These "servants" from the country still made up at least 10 percent of the population of the cities. They painfully labored to build up a small nest egg, drawn from their wages, which after fifteen years would allow them to marry. Their employers were of modest means, and their jobs could easily be terminated, landing these women in the street. Their living conditions were at times atrocious, but with energy, perseverance, or luck, they were sometimes able to marry, either back home or in the city. Young women born in urban areas ran fewer material risks and were in a better situation. But in any case, for the vast majority of married women working in rural areas, marriage was first of all an economic enterprise in which they were key contributors. They were by no means housewives limited to domestic duties. City women with full-time jobs turned their children over to rural wet nurses. Too busy with their work, they did not have the time to nurse them. This was a far cry from Rousseauian pastoral scenes, but it was the soul of a family economy where women's role as workers was essential. The work load was astounding. This was at times a source of profit, as in the case of the female lace merchants of Velay who were the true heads of their families by virtue of their skills and energy, which contrasted with the indolence of their husbands. An economically-based matriarchy began to emerge, as it did in many households where the man was a seasonal laborer. The women made the financial and familial decisions essential to survival. Once widowed, they would continue to do so. If the wife died, however, the husband would often abandon their children to public assistance. For half of all French households, the work of all family members from the age of seven on was indispensable for maintaining their economic equilibrium. The difficulties entailed by a crisis in employment or subsistence items are clear. The problem of poverty was thus, in many ways, a familial one, for marriage created indigents. In these cases, the woman was both the center of the family and the source of the expedients that enabled it to survive. To this end, she would arrange for her children to become beggars and drifters, in cooperation with the religious directors in charge of private charities. Smuggling salt and prostitution in the cities were other means of survival for the populace and for women in times of crisis. Such were the prevailing realities for women workers, and these continued to characterize their lot during the Revolution. For them, this was yet another phase in their continuing struggle to save their vulnerable families from economic disaster.[9]

From the perspective of the popular classes, the Revolution was a time when the conditions of family life grew harsher. Women working in the cities especially, whose economic plight we have just described, carried many more responsibilities than their husbands. They were the first to face the daily problems of hunger and cold and were thus in the forefront of riots during the Revolution. The first great *journées* were orchestrated above all by women. But we can imagine the problems the fall of the *ancien régime* imposed on the traditional economy of poor families. With the abolition of the *gabelle* (a government salt monopoly that artificially raised prices) what was to become of the two hundred thousand families that smuggled salt for a living? In many cities, the destruction of ecclesiastical institutions put an end to public charity. The crisis in luxury industries resulted in an analogous slump. This was exacerbated by the failure of the Revolution's policy on public assistance, so that at the time of the Terror nothing was left for the poor but shortages and illness, poverty and inflation. Poor women had often placed great hope in the Revolution and its social promises. Some of them had supported it vigorously. Disillusionment, whose economic bases were all too obvious, turned them into determined enemies of the new political regime. Their patience gave way before major subsistence crises that were not always forestalled by the suppression of price limits. Even when these controls were lifted, it was the women who spent hours in long, often fruitless lines. In 1795, after many years of undernourishment, the Republic could offer them and their children nothing but the prospect of dying of starvation while the rich stuffed themselves. How could they help being nostalgic for the *ancien régime*, which had at least offered assistance? In the year III, in French cities from which public aid had all but disappeared, an impoverished populace made bitter comments about "the charity of the *philosophes*." The last female-led protest, which brought Paris the *journées* of germinal and prairial, was accompanied in Rouen, Besançon, and Vesoul by clamorings for peace. After this all that was left was resigned silence, a wave of suicides, and the resurgence of Catholicism among the people. We know how fervently they returned to religion, particularly the women, even in the cities where some of them had just recently contributed to raging anticlericalism and de-Christianization. Disappointed with the results, they left their clubs and returned to their priests and their churches. After the catastrophes of the Revolution, this conversion was something of an expiation for the blasphemies in which they had participated. The unfortunate Constitutional Church was the preferred target of these exorcisms. Olwen Hufton notes the unprecedented strength of popular faith, whch was henceforth anchored in visceral retrospective emotions. If at times it tended to view the White Terror as a divinely inspired phenomenon, it signified more generally a desire to return to a sorely missed past. For almost the entire eighteenth century, the direct effects of war and famine, which had just been visited on the people by the Revolution, had been unknown. These had undermined both religion and the economic bases of the family. The vast majority of French women were henceforth more moved by this than by all the grand official rhetoric about freedom. And their point of view should no doubt count for more in the eyes of historians than that of the rare female intellectuals of the time or the even rarer and all too famous female profiteers of the regime.[10]

DID THE FRENCH REVOLUTION CREATE A NEW MAN?

This is what its leaders and militants often hoped and sometimes believed. Historians are increasingly turning their attention to the desire for cultural regeneration that marked this decade. Serge Bianchi connects it with a people's movement in the year II. According to his view, the initial populism of a revolution that had sought to speak for all was succeeded by the egalitarianism of the *sans-culottes* and their power. Life was to begin anew, a veritable clean slate, as symbolized by de-Christianization and embellished by political teachings and revolutionary art. These transient but profound transformations were accompanied throughout France by new ways of living and thinking, whose failures before and after Thermidor sprang from a bourgeois reaction that soon ended the influence of the *sans-culottes*. This study of the everyday experience of the Revolution as a break with the past acknowledges that it was sought by only a small activist minority. Can such a movement be viewed as a popular one?[1]

It was the expression of a powerful desire to rebuild French society by denying its past: Time was to be abolished and history would start again from zero, as symbolized by the calendar adopted in 1793. These aspirations permeated the rhetoric of the Revolution, which dealt not with the drearily prosaic domain of political realities (struggling for power, exploiting a dominant position, using violence) but with a social vision concocted to conceal and transfigure them. This was the role of revolutionary aesthetics. Word and image remained above all a cloak for clashing interests, a way of justifying the powers that be, and a dreamy refuge from sordid reality. They in fact expressed class and party animosities as much as love of humanity and the nation.[2]

Lynn Hunt views the Revolution in terms of a new political culture. The poetics of power were expressed through the rhetoric the era produced so abundantly. The actors in this drama played out their roles in an atmosphere haunted at all times by the fear of conspiracy. But did the performers in this rather bad play actually help create an authentic community? Their language overflowed with symbolic representations of their political practices. These symbols proliferated from the first, ranging from cockades to liberty trees, the Phrygian cap and patriotic altars. Widely diffused through the context of the revolutionary festivals, they were meant to replace the symbols of popular religion. It is not clear that this effort was a total success. In the spring of 1799 the citizens of Toulouse seemed to prefer the return of the Black Virgin, patron of their city. The official signs of patriotism, in clothing styles for instance, scarcely changed prevailing habits, though they did give rise to a future republican tradition. This tradition also drew on revolutionary emblems and slogans. Initial thoughts of a masculine, Herculean representation of freedom gave way, in the period of Thermidorean peace, to the allegorical figure of a seated woman, which was itself soon to be replaced by Bonaparte's image. While the Revolution produced a fertile political culture, the weaknesses and fragility of its creations in this realm soon became obvious. Born amid such pain, the symbolic figure of Marianne soon disappeared and was slow to return.[3]

Robert Darnton has observed that for certain historians who have succumbed to its rhetoric the Revolution has become a sort of rite of passage into modernity, punctuated by a succession of crises in imagery. In their fascination with the abstractions of language and revolutionary symbolism they have nearly lost sight of the actions of the players in this political drama and of the concrete conditions of their experience. Yet these conditions were highly restrictive and resistant to exorcism by word or art. This is shown by the case of Marat, whose fate, in life as in death, followed the successive phases of the revolutionary movement. From its glorious heights to the gutter, the Revolution was not primarily a series of speeches or a cultural language, but rather a chaotic social and political reality, dismal and disappointing, difficult to endure or control. Noting its exaltation of brotherhood, Marcel David has observed the ordeal inflicted on this ideal by the violence during the Terror. Nothing is further from the *reality* of the Revolution than the powerful myths that upheld, fueled, and justified it. It spoke volumes about love and lived above all on hate. The guillotine was in this respect a significant symbol of its imaginary universe. This new machine, suited to the spirit of the time and soon raised to sacred status by revolutionary democracy, corresponded to the image of anonymity and efficiency the state tried to assume. It also offered to the people of the time one of its most impressive political spectacles, with a constantly changing cast of characters. It finally became boring from overuse.[4]

In the end, indeed, revolutionary imagery disappointed its audience. The "scythe of reform" changed the names of streets and places, but this ideological, linguistic, and pedagogical delirium is less significant than the speed with which it died out. Saints were back en masse by 1802. Revolutionary slogans disappeared entirely four years later. The desire to put an end to the Revolution, even on the semantic level, was as fervent as had been the effort to foment it. The victors of 1793 had concocted, among other notions, the idea of purging royalist references from classic theater. Racine was thus corrected, just as a part of the artistic legacy of the Middle Ages was destroyed because it was said to represent feudalism and fanaticism. The idea of having all the French wear matching clothes as an obvious proof of patriotism cropped up in the year II. In May 1794, David was commissioned to come up with suggestions for these outfits. Contrary to all reason and good taste, modern clothing was to be remodeled along the lines of antiquity in order to set the French apart from other peoples, who had remained slaves. For a time revolutionary artists enthusiastically pursued this plan for uniformization, echoing all the views expressed by official propaganda.[5]

Although it was abandoned after Robespierre's fall, the ambitious program of revolutionary festivals with which he was associated offers an opportunity for a close look at the cultural and ideological innovations brought about by the political transformations of the times. Jean Starobinski has traced the origins of the revolutionary festivals to Enlightenment thought. Iconoclastic ceremonies of community rebirth, they spurned the embellishments of *ancien régime* theater to create forms better suited to the purity of heart Rousseau dreamt of. But they merely conveyed a past embellished and reconstituted by fiction. The neoclassical ideal could not be revived, and the artists who tried to turn it into theater merely produced an imaginatively transfigured reality that had nothing to do with these pastiches of antiquity. Hardened into ritual, these didactic performances provoked little interest. Drawing collective psychological renewal from them was difficult, and the whole enterprise, according to Quinet as recalled by Mona Ozouf, did not bring down a single village saint. As a fantasy of reason or concession to human frailty, it was unable to overcome indifference, the most pervasive collective emotion at the time of the Revolution. When, under the Directory, Sébastien Mercier expressed his "radical, physical rejection" of these "festive phemonema" (Michel Vovelle) he was doubtless not alone in his views. This sentiment explains their speedy disappearance. Mona Ozouf, to whom we owe the best study of revolutionary festivals, has noted the contradictory attitudes of their organizers and celebrants. Contrary to their creators' hopes, they failed to attract the community, degenerated into parody, and in the end were unattended. A malicious pamphlet in 1807 described the *journée* of 18 brumaire as the most successful of these performances, in that it quietly managed to put an end to the Revolution and its festivals. These representations of utopia failed, perhaps, because they came too close to re-creating the boredom and disgust that their subject eventually inspired. The laborious elaboration of a more primitive initial impulse, the festival of July 14, 1790, was itself rather disappointing; it was, furthermore, not a day of celebration for all the French.[6]

The festivals that followed reflected the deepening of antagonisms. Starting in 1794, the clearest application of Enlightenment thought was the attempt merely to bring some order to initial chaos. But the spatial and temporal symbolism of these processions, which were intended to consecrate social regeneration or commemorate the chronology of a revolution so rich in contradictory or unfinished events, made them an extremely rudimentary school of civic instruction. Its images and words proved powerless against the "tenacious exuberance of customs" in popular life. The revolutionary leaders saw this with surprise, fear, or contempt. They had a great deal of trouble realizing their wish to do away with crosses and church bells. Throughout the country, this anti-popular ambition provoked rebellions by the peasants, who were attached to their true festivals, the traditional ones. It fed resistance to the rational utopia so dear to the new authorities. It failed primarily because of the stubborn adherence of the Catholic populace to the celebration of Sundays and patron saints. Revolutionary symbolism coincided with peasant tradition only in the planting of liberty trees, which drew on the May celebrations of folklore. Even so, we must note that the Vendéan insurgents, rural people of another stripe and another time from those of Périgord, took care to uproot the liberty trees in 1793. They were thus rejecting the transfer of sacred significance that the leaders of the First Republic were unable to impose on France. Its rural inhabitants, in particular, retained their religious loyalties, rejecting any substitute liturgy made up of borrowings and deletions. The Republic tried to reshape the world according to the backward-looking model of the egalitarian golden age of the republics of antiquity. This undertaking did not immediately succeed in creating the man it dreamed of.[7]

The architects of the revolutionary period had no more success carrying out their plans to rebuild society completely, both its monuments and its civic structure. The *philosophes*'s naturally iconoclastic attitude towards the past, which inspired Condorcet to request that the Legislative Assembly have the archives destroyed, was replaced, under the Republic, by an unprecedented preoccupation with preserving the heritage of the past. The Revolution had a great interest in developing museums, an enterprise which would soon be facilitated by the pillage of a vanquished Europe. On the cultural level, the revolutionary period thus seems to show signs of both continuity and discontinuity. It completed the eighteenth century while repudiating it, and challenged the values of rationality and progress after attacking those of tradition and order. The temporary collapse of the old world had brought neither freedom nor happiness. Dissatisfaction and apprehension, malaise and nostalgia dominated the generation that came after 1800 because it understood better than its predecessors the limits of politics and the power of evil. It was haunted by the shadow of Sade, that lucid negation of the link between nature and virtue, truth and good. Sénac de Meilhan's *The Emigré*, published in 1797, sought to shatter prerevolutionary myths. This novel about the stripping off of masks and the loss of illusions understood that Enlightenment ideals had been nothing but a ruse conjured up by history to unleash the reality of violence. Their complacent optimism had seen its day, for a democratic revolution, built on the model of antiquity, had led only to the reign of oppression, anarchy, and a new inequality. The experience of the First Republic had taught this aristocrat to reject all utopias.[8]

Such criticism helped to turn people away from the rationalist social message of the eighteenth century *philosophes*. The Revolution had not substantially changed the terms of a controversy that pitted the Enlightenment heritage against the new conception of nature. Attitudes about death, as revealed in John McManners's immense study, illustrate this intellectual continuity. The dissolution of the learned societies in August 1793 did not lead to any cultural subversion. This democratization of academic life in no way challenged the ascendancy of the scientific model. With the creation of the institute, the Revolution ended, in this respect, with an effort at reconciliation. In the first rush of egalitarian protest it had proceeded to accomplish an indispensable reorganization of research that made scholars even more dependent on the state. In this area, as in so many others, the revolutionary phase served simply as a transition between Colbert and Napoleon.[9]

Changes in the art world did not go any deeper. The triumph of the neoclassical aesthetic, launched before 1789, continued under the Revolution, but David had no trouble maintaining his status as the favorite of both Napoleon and Robespierre by celebrating both military dictatorship and the dying Marat. His utopian aspirations had adapted to the most sordid realities of power, whether of the Terror or the empire. Ronald Paulson maintains that in Europe during this period David and his disciples were rather conservative aesthetically, while the revolutionary spirit found its true echo in Blake's England and Goya's Spain.

He considers reactionary France's brand of iconoclasm that, challenged by Catholicism, could do no more than revise its liturgy; he finds Gillray's counterrevolutionary caricatures more subversive than David's respectable canvases.[10]

The most important cultural choice the revolutionaries had to make was the adoption or rejection of the republican myth of liberty in the style of antiquity. Rousseau's teachings were symbolic of this and were profoundly hostile to economic development. This ignorance of the laws of capitalism was linked, as in the case of Saint-Just or Billaud-Varenne, with a moral and pedagogical emphasis on institutions that would shape "public awareness." This Jacobin dream was challenged, after Thermidor, by men like Hassenfratz, professor at the École Polytechnique and prophet of future industrialization. He correctly observed that "it was not by means of festivals that the English [had] achieved ascendancy over the political balance of Europe" or that the United States of America was in the process of becoming "a flourishing people." Throughout the entire revolution other authors attacked a Rousseauian primitivism that viewed private ownership of the means of production as a crime, whereas it was the driving force of prosperity. The ideologues studied by Sergio Moravia and Marc Regaldo expanded on these arguments, which did not view the Revolution as a process of total rebirth breaking completely with tradition. They attributed this Robespierrist ambition to a verbal, abstract fanaticism divorced from the reality of time. These descendants of the *philosophes* had difficulty formulating a political program that would confer authority on representatives of various interests without transforming them into a self-centered elite. Aware of the inevitable inequality of ability as well as the desirability of "equal access to happiness," they aspired to a regime that would reconcile the exigencies of order with those of progress. Like the Jacobins, but in another way, they believed in the power of education. It was, however, to be scientific and economically-oriented education, or nothing at all. At the time of the Thermidoreans, the ideologues, despite their influence on all the institutions of the Republic, failed to carry out this program, which would have turned the French Revolution into a victory for Adam Smith. Habits ingrained in the classical ethos and literary culture made this impossible; the pretext involved was the atheistic materialism for which the defenders of political economy were criticized. Traditional disciplines such as history and geography played their role in this defeat of the social sciences. Their supporters considered it necessary to base public morality on the latest scientific knowledge. This plan risked colliding with the religious conservatism that had been strengthened by the disappointments of the decade. Under Napoleon, the dominant role of science, backed by the

government, was eroded by the establishment of a university faithful to
ancien régime thought. This development reflected the aspirations of a
society that, in the wake of the Revolution, preferred security to productivity and calm to bold undertakings.[11]

Maurice Agulhon has noted the continuation of folk life in the year
of 1800 along with the resurgence of fraternal societies. Popular games
carried on the traditions of the old saints' days festivities. In all Provence
traditional celebrations held firm against the Revolution, which tried to
bring back carnival-style entertainments. Albert Soboul has pointed out
that the mores and customs of the French countryside were affected by
revolutionary upheavals only to a limited degree. Traditional mentalities
continued to make taverns and visits to neighbors the two basic components of village social life. Peasant diversions, including dancing, remained linked with religious beliefs and work in the fields. Fairs in the
west continued to draw inhabitants of the wooded areas, while rural
people remained attached to their traditional holidays. They resisted the
Directory's efforts in this area, responding to them with a veritable
explosion of religious festivals. There was thus a very rapid return almost
everywhere to the leisure activities of the prerevolutionary period. City
people, for their part, responded to political tension primarily by setting
up countless public dances after Thermidor, for their revenge against
Jacobin austerity. The workers of Paris, moreover, had never lost their
marked taste for taverns and boisterous drinking bouts. With the failure
of the Revolution's prohibitions and initiatives, traditional customs reappeared in all the cities of France: donkey rides, rough music, grand
festivals that had been momentarily forgotten, brotherhoods of archers,
all returned in force. Folklore, scorned by the *philosophes*, had won out
against the Revolution. The leaders of the Convention had become aware
of their linguistic preponderance in the wild rural areas of France where
patois was spoken more than French. Learned medicine was less popular
than traditional quackery.[12]

The Revolution's most serious cultural failure was in the area of
education. Furthered, no doubt, by other means, literacy advanced overall during this period, despite the dismantling of the old school system.
The Revolution did not bring any innovations in the principles or methods of teaching. It inherited a primary and secondary school system that
was certainly mediocre, but despite its theoretical proclamations did not
improve it. A large part of the teaching corps remained attached to the
ancien régime system; the majority of private schools, which were heavily
attended, remained in the hands of priests or nuns to whom parents
preferred to entrust their children. The public schools were handicapped
by the requirement that teachers take their pupils to the *décadaire* fes-

tivals. Large numbers of clerics who had taught under the *ancien régime* were kept on as instructors despite their outright opposition to the Republic, whose recruitment of teachers was hampered by the unattractive conditions it offered them. The inertia of local authorities starting in 1792 was the main obstacle to the establishment of public schools. The Revolution did not set up an efficient system of public education, and when it was over, the system reverted to exactly what it had been under the *ancien régime*. The case of Vendômois confirms this: The Republic's primary school was late in coming, had enormous difficulties scraping by, and wound up a failure. Minimal supplies were not necessarily provided, schools were very poorly attended, and the Revolution did nothing to advance the spread of literacy in the region. Material difficulties account for this fact even more than any ideological objections of the people. The Republic's elementary schools failed primarily in their educational mission, much like the *ancien régime* schools they so closely resembled. Alien to the rural world, this institution for the transmission of urban culture was greeted with indifference by peasants for whom access to the written word did not mean cultural inclusion. They were no doubt baffled, for example, by the constitutional texts that were assigned, and thrown off by the metric system they were being forced to substitute for the complex ancestral measures they knew so well. The new revolutionary calendar, which attacked age-old rites by eliminating traditional holidays, held no more appeal. Seen from this point of view, the republican primary schools of the 1790s were simply another phase, and a failed one at that, in the attempt to introduce the values of the elite into the countryside.[13]

Secondary education fared no better. In the north, for example, private schools were widely maintained. In the eyes of the parents, these had the advantage of carrying on the admissions policies and educational philosophy handed down from the *ancien régime*. The new centralized schools were in total disarray and vehemently criticized. Mandated in 1795, these institutions took different forms in the various departments. A maximum of fifteen thousand students attended annually; they came primarily from the urban bourgeois families linked with the administration and the liberal professions; very few of them received an education worthy of the name, and these institutions were viewed by most as "privileged places of specialization." On the cultural level, the Republic failed to sink roots in the country. Its achievements fell short of its rhetoric.[14]

Hence the disappointing impression left by the individual destinies of "average revolutionaries." Benoît Lacombe, a wholesaler from Bordeaux who was studied by Joël Cornette, started off in Gaillac as a "vineyard

Danton," buying up nationalized lands in quantity and defending the guillotine. He was soon accused of using the Revolution for his own profit and, along with others, withdrew almost entirely from public life in 1794. All that was left him of this political interlude was a melancholy memory of defeat and disillusion. The national turmoil had no doubt made a rich man of this citizen who had aspired to aristocracy under the *ancien régime*. But it had also brought him the irreparable experience of hatred and betrayal. A minor figure in the history of the Revolution, he was, like so many of his compatriots, above all its victim in terms of his private life. This was also true of the Gounon family, prominent citizens of Toulouse who had become aristocrats through the purchase of a seigneury in the eighteenth century. Their attitude toward the Revolution's restructuring of society moved from one of reasoned reformism to opposition to a Republic that was destroying the equilibrium of their lives. They nevertheless adapted to it, pledging their loyalty to create an impression of patriotism. They made their appearance at the Temple of Reason and at popular festivals. Their double life henceforth included a cover of ritual observance and an underground lifeline made up of tested friends. These born suspects were still trembling with fear in 1797. Although their strategy of disguise and retreat paid off, the Revolution fell far short of fulfilling their pre-1789 dreams. For a while, indeed, its new redistribution of powers and freedoms had come close to erasing the borders of private and public life.[15]

12. AN IDEOLOGICAL
LEGACY?

A*ny assessment of the French Revolution must take into account its continuing ideological effects. In this sense, it has not ended and still provokes impassioned debate. This is particularly true in France, where its influence on modern political life has been considerable. The republican system gradually emerged from sustained reflection on the nation's revolutionary heritage. Still a subject of controversy, this ongoing process of refashioning the founding myth of France easily transforms its commemoration into a debate bristling with conflict. The Revolution's symbols of unity are easier to accept when the exact conditions of the divisive event that produced them are forgotten or unknown. Its adoption and spread abroad have been more unanimously and enthusiastically hailed. But since 1917, the Leninist form of its socialist variant has given rise to revolutionarly movements that reveal even more starkly the original contradictions between 1789 and 1793, the rights of man and the Terror.*

DOES THE SHADOW OF THE REVOLUTION COLOR
CONTEMPORARY FRENCH POLITICS?

René Rémond has stressed the posthumous fruitfulness of the revolutionary period, during which public opinion entered public life. Thus was born the modern French form of public opinion, replacing the old one that was fragmented and hampered by the precariousness of freedoms and limited means of expression. Precedents established during the prerevolutionary crisis were to engender customs and a public spirit accustomed to "looking to the past for answers to present problems." The first legacy of the Revolution is an attachment to historical memories, which was to lead to periodic plans for a "convocation of the Estates-General." In 1789 politics became for the first time common property, invested with the mission of totally reconstructing society. This decisive change in principle and orientation broadened the field of political action and brought new forces into play. As we have seen, they were to prevent the securing of the peaceful rebirth that had been envisioned. The Revolution willed to the future an unfulfilled desire for national unanimity. It to embodied an analogous contradiction by worshiping the cult of law and violating it repeatedly by successive coups d'état. All the modern history of France was to be marked by this instability and insecurity. The Revolution schooled the country in violence. The populace received its political education in a period of forcible permanent changes. From it the nation acquired an enduring tolerance of illegality, disputes about rules, and the practice of revolt.[1]

It also learned to play the electoral game. The Revolution was, in this respect, a testing ground for the politics of the future. It anticipated various aspects of democratic life: the consultation of public opinion, the appointment of its representatives, the relations among the branches of power, the activities of official groups, and the exercise of freedoms. In France and elsewhere, future history was to depend on the various solutions adopted at that time, which were to create lasting traditions. The principle of national sovereignty led to elections starting in 1789. In its early phase, the Revolution even selected judges, National Guard officers, and parish priests by election. It effected an overall renewal of the power structure that was carried out throughout the entire country even though it directly affected only a minority. The legislative assemblies that were the focal point of political life constituted a decisive innovation over *ancien régime* practices, one destined for a great future, for it, too, began a tradition that still lives today. The concepts of a political left and right sprang up within the context of the assemblies' deliberations, and it was there, too, that the spectacular power of oratory was first demonstrated. They had to establish from scratch the conditions of parliamentary operations, including the organization of debates and the relations between powers. The decisions they made had an incalculable impact on modes of political procedure, thought, and action. But, besides all this, the Revolution instituted a militant, spontaneous democracy that allowed for citizen involvement beyond the exercise of the right to vote. This reflection of public opinion influenced those in power and often competed with them. It also served as an example to future revolutionaries of "the possibilities for action by the forces of the people." The societies that embodied these forces were the training ground and forerunners of future parties, whose role they already played within the state: As a structuring agent, they were to lend efficiency and continuity to the revolutionary movement. Created by activist minorities, they reflected the French penchant for very limited participation in political groups. Their egalitarian ideology, which was totally alien to the realities of modern society, was to influence the republican tradition of the nineteenth and twentieth centuries.[2]

The Revolution proclaimed, in addition, the essential freedoms that protect citizens' participation in political life. This did not, however, prevent the principle of freedom of opinion from being violated and sacrificed for reasons of state. Freedom of expression, unknown in the *ancien régime*, was instituted and then withdrawn. The future would not forget this connection between the statement of a principle and the limiting of its application. But the power of the press, as well as the link between its relative freedom and the existence of a government responsive to public opinion, was born during the revolutionary period. On the other hand, while granting the freedom to hold meetings, the Revolution strongly opposed the freedom to form associations. It turned congregating into a veritable crime, was distrustful of political pressure groups, and in its passion for unity even opposed the official recognition of parties. The popular societies did not escape this distrust, which was to prove enduring. The freedom to petition followed the same curve and scarcely survived the revolutionary phase. In sum, the Revolution simultaneously posited freedoms in principle and invented ways of limiting their exercise. Succeeding democratic governments were to heed this double-edged lesson.[3]

They also had to take into account the experience of the Terror, which, contrary to the hopes of 1789, had placed justice in the service of political expediency. This process long seemed inseparable from revolutionary practice. It was linked to the desire to change mankind, which turned Jacobinism into a moral doctrine hostile to the seductions of luxury and given to identifying democracy with simplicity of manners. The Revolution thus handed down its own liturgy of political life as celebrated in its didactic festivals. The picture that emerged from René Rémond's study impressed him with a heritage that set forth the main postulates of contemporary society, defined its centers of action, and laid down the rules and customs governing them. The achievements of the revolutionary period, moreover, were the source of the traditions of both parliamentary democracy and its socialist variant. As a seminal event, it molded political outlooks and sensibilities. A radical and violent departure from the past, it gave the French a taste for sudden and complete change. The abrupt reversals of France's modern history, with its frequent reshuffling of regimes, numerous constitutional experiments and attendant crises, and permanent instability orginated in it. The Revolution set a precedent for recourse to irregular procedures in the conduct of public affairs, resulting often in mounting opposition that paralyzed the centers of authority. There was no normal political life, for the risk of drastic change was preferred to reliance on the healing possibilities of the passage of time. The idealism handed down from the Revolution always led French intellectuals, and often the general public as well, to prefer a complete break to adaptation. A rejection of rules and a preponderance of struggle came to characterize the conflict-prone society of France. It became a point of honor to be attracted to extremes, to be contemptuous of legality, to practice the *politique du pire*, and await revolt. The interplay of revolutionary factions was prolonged in France by permanent challenges to the very bases of whatever regime was in power.[4]

Just before 1968 René Rémond felt that the Revolution remained "alive in our midst." He observed that while the right and the left alike drew some of their attitudes from it, their disagreements over its meaning continued to divide them. Having made conflict a central aspect of political life, the Revolution itself became the subject of disagreements over the acceptance or rejection of its outcome. The entire nineteenth century debated it and could be categorized with regard to this issue. Today, like twenty years ago, though the achievements of the Revolution have become irrevocable, it continues to inspire insurmountable aversion in those who view it as the source of all our troubles. It is impossible to speak of unanimous, universal acceptance. The old history of the Republic, which many citizens still recall, provides them with contrasting images of 1789 and 1793. These helped to inspire the actions of the Resistance generations. As for memories of the counterrevolution, they are as alive as those of its nemesis, as Jean-Clément Martin has recently shown, with respect to the Vendée. If Napoleon seemed for a moment to have laid waste to much of the heritage of the Revolution, the gradual restoration of freedoms, elections, and assemblies was to reinstate it in all its importance in modern France.[5]

Its complexity becomes evident, for example, upon examination of the problem of decentralization. The democratization of local administration, instituted in 1789, was totally suppressed at the end of the Revolution, which witnessed a return to the practices and spirit of the *ancien régime* in this area. This repudiation of its initial liberalism had already occurred during the Jacobin phase because of extraordinary circumstances arising from both the civil and foreign wars. Made up of hopes and betrayals, ideals and renunciations, the Revolution's legacy will always be a complicated one. Individual histories confirm this resistance to simplification. Daniel Encontre was a Calvinist who sympathized with the religious revival but had come to support the Restoration, during which he was dean of the school of theology of Montauban. For all his well-earned reputation for orthodoxy and traditionalism, he had been, in the spring of 1794, a devoted believer in Robespierre and his virtue and knowledge. French liberals remained revolutionaries until 1830, and have continued to link themselves to the Revolution, at least to some degree, ever since. Early in the Second Empire Charles de Rémusat observed that unlike the Englishman Burke in 1790, they were in no position to oppose the Revolution in the name of a liberal political tradition non-existent in France before 1789. In this respect the *ancien régime* left to posterity nothing but absolutism and its impasses. Under the Restoration, Paul-Louis Courier and Stendhal were its sworn enemies and dedicated admirers of the Revolution, or at least the Revolution that signified freedom, which was not that of either the Jacobins or of Bonaparte.[6]

The 1840s revived memories of the Terror. Raymond Huard has recently shown how true this was of the department of Gard, which was deeply attached to its traditions. In 1848 popular democrats there proclaimed their ties to their *sans-culotte* ancestors, while the women, with their more down-to-earth concerns, recalled that the Republic meant above all a lack of freedom and the rationing of food. The Revolution lived on here, above all, as a family and cultural heritage about which feelings were already violently split between admirers of 1789 and champions of 1793. Words and images, songs and celebrations continued to re-create these heroic times. In Bagnols, on January 21, 1850, there were cries of "Long live the guillotine!" while in Nîmes a bust of Robespierre became an object of considerable veneration. He was hailed as the man who had known how to "destroy the aristos." These republican supporters of the Terror still conjured up images of bloodshed in their festivals, declaring themselves eager to dip their hands in gore and evoking "the sweet pleasure of watching heads roll." In the red Midi this infatuation with the scaffold remained one of the Revolution's clearest legacies. The leftist mentality there equated victory with the physical annihilation of the enemy. Direct democracy by means of the total eradication of the state and the affirmation of the right to work also figured in this view. The movement's emphasis on moral considerations and its ignorance of economic realities cemented its ties to Rousseauian dreams.[7]

On the occasion of the centenary of the commune of Paris, Albert Soboul contrasted the continuity of this revolutionary tradition, linked to a mass movement and the notion of popular sovereignty, with the hierarchical centralizing tendencies typical of the Jacobin bourgeoisie. Revolutionary tradition focused on concepts of unity, unanimity, and brotherhood, whereas the Jacobin bourgeoisie was more concerned with revolutionary techniques and practices. Contradictory opinions of Robespierre and Marat sprang from this duality, itself the product of

the realities of the Revolution, past and future, torn between its desire
to speak for the masses and its concern with efficacy. The latter impulse
led it to hand over to an authoritarian elite the task of deciding what
was good for the people, irrespective of their wishes. This was the ultimate message of Babeuf's followers, who were to hand it down, by
way of Blanqui, through the entire nineteenth century to the state
founded by Lenin.[8]

Buonarroti felt, in 1830, that the only justification for 1793 lay in its
desire for total regeneration. This dream lived on in the spirit of the
French generation of the Liberation, with Jean Cassou contending in
1947 that the Revolution "was not over" and that there had been "in
the history of our country, ever since 1794, something waiting, unresolved." He was sorry to see France still under the boot of the Thermidoreans and called for "another revolution, in different conditions,
to take up the old dream and fulfill it." At a time when the Russian
revolution was proclaiming its debt to the French one, he was awaiting
"another act of the French people" to "bring Saint-Just back among
us," and declared, "We are now in a better position than any other
generation to see Saint-Just and the Terror in all their simplicity and
glory." In his commitment to activism, he claimed to be driven by "a
fierce desire for cleansing and justice" to purge "the Indulgents of our
times." These ideological rantings, less individual than collective, that
subscribed to "a doctrine of revolutions . . . particularly illuminated by
Marxism" and proclaimed that "the people" were "the fundamental
element in progress and revolutions," closed with a lyrical declamation,
according to which "hatred of enemies is a sacred sentiment," and with
this astonishing plea: "O, Saint-Just, we need you. . . . We call upon
you. . . . Light the way out of our confusion! . . . Your struggle continues
for us and pushes us forward. . . . Pass this torch on to those whose
victories, in the hidden byways of the future, are trembling to join yours.
Engrave in hearts worthy of following after you the example of your
unrelenting virtues."[9]

An entire segment of France shared these aspirations at the time. The
precedent of the Revolution was not recalled solely from the perspective
of brotherhood, and the Terror was never far from view. Healthy mass
violence was justified by the rage of the vanquished, and patriotic massacres seemed to be a necessary accompaniment to historical progress.
This position has been abandoned in view of recent developments in the
resolution of political conflicts and the disillusionment caused by the
experience of communism. The majority of the French, though not fundamentally hostile to it, are much more aware today of the Revolution's
imperfections and contradictions. They repudiate, in particular, its point-

less violence, and do not think it succeeded in instituting a valid model of democracy. Seeing in it the degradation of an ideal rather than the realization of a utopia, they are beginning to judge it as an event that was no doubt extraordinary and significant, but banal, prosaic, and ultimately disappointing in its details—in a word, like many others. Polled during the summer of 1983 about their attitudes to its participants, they rated La Fayette in first place, followed by Bonaparte. But the Revolution's initial champion received only a 6 percent unfavorable rating, as opposed to 21 percent for its liquidator. Both placed far ahead of Louis XVI or Danton, Marat, or Robespierre. The last, of whom Georges Marchais has at times proclaimed himself the successor, received a positive rating from only 8 percent of the population, a fifth of La Fayette's or Bonaparte's share. The French clearly prefer the image of a revolution that made modest contributions to the establishment of an acceptable liberal order to the tumultuous and militant image of a revolution that ushered in an uninterrupted wave of progress achieved by violence.[10]

DID THE FRENCH REPUBLIC
ORIGINATE FROM THE REVOLUTION?

Claude Nicolet has recently restored the developments in the French concept of a republic to their full importance. If they reached their high point with the definitive adoption of this regime at the end of the nineteenth century, the Revolution occupies an essential place in their origins and success. The defining characteristic and difficulty of the republican spirit is that it developed during this phase of history, with all its contradictions. The revolutionary occurrence that began in 1789 represents its absolute origin, as the incarnation does for Christianity. We return to it always because it is the beginning of everything. It is in this way, for example, that the Enlightenment is more or less firmly linked with the Republic. The recognition of this collective heritage eventually transformed the eighteenth-century *philosophes* into Fathers of the Republican Church. But it, in turn, began only with the Revolution, of which the republicans were the sons. They considered it a religious phenomenon whose symbols were at the heart of their doctrine and whose principles dictated their activities. They even had a tendency to turn this tumultuous and varied period, against all evidence, into a monolithic ideological bloc. The official historiography of the Revolution until our day was thus transformed into a single-minded enterprise whose high priests took pains to preserve this myth and provide for its eventual enrichment. This republican reading of the Revolution has always elevated the event to sacred status by transforming it into the absolute beginning of Good and end of Evil and imaginatively transfiguring it into an epic.[1]

The ideologues of the Directory were a key intellectual source for the future Republic. The republican spirit, however, had to survive a long internal exile during the first two thirds of the nineteenth century before gaining sway in France. It achieved it in the 1870s by establishing a new legitimacy that was able to lay down both a form of government and the principles of a regime fit to become definitive. The cult of the Revolution was an essential part of it, associated with the affirmation of an ideal republic that official policy was duty-bound to embody in society, as it was for Littré and his positivist friends. In order to triumph, this successor of the Revolution was forced, in this respect, to be at once conservative and liberal. This it very clearly was in the case of its opportunistic founders, who were even more preoccupied with strengthening the state than with carrying out justice. Their sole concern was to confirm the nation's acceptance of the civil order that grew out of the Revolution. Their teachings served this ideology, emphasizing a conception of science, history, and morality obsessed with the intangible character of the founding principles of 1789. Under the Republic, these came, in effect, to define the connection between society and politics. Fidelity to the Revolution became, in essence, the highest of virtues. The inevitable necessity of supplementing this heritage turned out to be the source of many difficulties.[2]

Claude Nicolet has pointed out how much the mental, or rather mythical, structure thus created by France's modern-day history suffers by comparison with that which prevailed during the *ancien régime*. In both cases, a dogma and a state found themselves at once inextricably linked and radically separated, while the sacred character attributed to both in no way simplified matters. An obsession with unity can be easily explained in light of this diversity. A successful reconciliation was made between the concepts of the nation and the Republic. In conformity with a certain tradition handed down from the Revolution, it was important to define the latter in terms of the supremacy of the legislative branch. Abuses of the representative and parliamentary system, however, led to a certain erosion of the concept of the state, which also had difficulty imposing "the spiritual unity necessary for the Republic" within a secular context. A "state of nontotalitarian law," it was at the same time a "unified and centralized state." This contradiction, inherited from the Revolution, was not always easy to live with. It was accompanied by another one, arising from the fact that *for Europe and the world*, the events of 1789 by no means ushered in the period of modernity. This was created not by the proclamation of the rights of man, but rather by developments linked to the growth of industrial capitalism. Revolutionary France experienced the latter to a very limited degree, preferring the ancient model of an Athenian Republic that was handed down from Rousseau to Mendès France by way of the Jacobins and Gambetta. The French concept of democracy remains a creation of philosophical thought, not a result of historical evolution. Offspring of the Revolution, the Republic also inherited its utopian aspects and its original enemies. From the time of Saint-Just on, it has been unable to separate morality from politics, as it has always tended to invest the latter with a religious dimension. One might well wonder whether the new forms, and especially the new spirit, introduced since 1958 have profoundly altered this revolutionary tradition.[3]

This tradition, moreover, has never been uncomplicated, as shown in the mid-1860s by the debate spurred by the publication of a work in which Quinet condemned the Terror. Applauded by Ferry, it was criticized by Robespierre's defenders. The symbolism surrounding the repository of memories that the Republic has become today is characterized by an analogous ambiguity. In these memories the Revolution partakes more of the mystery of origins than the clarity of new beginnings. It has handed down to us, however, the symbol of national legitimacy, the source of a modern cult of the military, and proof that the Republic is the culmination of French history. This myth of origins is a distortion of memory. The revolutionary calendar, which was to command eternity by subjugating time, withstood the resistance it encountered for only twelve years. The emptiness of its promises soon transformed it into a dying institution. *La Marseillaise* enjoyed greater success, as this war song exalting freedom has become a national and even international hymn. Its revolutionary origins have never kept it from being pressed into the service of all the various manifestations of patriotism.[4]

Under the Revolution the Pantheon embodied the collective will of a century hungry for celebration. But the Republic was unlucky in those it chose to commemorate. Already before 1799 Mirabeau and Marat were excluded from it. This symbol of national unity became a battleground among the French, as the events in 1981 illustrate. We no longer believe in the eighteenth-century's concept of great men, nor in the idea of art as "propagandistic and educational." The republican slogan on the town halls of France has stood up better than this empty monument because it is linked to the posthumous triumph of the principles of 1789. Maurice Agulhon observes that it is *only in the past hundred years* that the gradual popularization of local democracy has metamorphosed the "symbolic vocabulary of French culture." We owe this success to the Revolution only insofar as it was the inspiration for the Third Republic. This decisive link is the main factor accounting for the significance of 1789 in French history. Ernest Lavisse made it official in a grade school textbook whose central theme was the revolutionary destiny of France's national history. It increasingly glorified or excused the Revolution, and vilified the *ancien régime* in the name of the clearcut national interest. The nation's well-being was likewise identified with the transition from the despotism of the monarchy to the liberty of the Republic. This legitimization of a new regime in terms of national unity was, as Pierre Nora noted, a secular transposition of the justifications formerly advanced by royalty.[5]

The 1870s and the 1880s were marked by the celebration of the centenaries of Voltaire, Rousseau, and the Revolution, as well as the designation of July 14 as the national holiday. At the dawn of the Third Republic the two great philosophers of the eighteenth century were seen above all from the perspective of a revolution they symbolized and in the context of an obvious link between the Enlightenment and the new regime. Their promotion to sacred status transformed France's intellectual past into a messianic prefiguration of the republican future. Two years later, in 1880, July 14 was adopted as a national holiday. The Revolution had not yet become what it is today for 70 percent of the French people—that is, a pervasive myth of origins that is capable only of stirring up retrospective passions. On the contrary, the choice of July 14 signified that the new regime was affiliating itself with a symbol of freedom and the notion of a break with established order. Confusion with July 14, 1790, added overtones of fraternal festivals. Official and popular rituals gradually sprang up, helping to fix the Republic in people's awareness. Although it has since then become a part of the national heritage, the details of its history still provoke controversy.[6]

It was even more natural that this should have been the case in 1889, the centenary of a patrimony claimed by those in power at the time. In the face of conservative criticism, they put the finishing touches on a republican interpretation of national history, promulgating edifying images of the Revolution and organizing huge ceremonies in its honor. The museum commemorating the Revolution was the centerpiece of the Exposition that opened that year. Mythic celebrations of the Revolution went hand in hand with the moderate tendencies of this opportunistic republic. This is what Pascal Ory has neatly referred to as "the proof by '89." We may wonder whether, a hundred years later, under the leadership of Edgar Faure and his successor, it will not be pressed into service once more. Times, it is true, have changed. Both the Revolution and the Republic have gained much more solid national backing. If their image has taken a backseat to France's other concerns, Pierre Nora is nonetheless correct in detecting, along with the "return of national awareness," a "return to the old basic values of the Republic." In this respect, even though it is definitely over, the Revolution has not outlived its usefulness.[7]

Some historians have credited it with lifting political and social values to unprecedented heights. It is clear that the nexus "modern, secular, and liberal" that was forged at that point among "rights, freedom, and the fatherland" still holds, thus creating "a new legitimacy and a heritage that has henceforth been inviolable." In this sense, for republicans who are still rejoicing over this, the French Revolution was indeed "the beginning of time." Lynn Hunt sees the political geography of the First Republic's elections as a prefiguration of France's future divisions. Her cartography seems less instructive in this respect than one based on reactions to the Civil Constitution of the Clergy. This historian is on more solid ground when she affirms the emergence during the Revolution of a new political class with easily traceable sociological outlines. These shopkeepers and artisans were the embodiment of a democratization of public life that was brutally interrupted by Brumaire, but which presaged nineteenth-century developments up to Gambetta. Lynn Hunt sees the cultural rise of the lower- and mid-level urban bourgeoisie as proof of the modernization ushered in by the Revolution. Thanks to it and the new, more egalitarian type of power that it created, France embarked on its apprenticeship as a Republic.[8]

We have had difficulty leaving the Revolution behind in our own times. In 1968, Marat competed with Sade in the imaginary pantheon of revolutionary intellectuals. Alain Jouffroy was quick to inform his readers that "the idea of Revolution is the best and most efficient safeguard of individuality." Claude Roy, a short time before, had traded polemics with Jean Massin over the best way to celebrate the incomparable Marat, prototype of the leftist then in style. At the Cartoucherie de Vincennes Ariane Mnouchkine presented a theatrical vision of the Revolution inspired by Michelet's mythology and dominated, likewise, by the figure of Marat as the prophet of the people. Even a historian as lucid as Michel Pertué, in describing the makeup of the Convention, was moved by a desire for rationalism to interpret it as if it were some National Assembly today: From the reactionary ultraright to an exaggerated extreme left, by way of a conservative center right and a democratic center left made up of opportunists and radicals, the whole political spectrum is covered. It is almost as if we were there. For many, the story begun in 1789 has not ended.[9]

CAN MODERN REVOLUTIONS BE TRACED BACK TO THE ONE IN 1789?

John Pocock, who can hardly be accused of excessive sympathy for the French Revolution, has observed the extent of its influence. For many it gave rise to a new conception of world history. Political culture often was defined in relation to it, as the revolutions of the nineteenth and twentieth centuries demonstrate. They were so indebted to the event of 1789 because it invented the notion of revolution as a political change that was at once voluntary and total. Subsequent revolutions attempted to bring about similar transformations, making good use of the nationalistic ideology associated with a revolution that brought the fatherland to arms. This strange permutation of Enlightenment thought was not so much theorized as experienced anonymously by the entirety of a community. It is pointless to speculate whether the nationalism born of the victorious revolution really corresponded to the mentality of its leaders. It resulted above all from the events of the Revolution, from which its successors drew its lessons. The idea of a nation was new for France in 1789. With this impetus, it was to travel around the world, from a Europe trampled by its armies to Latin America, before spreading to the states born of decolonization. This creation of the political culture of the Revolution is, today, an essential element of France's prestige. The Revolution also produced the modern concepts of political terrorism and of a vanguard party. It created conditions that spurred the development of conservative thought and the early stages in the elaboration of socialism. Attitudes toward history and social order could no longer be the same after 1799 as they had been before 1789. An ideological tidal wave, the French Revolution was, in this sense, the cradle of the modern world. Its long-range influence was to prove more important in this respect than in its immediate effects.[1]

It provided a decisive element to German philosophy in the early nineteenth century and was related, along with the Romantic tradition, to the rise of German nationalism, if only by provoking a backlash. In 1794 Hungarian Jacobins were executed, while their Polish counterparts, who had risen up against the Russian army, dreamed of an international revolutionary brotherhood of European democrats. During the first half

of the nineteenth century the historiography of the French Revolution
was the common property of all the intellectuals of the Continent. From
it they drew their plans for a repeat version, splitting into the camps of
the liberals, who stopped with 1789, and the radicals, who did not reject
the example of 1793. The young Hungarian Jozsef Irinyi thus declared
in 1846, "The Revolution begun in 1789 is not yet over." Two years
later his compatriot Vasvari was to write that "the tree of liberty must
be watered with blood." Like Petöfi, this admirer of Robespierre and
his revolution, the world's new gospel and humanity's bible, was killed
in a desperate fight to which he had been pushed by moral imperatives
springing from his adherence to the ideology born in 1789. These heroes
were emulated in 1956 during Budapest's revolt against a Stalinist Soviet
order.[2]

Of all the European countries, Italy was the most profoundly shaken
by the French Revolution. Its mid-nineteenth-century national unity
movement owed much to this contact after 1796. In many ways the
culture of postrevolutionary Italy no doubt grew out of the reformist
tradition of the Enlightenment. But Italian democrats proclaimed their
allegiance to the example of 1789 even more strongly. Among them
Mazzini was especially significant, as he moved from justifying the Montagnard Terror in the early 1830s to opposing it, claiming that a repeat
of 1793 would be fatal to the interests of the republican party and the
Italian revolution. Its leaders nevertheless constantly harked back to the
French Revolution. In 1870 its mythic aura likewise surrounded the
nascent Italian socialist movement, which was more appreciative than
Mazzini in his later years of the accomplishments of the Terror.[3]

Even those authors least admiring of the French Revolution have
noted the prestige it gained abroad when its legend was elevated to
sacred status. It has contributed much more than memories of the *ancien
régime* to the glory of France, for it is considered a decisive phase in
mankind's history, the time and place where the various nations of the
world began to learn the lessons of freedom. This symbolism spread
through all of Latin America, where in the nineteenth century a number
of republics were created on the French model. And this movement was
to be repeated in our own era during the period of decolonization. To
understand this one needs only to have witnessed one of black Africa's
countless revolutions, which occurred, naturally, on the night of August 4: The power that was to be unseated was at the heart of a Committee of Public Safety; the new leaders called for people to be wary of
enemies both within and without, to achieve victory or die for the fatherland, and to form, posthaste, committees for the defense of the
revolution. The weary Hexagon can no longer match these tropical

passions, and the memory of 1789 has long been more alive in Mexico City or Brazzaville than in Paris.[4]

The historical fortunes of Marxism also explain this shift. Its founders always granted key importance to the French Revolution, from the writings of the young Marx to those of Lenin, who created or inspired large numbers of governments that still trace their roots, in part, to their 1793 precursor. The events of 1789 do indeed constitute a source of Marxism since, as Hans-Peter Jaeck reminds us, this date served to pinpoint a period of world history in which feudalism and the *ancien régime* stood opposed to the rise of the bourgeoisie. This was made possible, according to Marx and Engels, only by the "community of revolutionary interests within the third estate." On a deeper level, Ferenc Fehér has just shown that the French Revolution provided the model for the Marxist conception of politics. It should be noted, moreover, that on these two points Marx's thought is not truly original, since it overlaps with Guizot's and Thiers's. But the founders of Marxism perceptively observed the dual character of the Revolution of 1789, which was at once the founding act of democracy and the first mirror of its contradictions. As Jaurès was to say, socialism was conceived primarily to resolve these, and thus to carry out the legacy of the French Revolution.[5]

This was one of the ambitions of Lenin, who was always fascinated by the period of Jacobin predominance. Before turning late in life to the writings of Marat, he had accepted the comparison made in 1904 by his Menshevik adversaries between their struggle and the one that had split the Girondins and the Montagnards. This interpretation made the Bolsheviks, in turn, the conscious organizers of the revolution. Its leaders in early-twentieth-century Russia viewed their conflict in terms of the history of the Convention. Their concept of dictatorship was that of Robespierre and Saint-Just and their main goal was to imitate the great movement of 1789. In 1905 Lenin evoked with relish the prospect of a Terror and "several Vendées." Faced with an eventual counterrevolution, he openly proclaimed his adherence to Jacobin psychology and policy, which he viewed as authorizing the use of "revolutionary violence." In 1917 he identified his activities with the Jacobin example of "democratic revolution and defiance to the coalition of monarchs against the Republic." He praised the implacability of the Convention at its height and observed that its memory, loathed by the bourgeois and feared by the petty bourgeoisie, remained dear to the oppressed, for it bought them the hope of people's power. This concept of history stressed a hypothetical hegemony of the masses during the year II. Pressed into the service of the communist cause, it long dominated a historiography that refused, along with George Lefebvre, to see the Mountain's dictatorship during the Terror as an enterprise that repressed the plebeian movement. Victor Daline noticed the echoes of Robespierre in the Lenin of 1917 who wanted to take away from "the capitalists their bread and all their boots," while hoping he would not be forced to send defenseless people to the guillotine. He too was soon obliged to justify his own Terror by the force of circumstances. The whole history of Bolshevism in power was written in the shadow of the Convention, and 1793 remained an essential point of reference. Lenin ended his career contemplating, like many of his eventual successors, the possiblity of a Soviet Thermidor. This obsession brought Russia one step closer to eighteenth-century France. Lenin alluded several times to this in his public speeches and private notes. He was afraid that 1921 might be a repeat of 1794, but took comfort in the popular support he believed his government enjoyed.[6]

Subsequent communist revolutions, from Peking to Havana, have not escaped this mythology, particularly since their debt to Leninism is immense and they view modern world history through its deforming prism. It was perhaps not wrong to place the French Revolution at the center of the comparative study of revolutions, since its image remains at the heart of the social and ideological movements of the nineteenth and twentieth centuries. One possible explanation, offered by Theda Skocpol, involves the concept of modernization, with revolution offering the advantage of political mobilization of the masses in the service of economic progress. Valid as it is for most of the revolutions of the twentieth century, this view does not seem to hold for that of 1789. For them, as for modern history as a whole, it served rather as a political educator. Its importance stems not only from its creation of the socioeconomic classes of the bourgeoisie and the proletariat, which did not exist before it, but also from the astonishing inventiveness with which, over the course of ten years, it tried out almost all the possible forms of modern government: constitutional monarchy, republic based on property qualifications, democratic republic, oligarchical republic, popular dictatorship, direct municipal democracy, military dictatorship, etc. An astounded world witnessed the rapid succession of these various notions of power on the French political scene. An incredibly fertile proving ground, the Revolution handed down to the future all its political games and all their rules after having created an enduring model for each.[7]

The English-speaking countries have been almost the only ones untouched by this creativity and its influence, insofar as they had their own liberal tradition which proved, in practice, rather difficult to export. France dissociated itself likewise from them, at the time, by its rejection of the economic manifestations of modernity. Choosing political, rather than industrial revolution, it quickly elevated the state to sacred status, retaining its rural myths of a traditional society drawn from both its *ancien régime* heritage and the lessons of the republics of antiquity. What the world remembered of the French Revolution was its emphasis on class antagonisms and party conflict, and its taste for ideological radicalization and extreme solutions throughout the tumult of war at home and abroad. Since then, it has often been believed that nations and regimes were necessarily formed and dissolved after this pattern. The Revolution's greatness, and no doubt its curse as well, is that it invented modern politics.[8]

CONCLUSION

Tocqueville and Taine correctly viewed Napoleonic centralization as the foremost result of the Revolution. This culmination of a millennial process created a ruling class that was politically emasculated and even less favorable to economic development than the nobility of the *ancien régime*. The legal and fiscal bases of this predominance of the notables were to last until the beginning of the twentieth century. Such an outcome certainly represented a failure in terms of the major ideals of the pre-revolutionary period. Many enlightened French citizens had hoped at that time to replace royal despotism with a constitution inspired by the spirit of the Enlightenment. Opposition by a segment of the aristocracy to certain key aspects of this system lent revolutionary overtones to the events of 1789. They did not occur in an atmosphere of unanimity and affected above all the cities, with their populations of bourgeois and artisans. Even in those circles, participation in the revolutionary movement involved only a narrow militant minority. The violence it engendered was related to this fact.

It enjoyed even less support in the countryside, and generally speaking, was greeted very coolly by those Frenchmen who did not own land. The majority of the rural population, the poor and the marginal elements, remained uncommittted or indifferent to it until religious difficulties transformed them into its sworn enemies. Their resistance and the repression it brought on completed the disruption and weakening of the nation's economy. During this period a third of the departments underwent some deindustrialization, while urban progress came to a standstill. In the wake of their revolution, the French were, on the whole, poorer than before, and they lagged further than ever behind England. The Terror, occurring in the context of a foreign war, had even more serious consequences. By attributing all its problems to internal enemies the government created a vicious circle in which refusal to make the requisite sacrifices simultaneously strengthened those elements hostile to the Revolution and the effort made to liquidate them. The dictatorship of the Terror itself was unable to carry out its program as a whole. Divided as to its own goals, it succeeded mainly in surrounding itself with an atmosphere of fear and hatred. After Thermidor, the fragmentation of the revolutionaries and their separation from the nation only increased. Under these conditions, France was practically ungoverned in many regions.

The breakdown of representative institutions explains the return at the end of the Directory to an authoritarian regime. The main concern of the ruling clique brought to power by the Revolution was to keep public opinion from playing a decisive political role. This was the basis for its support of Bonaparte, who would also settle external affairs to its satisfaction. The new state, by means of the Concordat, proved to be the only one capable of ending the endemic disorders caused by the religious issue for the last ten years. In this sense, it was pressure by the traditional peasantry and the concessions that had to be granted it that led France to the Napoleonic system. Many ideals adopted in 1789 were dropped or diminished in the process. The partial failure of the Revolution thus stems from the fact that it was a popular movement only to a very limited degree. On the contrary, it increasingly incurred the hatred of the masses.[1]

This conclusion of Donald Sutherland's is a reminder of the key ways in which the course of the Revolution was shaped by those who opposed it. They were complex, as the Rennes colloquium underlined in 1985, and the counterrevolution's history, like the Revolution's, must be written in the plural. Their essence, in the image of the country that nurtured them, was diversity. Norman Hampson has even wondered, with typical British wit, if the huge number of counterrevolutionaries, among whom figured many former supporters of the Revolution, made it meaningless to lump them together in one category. Far from a monolithic phenomenon, the Revolution was experienced in very different ways by groups and individuals. The viewpoint of the majority of peasants was totally unrelated to that of the deputies, other politicians, or the enlightened citizenry. Wholesale traders were, for the most part, poorly disposed toward a revolution that was supposedly capitalistic, just as the humble people were cool to one that claimed to speak for them. As for individuals, caught in a sometimes absurd web of circumstances, their choices were often dictated by accidents of time and place. The unity of the revolutionary movement, like that of its opposition, is a myth. What fueled, built, or weakened each was a fight to the death for power, transformed by its participants into a struggle between Good and Evil. Historians should neither repeat that era's illusion nor oversimplify this most complex situation. The overturning of customs or interests, along with progressive and successive disillusionments, weighed ever more heavily on the course of the Revolution. Proclaimed or awaited by those who launched it as an apocalyptic event, it embodied above all the dreary banality of existence for most of those who lived through it.[2]

The chief merit of recent research on the Revolution by English-speaking historians lies in their simultaneous grasp of its continuities with the *ancien régime* and its irreducible diversity. Traditional economic constraints and social, familial, local, and personal antagonisms did not magically disappear in 1789. They dragged on, with the mentalities that either caused or grew out of them, until well into the nineteenth century. In this respect, the Revolution marks no break in a long historical period that, *from the perspective of the masses*, extends uninterrupted from Louis XIV's France to the France of 1848. This is forgotten when too much emphasis is placed on superficial political machinations. But the Revolution did nothing to change the lot of women, the poor, or children. It barely touched hierarchies and fundamental balances. We have seen that it scarcely affected popular leisure activities or beliefs, which resisted its inducements. Yves-Marie Bercé has compared the rural revolts of the seventeenth century with those of the peasants of Aquitaine in the revolutionary period. The eradication of seigniorial dues gave rise to the same ambiguities as the land-tax exemptions formerly granted by the king. The movements that followed were directly linked "in their motives, their ways of taking up arms, and of diffusion" to the old myth about tax exemptions and the riots they would induce. Later struggles, whether against taxes or grain distribution policies, were likewise a carryover from the *ancien régime*. As chief of state, Bonaparte put former associates of Calonne and Brienne at the head of his financial system and called on Maupeou's former right-hand man, along with Lebrun, to help him govern France. From the other side of the revolutionary interlude, the new despotism reached out to the old.[3]

The Revolution was astonishingly varied from one region to another. Each refracted the shock through its own structures and customs. The excessive attention paid to what was going on in Paris and the assemblies has often obscured this fact, which undermines the myth of national unity. For the faraway French islands, for example, the problem of slavery was by far the most important issue. The Constituent Assembly, which proclaimed the Rights of Man, was careful not to interfere with this fundamental element of colonial trade. There followed in 1791 a tremendous uprising, which culminated twelve years later in the creation of the Republic of Haiti. The rest of the French West Indies had to wait a long while before benefiting from the principles of 1789. On the island of Réunion, likewise, a hopeful period was followed by disillusionment and disappointment. Even though *sans-culottes* were in power for a year beginning in the spring of 1794, there, too, the revolutionary period ended in economic disaster, social tensions, and political divisions. Early enthusiasms had died a sad death amid "general indifference." At the end of the *ancien régime* Corsica, more recently annexed by France, had enjoyed the benefit of an interesting experiment with a brand of enlightened despotism concerned with reestabishing order and promoting development. This bureaucratic pragmatism, vigorously opposed to privilege, represented an original attempt at regeneration. This was perhaps why revolutionary sentiment in Corsica differed from that in France. It was even more marked by party spirit, the outgrowth of a clan mentality. Corsican political leaders used networks of family influence and trampled the rights of citizens with impunity. They made a travesty of the elections they participated in and energetically distributed spoils to the satisfaction of their friends and relatives. In Corsica "the role of personal loyalty to the leader" was far more important than "general motivations of a public nature." This was particularly true of local community life at the time of the Revolution. Elections often came down to armed battles or sordid buy-offs, and abuses of power were rampant. The administrative authorities could only show their distress at this situation that unleashed rivalries. Religious and political oppositions, as well as those between city dwellers and village folk, added to these confrontations.[4]

More than one region of France resembled Corsica in this respect between 1789 and 1799. The Revolution opened the floodgates, above all, to a multitude of small civil wars. The ultimate recourse to authoritarianism and centralization grew out of this tendency to generalized fragmentation. A large part of the Midi and almost all the west clearly experienced this. Jean-Clément Martin's fine book about the Vendéan tragedy has shown how typical was a regional revolt linked to the social and ideological contradictions of the Revolution and its tendency to solve them by repression. No doubt the logic of destruction did not spread the bitter fruits of the Terror as much everywhere as it did here. But a minority republic often left memories of disaster with its enemies. Along with pointless massacres, the scope of devastation and ruin shows the seriousness of this trauma. Less severe elsewhere, it marked Provence, the Lyonnais, and several areas of the Languedoc and Brittany. The Parisian basin and the northwest were more affected by a food catastrophe that recalled the worst moments of Louis XIV's reign. On the whole, no region was spared the scourges born of inflation, religious or political persecution and reprisals, or the disorders produced by draft dodging, brigandage, and insecurity. Mythology and legend had associated the French Revolution with images of celebration, glory, and happiness. In reality, especially for the humble, it brought above all misfortune, with its complement of material and moral scars. It was no more able to lighten the burden of human misery than the "old refrain" it claimed to succeed. At best, it managed to lull it with heroic dreams and remote promises.[5]

These dreams and promises were often fulfilled later. The reality of the French Revolution is greater than the sum of its more or less disappointing meanderings. Our modern societies owe to it the principles of civil equality, national sovereignty, public freedoms, and the secular state. Along with authoritarian socialism, liberal democracy and democratic socialism are the direct inheritors of 1789 and 1792. In France, for example, all the political parties, including those of the right, claim this heritage, which culminated in the Constitutional Republic of France.

Its triumph gave rise to a mythic vision of its origins, mixed with the new secular, monolithic cult of the national state. From Thiers to Soboul, by way of Michelet, Mathiez, Furet, and Richet, the predominant historiographical tendency has been to focus on the debates of the Paris tribunes and the development of revolutionary forces. Little attention has been paid to the silence of the disaffected, to regional, cultural, and social diversity, and to the weight of popular traditions.

In the last twenty years, especially among scholars of the English-speaking world, a new vision of the past, more respectful of individual, social, and ideological contradictions and less obsessed with the mechanisms peculiar to general political evolution has gained currency. I have tried to point this out. It seems to me to correspond to many exigencies of our time, less infatuated than earlier eras with the virtues of centralization and the heroic legend of the giants of year II. Although this revised view makes it impossible to repeat the old saws, it does not authorize the excesses of their usual adversaries. It in no way detracts from the extraordinary fruitfulness of an event whose far-reaching consequences are more important than its immediate achievements. French public life still rests on the principles it set forth, as elaborated by subsequent generations. In this sense, like it or not, whatever one may say about it, the French Revolution is at the root of our world today.

This is why the French today are grateful that it existed, despite its faults or deficiencies. They know they are indebted to it for the juridical origins of their democratic institutions. The critical reassessment of the history of the Revolution draws its inspiration from values it shared (concern for the downtrodden and the wronged, the rights of people and conscience, respect for differences) but was unable to put into practice, leaving this task to its heirs. It is in its name that the legitimate oppositions (religious, regional, and social) that it encountered are being rehabilitated. Jaurès may have been unable to understand this, but this is no reason to adopt the distorted, incomplete interpretation of Taine and his followers. To limit the historical impact of the French Revolution to its terrorist and bureaucratic aftermath, from whatever ideological bias, is an error in judgment.

It comes of forgetting the truth expressed by Bolívar when he said, "To understand revolutions and those who take part in them, one must simultaneously view them from very close and judge them from afar."[6]

GLOSSARY

CAHIERS OR CAHIERS DE DOLÉANCES: the list of grievances drawn up by each of the three orders for presentation to the Estates-General.

COUR DES AIDES: sovereign tax court.

FERMIERS GÉNÉRAUX: a group of financiers who in return for a special lease or bail (*ferme*) collected the indirect taxes and the income from the royal domains and royal monopolies.

INTENDANT: an official in charge of one of the 34 *généralités* into which France was divided in 1789.

JOURNÉE OR JOURNÉE POPULAIRE: day of collective popular intervention.

LEVÉE EN MASSE: mass conscription.

MAÎTRES DES REQUÊTES: councillors who held their offices by appointment (as opposed to venality) and were directly responsible to the royal councils.

PARLEMENT: sovereign judicial court.

PHILOSOPHE: Enlightenment man of letters and thinker.

SÉANCE ROYALE: enforced registration of a royal edict in a *parlement* in the presence of the king.

CHRONOLOGY

I. THE ORIGINS OF THE REVOLUTION

1748

Montesquieu: *L'Esprit des lois*. Grain crisis. Treaty of Aix La Chapelle.

1749

Buffon: *Théorie de la terre*. Edicts by Machault d'Arnouville establishing the *vingtième* tax on all income.

1750

Rousseau: *Si le rétablissement des sciences et des arts a contribué à épurer les moeurs*. Voltaire in Potsdam, with Frederick II. "Tax war": the privileged classes against Machault.

1751

Publication of the first two volumes of the *Encyclopédie*. Founding of the *Journal économique*. Edict suspending the application of the *vingtième* to the clergy.

1752

Affair of the *billets de confession*.

1753

"Great Remonstrances," exile, then recall of *parlement* over this affair.

1754

Rousseau: *Discours sur l'orgine et les fondements de l'inégalité parmi les hommes.* Machault d'Arnouville resigns as controller general of finances.

1755

Death of Montesquieu. France and England cut off diplomatic relations.

1756

Edict creating a new *vingtième*. Agitation by the *parlements*. Beginning of the Seven Years War.

1757

Damiens attempts to assassinate Louis XV. Resignation of Machault d'Arnouville as naval minister.

1758

Quesnay: *Tableau économique.* Choiseul becomes secretary of foreign affairs.

1759

Voltaire: *Candide, ou l'optimisme.* Quebec surrenders.

1760

Voltaire moves to Ferney. Montreal surrenders.

1761

Rousseau: *Julie, ou la Nouvelle Héloïse.* Decree granting "inducements to those who cultivate new land." Turgot, *intendant* in the Limousin. Pondicherry surrenders.

1762

Rousseau: *Du contrat social ou Principes du droit politique; Emile, ou De l'éducation. Parlement* declares the statutes of the Company of Jesus contrary to public order and forbids Jesuits to teach. Abolition of feudal duties in Savoy.

1763

Voltaire: *Traité sur la tolérance.* Decree freeing the domestic grain trade. Founding of the *Gazette du commerce.* Treaty of Paris ends the Seven Years War. France retains only the last vestiges of its first colonial empire.

1764

Voltaire: *Dictionnaire philosophique.* Society of Jesus in France dissolved.

1765

Founding of the *Ephémérides du citoyen.* Disturbances in Brittany: The *parlement* of Rennes resigns.

1766

Turgot: *Réflexions sur la formation et la distribution des richesses.* New royal declaration encouraging cultivation of land. Lorraine annexed to France. The monarchy and the *parlement* of Paris clash over the situation in Brittany. Bougainville's voyage to the South Seas.

1767

D'Holbach: *Le Christianisme dévoilé.* Le Mercier de La Rivière: *L'Ordre naturel et essentiel des sociétés politiques.*

1768

Quesnay: *Physiocratie ou Constitution naturelle du gouvernement le plus avantageux au genre humain.* Maupeou becomes chancellor. France acquires Corsica.

1769

Diderot: *D'Alembert's Dream.* Suppression of the charter of the Compagnie des Indes. Abbé Terray becomes controller general of finance.

1770

D'Holbach: *Système de la nature; Essai sur les préjugés.* Raynal: *Histoire philosophique et politique des établissements et du commerce des Européens dans les deux Indes.* Abbé Galiani: *Dialogues sur le commerce des blés.* Economic crisis strikes most of France. Choiseul disgraced. The dauphin marries Marie-Antoinette.

1771

Lavoisier analyzes the composition of air. Monge invents analytic geometry. Abbé Terray forbids the exportation of grains. Judiciary reforms by Maupeou and suppression of *parlements.* Kerguelen's voyage to the South Seas. Abolition of serfdom in Savoy.

1772

Publication of the *Encyclopédie* is completed.

1773

Diderot goes to Russia. Formation of *Grand-Orient* of France. The pope dissolves the Jesuit order.

1774

Death of Louis XV. Louis XVI becomes king. Vergennes becomes secretary of state for foreign affairs. Turgot becomes controller general of finance. *Parlements* reinstated. Free domestic grain trade.

1775

Stabilization of the long-term rise in agricultural prices. "Flour Wars."

1776

Adam Smith: *Inquiring into the Nature and Causes of the Wealth of Nations*. First pig iron rails manufactured in France. Jouffroy operates a steamboat on the Doubs. Guilds suppressed, then reinstated after Turgot's disgrace. Franklin goes to Paris.

1777

Widespread crisis of vineyards. Necker becomes director general of finance. La Fayette goes to America.

1778

Deaths of Voltaire and Rousseau. Creation of the Discount Bank of Paris and a provincial assembly in Berry. French-American Treaty of Alliance and beginning of struggles between France and England.

1779

Gluck: *Iphigénie*. Abolition of serfdom in the royal domain. French-Spanish alliance.

1780

Abolition of torture. Rochambeau goes to America.

1781

Publication of Rousseau's *Confessions*. Founding of the Creusot factory. Necker's *Compte rendu* to the king and his resignation on May 19. Edict requiring all officers to prove four degrees of nobility.

1782

Choderlos de Laclos: *Les Liaisons dangereuses*. Suffren goes to India.

1783

First performance of Beaumarchais's *Marriage of Figaro*. David: "Andromaque." Calonne becomes controller general of finance. Treaty of Versailles recognizing the independence of the United States of America.

1784

Bernardin de Saint-Pierre: *Études de la nature*. Death of Diderot. David: "Oath of the Horatii." Ledoux begins building customs posts in Paris.

1785

Necker: *De l'administration des finances de la France*. Cagliostro in Paris. "Affair of the Diamond Necklace." Forage crisis throughout France. First casting of coke ore by the Creusot factory. Calonne reestablishes the Compagnie des Indes. La Pérouse's voyage.

1786

Condorcet: *Vie de Turgot*. French-English trade treaty. Calonne's program for financial reform.

II. THE COURSE OF THE REVOLUTION

1787

FEBRUARY 22 Meeting of the Assembly of Notables.

APRIL 8 Calonne dismissed, replaced by Loménie de Brienne.

MAY 12 Dismissal of the Assembly of Notables.

NOVEMBER Edict granting civil status to Protestants.

1788

MAY 8 Judiciary reform by Lamoignon.

JUNE 7 Popular uprising in Grenoble in support of the parliamentary opposition.

JULY 21 Dauphiné's three estates demand national reforms and provincial liberties.

AUGUST 8 Decision to convoke the Estates-General on May 1, 1789.

AUGUST 25 Necker reinstated as controller general of finance.

SEPTEMBER 23 Reconvened *parlement* demands the convocation of the Estates-General its 1614 format.

DECEMBER 27 Louis XVI agrees to double the size of the Third Estate.

1789

JANUARY 24 Letter convoking and setting forth electoral rules for the Estates-General.

MARCH Agrarian revolts in Provence, Picardy, the Cambrésis.

APRIL 27 Riot in the Faubourg Saint-Antoine.

MAY 5 Opening session of the Estates-General in Versailles.

MAY 6 The Third Estate adopts the title Assembly of the Commons and demands verification of credentials in common.

JUNE 17 The Commons adopt the title National Assembly.

JUNE 20 Tennis court oath.

JUNE 23 *Séance royale:* The Third Estate refuses to disband.

JUNE 27 The king orders the deputies of the clergy and the nobility to join the Third Estate.

JULY 9 The National Assembly proclaims itself a Constituent Assembly.

JULY 11 Dismissal of Necker.

JULY 12 Disturbances in Paris.

JULY 13 Formation of a permanent committee and a bourgeois militia in Paris.

JULY 14 Fall of the Bastille.

JULY 16 Necker recalled.

JULY 17 Louis XVI at the Hotel de Ville in Paris: Bailly presents him with the tricolor cockade. Emigration of the Comte d'Artois.

LATTER HALF OF JULY: Municipal revolts and peasant risings in the provinces.

JULY 20 Beginning of the Great Fear.

AUGUST 4 Abolition of privileges and partial abolition of feudalism.

AUGUST 26 Adoption of Declaration of the Rights of Man and the Citizen.

SEPTEMBER 11 Constituent Assembly grants the king a suspensive veto on legislation.

OCTOBER 1 Banquet of the bodyguards and officers of the Flanders regiment.

OCTOBER 5-6 Women march from Paris to Versailles: The king brought back to Paris.

OCTOBER 12 The Assembly installed in Paris.

OCTOBER 21 Martial law decreed.

NOVEMBER 2 Church property nationalized.

NOVEMBER 29 Federation of the National Guard of Dauphiné and Vivarais.

DECEMBER 14 Creation of the *assignat*, pegged to the nationalized church property.

1790

JANUARY Election of new municipalities. Peasant risings in Brittany, Périgord, Quercy.

FEBRUARY Founding of the first popular society.

FEBRUARY 13 Perpetual monastic vows prohibited.

MARCH 15 Decree on redemption of feudal dues on lands.

APRIL Creation of the Cordelier Club.

MAY Discussion of the right to peace and war. Mirabeau sells his services to the court. Creation of the Commission on Weights and Measures.

JUNE 21 Avignon requests annexation to France.

JULY 21 Civil Constitution of the Clergy passed.

JULY 14 Festival of the Federation celebrated in Paris.

AUGUST 26 The Constituent Assembly rescinds the Family Compact with Spain.

AUGUST 27 The *assignat* becomes a paper currency.

AUGUST 31 Massacre of rebellious Swiss soldiers in Nancy.

NOVEMBER 27 The Constituent Assembly requires the clergy to take an oath of loyalty to the Civil Constitution.

1791

MARCH 2 Abolition of guilds.

MARCH 11 The Pope condemns the Civil Constitution of the Clergy.

APRIL 2 Death of Mirabeau.

MAY 7-15 Discussion of the political rights of free men of color.

JUNE 11 Voltaire's ashes transferred to the Pantheon.

JUNE 14 Passage of the Le Chapelier law prohibiting coalitions and strikes.

JUNE 20–21 King's flight and arrest at Varennes.

JULY 6 Leopold II calls for sovereign powers to unite against the Revolution.

JULY 15 The Constituent Assembly exonerates the king.

JULY 16 Founding of the Feuillant Club.

JULY 17 Champ de Mars massacre.

AUGUST 27 Electoral law revised: Property qualification increased. Declaration of Pilnitz: Foreign powers issue a warning to revolutionary France.

SEPTEMBER 12 Avignon annexed to France.

SEPTEMBER 14 Louis XVI swears allegiance to the Constitution.

SEPTEMBER 30 Constituent Assembly dissolves.

OCTOBER 1 Legislative Assembly meets.

OCTOBER 16 Unrest in Avignon; la Glacière massacre.

NOVEMBER 9 Decree against émigrés.

NOVEMBER 16 Petion elected mayor of Paris over La Fayette.

NOVEMBER 29 Decree against refractory priests.

DECEMBER 9 Creation of a Feuillant ministry.

DECEMBER 12 Robespierre's first antiwar speech to the Jacobins.

DECEMBER 14 Ultimatum to the Elector of Trèves to order the dispersal of émigré assemblies.

1792

JANUARY 6 The Elector of Trèves disperses émigrés.

JANUARY 23 Unrest in Paris over sugar and coffee.

FEBRUARY–MARCH Agrarian disturbances and popular price-fixing in markets in the provinces.

MARCH 10 Indictment of Lessart, minister of foreign affairs.

MARCH 15 Formation of a Girondin ministry.

APRIL 20 Declaration of war against the "king of Bohemia and Hungary."

APRIL 24 Rouget de Lisle composes the *Chant de guerre pour l'armée du Rhin* (the *Marseillaise*).

APRIL 29 First defeats on the frontiers.

MAY 27 Decree against refractory priests.

MAY 29 King's constitutional guard dissolved.

JUNE 8 Creation of a camp of twenty thousand National Guardsmen at Paris.

JUNE 11 Royal veto of decree against refractory priests and decree creating the camp in Paris.

JUNE 13 Dismissal of Girondin ministry.

JUNE 20 Demonstration at the Tuileries. The king maintains his veto.

JULY 11 Legislative Assembly declares the country in danger.

JULY 17 *Fédérés* in Paris demand the suspension of the king's powers.

JULY 20 Girondins negotiate secretly with the court.

JULY 25 Brunswick Manifesto threatening Paris with total subversion.

AUGUST 3 Forty-seven of Paris's 48 sections demand that the king be deposed.

AUGUST 10 Insurrection, storming of the Tuileries, and suspension of the king from his functions. Convocation of a National Convention.

AUGUST 14 Unsuccessful attempt by La Fayette to take over Paris with his army. He emigrates on the nineteenth.

AUGUST 23 Longwy surrenders.

SEPTEMBER 2 Verdun surrenders.

SEPTEMBER 2–6 Paris prison massacres.

SEPTEMBER 20 Civil status secularized, divorce instituted, Legislative Assembly disbands. Convention meets. Victory at Valmy.

SEPTEMBER 21 Monarchy abolished.

SEPTEMBER 24 French troops enter Nice.

OCTOBER 1 French troops enter Mayence.

NOVEMBER 6 Victory at Jemmapes. Belgium conquered.

NOVEMBER 19 Propaganda war organized.

NOVEMBER 20 King's secret documents discovered at the Tuileries.

NOVEMBER 22 Rural unrest in Beauce.

NOVEMBER 27 Savoy annexed.

DECEMBER 8 All controls on grain trade lifted.

DECEMBER 11 Louis XVI's trial begins.

DECEMBER 15 Revolutionary administrations set up in conquered territories.

1793

JANUARY 14 Deliberations begin on the fate of Louis XVI.

JANUARY 21 Louis XVI executed.

JANUARY 31 Nice annexed.

FEBRUARY 1 Declaration of war against England and Holland.

FEBRUARY 21 Consolidation of line regiments and volunteer battalions.

FEBRUARY 24 Three hundred thousand men called up.

FEBRUARY 25–26 Grocery stores in Paris looted.

MARCH 7 Declaration of war against Spain.

MARCH 9–10 Attempted uprising in Paris.

MARCH 10 Establishment of the Revolutionary Tribunal. Beginning of Vendéan revolt.

MARCH 18 Dumouriez defeated at Neerwinden. Withdrawal from Belgium.

MARCH 21 Creation of revolutionary surveillance committees.

MARCH 28 Émigrés subjected to "civic death" and permanently banned.

APRIL 5 Creation of the Committee of Public Safety. Dumouriez deserts to the enemy.

APRIL 11 Imposition of *assignat* as legal tender.

MAY 4 First Maximum prices of grains and flour set by departments.

MAY 29 Anti-Jacobin uprising in Lyons.

MAY 31–JUNE 2 *Journées* in Paris. 27 Girondin deputies arrested.

JUNE 7 Federalist revolt in Calvados and Bordeaux.

JUNE 10 Decree on the division of communal lands. Museum of Natural History established.

JUNE 24 Passage of a new declaration of rights and the Constitution of 1793.

JUNE 25 Jacques Roux petitions for fixed prices and the death penalty for hoarders.

JUNE 26–28 Unrest over soap shortages in Paris.

JULY 10 Restructuring of the Committee of Public Safety: Danton eliminated.

JULY 13 Marat assassinated.

JULY 17 Final abolition of feudal rights.

JULY 23 Fall of Mayence.

JULY 26 Death penalty for hoarders.

JULY 27 Robespierre joins the Committee of Public Safety.

AUGUST 1 Fall of Valenciennes. Decree establishing the metric system.

AUGUST 8 Kellermann's army surrounds Lyons.

AUGUST 23 Universal obligation to military service (*lévee en masse*) decreed.

AUGUST 24 Decree instituting the Grand Register of Public Accounts.

AUGUST 25 Marseille in revolt; Convention's troops enter.

AUGUST 29 Toulon delivered to the English.

SEPTEMBER 4–5 Popular *journées* in Paris. The Terror is henceforth the order of the day.

SEPTEMBER 6–8 Hondschoote victorious against Anglo-Dutch forces.

SEPTEMBER 11 National Maximum price on grains and flour.

SEPTEMBER 17 Law of Suspects.

SEPTEMBER 29 General Maximum on prices and salaries.

OCTOBER 5 Adoption of Republican calendar.

OCTOBER 9 (18 vendémiaire year II) Lyons surrenders. English merchandise prohibited.

OCTOBER 10 (19 vendémiaire year II) Government is declared "revolutionary until peace."

OCTOBER 16 (25 vendémiaire year II) Marie-Antoinette executed. Wattignies defeats Austrians.

OCTOBER 31 (10 brumaire year II) Girondins executed.

OCTOBER–NOVEMBER (brumaire, year II) De-Christianization movement.

NOVEMBER 6 (16 brumaire year II) Municipalities allowed to renounce the Catholic faith.

NOVEMBER 10 (20 brumaire year II) Festival of Reason at Notre-Dame in Paris.

NOVEMBER 13 (23 brumaire year II) Vendéans defeated at Granville.

NOVEMBER 17 (27 brumaire year II) Compagnie des Indes scandal uncovered.

NOVEMBER 21 (1 frimaire year II) Robespierre opposes de-Christianization.

DECEMBER 4 (14 frimaire year II) Law constituting the revolutionary government.

DECEMBER 5 Desmoulins begins his campaign for leniency.

DECEMBER 8 Robespierre decrees freedom of religion.

DECEMBER 12 Vendéans defeated at Le Mans.

DECEMBER 19 Toulon recaptured. Decree instituting free mandatory primary schooling.

DECEMBER 23 (3 nivôse year II) Vendéans defeated at Savenay.

DECEMBER 26 Hoche's victory at Geisberg.

1794

FEBRUARY 4 (16 pluviôse year II) Slavery abolished in the colonies.

FEBRUARY 26 (8 ventôse year II) Confiscation of suspects' property.

MARCH 3 (13 véntôse year II) This property to be used for compensating "indigent patriots."

MARCH 6 Barère's report on the elimination of begging.

MARCH 7 André Chénier arrested.

MARCH 14 Hébert and Cordelier leaders arrested.

MARCH 24 (4 germinal year II) Hébertists executed.

APRIL 14 Jean-Jacques Rousseau's ashes transferred to Pantheon.

MAY 7 (18 floréal year II) Decree instituting the Cult of the Supreme Being.

MAY 11 Decree instituting the Great Book of National Charity.

JUNE 8 (20 prairial year II) Festival of the Supreme Being.

JUNE 10 Law reorganizing the Revolutionary Tribunal.

JUNE 26 (8 messidor year II) Fleurus's victory over Austrians.

JULY 8 (20 messidor year II) French troops enter Brussels.

JULY 14 First performance of the *Chant du départ* (the *Marseillaise*).

JULY 23 (5 thermidor year II) Forced salary reductions in Paris.

JULY 26 Robespierre's last speech.

JULY 27 Robespierrists arrested.

JULY 28 Robespierrists executed.

AUGUST 24 (7 fructidor year II) Reorganization of revolutionary government.

SEPTEMBER 18 (2nd *sans-culottide* year II) Elimination of religious budget.

OCTOBER 10 (19 vendémiaire year III) National Conservatory of Arts and Industries founded.

OCTOBER 30 (9 brumaire year III) *École normale supérieure* founded.

NOVEMBER 19 (29 brumaire year III) Jacobin Club closed.

DECEMBER 8 (18 frimaire year III) Deputies who protested against June 2, 1793, reinstated in the convention.

DECEMBER 24 (4 nivôse year III) Maximum abolished.

DECEMBER 27 French troops enter Holland.

1795

JANUARY 30 (11 pluviôse year III) Pichegru captures the Dutch fleet.

FEBRUARY 17 (29 pluviôse year III) Amnesty and freedom of religion granted to Vendéans.

FEBRUARY 21 (3 ventôse year III) Reaffirmation of separation of church and state.

MARCH 8 (8 ventôse year III) Recall of outlawed Girondin deputies.

MARCH 30 (10 germinal year III) *École des langues orientales* founded.

APRIL 1 (12 germinal year III) Attempted popular uprising in Paris.

APRIL 6 Treaty of Basle between France and Prussia.

MAY 16 (27 floréal year III) Treaty of the Hague between France and Holland.

MAY 20 (1 prairial year III) Popular uprising in Paris.

MAY 22 Faubourg Saint-Antoine disarmed.

JUNE 21 (3 messidor year III) Sliding scale of depreciation of the *assignat*.

JULY 4 (16 messidor year III) Discussion of Constitution of Year III begins.

JULY 15 Émigrés land at Quiberon. Hoche sends them back to sea.

JULY 22 (4 thermidor year III) Treaty of Basle between France and Spain.

JULY 23 Constitution of Year III voted.

AUGUST 30 (13 fructidor year IV) Law of the Two-Thirds.

OCTOBER 5 (13 vendémiaire year IV) Attempted royalist insurrection in Paris.

OCTOBER 25 (3 brumaire year IV) Establishment of central schools and the *Institut National* for the training of teachers.

OCTOBER 26 Convention disbands.

NOVEMBER Beginning of the Directory.

NOVEMBER 7 (16 brumaire year IV) Pantheon Club opens.

NOVEMBER 30 (9 frimaire year IV) Publication of the "Manifesto of the Plebians" in Babeuf's *Tribun du peuple*.

1796

FEBRUARY 19 (30 pluviôse year IV) *Assignats* discontinued.

FEBRUARY–MARCH (pluviôse-ventôse year IV) *Chouannerie* repressed.

MARCH 2 (12 ventose year IV) Bonaparte becomes general of the army of Italy.

MARCH 18 Creation of the territorial note, replacing the *assignat*.

MAY 10 (21 floreal year IV) Babeuf and his coconspirators are arrested.

MAY 14 French troops enter Milan.

MAY 15 The king of Piedmont cedes Savoy and Nice to France.

NOVEMBER 14–17 (24–27 brumaire year V) Battle of Arcola.

DECEMBER 16–29 Hoche attempts to land in Ireland.

DECEMBER 31 (11 nivôse year V) Bonaparte establishes the Cispadane Republic.

1797

JANUARY 14 (25 nivôse year V) Bonaparte's victory at Rivoli.

FEBRUARY 4 (16 pluviôse year V) Return to metal currency.

FEBRUARY 19 (1 ventôse year V) The pope recognizes the transfer of Avignon to France.

MARCH–APRIL (germinal year V) Elections to the councils strengthen the monarchist right.

APRIL 18 Preliminaries of Treaty of Leoben with Austria.

MAY 19 (30 floréal year V) Barthélemy elected director.

MAY 26 (7 prairial year V) Babeuf sentenced to detah.

JULY 9 (21 messidor year V) Cisalpine Republic created.

AUGUST 24 (7 fructidor year V) Repressive measures against refractory priests abolished.

SEPTEMBER 4 (18 fructidor year V) Directory's coup d'état against the councils.

SEPTEMBER 30 (9 vendémiaire year VI) Bankruptcy of the Two-Thirds.

OCTOBER 18 (27 vendémiaire year VI) Treaty of Campoformio with Austria.

NOVEMBER 12 (8 frimaire year VI) Reorganization of the Administration of Direct Taxes.

NOVEMBER 28 (8 frimaire year VI) Beginning of the Congress of Rastatt, concerning German affairs.

1798

JANUARY 18 (29 nivôse year VI) Authorization to seize all neutral vessels transporting English merchandise.

JANUARY 22 (3 pluviôse year VI) Establishment of Batavian Republic.

JANUARY 28 Mulhouse becomes part of France.

FEBRUARY 5 Roman Republic established.

APRIL (germinal year VI) Council elections strengthen Jacobin opposition.

MAY 11 (22 floréal year VI) Directory's coup d'état against the councils.

MAY 19 Bonaparte heads expedition to Egypt.

JULY 23 (5 thermidor year VI) Fall of Cairo.

AUGUST 1 Nelson destroys French fleet at Aboukir.

SUMMER Formation of second coalition against France.

SEPTEMBER 5 (19 fructidor year VI) Jourdain Law institutes military conscription.

SEPTEMBER 15 French troops occupy Turin.

SEPTEMBER 22–OCTOBER 1 (1–10 vendémiaire year VII) Industrial exposition at the Champ-de-Mars.

NOVEMBER 24 (4 frimaire year VII) Door and window tax instituted.

DECEMBER 12 Law establishing the Registration Administration.

1799

MARCH 25 (4 pluviôse year VII) Creation of the Parthenopean Republic after Championnet captures Naples.

APRIL 28 (9 floréal year VII) French diplomats attacked at Rastatt.

MAY 16 (27 floréal year VII) Sieyès elected to the Directory.

JUNE 17–19 (29 prairial–1 messidor year VII) Russian army under Suvorov defeats Macdonald at Trevi.

JUNE 18 Councils stage coup d'état against the Directory; neo-Jacobin upsurge.

JUNE 28 Forced loan on the rich.

JULY 6 (18 messidor year VII) Opening of the Manège neo-Jacobin club.

JULY 12 Law of Hostages.

AUGUST 1 (4 thermidor year VII) Abrogation of restrictions on the freedom of the press.

AUGUST 15 Joubert defeated at Novi. Italy lost to the French.

AUGUST 22 (5 fructidor year VII) Bonaparte abandons his army and leaves Egypt.

AUGUST 27 Anglo-Russian forces arrive in Holland.

SEPTEMBER 25–27 (3–5 vendémiaire year VIII) Masséna defeats Korsakov's Russian army at Zurich.

OCTOBER 9 (17 vendémiaire year VIII) Bonaparte arrives at Frejus.

OCTOBER 16 Bonaparte arrives in Paris.

OCTOBER 18 Anglo-Russian troops leave Holland.

OCTOBER 23 (1 brumaire year VIII) Lucien Bonaparte president of the Council of Five Hundred.

NOVEMBER 9 (18 brumaire year VIII) Elders vote to have the councils transferred to Saint-Cloud.

NOVEMBER 10 Coup d'état, Bonaparte named First Consul.

III. THE IMMEDIATE LEGACY OF THE REVOLUTION

1799

NOVEMBER 24 (3 frimaire year VIII) Administration of Direct Taxes created.

NOVEMBER 27 Reserve Fund created.

DECEMBER 24 (3 nivôse year VIII) Constitution of the Year VIII takes effect.

DECEMBER 26 Council of State created.

1800

FEBRUARY 13 (24 pluviôse year VIII) Bank of France created.

FEBRUARY 17 Local administration reorganized.

FEBRUARY 28 (9 ventôse year VIII) Plebiscite on the Constitution of Year VIII.

MARCH 3 Émigré list closed.

MARCH 18 Tribunals reorganized.

JUNE 14 Battle of Marengo.

DECEMBER 24 (3 nivôse year IX) Rue Saint-Nicaise attack.

DECEMBER 25 Armistice with Austria.

1801

JANUARY 5 "Jacobins" deported without trial.

FEBRUARY 9 Treaty of Lunéville with Austria.

JULY 16 (27 messidor year IX) Signing of the Concordat.

1802

JANUARY 24 Bonaparte becomes president of the Italian Republic.

MARCH 25 Treaty of Amiens with England.

APRIL 1 (11 germinal year X) Purge and reorganization of the Tribunate.

APRIL 8 Vote on Concordat and Organic Articles.

APRIL 26 (6 floréal year X) Amnesty for émigrés.

MAY 1 *Lycées* created.

MAY 19 Legion of Honor established.

AUGUST 2 (14 thermidor year X) Bonaparte named Consul for Life by plebiscite.

AUGUST 4 Constitution of the Year X.

SEPTEMBER Piedmont annexed.

DECEMBER 24 (3 nivôse year XI) Chambers of Commerce created.

1803

FEBRUARY 19 Helvetian Confederation organized.

FEBRUARY 25 Reorganization of Germany.

MARCH 28 (7 germinal year XI) Law setting value of the franc.

APRIL 12 Worker coalitions prohibited.

APRIL 14 Reorganization of the Bank of France.

MAY 12 Treaty of Amiens broken.

DECEMBER 1 (9 frimaire year XII) Workers' passbook instituted.

1804

FEBRUARY 25 Administration of Amalgamated Duties established.

MARCH 21 Duc d'Enghien executed. Civil Code promulgated.

MAY 18 (28 floréal year XII) Empire established.

DECEMBER 2 Coronation of Napoleon.

1805

MAY 26 Napoleon proclaimed king of Italy.

JUNE 4 Annexation of Genoa.

AUGUST 26 Army recruitment system definitively organized.

SEPTEMBER Beginning of financial crisis.

NOVEMBER 13 Napoleon occupies Vienna.

DECEMBER 2 Battle of Austerlitz.

DECEMBER 27 Napoleon unseats Bourbons of Naples. Completion of Simplon highway.

1806

MAY 10 Creation of the Imperial University.

AUGUST 1 Napoleon proclaims the end of the Holy Roman Empire.

OCTOBER 27 Napoleon occupies Berlin.

NOVEMBER 27 Napoleon occupies Warsaw.

1807

JULY 7 French-Russian alliance.

AUGUST 19 Suppression of the Tribunate.

SEPTEMBER 11 Publication of the Commercial Code.

NOVEMBER 13 Napoleon unseats Portugal's Bragance dynasty.

NOVEMBER 30 Junot occupies Lisbon.

1808

FEBRUARY 2 Rome occupied under Napoleon's orders.

MARCH 1 Imperial nobility created.

MARCH 23 Murat enters Madrid.

MARCH 24 Magistrate purged.

JUNE 9 General Malet's first conspiracy.

SEPTEMBER 17 Organization of the Imperial University.

NOVEMBER 5 Napoleon in Spain.

1809

APRIL 10 Austria goes to war.

JUNE 10 Pius VII excommunicates Napoleon.

JULY 6 Battle of Wagram.

DECEMBER 15 Napoleon divorces.

1810

FEBRUARY 5 Censorship reestablished.

MARCH 3 State prisons reestablished.

APRIL 28 Judiciary administration reorganized. Publication of the Penal Code.

JULY 9 Holland annexed.

1811

JANUARY 22 German shores of the North Sea annexed.

JUNE 17 National Synod of Paris opens.

NOVEMBER 15 University's monopoly strengthened.

1812

FEBRUARY 23 Napoleon violates the Concordat.

MARCH Subsistence crisis. Rioting in Caen.

MAY 8 Maximum grain price reestablished.

SEPTEMBER 14 Moscow is captured.

OCTOBER 23 General Malet's second conspiracy.

NOVEMBER 26–28 Crossing of the Berezina.

1813

JANUARY 25 Concordat of Fontainebleau.

MARCH 16 Prussia declares war on Napoleon.

MAY 20–23 Panic in the Paris stock market.

AUGUST 12 Austria declares war on Napoleon.

OCTOBER 8 Wellington invades the Midi.

NOVEMBER 2–4 Napoleon retreats behind the Rhine.

1814

MARCH 21 The Austrians capture Lyons.

MARCH 30 Paris surrenders.

APRIL 2 The Senate deposes Napoleon.

APRIL 6 The Senate calls upon Louis XVIII. Napoleon abdicates.

MAY 30 First Treaty of Paris.

JUNE 4 Publication of the charter.

1815

MARCH 1 Return from the Island of Elba.

MARCH 20 Napoleon reaches Paris.

JUNE 1 Supplementary act to the Constitutions of the Empire.

JUNE 18 Waterloo.

JUNE 22 Napoleon's second abdication.

JULY 3 Paris surrenders.

JULY 8 Louis XVIII returns to Paris.

AUGUST 14–22 Election of the Incomparable Chamber. White Terror.

SEPTEMBER 26 Holy Alliance.

OCTOBER 13 Murat executed.

NOVEMBER 20 Second Treaty of Paris.

DECEMBER 7 Execution of Marshal Ney.

NOTES

ABBREVIATIONS

A.E.S.C.	*Annales (Économie Sociétés Civilisations)*
A.H.R.	*American Historical Review*
A.H.R.F.	*Annales historiques de la Révolution française*
B.S.H.M.	*Bulletin de la Société d'histoire moderne*
C.H.	*Cahiers d'histoire*
E.H.R.	*English Historical Review*
E.S.R.	*European Studies Review*
F.H.S.	*French Historical Studies*
J.M.H.	*Journal of Modern History*
P.P.	*Past and Present*
P.U.F.	*Presses Universitaires de France*
R.H.	*Revue historique*
R.H.E.F.	*Revue de l'histoire de l'Église de France*
R.H.M.C.	*Revue d'histoire moderne et contemporaine*
S.S.	*Studi storici*

INTRODUCTION

1. Georges Lefebvre, *La Révolution française*, P.U.F., 1951.

2. Alice Gérard, *La Révolution française: Mythes et interprétations (1789–1970)*, Flammarion, 1970. According to Jeremy Popkin, "Recent West German Work on the French Revolution," *J.M.H.*, 1987, 737–750, contemporary West German historians stress the opposition between the *philosophes* and the Revolution while denying the fundamentally "bourgeois" character of the latter.

3. Alfred Cobban, *Le Sens de la Révolution française*, Julliard, 1984. George C. Comninel, *Rethinking the French Revolution: Marxism and the Revisionist Challenge*, Verso, 1987, has recently recognized that the traditional interpretation of the events of 1789 as a bourgeois revolution cannot be supported *from a Marxist point of view*. He attributes this error of Marx's

to his being excessively influenced by liberal historians such as Mignet and Guizot. Gwynne Lewis gives an interesting account of this work in the *Times Literary Supplement* of March 11–17, 1988. In his article, entitled "In Course of Revision," he correctly points out that the whole body of interpretations of the French Revolution is constantly being revised because of primary research. On this subject, see Bill Edmonds, "Successes and Excesses of Revisionist Writing about the French Revolution," *European History Quarterly*, 1987, 195–218.

4. William Doyle, *Origins of the French Revolution*, Oxford, 1980.

5. Donald M. G. Sutherland, *France 1789–1815: Revolution and Counterrevolution*, William Collins 1985; cf. Jacques Godechot, *R.H.*, 1986, p 197. For an important bibliographical contribution of this sort to the renewal of historiography, see R. J. Caldwell, *The Era of French Revolution*, Garland, 1985. Jean Tulard, Jean-François Fayard, and Alfred Ferrio, *Histoires et Dictionnaire de la revolution française 1789–1799*, Robert Laffont, 1987, is a useful tool. Colin Lucas has also edited an impressive publication of one million pages on microfiche with thirty-five thousand illustrations that will be published by Pergamon Press between 1989 and 1992 under the title *The French Revolution, Research Collection and Video-disk*, *L'État de la France pendant la Révolution*, published under the direction of Michel Vovelle in 1988 by Éditions La Découverte, gives a good idea of recent historigraphical developments. On this subject see Gwynne Lewis, *E.H.R.*, 1988 746ff. A useful film of the events is to be found in Jean Favier, ed., *Chronique de la Révolution*, Larousse, 1988.

6. Augustin Cochin, *L'Esprit du jacobinisme: Une interprétation sociologique de la Révolution française*, P.U.F., 1979. For interesting evidence on the enduring opposition of intellectuals to the Revolution, see *Vu de haut*, no. 5, "1789: l'injustice," Éditions Fideliter, 1986. Contributors include serious historians such as Réné Pillorget and Jean de Viguerie.

7. Hippolyte Taine, *Les Origines de la France comtemporaine*, 2 vols., Laffont, 1986.

8. Pierre Gaxotte, *La Révolution française*, college edition by Jean Tulard, Fayard, 1975. In 1988 Jean Tulard reissued Pierre Gaxotte's *La Révolution Française*, with an introduction and supplementary notes, for Éditions Complexe.

9. François Furet, *Penser la Révolution française*, Gallimard, 1978. For an excellent introduction to the most recent issues, see T. C. W. Blanning, *The French Revolution: Aristocrats versus Bourgeois?*, Macmillan, 1987. He sees the Revolution as a political transformation with social consequences, rather than the opposite. See also Louis Trénard, "Le Bicentenaire de la Révolution française," *L'Information Historique*, 1988, 26–32. Also François Furet and Mona Ozouf, eds., *Dictionnaire critique de la Révolution française*, Flammarion, 1988. The first of these two authors also has recently written *La Révolution De Turgot à Jules Ferry 1770–1880*, Hachette, 1988.

10. Alexis de Tocqueville, *L'Ancien Régime et la Révolution*, 2 vols., Gallimard, 1952–1953.

1. A TRIUMPH OF THE ENLIGHTENMENT?

Was Enlightenment thought an integral part of the French mentality on the eve of the Revolution?

1. Daniel Mornet, *Les Origines intellectuelles de la Révolution française*, A. Colin, 1933. Amos Horman, "The Origins of the Theory of the *Philosophe* Conspiracy," *French History*, 1988, 152–172, has recently pointed out that the theory of the intellectual origins of the Revolution was first set forth *under the ancien régime* by supporters of the traditional order. The group associated with the *Année littéraire*, founded in 1754 by Elie Fréron, who led it until his death in 1776, fueled this anti-Enlightenment campaign, accusing the intellectuals it opposed of fomenting a widespread subversive conspiracy starting in 1772. The Abbé Royou, founder of the *Ami du Roi* in 1790, and the Abbé Barruel, who judged in 1785 that nations transformed the writings of the wise into concrete acts, followed Fréron's footsteps. It was Royou's publication that affirmed in December 1789: "It was Enlightenment thought that made the Revolution possible." Its editors always asserted that criticizing Catholicism amounted to attacking the entire social structure. They therefore considered Protestants to be

the precursors of subversion. Their campaign simply became pervasive at the time of the Revolution. Thus Barruel, during the Directory, would merely return to his old interpretation, which he considered confirmed by events. His weakness was his failure to undertake a concrete analysis of Jacobin activity. Cochin supplied this.

2. Donald M. G. Sutherland, *France 1789–1815*, 35.

3. Daniel Roche, "Négoce et culture dans la France du *XVIIIᵉ* siècle," *R.H.M.C.*, 1978, 375–395.

4. William Doyle, *Origins of the French Revolution*, 116–121.

5. Daniel Mornet, *La Pensée française au XVIIIᵉ siècle*, A. Colin, 166–171.

6. Jean-Marie Goulemot, "Démons, merveilles et philosophie à l'âge classique," *A.E.S.C.*, 1980, 1223–1250. The special 1986 issue of the magazine XVIIIᵉ *Siècle* devoted to "popular literature" illustrates the unusual and diverse relationships between the popular classes and the written word.

7. George V. Taylor, Les cahiers de 1789; aspects révolutionnaires et non révolution-naires," *A.E.S.C.*, 1973, 1495–1514; André Burguière, "Société et culture à Reims à la fin du XVIIIᵉ siècle: la diffusion des 'Lumières' analysée à travers les cahiers de doléances," *A.E.S.C.*, 1967, 303–339; Roger Chartier, "Culture, Lumières, doléances de 1789," *R.H.M.C.*, 1981, 68–93.

8. François Bluche, *La Vie quotidienne au temps de Louis XVI*, Hachette, 1980, 150–187.

9. Michel Vovelle, *Piété baroque et Déchristianisation en Provence au XVIIIᵉ siècle*, Le Seuil, 1978.

10. Jean de Viguerie, "Quelques aspects du catholicisme des Français au XVIIIᵉ siècle," *R.H.*, 1981, 335–370. Confirmation of this point of view with respect to the case of Provence comes from Marie-Helene Froeschle-Chapard, "Lieux de culte et peuple des saints au XVIIIᵉ siècle, enquête en cours," *R.H.E.F.*, 1985, 281–310.

11. Norman Hampson, *Le Siècle des Lumières*, Le Seuil, 1972, 218.

12. Haydn Mason, *French Writers and Their Society, 1715–1800*, Macmillan, 1982; Marie-Hélène Huet, "Roman libertin et réaction aristocratique," *XVIIIᵉ Siècle*, 1974, 137–142.

13. Monique Cubells, "Franc-maçonnerie et société: le recrutement des loges à Aix-en-Provence dans la deuxième moitié du XVIIIᵉ siècle," *R.H.M.C.*, 1986, 463–484.

14. Robert Darnton, "Sounding the Literary Market in Prerevolutionary France," *Eighteenth Century Studies*, 1984, 484; cf. Michael P. Fitzsimmons, *The Parisian Order of Barristers and the French Revolution*, Harvard 1987, who shows that the vast majority of Parisian lawyers were against the Revolution.

15. Dieter Gembicki, "La condition historienne à la fin de l'Ancien Régime," *XVIIIᵉ Siècle*, 1981, 271–287.

16. Furio Diaz, *Filosofia e Politica nel Settecento Francese*, Einaudi, 1962, 638.

Was Enlightenment thought revolutionary?

1. William H. Sewell, Jr., "Ideologies and Social Revolutions. Reflections on the French Case," *J.M.H.*, 1985, 57–85. See "Corps et communautés d'Ancien Régime" (*A.E.S.C.*, 1988, 295–299) by Jacques Revel for an excellent recent presentation of a new historiographic vision in which a corporatist type society in prerevolutionary France is thought to constitute a fundamental framework (much more so, in fact, than during the feudal period) and a phenomenon that was neither backward nor doomed to extinction by virtue of the liberating impact of the bourgeoisie. These bodies and communities were even, as forms of association, the basis of a type of political interaction that the future would show to be extremely prolific. Cf. the statement by the same author at the colloquium at Chicago in 1986 in Keith Baker, ed., *The French Revolution and the Creation of Modern Political Culture*, Vol. I, *The Political Culture of the Old Regime*, Pergamon, 1987, 225–242. For commentary on this work, see J. R. Censer, "The Coming of a New Interpretation of the French Revolution," *Journal of Social History*, 1987, 295–309.

2. William Doyle, *Origins of the French Revolution*, 25, 78, 84.

3. David D. Bien, "Catholic Magistrates and Protestant Marriage in the French Enlightenment," *F.H.S.*, 1962, 409–429. Cf., regarding the Protestants, the "Actes des Journées

d'Étude sur l'édit de 1787," in *Bulletin de la Société d'Histoire du Protestantisme Français*," April–June 1988.

4. William F. Church, "The Decline of the French Jurists as Political Theorists, 1660–1789," *F.H.S.*, 1967, 25–40; Jacques F. Traer, "From Reform to Revolution: The Critical Century in the Development of the French Legal System," *J.M.H.*, 1977, 73–88.

5. Robert Darnton, "In Search of the Enlightenment: Recent Attempts to Create a Social History of Ideas," *J.M.H.*, 1971, 113–132. Cf., more recently, L. J. Jordanova, "Toward the Light?: Science, Politics and the Enlightenment," *E.S.R.*, 1982, 479–488.

6. Denis Richet, "Autour des origines idéologiques lointaines de la Révolution française: élites et despotisme," *A.E.S.C.*, 1969, 1–23.

7. Cf. Furio Diaz, *Settecento Francese*; Paolo Alatri, "Problemi e figure del Settecento politico francese nella recenti storiografia," *S.S.*, 1964, 137–168, 333–379; Norman Hampson, *La Siècle des Lumières*; Eric Walter, "Sur l'intelligentsia des Lumières," *XVIIIᵉ Siècle*, 1973, 173–201. A good example of the persistence of oversimplification in a certain kind of Marxist historiography can be found in Michael Nerlich's work, *Kritik der Abenteuer-Ideologie: Beitrag zur Erforschung der burgerlicher Bewussteinsbildung, 1100–1750*, Akademie-Verlag, 1977. This is to be contrasted with the interesting contributions of Guy Lemarchand ("Les Caractères nouveaux spécifiques apportés par la Révolution"), Jean Dhombres ("La formation des Cadres"), or Roger Dupuy ("L'abolition de la féodalité: condition de passage au capitalisme ou du comprimis physiocratique entre bourgeois et paysans") in *Cahiers d'Histoire de L'Institut de recherches marxistes*, no. 32, proceedings of a colloquium organized in May 1987 in Paris.

8. *XVIIIᵉ Siècle*, 1974, "Lumières et Révolution." See also the judicious conclusions in an excellent book by Jean-Marie Goulemot, *Discours, Révolutions et Histoire: Représentations de l'histoire et discours sur les Révolutions de l'Age Classique aux Lumiéres*, Union Générale d'Éditions, 1975.

9. Daniel Roche, *Le Siècle des Lumières en province: académie et académiciens provinciaux, 1680–1789*, 2 vols., Mouton, 1978. For a confirmation of the information found in "Musées et lycées parisiens (1780–1830)," see Hervé Guénot (*XVIIIᵉ Siècle*, 1986, 249–267)

10. Keith Michael Baker, "Enlightenment and Revolution in France: Old Problems, Revewed Approaches," *J.M.H.*, 1981, 281–303; Renato Pasta, "Illuminismo e organizzazione della cultura," *S.S.*, 1981, 251. On p. 363 of *Reform und Revolution bei Condorcet*, Bonn, 1973, Rolf Reichardt shows, with respect to this particular case, that the *philosophes*, who may have unknowingly paved the way for the Revolution, were by no means directly responsible for it. Daniel Roche elaborated on his work at a colloquium in Chicago in 1986 by stressing that the cultural interchanges fostered the development of public opinion ("Académies et politique au siècle des Lumières," in K. M. Baker, ed., *Modern Political Culture*, 331–343). However, he recognizes that a global crisis (more political, in our view, than social) was needed for this enlightened outlook to become, through the press of events, involved in the fight for a radical transformation. Cf. more recently by the same author, *Les Républicains des Lettres: Gens de culture et Lumières au XVIIIᵉ siècle*, Fayard, 1988.

11. Christian Desplat, "Le barreau béarnais et la signification des Lumières en province (1770–1789)," *XVIIIᵉ Siècle*, 1974, 109–113.

12. Suzanne Turcoo-Chala, "La diffusion des Lumières dans la seconde moitié du xviiiᵉ siècle: Ch. J. Panckoucke, un libraire éclairé (1760–1799)," *ibid.*, 115–128; David Hume, *Of Civil Liberty, Works*, Vol. III, 159.

13. George V. Taylor, "Les cahiers de 1789."

14. Henry Wyverberg, "Limits of Nonconformity in the Enlightenment: The Case of Simon-Nicolas-Henri Linguet," *F.H.S.*, 1970, 474–491; Darline Gay Levy, *The Ideas and Careers of S. N. H. Linguet: A Study in Eighteenth-Century French Politics*, University of Illinois, 1980.

15. Frank A. Kafker, "Les encyclopédistes et la Terreur," *R.H.M.C.*, 1967, 284–295. Angélique, the daughter of Diderot, who was enlightened by the family hardships undergone during year II, opined in 1848 that "revolutions destroy a sense of morality" (*XVIIIᵉ Siècle*, 1987, 295). Cf., in the same vein, the interesting and melancholy account of the *Mémoires de l'abbé Morellet, sur le 18ᵉ siècle et la Révolution*, Mercure de France, 1987.

16. Alan Charles, "The Myth of the Coterie holbachique," *F.H.S.*, 1976, 573–595.

17. Roland Mortier, "Les héritiers des 'philosophes' devant l'expérience révolutionnaire," *XVIIIe Siècle*, 1974, 45–57.

18. John M. Roberts, *The Mythology of the Secret Societies*, Secker & Warburg, 1972; Gérard Gayot, *La Franc-Maçonnerie française. Textes et pratiques (xviiie-xixe siècles)*, Gallimard / Julliard, 1980; Maurice Agulhon, *Pénitents et Francs-Maçons de l'ancienne Provence. Essai sur la sociabilité méridionale*, Fayard, 1968; Jacques Brengues, "Pour une linguistique maçonnique au xviiie siècle," *A.H.R.F.*, 1977, 57–75; *Franc-Maçonnerie et Lumières au seuil de la Révolution française: Actes du colloque d'avril 1984*, Publications de l'Institut d'études et de recherches maçonniques, 1985; Jacques Lemaire, *Les Origines françaises de l'antimaçonnisme*, Editions de l'université de Bruxelles, 1985; cf. also the special issue *XVIIIe Siècle*, 1987.consacré à "La franc-maçonnerie." Michel Taillefer (*La Franc-Maçonnerie toulousaine, 1741-1799*, historical commission on the French Revolution, "Mémoires et documents," XLI, 1984) has described an unusual adaptation of the lodges to the revolutionary upheavals in this exceptional case.

19. Robert Darnton, *Le Grand Massacre des chats*, Laffont, 1986, 246–295; Richard Howard Powers, "Rousseau's 'Useless Science': Dilemma or Paradox," *F.H.S.*, 1962, 450–468; Roger Barny, "Les aristocrates et Jean-Jacques Rousseau dans la Révolution," *A.H.R.F.*, 1976, 534–568; "Jean-Jacques Rousseau dans la Révolution," *XVIIIe Siècle*, 1974, 59–98; Raymond Trousson, "Quinze années d'études rousseauistes," *XVIIIe Siècle*, 1977, 343–386; Jan Marejko, *Jean-Jacques Rousseau et la Dérive totalitaire*, L'Âge d'homme, 1984; Roger Barny, *Prélude idéologique à la Révolution française: Le rousseauisme avant 1789*, Les Belles Lettres, 1985.

Did a revolutionary mentality exist on the eve of 1789?

1. William Doyle, *Origins*, 29, 93ff.

2. Robert Darnton, *Bohème littéraire et Révolution: Le monde des livres au xviiie siècle*, Gallimard / Le Seuil, 1983, 7–41.

3. *Ibid.*, 43–69.

4. *Ibid.*, 71–109.

5. *Ibid.*, 111–208; Henri-Jean Martin, "La librairie française en 1777–1778," *XVIIIe Siècle*, 1979, 87–112; Robert Darnton, *The Business of Enlightenment: A Publishing History of the "Encyclopédie" 1775–1800*, Cambridge University Press, 1979; David I. Kulstein, "The Ideas of Charles-Joseph Panckoucke, Publisher of the *Moniteur universel*, On the French Revolution," *F.H.S.*, 1966, 304–319.

6. Nina R. Gelbart, " 'Frondeur' Journalism in the 1770s Theater Criticism and Radical Politics in the Prerevolutionary French Press," *Eighteenth Century Studies*, 1983, 493–514; Jean-Paul Marat, *Journal de la République française*, January 14, 1793. One gets a sense of the megalomania of the revolutionaries in the way in which Babeuf describes himself to his wife on April 17, 1793, as being the one "whom the entire universe would bless and all the nations and all the centuries would consider the Savior of the human species" (Victor Daline, *Gracchus Babeuf à la veille et pendant la Révolution française*, Editions du Progrès, 1987, 434). Regarding the origins of revolutionary journalism during the *ancien régime*, see an excellent study by Jeremy Popkin, "The Pre-Revolutionary Origins of Political Journalism," in Keith Michael Baker, ed., *The French Revolution and the Creation of Modern Political Culture*, Vol. I, *The Political Culture of the Old Regime*, Pergamon, 1987, 203–223. Cf. also Jack Cense and Jeremy Popkin, ed., *Press and Politics in Pre-Revolutionary France*, University of California Press, 1987.

7. Alexis de Tocqueville, *L'Ancien régime et la Révolution*, Vol. II, *Fragments et Notes inédites sur la Révolution*, Gallimard, 1953, 34–47. For a broad and interesting perspective see Hans Erich Badecker and Ulrich Hermann, *Aufklärung als Politizierung-Politizierung der Aufklarung*, Hamburg, 1987. If the politicization of the *philosophes* is seen primarily as a pragmatic and prudent reaction, their emergence appears to herald a new kind of society whose behavior and outlook are still our own.

8. Auguste Viatte, *Les Sources occultes du romantisme. Illuminisme-théosophie, 1770–1820*, 2 vols., Vrin, 1928; Robert Darnton, *Mesmerism and the End of Enlightenment in*

France, Cambridge University 1968; Guy Chaussinand-Nogaret, "Gagliostro et la chute de l'Ancien Régime," *L'Histoire*, February 1986, 30–36.

9. Nicole Chaquin, "Le citoyen Louis-Claude de Saint-Martin, théosophe révolutionnaire," *XVIIIe Siècle*, 1974, 209–224. Eugen Weber has recently noted the importance in various social strata of the magical way of thinking that was to take advantage of the forthcoming crisis of the established church and spread ("Religion and Superstition in Nineteenth-Century France," *The Historical Journal*, 1988, 399–423).

10. Catherine-Laurence Maire, *Les Convulsionnaires de Saint-Médard: Miracles, convulsions et prophéties à Paris au XVIIIe siècle*, Gallimard / Julliard, 1985, 27, 227–231, 238–240.

11. Clarke W. Garrett, *Respectable Folly: Millenarians and the French Revolution in France and England*, Johns Hopkins, 1975.

12. Ran Halévi, "Les représentations de la démocratie maçonnique au XVIIIe siècle," *R.H.M.C.*, 1984, 571–596; Keith Michael Baker, "Enlightenment and Revolution," *J.M.H.*, 1981, 297.ff.

13. Robert R. Palmer, *The Age of Democratic Revolution: A Political History of Europe and America, 1760–1800*, Vol. I., *The Challenge*, Princeton University, 1959, 237–282; Saint-John de Crèveceur, *Lettres d'un cultivateur américain*, 2 vols., Genève, Éditions Ressources, 1979; Durand Echeverria, "L'Amérique devant l'opinion française, 1734–1870: Questions de méthode et d'interprétation," *R.H.M.C.*, 1962, 51–62; Bronislaw Baczko, "The Shifting Frontiers of Utopia," *J.M.H.*, September 1981, 468–476; André Delaporte, *L'Idée d'égalité en France au XVIIIe siècle*, P.U.F., 1987.

14. Robert Favre, "Les Lumières . . . ou la mort! Fécondité d'un mythe: la 'dépopulation' en France au XVIIIe siècle," *C.H.*, 1977, 13–35; Antonio Santucci, "Diderot collaboratore di Raynal," *S.S.*, 1982. 453–459; Gianluigi Goggi, "Diderot et l'*Histoire des deux Indes*: reflessioni sulla storia," *Studi Francesi*, 1982 32–43. The best overall study remains beyond a doubt that of Albert Soboul, "Lumières, critique sociale et utopie pendant le 18e siècle français," in Jacques Droz, ed. *Histoire Générale du Socialisme*, Vol. 1, P.U.F., 1972 103–194.

15. John Pappas, "D'Alembert et la nouvelle aristocratie," *XVIIIe Siècle*, 1982, 335–343; Thomas E. Crow, *Painters and Public Life in Eighteenth-Century Paris*, Yale, 1985; C. G. Stricklen, "The *Philosophe*'s political mission: The creation of an idea, 1750–1789," *Studies on Voltaire and the Eighteenth Century*, 1971; Michel Delon, "*L'idée d'énergie au tournant des Lumières (1770–1820)*," P.U.F., 1988. Robert Darnton has recently elaborated on the sociology of the prerevolutionary intelligentsia ("The Facts of Literary Life in Eighteenth-Century France," in K. M. Baker, ed. *Modern Political Culture*, 26191). It is interesting on a semantic level to note with Jean Starobinski (*ibid.*, 320) the academic origins of the glorification of the concept of the Revolution of 1789. This term, after having been used in a very general sense, as by Condorcet in 1782, was successively applied to a political event that was fortunately to come about, then transformed into an irreducible entity with various earlier related vicissitudes. For an analysis of the continuity of this theme from the prerevolutionary period to the Revolution, based on contemporary pamphlets, see Antoine de Baecque, "L'Homme Nouveau est arrivé: La régénération du Français en 1789," *XVIIIe Siècle*, 1988, 193–208. This theme figures in the novels of the period, according to Malcolm Cook, *ibid.*, 228.

16. Jacques-Pierre Brissot, *Correspondance et Papiers*, Paris, 1912, 18; Robert R. Palmer, *A Political History*, 472.

2. A DEFEAT OF DESPOTISM?

Was the monarchy capable of reform before 1787?

1. François Bluche, *La Vie quotidienne au temps de Louis XVI*, Hachette, 1980, 46–80.

2. William Doyle, *Origins*, a53–65; cf. Jean-François Labourdette, "Vergennes ou la tentation du 'ministériat,' " *R.H.*, 1986, 73–107. Munro Price describes with insight the problems affecting the functioning of the government of Louis XVI ("Vergennes 'Principal Ministre' in 1783," *Revue d'Histoire Diplomatique*, 1987, 323–334). One can note, with respect to the monarchy of the *ancien régime*, the development of a road and postal system beginning in

1740 (cf. Guy Arbellot and Bernard Lepetit, *Atlas de la Révolution Française*, Éditions de l'École des Hautes Études en Sciences Sociales, Vol. I, *Routes et Communications*; l'École des Hautes Études en Sciences Sociales, 1987). This relative standardization of the national geography began to unify the territory and gave new dimensions to the future Revolution. See, however, the cogent observations of Gail Bossenga on the responsibility of the monarchy for the political unhappiness of numerous groups within the elite in French villages on the eve of the Revolution ("City and State: An Urban Perspective on the Origins of the French Revolution," in Keith Michael Baker, ed., *The French Revolution and the Creation of Modern Political Culture*, Vol. I, *The Political Culture of the Old Regime*, Pergamon, 1987, 115–140)

3. David Hudson, "In Defense of Reform: French Government Propaganda during the Maupeou Crisis," *F.H.S.*, 1973, 51–76.

4. William Doyle, "The Parliaments of France and the Breakdown of the Old Regime," *F.H.S.*, 1970, 415–458.

5. Bailey Stone, "Robe against Sword: The *Parlement* of Paris and the French Aristocracy, 1774–1789." *F.H.S.*, 1975, 278–303; *The Parlement of Paris, 1774–1789*, University of North Carolina Press, 1981; *The French Parlements and the Crisis of the Old Regime*, University of North Carolina Press, 1987.

6. Gérald J. Cavenaugh, "Turgot: The Rejection of Enlightenment Despotism," *F.H.S.*, 1969, 31–58.

7. Olwen Hufton, *Europe: Privilege and Protest, 1730–1789*, Fontana, 1980, 299–347. H. M. Scott, "Whatever Happened to the Enlightened Despots?", *History*, 1983, 245–257, correctly stresses the vitality of the reform movement under the *ancien régime* in Europe at the end of the eighteenth century and rejects efforts to dismiss this period as a simple preparation for the French Revolution.

8. A. d'Anerth and J. Flammermont, *Correspondance secrète du comte de Mercy-Argenteau avec l'empereur Joseph II*, Vol. I, Paris, 1889, 223–229; Betty Behrens, *L'Ancien Régime*, Flammarion, 1969, 163–184.

9. François-Xavier Emmanuelli, *Pouvoir royal et Vie régionale en Provence au déclin de la monarchie*, 2 vols., université de Lille-III, 1974; Albert Mathiez, *La Vie politique de la France dans la seconde partie du XVIIIᵉ siècle*, a course given at the faculty of letters in Paris, 1929–1930, Librairie classique R. Guillon, part IV, 187; part V, 204–216.

10. Régine Robin, "La natura dello stato alla fine dell' 'Ancien Régime': Formazione sociale, stato e transizione," *S.S.*, 1973, 642–669; William Doyle, *Origins of the French Revolution*, 43–52. James C. Riley has recently shown ("French Finances, 1727–1768," *J.M.H.*, 1987, 209–243) that the French paid much less in taxes at the end of the reign of Louis XV than at the beginning.

11. William Doyle, *Origins*, 38; John F. Bosher, *French Finances, 1770–1795: From Business to Bureaucracy*, Cambridge University, 1970; "The *premiers commis des Finances* in the Reign of Louis XVI," *F.H.S.*, 1964, 475–494. George V. Taylor had shown in 1962 ("The Paris Bourse on the Eve of the Revolution, 1781–1789," *A.H.R.*, 952–977) the power of financiers over the monarchy and the later influence of their spirit of speculation on revolutionary politics. But he has pointed out that these forward-looking speculators remained associated with the traditional economic activity that was tied to the French court rather than the capitalism of the future.

12. *Gestionnaires et Profiteurs de la Révolution: L'Administration des finances françaises de Louis XVI à Bonaparte*, Olivier Orban, 1986, 23–48.

13. Robert D. Harris, "Necker's *Compte rendu* of 1781: A Reconsideration," *J.M.H.*, 1970 161–183; "French Finances and the American War, 1777–1783," *J.M.H.*, 1976, 233–258; *Necker: Reform Statesman of the Ancien Régime*, University of California Press, 1979; *Necker and the French Revolution*, Princeton, 1986; Jean Egret, *Necker, ministre de Louis XVI*, Champion, 1975; James C. Riley, *The Seven Years War and the Old Regime in France: The Economic and Financial Toll*, Princeton University, 1987.

*Did the aristocrats' victory in 1788 represent the triumph of
liberal ideas or of traditional privilege?*

1. William Doyle, *Origins* 35–37; Jean Egret, *Louis XV et l'Opposition parlementaire,
1715–1774*, P.U.F., 1970. Durand Echeverria, *The Maupeou Revolution: A study in the
History of Libertarianism, France, 1770–1774*, Baton Rouge, 1985. For a traditional and
debatable eulogizing of the coup d'état, see Michel Antoine, "La Monarchie Absolue" in Keith
Michael Baker, ed., *The French Revolution and the Creation of Modern Political Culture*, Vol.
I. *The Political Culture of the Old Regime*, Pergamon, 1987, 3–24. For an excellent summary
of an opposing view on the strengths and weaknesses of the *parlements* of the eighteenth
century, see William Doyle, *Origins*, 157–167.

2. William Doyle, *Origins*, 66–77, 85–95; Keith Michael Baker, "Politique et opinion
publique sous l'Ancien Régime," *A.E.S.C.*, 1987, 41–71; Sarah Muza, "Le tribunal de la
nation: Les mémoires judiciaires et l'opinion publique à la fin de l'Ancien Régime," *ibid.*,
73–90. J. S. Branley has called the *parlementaires* of the eighteenth century, more than the
philosophes, the creators of the concept of national sovereignty and the true educators of the
sans-culottes ("the decline of absolute monarchy" in J. Wallace-Hadrill and J. McManners,
eds., *France: Government and Society*, 2nd ed., 1970, cited by T. C. W. Blanning in *The
French Revolution*, Macmillan, 1987, 29). Based on the Marquis of Argenson's 1754 remark
on the new popularity of the idea of the nation and its rights, Keith Baker believes that a new
antiabsolutist political culture was born at this moment in France ("On the problems of the
ideological origins of the French Revolution" in Dominick La Capra and Steven L. Kaplan,
eds., *Modern European Intellectual History: Reapraisals and New Perspectives*, Cornell University Press, 1982, cited by T. C. W. Blanning, *ibid*, 30).

3. William Doyle, *Origins*, 73–90. For an interesting overview on the debates of 1788
regarding the idea of a French constitution, see Marina Valensise in Keith Michael Baker, ed.,
Modern Political Culture, 441–467. Those who offered the standard traditional defense and
those who deplored the lack of a French constitution and demanded its creation were indeed
the precursors of the counterrevolution and the liberal tendencies of the future. Le Mounier,
who in 1792 accused his revolutionary adversaries of 1789 "of assuming France to be without
a government, without legitimate authority, and to be a country of savages who joined together
to choose their leaders and to create their laws," was in hindsight closer to the counterrevolutionaries than to the liberals (quoted by Bronislaw Baczko, *ibid.*, 497). One can compare
this statement to the remarks of Lurien Jeame, "Citoyenneté et souveraineté: le poids de
l'absolutisme," *ibid.*, 515–534.

4. Donald M. G. Sutherland, *France 1789–1815*, 27–33. The social exclusiveness of the
parlementaires that Monique Cubells pointed out in the case of Aix (*La Province des Lumières:
les parlementaires d'Aix au XVIIIe siècle*, Maloine, 1984) was not a general phenomenon, for
Doyle did not find it to apply in Bordeaux (cf. *J.M.H.*, 1986, 943). This exclusiveness did not
prevent the *parlements* from playing the role of political educators of the enlightened elite
during the second half of the eighteenth century. According to the view of Denis Richet (*La
France moderne, L'esprit des institutions*, 1973, quoted by T. C. W. Blanning, *The French
Revolution*, Macmillan, 34), the fall of Calonne was no more than the defeat of authoritarian
reformism and the victory of the liberals.

5. Eberhard Schmitt, *Repräsentation und Revolution. Eine Untersuchung zur Genesis der
kontinentalen Theorie und Praxis parlementarischer Repräsentation aus der Herrschaftspraxis
der Ancien Regime in Frankreich (1760–1789)*, Munich, 1969; Jacques Godechot, *Les Institutions de la France sous la Révolution et l'Empire*, P.U.F., 1968, 110. Monique Cubbels has
pointed out (*XVIIIe Siècle*, 1988, 174) that nearly two thirds of the members of the municipal
council of Aix-en-Provence in 1790 performed similar functions under the *ancien régime*.

6. Eugenio Di Rienzo, "Istituzioni e teorie politiche nella Francia moderna," *S.S.*, 1982,
329–353. Pierre Lamarque has correctly pointed out the repeated use of the term "representatives of the nation," which was applied to members of the Estates-General by Louis XVI in
his speech on May 5, 1789 (*XVIIIe Siècle*, 1988, 117).

7. Keith Michael Baker, "A Script for a French Revolution: The Political Consciousness
of the Abbé Mably," *Eighteenth Century Studies*, 1981, 235–263.

8. Dale K. Van Kley, "Church, State and the Ideological Origins of the French Revolution: The Debate Over the General Assembly of the Gallican Clergy in 1765," *J.M.H.*, 1979, 629–666; *The Damiens Affair and the Unravelling of the Ancien Régime, 1750–1770*, Princeton, 1984. Confirmation comes from Yann Fauchois, "Jansénisme et politique au XVIIIᵉ siècle: légitimation de l'État et délégitimation de la monarchie chex G. N. Maultrot," *R.H.M.C.*, 1987 473–491, and in Jeffrey Merrick, "Conscience and Citizenship in Eighteenth-Century France," *Eighteenth Century Studies*, 1987, 48–70. The same author has noted ("Disputes over Words and Constitutional Conflict in France, 1730–1732," *F.H.S.*, 1986 497–520) the length of the process of demystification that the French monarchy had to face during the political and religious conflicts of the eighteenth century that gradually deepened its ideological contradictions and prepared the way for the final crisis. Dale Van Kley has recently provided a persuasive account in "The Jansenist Constitutional Legacy in the French Pre-Revolution," in Keith Michael Baker, ed., *Modern Political Culture*, 169–201. From his ideological and linguistic analysis, it becomes clear that, if the Revolution of 1789 broke out too late to be principally religious in nature, it could not, on the other hand, avoid the influence of its Christian heritage, however secularized or denied.

9. Keith Michael Baker, "French Political Thought at the Accession of Louis XVI," *J.M.H.*, 1978, 279–303; Marina Valensise, "Le sacre du roi: stratégie symbolique et doctrine politique de la monarchie française," *A.E.S.C.*, 1986, 543–577; Clarke W. Garrett, "The *Moniteur* of 1788," *F.H.S.*, 1968, 263–273. For an overview, see K. M. Baker, ed., *op. cit.*, based on the proceedings of a colloquium in Chicago in September 1986. Baker asserts in this work's introduction (pp. xi-xxiii) that the overthrow of the traditional monarchy was due to the development of a new political culture, enlightened and soon to be revolutionary, but that this phenomenon, which was the product of political events, cannot be related to any of the preceding intellectual movements: It was a radical departure from all that preceded it. According to the analysis of Nannerl Keohane, *Philosophy and the State in France*, Princeton University, 1980, the old conflict between absolutism and aristocratic traditionalism was probably modified during the eighteenth century under the influence of the Enlightenment. These developments probably brought about a liberalization and modernization of absolutism and a split within the aristocratic opposition between constitutional liberals, who would form the core of the national and patriotic party, and the supporters of an aristocratic constitutionalism that was particularly strong among the *parlementaires*. As Kenneth Morgensen points out, however ("History, Representative Institutions, and Political Rights in the French Pre-Revolution [1787–1789], *F.H.S.*, 1987, 68–98), political debate in France would remain dominated by fundamentally traditional perspectives until the beginning of the Revolution. See also K. M. Baker in D. La Capra and S. Kaplan, eds., *Modern European Intellectual History*, 197–219. The same author, in his collection (Modern Political Culture, 1987, 471–492), shows that the concept of political representation, adopted in 1789 and replete with future ambiguities, departed from the theories that were in favor under the *ancien régime* without subscribing to the nihilism expressed by the Rousseauian myth of the general will.

10. Viviane R. Gruder, "Les notables à la fin de l'Ancien Régime: l' 'Avertissement' de 1787," *XVIIIᵉ Siècle*, 1982, 45–55; "A Mutation in Elite Political Culture: The French Notables and the Defense of Property and Participation, 1787," *J.M.H.*, 1984, 598–634. The same author has emphasized ("Paths to Political Consciousness: The Assembly of Notables of 1787 and the Pre-Revolution in France," *F.H.S.*, 1984, 323–355) the importance of this episode for the development of the political awareness of the French elite on the eve of the Revolution.

11. Jean Egret, *La Prérévolution française, 1787–1788*, P.U.F. 1962 (cf. the account of Marcel Reinhard, *R.H.M.C.*, 1963, 309–310); William Doyle, "The Parliaments of France," *F.H.S.*, 1970, 415–458.

Did the monarchy abdicate all responsibility just before and during the early stages of the revolution?

1. William Doyle, *Origins*, 114, 139–157, 168–177.

2. *Ibid.*, 187–190, 204, 210–212; Guy Chaussinand-Nogaret, *La Bastille est prise La Revolution commence*, Editions Complexe, 1988. For a good analysis of the motivations of

the monarchy, see Vivian R. Gruder, "The Bourbon Monarchy: Reforms and Propaganda at the End of the Old Regime," in K. M. Baker, ed., *Modern Political Culture*, 1987, 347–374. In his excellent study "La Monarchie et le règlement èlectoral de 1789," *ibid.*, 375–386, François Furet asserts, for his part, that the monarchy bequeathed "democracy to the Revolution." Ran Halévi (*ibid.*, 387–402) appears to confirm this while implying rather curiously, in the manner of Cochin, that the elections also may have marked what he calls the first purge of the Revolution. One contrasts this view with that of Bronislaw Baczko, who believes that Sieyès's statements made at the beginning of 1789 show that he was already in favor of excluding the enemies of the nation from the political arena (*ibid.*, 499).

3. Donald M. G. Sutherland, *France 1789–1815* 33–48, 63–68, 82–85; Olwen Hufton, *Europe: Privilege and Protest, 1730–1789*, Fontana, 1980, 351, 353–355.

4. Pierre Goubert and Michel Denis, *1789: les Français ont la parole*, Julliard, 1964. Recent confirmation comes from Michel Vovelle, "La représentation populaire de la monarchie," in K. M. Baker, ed., *Modern Political Culture*, 77–86.

5. Cf. Maurice Agulhon, "Conflits et contradictions dans la France d'aujoud'hui," *A.E.S.C.*, 1987, 595–610.

3. A VICTORY FOR THE BOURGEOISIE?

Was there a class struggle between the nobility and the bourgeoisie before 1789?

1. Régine Robin, *La Société française en 1789: Semur-en-Auxois*, Plon. 1970; Jean Sentou, *Fortunes et Groupes sociaux à Toulouse sous la Révolution (1798–1799): Essai d'histoire statistique*, Privat, 1969; Georges Lefebvre, "Urban Society in the Orleanais in the Late Eighteenth Century," *P.P.*, 1961, 46–75; I. Cervelli, "Sul concetto di Rivoluzione borghese," *S.S.*, 1976, 147–155; Jean Nicolas, *La Savoie au XVIIIe siècle: Noblesse et bourgeoisie*, 2 vols., Maloine, 1978; James A. Leith, "Les origines de la Révolution française remises en question," *A.H.R.F.*, 1982, 632–639.

2. George V. Taylor, "Non-Capitalist Wealth and the Origins of the French Revolution," *A.H.R.*, 1967, 469–496.

3. Colin Lucas, "Nobles, Bourgeois and the Origins of the French Revolution," *P.P.*, 1973, 469–496.

4. Guy Chaussinand-Nogaret, "Aux origines de la Révolution: noblesse et bourgeoisie," *A.E.S.C.*, 1975, 275–278. The same author published in the same year a series of key texts for *Une histoire de l'Élite 1700–1848*, Mouton. His theory has recently been called into question by Diego Venturino, "L'idéologie nobiliare nella Francia d'Antico Regime: Note sul dibattito storiografico recente," *S.S.*, 1988, 61–101. His skepticism is based above all on the views of Tocqueville.

5. William Doyle, *Origins*, 11–24, 116–127.

6. *Ibid.*, 128–138; Michel Vovelle, ed., *Bourgeoisies de province et Révolution*, Presses universitaires de Grenoble, 1987. William M. Reddy, in his impressive book, *The Rise of Market Culture: The Textile Trade and French Society, 1750–1900*, Cambridge University, 1984, has described industrial and bourgeois France of the prerevolutionary and revolutionary period as a world without entrepreneurs.

7. Donald M. G. Sutherland, *France 1789–1815*, 15–21; Jean Meyer, "Un problème mal posé: la noblesse pauvre. L'exemple breton au XVIIIe siècle," *R.H.M.C.*, 1971, 161–188; Guy Richard, *Noblesse d'affaires au XVIIIe siècle*, A. Colin, 1974; Norbert Elias, *La Sociéte de cour*, Flammarion, 1985, 307–316; Jean Bastier, *La Féodalité au siècle des Lumières dans la région de Toulouse (1730–1790)*, Commission d'histoire économique et sociale de la Révoltion, "Mémoires et documents," XXX, 1975; Guy Chaussinand-Nogaret, *La Noblesse au XVIIIe siècle: De la féodalité aux Lumières*, Hachette, 1976.

8. Philippe Goujard, " 'Féodalité' et Lumières au XVIIIe siècle: L'exemple de la noblesse," *A.H.R.F.*, 1977, 103–118.

9. Guy Chaussinand-Nogaret, "Un aspect de la pensée nobiliaire au XVIII° siècle: l' 'antinobilisme,' " *R.H.M.C.*, 1982, 442–452.

10. William Doyle, "The Price of Offices in Prevolutionary France," *The Historical Journal*, 1984, 831–860.

11. William Doyle, "Was there an Aristocratic Reaction in Prerevolutionary France?", *P.P.*, 1972, 97–122.

12. David D. Bien, "La réaction aristocratique avant 1789: l'exemple de l'armée," *A.E.S.C.*, 1974, 23–48, 505–534; "The Army in the French Enlightenment: Reform, Reaction and Revolution," *P.P.*, 1979, 68–98; Melvin Edelstein, "La noblesse et le monopole des fonctions publiques en 1789," *A.E.S.C.*, 1982, 440–443.

13. Betty Behrens, "A Revision Defended: Nobles, Privileges and Taxes in France," *F.H.S.*, 1976, 521–527; Ralph E. Giesey, "Rules of Inheritance and Strategies of Mobility in Prerevolutionary France," *A.H.R.*, 1977, 271–289. For recent confirmation, see David D. Bien in Keith Michael Baker, ed., *The French Revolution and the Creation of Modern Political Culture*, Vol. I, *The Political Culture of the Old Regime*, Pergamon, 1987, 89–114 (cf. his French translation in *A.E.S.C.*, 1988, 379–404, under the title "Les Offices, les corps et le crédit d'état: l'utilisation des privilèges sous l'Ancien Régime").

Was the political revolution of 1789 caused by the bourgeoisie?

1. Philip Dawson, "The 'bourgeoisie de robe' in 1789," *F.H.S.*, 1965, 1–21; Elizabeth L. Eisenstein, "Who Intervened in 1788? A Commentary on *The Coming of the French Revolution*," *A.H.R.*, 1965, 77–103.

2. Jeffry Kaplow, "On 'Who Intervened in 1788?' ", *A.H.R.*, 1967, 496–502; Gilbert Shapiro, "The Many Lives of Georges Lefebvre," *ibid.*, 502–514; Lynn A. Hunt, "Local Elites at the End of the Old Regime, Troyes and Reims. 1750–1789," *F.H.S.*, 1976, 379–399; *Revolution and Urban Politics in Provincial France: Troyes and Rheims, 1786–1790*, Stanford University, 1978.

3. William Doyle, *Origins*, 139–157.

4. *Ibid.*, 168–177. Inspired by Tocqueville, Lynn Hunt ("The National Assembly" in K. M. Baker, ed., *Modern Political Culture*, 403–415) believes that the decisive revolutionary and political break with the monarchy's past, with respect to the future leaders of the Constituent Assembly, occurred between July 1788 *and January 1789*. As Bronislaw Baczko has noted (*ibid.*, 523, n. 16), it is in fact difficult to be categorical about texts that are both similar to and different from the future revolutionary discourse.

5. Donald M. G. Sutherland, *France 1789–1815*, 33–48, 68–69. For material on the origins, nature, and significance of the "spirit of Vizille," see the recently edited collection by Vital Chomel, *Les Débuts de la Révolution en Dauphiné 1788–1791*, Presses Universitaires de Grenoble, 1988. This can be supplemented by the excellent study by Jean Sgard with the same publisher, *Les Trente récits de la Journée des Tuiles*, 1988.

6. Daniel L. Wick, "The Court Nobility and the French Revolution: The Example of the Society of Thirty," *Eighteenth Century Studies*, 1980, 263–284.

7. George Armstrong Kelly, "The Machine of the Duc d'Orléans and the New Politics," *J.M.H.*, 1979, 667–684.

8. Abel Poitrineau, "Les assemblées primaires du bailliage de Salers en 1789," *R.H.M.C.*, 1978, 419–441.

9. James Murphy and Patrice Higonnet, "Les députés de la noblesse aux états généraux de 1789," *R.H.M.C.*, 1973, 230–243.

10. Guy Chaussinand-Nogaret, *Mirabeau*, Le Seuil, 1982; Louis Gottschalk and Margaret Maddox, *La Fayette in the French Revolution through the October Days*, Chicago, 1969. For a good account of the continuity and the coherence of La Fayette's revolutionary views until the end of his life, see Lloyd S. Kramer, "The Rights of Man: La Fayette and the Polish National Revolution, 1830–1834," *F.H.F.*, 1986, 521–546.

11. Elna Hindie Lemay, "La composition de l'Assemblée nationale constituante: les hommes de la continuité?" *R.H.M.C.*, 1977, 341–363; William H. Sewell, Jr., article previously cited,

J.M.H., 1985, 66–69; Gail Bassenga, "From 'Corps' to Citizenship: The *Bureaux des Finances* before the French Revolution," *J.M.H.*, 1986, 643–668.

Was the social revolution of 1789 a bourgeois phenomenon?

1. William Doyle, *Origins*, 202–213. One has here, it seems to me, the best answer to the question asked by Colin Lucas in the *Times Literary Supplement* of May 8, 1981: Could an assembly of notables such as the Constituent Assembly have unleashed a revolutionary movement as far reaching as that of 1789? The feverish atmosphere that had been growing for almost three years and particularly since the spring in all social strata is, to a large degree, a sufficient explanation.

2. Donald M. G. Sutherland, *France 1789–1815*, 76–82, 86–88.

3. William H. Sewell, Jr., article previously cited, *J.M.H.*, 1985, 69–71; Jean-Pierre Hirsch, *La Nuit du 4 Août*, Gallimard / Julliard, 1978.

4. Guy Chaussinand-Nogaret, "Aux origines de la Révolution: noblesse et bourgeoisie," *A.E.S.C.*, 1975, 277; Roberto Zapperi, "Sieyès e l'abolizione del feudalesimo nel 1789," *S.S.*, 1970, 415–444. Michael P. Fitzsimmons, "Privileges and the Polity in France, 1786–1791," *A.H.R.*, 1987, 269–295, has recently confirmed both the depth of the ideological schism that occurred regarding the notion of privilege between 1787 and 1789, and the spirit of unity among the French elite that was maintained during the summer of 1789. See a recent study by Jean-Denis Bredin on a key figure of the period, *Sieyès: La Clef de la Révolution française*, Éditions de Fallois, 1988.

4. A PEOPLE'S REVOLUTION?

Was the popular intervention of 1789 an unprecedented uprising by the poor?

1. Robert R. Palmer, *The Age of Democratic Revolution: A Political History of Europe and America, 1760–1800*, Vol. I, *The Challenge*, Princeton University, 1959, 479; Donald M. G. Sutherland, *France 1789–1815* 49. Ulrich Ricken has pointed out in an insightful article ("Oppositions et polarités d'un champ notionnel: les philosophes et l'absolutisme éclairé," *A.H.R.F.*, 1979, 547–557) that for Voltaire, according to a confidential remark that he made to Frederick II, "the riffraff [was] not worth enlightening." Billaud-Varenne was still asserting in 1789 (*Dernier Coup porté au Préjugé et à la Superstition*, 119) that the popular classes never had "the sensitivity of feelings that constitutes honor."

2. William Doyle, *Origins*, 158–167. For a good bibliographic overview, see Rolf Reichardt, "Bevölkerung und Gesellschaft Frankreiches im 18. Jahrhundert: Neue Wege und Ergebnisse der sozial historischen Forschung 1950–1976," *Zeitschrist Für historische Forschung* IV, 1977. For a useful reminder about the fundamental importance of barter, self-sufficiency, and the subsistence economy in France at the end of the *ancien régime*, see Abel Poitrineau ("Minimum vital catégoriel et conscience populaire: les retraites conventionnelles des gens âgés dans le pays de Murat au xviiie siècle," *F.H.S.*, 1981, 165–176). One can add to this list the key role of work performed by women and children within the framework of the family economy as described by Guy L. Gullickson, "The Sexual Division of Labor in Cottage Industry and Agriculture in the Pays de Caux: Auffray, 1750–1850," *ibid.*, 177–199. For a study in one particular case of the disastrous economic consequences of population pressures that existed in France at the end of the *ancien régime*, see Edmond N. Allen, "Deforestation and Fuel Crisis in Pre-Revolutionary Languedoc, 1720–1789," *ibid.*, 1984, 455–473. See also the study by Daniel Hickey on the deeply rooted origins of the Revolution's economic problems in the distant past in *ibid.*, 1987, 208–240, ("Innovation and Obstacles to Growth in the Agriculture of Early Modern France: The Example of Dauphiné"). Cf. Also Marie Donoghay, "The Best Laid Plans: French Execution of the Anglo-French Commercial Treaty of 1786," *European History Quarterly*, 1984, 401–422.

3. Donald M. G. Sutherland, *France 1789–1815* 49–63; Olwen Hufton, "Begging, Va-

grancy, Vagabondage and the Law: An Aspect of the Problem of Poverty in Eighteenth-Century France," *E.S.R.*, 1972, 97–123; Muriel Jeorger, "La structure hospitalière de la France sous l'Ancien Régime," *A.E.S.C.*, 1977, 1025–1051; Marie-Claude Dinet-Lecomte, "Recherche sur la clientèle hospitalière aux xviiᵉ et xviiiᵉ siècles: L'exemple de Blois," *R.H.M.C.*, 1986, 345–373. For a recent confirmation of the final economic crisis of the *ancien régime* that was marked particularly by stagnating land prices, see Gérard Béaur, *Le Marché foncier à la veille de la Révolution: Les mouvements de propriété beaucerons dans les régions de Maintenon et de Jarville de 1761 to 1790*, Éditions de l'École des hautes études en sciences sociales, 1984. For a cogent study of the revolutionary nature of the events immediately preceding the summer of 1789, albeit in an admittedly special case, see Monique Cubells' *Les Horizons de la Liberté: Naissance de la Révolution en Provence 1787–1789*, Edisud, 1987. Regarding the problems surrounding public assistance, see also Colin Jones and Michael Sonenscher, "The Social Functions of the Hospital in Eighteenth-Century France: The Case of the Hôtel-Dieu de Nîmes," *F.H.S.*, 1983, 172–214.

4. Jean Nicolas, *Actes du colloque de Paris, mai 1984: Mouvements populaires et Conscience sociale, xviᵉ–xixᵉ siècles*, Mouton, 1985; "Ephémérides du refus pour une enquête sur les émotions populaires au xviiiᵉ siècle: Le cas de la Savoie," *A.H.R.F.*, 1973, 593–607; *A.H.R.F.*, 1974, 111–153. William M. Reddy, *The Rise of Market Culture: The Textile Trade and French Society, 1750–1900*, Cambridge University, 1984, considers this widespread demand for a more equitable economy the principal cause of France's social problems from the middle of the eighteenth century to the beginning of the twentieth century. George V. Taylor has pointed out ("The bourgeoisie at the beginning of and during the Revolution" in Eberhard Schmitt and Rolf Reichardt, eds., *Die Französische Revolution: zufälliges oder notwendiges Ereignis?*, 1983) this fundamental *coincidence* in 1789 between a political crisis and a socioeconomic crisis. For a good recent study, see "déstabilization de la société française" on the eve of the Revolution by André Burguière in Jacques Dupâquier, *Histoire de la Population Française*, Vol. II, 1988, P.U.F., 475–493.

5. Charles Tilly, *La France conteste, de 1600 à nos jours*, Fayard, 1986. Note Jean Starobinski's remark (*1789: Les Emblèmes de la Raison*, Flammarion, 1979, 44): "The Revolution owes its success, its rhythm, and its catastrophic acceleration of events to the unforeseen coalition of Enlightenment thinkers (or, if one wishes, enlightened reform) and the obscure pressure of frustrated crowds."

6. Louise A. Tilly, "La révolte frumentaire, forme de conflit politique en France," *A.E.S.C.*, 1972, 731–757; Edward P. Thompson et. al., *La Guerre du Blé au XVIIIᵉ siècle*, Les Éditions de la Passion, 1988 (introduction by Florence Gathier and Guy-Robert Ikni). It is curious to note that Roger Chartier ("Culture populaire et culture politique dans L'Ancien Régime: quelques reflexions," in Keith Michael Baker, ed., *The French Revolution and the Creation of Modern Political Culture*, Vol. I, *The Political Culture of the Old Regime*, Pergamon, 1987, 243–258) neglects the key role of agricultural subsistence items.

7. Steven L. Kaplan, *Bread, Politics and Political Economy in the Reign of Louis XV*, 2 vols., Martinus Nijhoff, 1976; *Le Complot de famine: histoire d'une rumeur au xviiiᵉ siècle*, A. Colin. 1982. See an admirable study by the same historian ("The Paris Bread Riot of 1725," *F.H.S.*, 1985, 23–56) on the deep roots of Parisian revolutionary realities (including the connection between the problems of food supplies and the maintenance of order, the psychological aspects of the former, and the independent attitude of the inhabitants of the Faubourg Saint-Antoine, etc.) during the long pre-Revolution period. From this point of view, Paris was calm between 1725 and 1775, thanks to the thoughtful policy of a government that had been jolted by the riots at the beginning of the century. Nonetheless, the government remained at the mercy of a situation dominated by penury that could make a political crisis extremely dangerous.

Why did Paris rise up in 1789?

1. William Doyle, *Origins*, 178–191.

2. Donald M. G. Sutherland, *France 1789–1815*, 63–69, 83–86. See an interesting new edition thanks to Jacques Revel, of G. Lefebvre's *La Grande Peur*, followed by *Foules Révolutionnaires*, Armand Colin, 1988.

3. George Rudé, *The Crowd in the French Revolution*, Oxford, 1959. Michael Sonenscher, however, has recently pointed out ("Journeymen, the Courts and French Trades 1781–1791," *P.P.*, 1987, 77–109) the degree to which the struggles of the French workers at the end of the *ancien régime* occurred within the context of an official judiciary system. Cf. also David Garrioch and Michael Sonenscher, "*Compagnonnages*, Confraternities and Associations of Journeymen in Eighteenth-Century Paris," *European History Quarterly*, 1986, 25–45, which reminds us that the religious brotherhoods remained by far the most important associations for the Parisian working class on the eve of the Revolution. See also Haim Burstin, "Conditionnement économique et conditionnement mental dans le Monde du Travail parisien à la fin de l'Ancien Régime: le Privilège corporatif," *History of European Ideas*, 1982, 23–29. See also a good recent study by Colin Lucas, "The Crowd and Politics" in C. Lucas, ed., *The Political Culture of the French Revolution*, Pergamon, 1988, 259–285.

4. Daniel Roche, *Le Peuple de Paris: Essai sur la culture populaire au xviiie siècle*, Aubier, 1981. Thomas Brennan (*Public Drinking and Popular Culture in Eighteenth-Century Paris*, Princeton University, 1988) shows that the rituals surrounding the consumption of wine in taverns were important aspects of Parisian working-class culture in the *ancien régime*.

5. Christian Romon, "Le monde des pauvres à Paris au xviiie siècle," *A.E.S.C.*, 1982, 729–763; Charles Engrand, "Paupérisme et condition ouvrière dans la seconde moitié du xviiie siècle: l'exemple amiénois,": *R.H.M.C.*, 1982, 376–410.

6. Jean Lecuir, "Criminalité et 'moralité': Montyon, statisticien du parlement de Paris," *R.H.M.C.*, 1974, 445–493.

7. Jean Chagniot, "Le problème du maintien de l'ordre à Paris au sviiie siècle,", *B.S.H.M.*, no. 3, 1974, 32–39; "Le guet et la garde de Paris à la fin de l'Ancien Régime," *R.H.M.C.*, 1973, 58–71; *Paris et l'armée au xviiie siècle, Étude politique et sociale*, Edition, Economica, 1985. Emile G. Leonard (*L'armée et ses problemes au xviiie siècle*, Plon, 1958, cited by T. C. W. Blanning, *The French Revolution*, Macmillan, 1987, 38) has noted the political importance of the defection of the army *and of a good part of the aristocratic officers* at the end of the *ancien régime*. The Revolution was the result, above all, of the royal authorities' loss of the monopoly of organized force during the summer of 1789. (*Ibid.*, 41).

8. Arlette Farge and André Zysberg, "Les théâtres de la violence à Paris au xviiie siècle," *A.E.S.C.*, 1979, 984–1015.

9. Arlette Farge, *La Vie fragile: Violence, pouvoirs, pouvoirs et solidarités à Paris au xviiie siècle*, Hachette, 1986; Arlette Farge and Jacques Revel, *Logiques de la Foule, L'affaire des enlèvements d'enfants, Paris 1750*, Hachette, 1988. In the first issue of *Mentalités*, "Affaires de sang," Imago, 1988, Arlette Farge ("La Violence, les femmes et le sang au xviiie siècle") analyzes the later attitude of the famous *"Tricoteuses"* as a reaction to their exclusion from the political arena.

Did the rural upheavals of 1789 constitute an original and autonomous peasant revolution?

1. William Doyle, *Origins*, 192–202. See a remarkable recent synthesis by Peter M. Jones, *The Peasantry in the French Revolution*, Cambridge University, 1988.

2. Donald M. G. Sutherland, *France 1789–1815*, 69–76.

3. Nicole Castan, "Délinquance traditionnelle et répression critique à la fin de l'Ancien Régime dans les pays de Languedoc," *A.H.R.F.*, 1977, 182–203; Nicole and Yves Castan, *Vivre ensemble: Ordre et désordre au Languedoc au xviiie siècle*, Gallimard/Julliard, 1981. For an interesting recent confirmation of these phenomena, see Jacques Godechot, *La Révolution française dans le Midi toulousain*, Privat, 1986. He notes that in 1770 the representative of the Order of Malta in a parish in Lauragais considered peasants who challenged his seignorial dominance to be prorepublican. It is true that, four years later, a neighboring parish priest described the nobles and the bourgeois who no longer adhered to religious traditions in similar terms. In any case, in Gascogny, Comminges, Quercy, and everywhere, in fact, the revolt of the poor and the brigandage of the desperate festered (*ibid.*, 36–43). The study done by Jean Nicolas, since the colloquium organized by him in Paris in 1984, also shows the growth of riots involving adolescents, which tripled from the beginning to the end of the eighteenth

century. Cf. his presentation to the colloquium in Grenoble in 1988 on the pre-Revolution period in the provinces.

4. Olwen Hufton, "Le paysan et la loi en France au XVIIIᵉ siècle," *A.E.S.C.*, 1983, 679–701; Iain A. Cameron, "The Police of Eighteenth-Century France," *E.S.R.*, 1977, 47–75; Clive Emsley, "La maréchaussée à la fin de l'Ancien Régime," *R.H.M.C.*, 1986, 622–644. Cf., for a particularly important urban case, Agnès Barruol, "Delinquance ou contestation? Contrebandiers et agents des fermes à Marseille (1750–1789)," *Provence Historique*, 1987, 397–409. See also Steven G. Reinhardt, "The Selective Prosecution of Crime in Ancien Régime France: Theft in the Sénéchaussée of Sarlat," *European History Quarterly*, 1986, 3–24.

5. Hilton Lewis Root, "Challenging the Seigneurie: Community and Contention on the Eve of the French Revolution," *J.M.H.*, 1985, 652–681; *Peasants and King in Burgundy: Agrarian Foundations of French Absolutism*, University of California Press, 1987; "The Rural Community and the French Revolution" in Keith Michael Baker, ed., *Modern Political Culture*, Pergamon, 1987, 141–153.

6. Emmanuel Le Roy Ladurie, "Révoltes et contestations rurales en France de 1675 à 1788," *A.E.S.C.*, 1974, 6–22; Jean-Marie Constant, "Les idées politiques paysannes: étude comparée des cahiers de doléances (1576–178)," *A.E.S.C.*, 1982, 717–728.

7. Jean Nicolas, "Les mouvements populaires dans le monde rural sous la Révolution française: état de la question," *B.S.H.M.*, no. 3, 1986, 20–28; Yves-Marie Bercé, *Histoire des croquants*, Le Seuil, 1986, 379.

5. AN AVOIDABLE DERAILMENT?

Was a constitutional monarchy viable in 1790?

1. François Furet and Denis Richet, *La Révolution française*, Vol. I, Hachette, 1965; Donald M. G. Sutherland, *France 1789–1815*, 89ff.

2. *Ibid.*, 121 ff.

3. *Ibid.*, 90–93.

4. *Ibid.*, 93 ff.

5. *Ibid.*, 103–106; cf. Jean-Noël Luc, *Paysans et Droits féodaux en Charente-Inférieure pendant la Révolution française*, Commission d'histoire de la Révolution française, "Travaux historiques et scientifiques," 1984.

6. Guy Chaussinand-Nogaret, *Mirabeau*, Le Seuil, 1982.

7. Samuel F. Scott, "Problems of Law and Order During 1790, the 'Peaceful' Year of the French Revolution," *A.H.R.*, 1975, 859–863.

8. *Ibid.*, 863–871.

9. David D. Bien, article previously cited, *P.P.*, 1979, 95; Samuel F. Scott, "The Regeneration of the Line Army During the French Revolution," *J.M.H.*, 1970, 307–330; *The Response of the Royal Army to the French Revolution: The Role and Development of the Line Army During 1787–1793*, Oxford, 1978; Jean-Paul Bertraud, "Voies nouvelles pour l'histoire militaire de la Révolution," *A.H.R.F.*, 1972, 66–93; "Les travaux récents sur l'armée de la Révolution et de l'Empire," *B.S.H.M.*, no. 3, 1986, 2–7.

10. Samuel F. Scott, "Problems of Law and Order," article previously cited, *A.H.R.*, 1975, 871–876.

11. James N. Hood, "Protestant-Catholic Relations and the Roots of the First Popular Counter-Revolutionary Movement in France," *J.M.H.*, 1971, 245–275; "Patterns of Popular Protest in the French Revolution: the Conceptual Contribution of the Gard," *J.M.H.*, 1976, 259–293; "Permanence des conflits traditionnels sous la Révolution: l'exemple du Gard," *R.H.M.C.*, 1977, 602–640; "Revival and Mutation of Old Rivalries in Revolutionary France," *P.P.*, 1979, 82–115; Gwynne Lewis, "The White Terror of 1815 in the Department of the Gard: Counter-Revolution, Continuity and the Individual," *P.P.*, 1973, 108–135; *The Second Vendée: The Continuity of Counter-Revolution in the Department of the Gard, 1789–1815*, New York, 1978; Timothy Tackett, "Women and Men in Counterrevolution: The Sommières Riot of 1791," *J.M.H.*, 1987, 680–704.

12. Donald M. G. Sutherland, *France 1789–1815*, 107–114.

13. Hubert C. Johnson, *The Midi in Revolution: A Study of Regional Political Diversity, 1789–1793*, Princeton University, 1986; Roger Dupuy, "La contre-révolution (1780–1802): éléments d'un chantier," *B.S.H.M.*, no. 3, 1986, 16–19. For a more recent study of a particularly important aspect of this counterrevolutionary dynamic from 1789 to 1792, see W. J. Murray, *The Right-Wing Press in the French Revolution*, Boydell & Brewer. See also Jean-Paul Bertaud, *Les Amis du Roi, Journaux et journalists royalistes au début de la Révolution, 1789–1792*, Librairie Académique Perrin, 1984.

14. Samuel F. Scott, article previously cited, *A.H.R.*, 1975, 876–888.

15. Donald M. G. Sutherland, *France 1789–1815*, 99–103.

16. R. B. Rose, "Tax Revolt and Popular Organization in Picardy 1789–1791," *P.P.*, 1969, 92–108; Philippe Goujard, "L'abolition de la féodalité dans le pays de Bray (1789–1793)," *A.H.R.F.*, 1977, 287–294; Jean Boutier, "Jacqueries en pays croquant: les révoltes paysannes en Aquitaine (décembre 1789–mars 1790)," *A.E.S.C.*, 1979, 760–786; Guy Ikni, "Sur les biens communaux pendant la Révolution française," *A.H.R.F.*, 1982, 71–93; R. B. Rose, "The 'Red Scare' of the 1790s: The French Revolution and the 'Agrarian Law,' " *P.P.*, 1984, 113–130.

Did the revolutionary movement become radicalized before the flight to Varennes?

1. François Furet, *Penser la Révolution française*, Gallimard, 1978; William H. Sewell, Jr., art. cité, *J.M.H.*, 1985, 72–75. Lynn Hunt (*History and Theory*, no. 20, October 1981, 313–323) has correctly pointed out, with respect to Furet's theories, the dual phenomena of the importance of revolutionary rhetoric and its contrasts with reality. She correctly attributes the final defeat of the Revolution to this last point.

2. See the important special issue of *A.H.R.F.*, September–October 1986 (no. 226) devoted to the popular societies. Marie-Helene Froeschle-Chopard has recently demonstrated ("Pénitents et sociétés populaires du Sud-Est," *A.H.R.F.*, 1987, 117–157), along the same lines as M. Agulhon, the unusual characteristics of the societies in Provence that continued the tradition of the religious brotherhoods of the *ancien régime* within the framework of southern social customs. Five thousand five hundred communes had a political organization under the Revolution, according to the article by Jean Boutier and Philippe Bautry in the issue cited in *A.H.R.F.*, 365–398.

3. R. B. Rose, *The Making of the Sans-Culottes*, Manchester, 1983; Maurice Genty, "Mandataires ou représentants: un problème de la démocratie municipale à Paris, en 1789–1790," *A.H.R.F.*, 1972, 23–27; "Le mouvement démocratique dans les sections parisiennes (printemps 1790–automne 1792)," *A.H.R.F.*, 1982, 134–142; *L'Apprentissage de la citoyenneté. Paris, 1790–1795*, Messidor, 1987.

4. Michael L. Kennedy, "The Foundation of the Jacobin Clubs and the Development of the Jacobin Club Network, 1789–1791," *J.M.H.*, 1979, 701–733; *The Jacobin Clubs in the French Revolution*, Princeton University, 1981.

5. Michael L. Kennedy, "Les clubs des jacobins et la presse sous l'Assemblée nationale, 1789–1791," *R.H.*, 1980, 49–63; Melvin Edelstein, "*La Feuille villageoise*, the Revolutionary Press and the Question of Rural Political Participation," *F.H.S.*, 1971, 175–203; Jean-Paul Bertaud, *C'était dans le journal pendant la Révolution française*, Librairie Académique Perrin, 1988; Hugh Gough, "The Provincial Jacobin Club Press During the French Revolution," *European History Quarterly*, 1986, 47–76.

6. Jack-Richard Censez, *Prelude to Power: The Parisian Radical Press, 1789–1792*, Baltimore, 1976; Jean-Paul Marat, *Textes choisis*, Éditions sociales, 1950, 66ff., 75ff., 95ff. (particularly p. 102ff.).

7. R. B. Rose, "The 'Red Scare,' ", *P.P.*, 1984, 122–123; "Tax Revolt," *P.P.*, 1969, 101–105. Georges Weulersse has pointed out, in *Physiocratie à l'aube de la Révolution (1781–1792)*, edited in 1985 by l'École des hautes études en sciences sociales, the first revolutionary rhetorical attacks against private property rights. For the development of the thought of Babeuf until 9 thermidor, see Victor Daline, *Gracchus Babeuf à la veille et pendant la Révolution française 1785–1794*, Éditions du Progrès, 1987.

8. Jean Boutier, art. cité, *A.E.S.C.*, 1979, p. 767. See recent study by Norman Hampson, *Prelude to Terror: The Constituent Assembly and the Failure of Consensus 1789–1791*, Basil Blackwell, 1988.

Did the Revolution's reorganization of the Catholic church increase the risk of civil war?

1. André Latreille, *L'Église catholique et la Révolution française*, Vol. I, Hachette, 1946; Jean Dumont, *La Révolution française ou les Prodiges du sacrilège*, Criterion, 1984; Jean de Viguerie, *Christianisme et Révolution*, Nouvelles Éditions latines, 1986.

2. Bernard Plongeron, *La Vie quotidienne du clergé français au XVIIIᵉ siècle*, Hachette, 1974; Louis S. Greenbaum, *Talleyrand, Statesman-Priest: The Agent General of the Clergy and the Church of France at the End of the Old Regime*, Catholic University of America, 1970; B. de Brye, *Un évêque d'Ancien Régime à l'épreuve de la Révolution, le cardinal A.C.H. de La Fare (1752–1829)*, Publications de la Sorbonne, 1985.

3. Dominique Julia, "Le clergé paroissial dans le diocèse de Reims à la fin du XVIIIᵉ siècle," *R.H.M.C.*, 1966, 195–216; Timothy Tackett, *Priest and Parish in Eighteenth-Century France*, Princeton University, 1977; Paul Christophe, *1789, les prêtres dans la Révolution*, Le Cerf, 1986.

4. Jean Quéniart, *Les Hommes, l'Église et Dieu dans la France du XVIIIᵉ siècle*, Hachette, 1978; Michel Vovelle, "L'élite ou le mensonge des mots," *A.E.S.C.*, 1974, 49–72; Steven ,L. Kaplan, "Religion Subsistence and Social Control: the Use of Saint Genevieve," *Eighteenth Century Studies*, 1980, 142–168; Jeffry Kaplow, *The Names of Kings: Parisian Laborian Poor in the Eighteenth Century*, New York, 1972; B. Robert Kreiser, *Miracles, Convulsions and Ecclesiastical Politics in Early Eighteenth-Century Paris*, Princeton University, 1978. Dominique Julia has recently pointed out, however, the depth of the crisis in the relationship between the monarchy of the *ancien régime* and the leaders of the Gallican church beginning in 1750 ("Les Deux Puissances: chronique d'une séparation de corps," in Keith Michael Baker, ed., *The French Revolution*, Pergamon, 1987, 293–310). In the name of Enlightenment utilitarianism, the latter were increasingly tempted by the option of submission to state control in exchange for the recognition of their right to reform themselves on the eve of the Revolution.

5. Bernard Plongeron, *Conscience religieuse en révolution: Regards sur l'historiographie religieuse de la Révolution française*, Plon, 1969; Bernard Plongeron and Jean Godel, "1945–1970: un quart de siècle d'histoire religieuse de la génération des 'secondes Lumières' (1770–1820)," *A.H.R.F.*, 1972, 181–203, 352–389; Bernard Plongeron, "Le fait religieux dans l'histoire de la Révolution française: Objet méthodes, voies nouvelles," *A.H.R.F.*, 1976, 95–133; *Théologie et Politique au siècle des Lumières (1770–1820)*, Droz, 1973; "Théologie et applications de la collégialité dans l'église constitutionnelle de France," *A.H.R.F.*, 1975, 71–84; Ruth Graham, "The Revolutionary Bishops and the *Philosophes*," *Eighteenth Century Studies*, 1983, 117–140. The villagers of Périgord, at the beginning of the Revolution, hoped to liberate the good Lord by putting the tricolor cockade hat on the Holy Ghost and by opening the tabernacle (according to Mona Ozouf, *La Fête révolutionnaire, 1789–1799*, Gallimard, 1976, 151, where she cites a letter of Vergniaud dated January 16, 1790).

6. William Doyle, *Origins*, 151ff.; Ruth F. Necheles, "The Curés in the Estates-General of 1789," *J.M.H.*, 1974, 425–444; Louis Trénard, "Église et État: le clergé face à la Révolution dans les diocèses du nord de la France, 1788–1792," in *Christianisme et Pouvoirs politiques*, université de Lille-III, 1973, 57–90 "Église et Révolution (1780–1802)," *L'Information historique*, 1985, 36–42; "L'Église de France et la Révolution," *ibid.*, 78–80.

7. Donald M. G. Sutherland, *France 1789–1815*, 94–99.

8. *Ibid.*, 115–177.

9. Timothy Tackett and Claude Langlois, "Ecclesiastical Structures and Clerical Geography on the Eve of the French Revolution," *F.H.S.*, 1980, 352–370.

10. Timothy Tackett, *Religion, Revolution and Regional Culture in Eighteenth-Century France: The Ecclesiastical Oath of 1791*, Princeton University, 1986; cf. *L'Église de France et la Révolution: Histoire régionale*, Vol. I, *L'Ouest*, Vol. II, *Le Midi*, Beauchesne, 1983 and 1984. See also the commentary by Dominique Julia, "La Révolution, L'Église et la France," *A.E.S.C.*, 1988, 761–770.

11. Jean-Louis Ormières, "Politique et religion dans l'Ouest," *A.E.S.C.*, 1985, 1041–1066.

12. William H. Sewell, Jr., article previously cited from *J.M.H.*, 1985, 80. Cf. the episode recently studied by Jean-Marie Cabasse, "Un des premiers cas de résistance populaire à la Révolution: l'émeute du 25 janvier 1791 à Millau," *Bulletin de la Commission d'histoire de la Révolution française, 1984–1985*, 57–72. This involved Catholic women and children who clung to their religion and their clergy in the face of a nationalist mayor who wanted to take over the Capucine convent. In the spring, a reaction by the revolutionary bourgeois minority against the royalist majority of the town led to various incidents of violence and intimidation. In this town, anti-Protestant feelings united the two social extremes, the aristocracy and the popular classes.

6. AN IDEOLOGICAL WAR?

Was revolutionary France responsible for its conflict with Europe?

1. Donald M. G. Sutherland, *France 1789–1815*, 123–139. C.J. Mitchell, "Political Divisions Within the Legislative Assembly of 1791," *F.H.S.*, 1984, 356–389. See an interesting study by Patricia Chastain Howe ("Charles-François Dumouriez and the Revolutionizing of French Foreign Affairs in 1792," *ibid.*, 1986, 367–390) on the importance and the sincerity of the contribution of this politician and military adventurer to the war of liberation and the propaganda then supported by the Brissotins and their refugee allies (from Belgium in particular).

2. T. C. W. Blanning, *The Origins of the French Revolutionary Wars*, Longman, 1986, 36–130; Howard V. Evans, "The Nootka Sound Controversy in Anglo-French Diplomacy, 1790," *J.M.H.*, 1974, 609–640; H. A. Barton, "The Origins of the Brunswick Manifesto," *F.H.S.*, 1967, 146–169. According to Gerhard Wolf, during talks with the Allies in Brussels on the eve of Brunswick's manifesto, an envoy of Duport's insisted on the need to keep, after their victory, a constitutional monarchy similar to the one that existed in 1789. ("Les négotiations secrètes des feuillants: juin–juillet 1792," *111ᵉ Congrès national des sociétés savantes: "Histoires moderne et contemporaine,"* Vol. I, Part 2, Poitiers, 1986, 7–19).

3. T. C. W. Blanning, *op. cit.*, 131–172; Marc Bouloiseau, "L'organisation de l'Europe selon Brissot et les girondins à la fin de 1792," *A.H.R.F.*, 1985, 290–294; Paul Kelly, "Strategy and Counter-Revolution: The Journal of Sir Gilbert Elliot, September 1–22, 1793," *E.H.R.*, 1983, 328–348.

4. T. C. W. Blanning, *op. cit.*, 205–211.

5. *Ibid.*

6. Jacques Godechot, *La Grande Nation*, Aubier, 1983. The impact of the French Revolution in Canada was strong enough to give Genet the idea of liberating Quebec from the British in 1793 (*ᵉ Siècle*, 1988, 332, n. 20).

7. Michael L. Kennedy, "Le club jacobin de Charleston en Caroline du Sud (1792–1795)," *R.H.M.C.*, 1977, 420–438; William L. Blackwell, "Citizen Genet and the Revolution in Russia, 1789–1792," *F.H.S.*, 1963, 72–92; Jan L. Polasky, "Traditionalists, Democrats and Jacobins in Revolutionary Brussels," *J.M.H.*, 1984, 227–262; Karl H. Wegert, "Patrimonial Rule, Popular Self-Interest and Jacobinism in Germany, 1763–1800," *J.M.H.*, 1981, 440–467; T. C. W. Blanning, *The French Revolution in Germany: Occupation and Resistance in the Rhineland, 1792–1802*, Oxford, 1983 (reviewed by Claude Michaud, *A.E.S.C.*, 1986, 845–847); César-Frédéric de La Harpe, *Correspondance sous la République helvétique*, Vol. I., *Le Révolutionnaire, 1796–1798*, La Baconnière, 1985; Walter Grab, *"Ein Volk muss seine Freiheit selbst erobern," Zur Geschichte der deutschen Jakobiner*, Frankfort, 1984.

8. Jean-Pierre Bertaud, "Les travaux récents sur l'armée de la Révolution et de l'Empire," *B.S.H.M.*, no. 3, 1986, 2–7. Cf., by the same author, "Enquête sur les voluntaires de 1792," *A.H.R.F.*, 1988, 151–170.

9. Jean-Pierre Bertaud, *Valmy, la démocratie en armes*, Julliard, 1970; "Notes sur le premier amalgame (février 1793–janvier 1794)," *R.H.M.C.*, 1973, 72–83; "Voies nouvelles pour l'histoire militaire de la Révolution," *A.H.R.F.*, 1975, 64–94; "Le recrutement de

l'avancement des officiers de la Révolution," *A.H.R.F.*, 1972, 513–534; John Lynn, "Esquisse sur la tactique de l'infanterie des armées de la République," *ibid.*, 537–558; Samuel F. Scott, "The Regeneration of the Line Army During the French Revolution," *J.M.H.*, 1970, 307–330; *The Response of the Royal Army to the French Revolution: The Role and Development of the Line Army, 1787–1793*, Oxford, 1798; Steven T. Ross, "The Development of the Combat Division in Eighteenth-Century French Armies," *F.H.S.*, 1965, 84–94; Charles J. Wrong, "The *officiers de fortune* in the French Infantry," *F.H.S.*, 1976, 400–431; for a recent synthesis see John A. Lynn, *The Bayonets of the Republic: Motivation and Tactics in the Army of Revolutionary France, 1791–1794*, University of Illinois, 1984.

Was the mobilization of the people in 1792–93 favorable to the Revolution or the counterrevolution?

1. Donald M. G. Sutherland, *France 1789–1815*, 139–144.

2. *Ibid.*, 144–155.

3. *Ibid.*, 155–160.

4. *Ibid.*, 166–172. For a good study of the origins and limits of the "second Revolution," in one particularly significant case, see Michel Seyve, *Montélimar et la Révolution 1789–1792: Audaces et Timidités provinciales*, Editions "Notre Temps," 1987.

5. Jean Nicolas, article previous cited, *B.S.H.M.*, no. 3, 1986, 20–28; Guy Ikni, "Sur les biens communaux pendant la Révolution française," *A.H.R.F.*, 1982, 71–94; Melvin Edelstein, article previously cited, *F.H.S.*, 1971, 175–203; Albert Mathiez, *La Vie chère et le Mouvement social sous la Terreur*, Payot, 1927; David Hunt, "The People and Pierre Dolivier: Popular Uprisings in the Siene-et-Oise Department (1791–1792)," *F.H.S.*, 1979, 184–214; R. B. Rose, article previously cited, *P.P.*, 1984, 113–130.

6. George Rudé, *La Foule dans la Révolution française*, Maspero, 1982, 99–133; Maurice Genty, article previously cited, *A.H.R.F.*, 1982, 134–142; Morris Slavin, *The French Revolution in Miniature: Section Droits de l'homme, 1789–1795*, Princeton University, 1984; Raymonde Monnier, "Les classes laborieuses du faubourg Saint-Antoine sous la Révolution et l'Empire," *A.H.R.F.*, 1979, 119–124; Haim Burstin, "Le faubourg Saint-Marcel à l'époque révolutionnaire" *A.H.R.F.*, 1978, 117–126; Frédéric Bluche, *Septembre 1792: logiques d'un massacre*, Perrin, 1986; Suzanne Petersen, *La Question des subsistances et la Politique révolutionnaire à Paris, 1792–1793*, Munich, 1978; Florence Gauthier, "De Mably à Robespierre, un programme égalitaire," *A.H.R.F.*, 1985, 273–289; Michel Pertué, "Les luttes de classes et la question de la dictature au début de 1793," *A.H.R.F.*, 1977, 454–462; Anne-Marie Boursier, "L'émeute parisienne du 10 mars 1793," *A.H.R.F.*, 1972, 204–230; Paolo Viola, "Sur le mouvement populaire parisien de février-mars 1793," *A.H.R.F.*, 1974, 503–518; Jean-Paul Marat, *Textes Choisis*, Éditions sociales, 1950, 54.

7. James N. Hood, article previously cited, *P.P.*, 1979, 82–115; Michael L. Kennedy, "The Best and the Worst of Times: The Jacobin Club Network from October 1791 to June 2, 1793," *J.M.H.*, 1984, 635–666; Hugh Gough, "Politics and Power: The Triumph of Jacobinism in Strasbourg, 1791–1793," *The Historical Journal*, 1980, 327–352; Hubert C. Johnson, *The Midi in Revolution . . . , Princeton University*, 1986, 174–221; Takashi Koi, "Les 'Chaliers' et les sans-culottes lyonnais (1792–1793)," *A.H.R.F.*, 1978, 127–131; Antonio de Francesco, "Montagnard e san culotti in Provincia: il caso lionese (agosto 1792–maggio 1793)," *S.S.*, 1978, 589–626; David L. Longfellow, "Silk Weavers and the Social Struggle in Lyon During the French Revolution, 1789–1794," *F.H.S.*, 1981, 1–40. Michael L. Kennedy ("The Jacobin Clubs and the Press: 'Phase Two'," *F.H.S.*, 1984, 474–499) has pointed out that *until the spring of 1793* the Parisian newspaper most appreciated by the revolutionaries in the provinces remained that of the "Girondin" Carra. Carra, whose newspaper had at that point nearly a million readers scattered among more than twelve hundred popular socieites, was the deputy elected with the most votes at the National Convention. Cf., for a more recent and general work by the same author, *The Jacobin Clubs in the French Revolution: The Middle Years*, Princeton University, 1988.

8. Jacques Godechot, *La Contre-Révolution, 1789–1804: Doctrine et action*, P.U.F., 1961; John Gerard Gallaher, "Recruitment in the District of Poitiers: 1793," *F.H.S.*, 1963, 246–267; Harvey Mitchell, "The Vendée and Counter-Revolution: A Review Essay," *F.H.S.*,

1968, 405–429; Roger Dupuy, "A propos de 'la Vendée' de Charles Tilly," *A.H.R.F.*, 1971, 603–614; Claude Petitfrère, "Les grandes composantes sociales des armées vendéennes d'Anjou," *F.H.S.*, 1973, 1–20; *Blancs et Bleus d'Anjou (1789–1793)*, 2 vols., université de Lille-III, 1979; *La Vendée et les Vendéens*, Julliard, 1981; Jean-Clément Martin, "La Vendée et sa guerre: Les logiques de l'événement," *A.E.S.C.*, 1985, 1067–1085; *La Vendée et la France*, Le Seuil, 1987.

9. Claude Petitfrère, *La Vendée et les Vendéens*, 185–206; Roger Dupuy, "Chansons populaires et chouannerie en basse Bretagne," *B.S.H.M.*, no. 4, 1978, 2–11; Harvey Mitchell, "Resistance to the Revolution in Western France," *P.P.*, 1974, 94–131; Timothy Tackett, "The West in France in 1789: The Religious Factor in the Origins of the Counter-Revolution," *J.M.H.*, 1982, 715–745; T. J. A. Le Goff and Donald M. G. Sutherland, "The Revolution and the Rural Community in Eighteenth-Century Brittany," *P.P.*, 1974, 96–119; "The Social Origins of Counter-Revolution in Western France," *P.P.*, 1983, 65–87; *Mémoires de la marquise de La Rochejaquelein, 1772–1857*, Mercure de France, 1984, 167ff; Donald M. G. Sutherland, *The Chouans: The Social Origins of Popular Counterrevolutions in Upper Brittany, 1770–1796*, Oxford, 1982. See an excellent recent study by Roger Dupuy, *De la Revolution à la Chouannerie: Paysans en Bretagne 1788–1794*, Flammarion, 1988. Cf. also the study on "le problème des causes de la Contre-Revolution dans L'Ouest 1788–1794," *Historiens-Géographes*, no. 318, March–April 1988, 37–42. See also Claude Petitfrère, "The Origins of the Civil War in the Vendée," *French History*, 1988, 187–207.

Was the antagonism between the Girondins and the Montagnards insurmountable?

1. Donald M. G. Sutherland, *France 1789–1815*, 161–166.

2. *Ibid.*, 172–186.

3. *Ibid.*, 186–191. For a good commentary on the ways in which the history of the National Convention during its "heroic" phase would be distorted by future French thinkers from George Sand to Jaurès, see Dominique Aubry, *Quatre Vingt-Treize et Les Jacobins: Regards Littéraires du xixe siècle*, Presses Universitaires de Lyon, 1988. Their exaggerations are summed up by a phrase Victor Hugo wrote in 1874: "Never has anything so grand appeared on the horizon of men" (*ibid.*, 117).

4. Marc Bouloiseau, *La République jacobine*, Le Seuil, 1972; Albert Soboul, *Actes du colloque "Girondins et montagnards,"* Bibliothèque d'histoire révolutionnaire, Vol. 19, 1980; *La Civilisation et la Révolution française*, Vol. II, Arthaud, 1982; Jacqueline Chaumié, "Les girondins et les Cent-Jours," *A.H.R.F.*, 1971, 329–365; Alison Patrick, "Political Divisions in the French National Convention, 1792–1793," *J.M.H.*, 1969, 421–474; "The Montagnards and their Opponents: Some Comments," *J.M.H.*, 1971, 294–297; *The Men of the First French Republic: Political Alignments in the National Convention of 1792*, Baltimore, 1972. Marcel Dorigny has pointed out recently that the Girondins were well disposed toward the development of popular soicieties ("Les congrès des sociétés populaires de 1792 en Bourgogne: défense révolutionnaire et ordre social," *111e Congrès national des sociétés savantes*, Histoire Moderne, et Contemporaire, Vol. 1, Part 2, Poitiers 1986, 91–119).

5. Michael J. Sydenham, "The Montagnards and their Opponents: Some Considerations on a Recent Reassessment of the Conflicts in the French National Convention, 1792–1793," *J.M.H.*, 1971, 287–293; "The Girondins and the Question of Revolutionary Government," *F.H.S.*, 1977, 342–348; Theodore A. Dipadova, "The Girondins and the Question of Revolutionary Government," *F.H.S.*, 1976, 432–450; "The Question of Girondins Motives," *F.H.S.*, 1977, 349–352; Michel Pertué, review of a book by Alison Patrick, *A.H.R.F.*, 1982, 661–665; M. Slavin, *The Making of an Insurrection: Parisian Sections and the Gironde*, Harvard University, 1986.

6. Patrice Higonnet, "The Social and Cultural Antecedents of Revolutionary Discontinuity: Montagnards and Girondins," *E.H.R.*, 1985, 513–544; Gary Kates, *The Cercle Social, the Girondins, and the French Revolution*, Princeton University, 1984.

7. Albert Mathiez, *La Vie chère*; Guy Ikni, article previously cited, *A.H.R.F.*, 1982, 71–94; Takashi Koi, article previously cited, *A.H.R.F.*, 1978, 131; Antonio De Francesco, article previously cited, *S.S.*, 1978, 623; David L. Longfellow, article previously cited, *F.H.S.*, 1981,

22; Daniel Stone, "La révolte fédéraliste à Rennes," *A.H.R.F.*, 1971, 367–387; Michael J. Sydenham, "The Republican Revolt of 1793: A Plea for Less Localized Local Studies," *F.H.S.*, 1981, 120–138; Bill Edmonds, " 'Federalism' and Urban Revolt in France in 1793," *J.M.H.*, 1983, 22–53; Hubert C. Johnson, *The Midi in Revolution*, Princeton University, 1986, 222–249; Yves Delaporte, "Un 'montagnard' fédéraliste: Antoine C. Thibaudeau, député de la Vienne à la Convention nationale, 1792–1795," *111ᵉ Congrès national des sociétés savantes*, *op. cit.*, 121–135; Louis Trénard, "Lyon capitale d'une 'seconde Vendée'?" in *112ᵉ Congrès National des Sociétés Savantes, Histoire Moderne et Contemporaine*, Vol. III, Éditions du C.T.H.S., 1987, 69–90; Bill Edmonds, "A Jacobin Debacle: The Losing of Lyon in Spring 1793," *History*, 1984, 1–14; M. H. Crook, "Federalism and the French Revolution: The Revolt of Toulon in 1793," *ibid.*, 1980, 383–397.

7. A LOGIC TO THE TERROR?

Who were the instigators of the Terror, what was their program, and how was it carried out?

1. Mona Ozouf, "War and Terror in French Revolutionary Discourse (1792–1794)," *J.M.H.*, 1984, 579–597; Jacob L. Talmon, *The Origins of Totalitarian Democracy: Political Theory and Practice During the French Revolution and Beyond*, Secker & Warburg, 1952; Claude Lefort, *Essais sur le politique (xixᵉ-xxᵉ siècles)*, Le Seuil, 1986; Patrice Higonnet, article previously cited, *E.H.R.*, 1985, 513–544; *Class, Ideology and the Right of Nobles During the French Revolution*, Clarendon, 1981; Ferenc Feher, "The French Revolution: Between Class Identity and Universalist Illusions," *Review*, 1985, 335–351; Ferenc Feher, *The Frozen Revolution: An Essay on Jacobinism*, Maison des Sciences de l'Homme, 1987.

2. Noel O'Sullivan, ed., *Terrorism, Ideology and Revolution: The Origins of Modern Political Violence*, Wheatsheaf, 1985; William H. Sewell, Jr., article previously cited, *J.M.H.*, 1985, 74–76. T. C. W. Blanning (*The French Revolution: Aristocrats versus Bourgeois?*) has recently described the Terror (p. 45) as an exceptional and aberrant response to a situation that was equally atypical. One can compare this point of view with the "standard" one of Robert Palmer, *Twelve Who Ruled: The Year of the Terror in the French Revolution*, Princeton University, 1973.

3. Donald M. G. Sutherland, *France 1789–1815* 192–196. See an interesting study by Patrice Higonnet in F. Furet and M. Ozouf, *op. cit.*, 422ff. He points out the critique of Soboul positions by Richard M. Andrews ("Social Structure, Political Elites and Ideology in Revolutionary Paris, 1792–1793," *Journal of Social History*, Vol. 19, no. 1, Fall 1985), for whom the Parisian *sans-culotte* oligarchy of several thousand persons was not a "true popular manifestation" but a "revolutionary democracy" that was completely "ideological." P. Higonnet also places it at an equal distance between its cultural past (taste for violence, the posturings, and the archaisms) and its revolutionary future in the nineteenth century (social consciousness, politicization, and incipient feminism).

4. Richard Cobb, "The People in the French Revolution," *P.P.*, 1959, 60–72; "Quelques aspects de la mentalité révolutionnaire (avril 1793–thermidor an II)," *R.H.M.C.*, 1959, 81–120.

5. Richard Cobb, *The Police and the People: French Popular Protest, 1789–1820*, Oxford, 1970.

6. Marie-Thérèse Lagasquié, "Recherches sur le personnel terroriste toulousain," *A.H.R.F.*, 1971, 248–263; William Scott, *Terror and Repression in Revolutionary Marseille*, Macmillan, 1973; Alan Forrest, *Society and Politics in Revolutionary Bordeaux*, Oxford, 1975; Martyn Lyons, "The Jacobin Elite of Toulouse," *E.S.R.*, 1977, 259–284; David L. Longfellow, article previously cited, *F.H.S.*, 1981, 22–40. Philippe Barlet has recently described the revolutionary militants in a certain number of rural villages in the Indre ("les sans-culottes aux champs: mentalités révolutionnaires dans les comités de surveillance du district de La Châtre (Indre) en l'an II," *IIIᵉ Congrès national des sociétés savantes: "Histoires moderne et contemporaine,"* Vol. I, Part 2, Poitiers, 1986, 171–188). In these villages, property owners and the

professionals were overrepresented within this new elite. Dutifully attending meetings, even if not very active, this new elite opposed the old, more upper class, elite, which rejected the new revolutionary order. For an invaluable study on the complexity of the participation of the workers of Lyons in the Revolution, see Bill Edmonds, "A Study in Popular Anti-Jacobinism: The Career of Denis Mornet," *F.H.S.*, 1983, 215–251.

7. Donald M. G. Sutherland, *France 1789–1815*, 196–205; Albert Mathiez, *La Vie chère et le Mouvement social sous la Terreur*, Payot, 1927; Georges Lefebvre, *Études orléanaises*, Vol. II, *Subsistances et Maximum (1789–an IV)*, Commission d'histoire économique et sociale de la Révolution, "Mémoires et documents," 1963; J.-P. Fanget, "Aspects de l'abolition du régime seigneurial dans le département du Puy-de-Dôme: le brûlement des titres féodaux (août 1793–pluviôse an II)," *C.H.*, 1978, 169–192.

8. Donald M. G. Sutherland, *France 1789–1815*, 208–214; Antoine de Baecque, "Le corps meurtri de la Révolution: Le discours politique et les blessures des martyrs (1792–1794)," *A.H.R.F.*, 1987, 17–41. (on the subject of the regular display of these sufferings undergone in service of the Terror.)

9. Laura Maslaw Armand, "La bourgeoisie protestante, la Révolution et le mouvement de déchristianisation à La Rochelle," *R.H.M.C.*, 1984, 489–502; Yvan-Georges Paillard, "Fanatiques et patriotes dans le Puy-de-Dôme: La déchristianisation," *A.H.R.F.*, 1978, 372–404; Jacques Bernet, "Les origines de la déchristianisation dans le district de Compiègne," *ibid.*, 405–432; Philippe Goujard, "Sur la déchristianisation dans l'Ouest: La leçon des adresses à la Convention nationale," *ibid.*, 433–449; Michel Vovelle, *Religion et Révolution: La déchristianisation en l'an II*, Hachette, 1976; Serge Bianchi, "Manifestations et formes de la déchristianisation dans le district de Corbeil," *R.H.M.C.*, 1979, 256–285; "Les curés rouges dans la Révolution française," *A.H.R.F.*, 1982, 364–392; *A.H.R.F.*, 1985, 447–479; Jean-Claude Meyer, *La Vie religieuse en Haute-Garonne sous la Révolution (1789–1801)*, Publications de l'université Toulouse-Le Mirail, 1982; Albert Soboul, "Sur les 'curés rouges' dans la Révolution française," *A.H.R.F.*, 1982, 349–363.

10. Donald M. G. Sutherland, *France 1789–1815*, 214–217.

11. Jean Delumeau, "Au sujet de la déchristianisation," *R.H.M.C.*, 1975, 52–60; André Latreille, "La déchristianisation en France à l'époque moderne," *C.H.*, 1969, 13–35; Ruth Graham, article previously cited, *Eighteenth Century Studies*, 1983, 117–140; Jean de Viguerie, *Christianisme et Révolution*, Nouvelles Éditions latines, 1986, 152–177; Serge Bianchi, "La déchristianisation de l'an II: Essai d'interprétation," *A.H.R.F.*, 1979, 341–371; Gérard Cholvy, "Religion et Révolution: la Révolution française et la question religieuse," *L'Histoire*, no. 72, novembre 1984, 50–59; Jacques Bernet, "La déchristianisation dans le district de Compiègne (1789–1793)," *A.H.R.F.*, 1982, 299–305; *B.S.H.M.*, no. 4, 1964, 10.

12. Philippe Goujard, "L'homme de masse sans les masses, ou le déchristianisateur malheureux," *A.H.R.F.*, 1986, 160–180. See a recent synthesis by Michel Vovelle, *1793: La Révolution contre l'Église de la Raison à l'Être Suprême*, Éditions Complexe, 1988.

13. Donald M. G. Sutherland, *France 1789–1815*, 217–229; for a good clarification by Jean-Noël Bergeon, *Carrier et la Terreur nantaise*, Librairie académique Perrin, 1987. Richard Cobb has recently pointed out (*Times Literary Supplement* Jan. 29–Feb. 4, 1988) that Fouquier-Tinville, before becoming the public prosecutor of the Revolutionary Tribunal of 1793, had already sent the rioters of the flour war in 1775 to prison. Also consult the interesting *Actes du colloque Jean-Baptiste Carrier, Aurillac 30 mai 1987*, in *Revue de la Haute Auvergne*, October-December 1987 and January-March 1988.

14. Andrew Wheatcroft, *The World Atlas of Revolutions*, Hamish Hamilton, 1983; Richard Louie, "The Incidence of the Terror: A Critique of a Statistical Interpretation," *E.H.S.*, 1964, 379–389; Michel Morineau, "Mort d'un terroriste . . . Prolégomènes à l'étude d'un juste: 'Aristide' (ci-devant Georges) Couthon," *A.H.R.F.*, 1983, 292–339; Colin Lucas, *The Structure of the Terror: The Example of Javogues and the Loire*, Oxford, 1973; Martyn Lyons, *Revolution in Toulouse: An Essay on Provincial Terrorism*, University of Durham, 1978; Michel Pertué, "Note sur la mise hors la loi sous la Révolution française," *Bulletin de la Commission d'histoire de la Révolution française*, 1982–1983, 103–118; Olivier Blanc, *La Dernière Lettre: Prisons et condamnés de la Revolution, 1793–1794*, Laffont, 1984; George Armstrong Kelly, *Victims, Authority and Terror*, University of North Carolina, 1982; Jeremy D. Popkin, "The Royalist Press in the Reign of Terror," *J.M.H.*, 1979, 685–700. Paul Mans-

field, in his study "The Repression of Lyon, 1793–94: Origins, Responsibility and Significance," *French History*, 1988, 74–106, shows convincingly that what was involved here was
a *collective* responsibility of the Committee of Public Safety and, above all, of those who
supported Robespierre. Moreover, he points out this unshakable *unity* of the revolutionary
government regarding its policy of repression and the costly and senseless accumulation of
errors that this represented. Cf., in the same vein, the study on "Collot d'Herbois at the
Committee of Public Safety: A revaluation," *E.H.R.*, 1988, 565–587.

Why did the Terror become bureaucratized?

1. Donald M. G. Sutherland, *France 1789–1815* 205–208.

2. *Ibid.*, 229–239.

3. Albert Mathiez, *La Vie chère*; Michel Eude, *"Une interprétation 'non mathiézienne' de
l'affaire de la Compagnie des Indes," A.H.R.F.*, 1981, 239–250; Morris Slavin, "Jacques Roux:
A Victim of Vilification," *F.H.S.*, 1964, 525–553; Walter Markow, *Die Freiheiten des Priesters
Roux*, Akademie Verlag, 1967; Morris Slavin, "Jean Varlet as Defender of Direct Democracy,"
J.M.H., 1967, 387–404; Jacques Guilhaumou, "Discours et Révolution: du porte-parole à
l'événement discursif," *B.S.H.M.*, no. 3, 1986, 8–15. We are indebted to Daniel Guérin for
his pioneering work, *La Lutte des Classes sous la Première République*, 2 vols., Gallimard,
1946.

4. Jacques Bernet, "Le problème des sociétés sectionnaires sous la Révolution française:
l'exemple de Reims (1793–1794)," *111ᵉ Congrès national des sociétés savantes; "Histoire
moderne et contemporaine," op. cit.* (this part is entitled *Existe-t-il un fédéralisme jacobin?
Etudes sur la Révolution*), 7–19; Anne-Marie Duport, "Les congrès des sociétés populaires
tenus à Valence en 1793: résistance au fédéralisme et anticipations politiques," *ibid.*, 21–37;
François Wartelle, "Contre-pouvoir populaire ou complot maximaliste? Les fédérations mon-
tagnardes dans le nord de la France, octobre–décembre 1793," *ibid.*, 59–90; Jacques Guilhaumou, "Le congrès républicain des sociétés populaires des départements méridionaux de
Marseille (octobre–novembre 1793): programme et mots d'ordre," *ibid.*, 39–57; Yves Tripier,
"Les agents nationaux en Bretagne," *XVIIIᵉ Siècle*, 1986, 227–248.

5. Raymonde Monnier, "La dissolution des sociétés populaires parisiennes au printemps
de l'an II," *A.H.R.F.*, 1987, 176–191.

Why did the Jacobin dictatorship destroy itself on 9 thermidor?

1. Donald M. G. Sutherland, *France 1789–1815*, 239–247; George Rudé, *La Foule dans
la Révolution française*, Maspero, 1982, 150–163; Pierre Arches, "Les conséquences démo-
graphiques de la guerre de Vendée dans le nord des Deux-Sèvres," *111ᵉ Congrès national des
sociétés savantes, op. cit.*, 211–229; Anne-Marie Duport, "Le 'tribunal révolutionnaire' du
Gard, octobre 1793–thermidor an II," *Bulletin de la Commission d'histoire de la Révolution
française*, 1984–1985, 85–99. (This *regional* terrorist institution was never more actively
involved in deadly political repression than on the eve of 9 thermidor.) The same phenomena
could be seen in Bordeaux, where the military commission speeded up the death sentences
considerably during June and July 1794 under the direction of Marc-Antoine Jullien, Robespierre's agent, in comparison with the preceding months. (cf. Marie-Helene Bourquin, *Monsieur
et Madame Tallien*, Librarie Académique Perrin, 1987, 172). F. Furet has pointed out (*Dictionnaire critique*, 194) "that there is no significant difference between the Terror that ravaged
the Vendée and the revolutionary Terror in general." For an invaluable documentary study
on the responsibility of the Convention and the Committee of Public Safety of year II for the
genocidal policies that ravaged the Vendée during the first half of 1794, see Elie Fournier,
Turreau et les colonnes infernales ou l'échec de la violence, Albin Michel, 1985. See an insightful
and courageous study of the phenomenon by Anne Burnel, "Les Colonnes infernales (1794),"
in *Gavroche, Revue d'Histoire Populaire*, nos. 4–5, June–September 1982, 34–38.

2. Martyn Lyons, "The 9 Thermidor: Motives and Effects," *E.S.R.*, 1975, 123–146; Albert
Mathiez, *La Révolution française*, Vol. III, *La Terreur*, A. Colin, 1924, 223.

3. Patrice Bret, "Lazare Carnot, stratège de l'ambigu," *L'Histoire*, no. 94, November 1986,
42–49; Marc Martin, "Les journaux militaires de Carnot," *A.H.R.F.*, 1977, 405–428; Michel
Eude, "La loi de prairial," *A.H.R.F.*, 1983, 544–559; "Le Comité de sûreté générale en

1793–1794," *A.H.R.F.*, 1985, 295–306; "Point de vue sur l'affaire Catherine Théot," *A.H.R.F.*, 1969, 606–629.

4. Suzanne Grézaud, "Vadier à Montaut (Ariège) en 1793," *A.H.R.F.*, 1972, 420–425; Martyn Lyons, "M. G. A. Vadier (1736–1828): The Formation of the Jacobin Mentality," *F.H.S.*, 1977, 74–100.

5. Albert Mathiez, "Robespierre, l'histoire et la légende," *A.H.R.F.*, 1977, 5–31; Georges Lefebvre, "Robespierre," *B.S.H.M.*, no. 3, 1958, 11–12; Albert Soboul, "Robespierre and the Popular Movement of 1793–1794," *P.P.*, 1954, 54–70; David P. Jordan, "Robespierre," *J.M.H.*, 1977, 282–291; Joseph T. Sholim, "Robespierre and the French Revolution," *A.H.R.F.*, 1977, 20–38; Norman Hampson, *The Life and Opinions of Maximilien Robespierre*, Duckworth, 1974; Serena Torjnssen, "Saint-Just et ses biographes: Mécanique d'un mythe," *A.H.R.F.*, 1979, 234–249; Bernard Vinot, *Saint-Just*, Fayard, 1985. Mouza Raskolnikoff, "Volney et les Idéologues: Le refus de Rome," *R.H.*, 1982, 357–373, has noted that this former member of the Constituent Assembly pronounced a series of historical lessons at the new École Normale at the beginning of 1795 that strongly challenged the myth of the supreme value of the republics of antiquity. Myrian Revault d'Allonnes ("tacite et la Révolution française," *Esprit*, December 1987, 103–110) has recently shown, however, that the Jacobins' references to antiquity went beyond republican ideology and were connected to a profound political obsession with the idea of death as a precondition for rebirth.

6. George Armstrong Kelly, "Conceptual Sources of the Terror," *Eighteenth Century Studies*, 1980, 18–36; Jean Deprun, "A la Fête de l'Être suprême: Les 'noms divins' dans deux discours de Robespierre," *A.H.R.F.*, 1972, 161–180; Claude Lefort, *op cit.*, 139; Mona Ozouf, article previously cited, *J.M.H.*, 1984, 579–597; Lazare Carnot, *Révolution et Mathématique*, Vol. II, L'Herne, 1985, 204ff., 211ff.; Raymond Sechez, *Le Génocide franco-français: La Vendée-Vengé*, P.U.F., 1986; Jean-Clément Martin, *La Vendée et la France*, Le Seuil, 1987; Claude Langlois, "La Révolution malade de la Vendée," *XXᵉ Siècle*, no. 14, April–June 1987, 69–78; George Armstrong Kelly, *Mortal Politics in Eighteenth-Century France*, Waterloo University, 1987; Hugh Gough, "Genocide and the Bicentenary: The French Revolution and the Revenge of the Vendée," *The Historical Journal*, 1987, 977–988; Gerd van der Heuvel, "Terreur, terroriste, terrorisme," in R. Reichardt and E. Schmitt, eds., *Handbuch politisch-sozialer Greundbegriffe in Frankreich, 1680–1820*, Vol. 3, Munich, Oldenbourg, 1985, shows that these concepts were rooted in the thought of the *ancien régime* and discusses their revival and reversal during the Revolution.

8. AN INEVITABLE DICTATORSHIP?

Did the Thermidorean reaction mark the end of the Revolution?

1. François Furet and Denis Richet, *La Révolution française*, Vol. II, Hackette, 1966.

2. Donald M. G. Sutherland, *France 1789–1815* 248–255; Geroges Lefebvre, *Les Thermidoriens*, A. Colin, 1937; Denis Woronoff, *La République bourgeoise de Thermidor à Brumaire, 1794–1799*, Le Seuil, 1972.

3. Donald M. G. Sutherland, *France 1789–1815* 255–264; George Rudé, *La Foule dans la Révolution française*, Maspero, 1982, 164–182.

4. Donald M. G. Sutherland, *op. cit.*, 264–278; George Rudé, *op. cit.*, 183–201.

5. Pierre Massé, "*Les Mémoires* de Thibaudeau vus par l'exconventionnel Piorry," *A.H.R.F.*, 1972, 417–437; François Gendron, *La Jeunesse sous Thermidor*, P.U.F., 1983; Maurice Dommanget, *Pages choisies de Babeuf*, A. Colin, 1935, 161–203; Morris Slavin, article previously cited, *J.M.H.*, 1967, 400–402; Alexandre Jovicevich, "Le royaliste La Harpe en vendémiaire an IV, d'après un document inédit," *A.H.R.F.*, 1971, 441–458. Gracchus Babeuf, *La guerre de Vendée: Le système de dépopulation*, new edition, R. Secher and J.J. Brégeon, Tallandier, 1987.

6. Françoise Brunel, "Les derniers montagnards et l'unité révolutionnaire," *A.H.R.F.*, 1977, 385–404; "Sur l'historiographie de la réaction thermidorienne: Pour une analyse politique de l'échec de la voie jacobine," *A.H.R.F.*, 1979, 455–474; Françoise Brunel and Myriam

Revault d'Allonnes," Jacobinisme et libéralisme," *XVIIIe Siècle*, 1982, 103–115; Bronislaw Baczko, "Le Contrat social des Français: Sieyès et Rousseau," in Keith Michael Baker, ed., *Modern Political Culture*, Pergamon, 1987, 493–513.

7. Clive H. Church, "Du nouveau sur les origines de la Constitution de 1795," *Revue historique de droit français et étranger*, 1974, 594–627; "Bureaucracy, Politics and Revolution: The Evidence of the Commission des Dix-Sept," *F.H.S.*, 1970, 492–516; Jeremy D. Popkin, *The Right-Wing Press in France, 1792–1800*, University of North Carolina, 1980.

8. Richard Cobb, "Quelques aspects de la crise de l'an III en France," *B.S.H.M.*, no. 2, 1964, 2–5.

9. Richard Cobb, *The Police and the People: French Popular Protest 1789–1820*, Oxford, 1970; *Reactions to the French Revolution*, Oxford, 1972.

10. James R. Harkins, "The Dissolution of the Maximums and Trade Controls in the Department of the Somme in 1795," *F.H.S.*, 1970, 333–349.

11. Michéle Schlumberger, "La réaction thermidorienne à Toulouse," *A.H.R.F.*, 1971, 265–283; Gwynne Lewis, article previously cited, *P.P.*, 1973, 108–135; Gwynne Lewis and Colin Lucas, eds., *Beyond the Terror: Essays in French Regional and Social History, 1794–1815*, Cambridge University, 1983; Colin Lucas, "Violence thermidorienne et société traditionnelle: L'exemple du Forez," *C.H.*, 1979, 3–43; "Thermidorean Reaction," in S. F. Scott and B. Rothaus, eds., *Historical Dictionary of the French Revolution, 1789–1799*, Vol. II, Aldwych, 1985, 960–965.

Was the liberal Directory a viable experiment?

1. Donald M. G. Sutherland, *France 1789–1815*, 279–292.

2. *Ibid.*, 292–307. In June 1796, a refractory priest, who had taken refuge in Spain, was heartened by the collapse of the Constitutional Church, in Montpellier. He noted with satisfaction that all the churches there were closed and that the official religious life had been defunct for more than two years (Gérard Cholvy, "La crise révolutionnaire et le clergé de l'Hérault," *Bulletin de la Commission d'histoire de la Révolution française*, 1984–1985, 73–84). In addition, Raymond Dartevelle has recently shown ("La foi et la reconquête pastorale dans le diocèse de Gap et d'Embrun, 1795–1798," *Actes du 109e Congrès national des sociétés savantes*, Vol. I, Part 1, Dijon, 1984, 403–421; "les attitudes du clergé dans les Hautes-Alpes au lendemain du 18 Fructidor an V," *A.H.R.F.*, 1987, 192–218) the strength of the resistance of refractory priests and the vitality of popular piety in the southern part of this department.

3. Denis Woronoff, *op. cit.*; Georges Lefebvre, *La France sous le Directoire (1795–1799)*, edited by Jean-René Suratteau, Éditions sociales, 1977; Jean-René Suratteau, *"Le Directoire: Points de vue et interprétations d'après des travaux récents,"* *A.H.R.F.*, 1976, 181–214; Robert H. Wiede, *The Opening of American Society from the Adoption of the Constitution to the Eve of Disunion*, A. A. Knopf, 1984; Clive H. Church, "In Search of the Directory," in J. F. Bosher, ed., *French Government and Society, 1500–1850: Essays in Memory of Alfred Cobban*, Athlon, 1973; *Revolution and Red Tape: The French Ministerial Bureaucracy, 1770–1850*, Oxford, 1981. For a good summary of various research approaches, see Catherine Kawa, "Voies nouvelles pour une étude de la bureaucratie révolutionnaire," *A.H.R.F.*, 1988, 60–75. According to a letter of an activist from the Yonne to Grégoire on January 11, 1795, if the heart of the French people was perhaps republican, their habits remained monarchical (quoted by Suzanne Desan, *J.M.H.*, 1988, 24). See also a recent study by Georges Gusdorf, *Les Révolutions de France et d'Amérique: La Violence et la Sagesse*, Librairie Académique Perrin, 1988. Consult also a remarkable analysis by Vida Azimi on the changes between 1789 and 1792, including the transformation of the employees of the *ancien régime* into state civil servants thanks to remarkable verbal prestidigitation and group solidarity ("1789: l'écho des employés ou le nouveau discours administratif," *XVIIIe Siècle*, 1988, 133–150).

4. Colin Lucas, "The First Directory and the Rule of Law," *F.H.S.*, 1977, 231–260.

5. Harvey Mitchell, "Resistance to the Revolution in Western France," *P.P.*, 1974, 94–131.

6. T. J. A. Le Goff and Donald M. G. Sutherland, "The Social Origins of Counter-Revolution in Western France," *P.P.*, 1983, 65–87; Gérard Cholvy, "La Révolution française et la question religieuse," *L'Histoire*, November 1984, 50–59. Colin Lucas, "L'Église con-

stitutionelle dans la Loire après la Terreur," *C.H.*, 1985, 309–339, has shown that even in this region, where the constitutional clergy was in the majority, it underwent a profound crisis because of the resistance of the faithful and the ensuing developments. Suzanne Desan has recently focused ("Redefining Revolutionary Liberty: The Rhetoric of Religious Revival during the French Revolution," *J.M.H.*, 1988, 1–27) on the strategy of the Catholics who were not directly confronted by the counterrevolution in about half of France. Fully politicized, their campaign in favor of religious liberty borrowed shamelessly from a revolutionary rhetoric that was obviously multifaceted and that served here to denounce the despotism and tyranny that opposed the Catholic demands. One can certainly see here, as one of the principal cultural results of a revolution that sanctified politics, a strange blend of traditional religion and a new political culture.

7. Marc Martin, "Les journaux militaires de Carnot," *A.H.R.F.*, 1972, 405–428; Jacques Godechot, "Études récentes sur la presse révolutionnaire," *A.H.R.F.*, 1974, 310–317; Jeremy D. Popkin, "Les journaux républicains, 1795–1799," *R.H.M.C.*, 1984, 143–157; Isser Woloch, "The Revival of Jacobin in Metz During the Directory," *J.M.H.*, 1966, 13–37; *Jacobin Legacy: The Democratic Movement under the Directory*, Princeton University, 1970; Maurice Dommanget, *op. cit.*, 224–319; John L. Talmon, *The Origins of Totalitarian Democracy: Political Theory and Practice During the French Revolution and Beyond*, Secker & Warburg, 1952, 165–247; Richard M. Andrews, "Réflexions sur la conjuration des égaux," *A.E.S.C.*, 1974, 73–106. Steven Kaplan has recently confirmed brilliantly the unusual nature of the Faubourg Saint-Antoine, whose autonomy provoked fear in 1791 all the way up to Marat ("Les Corporations, les 'faux ouvriers' et le Faubourg Saint-Antoine au XVIIIᵉ siècle," *A.E.S.C.*, 1988, 353–378).

Was the Brumaire coup d'état a fatal blow?

1. Donald M. G. Sutherland, *France 1789–1815*, 308–320.

2. *Ibid.*, 320–334; Jean-Pierre Bertaud, *Bonaparte prend le pouvoir*, Editions Complexe, 1987.

3. T. C. W. Blanning, *The Origins of the French Revolutionary Wars*, Longman, 1986, 173–211.

4. Steven T. Ross, "The Military Strategy of the Directory: The Campaigns of 1799," *F.H.S.*, 1967, 170–187. Paul Schroeder ("The Collapse of the Second Coalition," *J.M.H.*, 1987, 244–290) has recently attributed the Allied defeat to the opposition between Austria and Anglo-Russian imperialist policy. It would be necessary to wait until 1814 for France's adversaries to reject short-term military calculations in favor of an overall political view of the situation in Europe. Cf., for Vienna's outlook, Karl A. Roider, Jr., *Baron Thugut and Austria's Response to the French Revolution*, Princeton University, 1987.

5. Jacques Godechot, *La Révolution française dans le Midi toulousain*, Privat, 1986, 279–301; *La Contre-Révolution. Doctrine et action, 1789–1804*, P.U.F., 1961, 347–376.

6. Jean Merley, "La situation économique et politique de la Haute-Loire à la fin du Directoire et le dressement consulaire," *C.H.*, 1971, 393–401; John A. Davis, "Les sanfédistes dans le royaume de Naples (1799): guerre sociale ou guerre civile?" in François Lebrun and Rogert Dupuy, eds., *Les Résistances à la Révolution*, Imago, 1987, 311–320; Guy Lemarchand, "Une contre-révolution impossible: le pays de Caux face à la basse Normandie, 1793–1800;" *ibid.*, 106–115; Alan Forrest, "Le recrutement des armées et la contre-révolution en France," *ibid.*, 180–190. Carlo Zaghi has recently shown *Potere, Chiesa e Societa. Studi e ricerche sull'Italia giacobina e napoleonice*, Naples, 1984; cf. his *Italia di Napoleone dalla Cisalpina al Regno*, Vol. VII of *Storia d'Italia*, dirigée par G. Galasso, Turin, 1986 that the real power in revolutionary and Napoleonic Italy remained that of the Catholic church. Marina Formica, "Tra Semantica e Politica: il concetto di popolo nel giacobinismo italiano (1796–1799)," *S.S.*, 1987, 699–721. For a striking confirmation of the inertia of the rural world with respect to the Revolution, see the article by Philippe Bourdin, "les paysans et le pouvoir directorial dans le Puy-de-Dôme," *A.H.R.F.*, 1987 314–337.

7. Lynn Hunt, David Lansky, and Paul Hamson, "The Failure of the Liberal Republic in France, 1795–1799: The Road to Brumaire," *J.M.H.*, 1979, 734–759. Mona Ozouf has shown (in Keith Baker, ed., *Modern Political Culture*, Pergamon, 1987, 431ff.) this horror of factions

and the dream of perfect unity and absolute uniformity that permeated the entire Revolution. Arguing against Benjamin Constant in 1796, Adrien Lezay-Marnesia correctly identified (*De la faiblesse d'un gouvernement qui commence et de la nécessité où il est de se rallier à la majorité nationale*, 61) the optimum equilibrium in France between the "two distinct parties, one of which defends the prerogative of the government . . . and the other popular liberties."

8. Raymonde Monnier, "De l'an III à l'an IX, les derniers sansculottes: Résistance et répression à Paris sous le Directoire et au début du Consulat," *A.H.R.F.*, 1984, 386–406; Albert Soboul and Raymonde Monnier, *Répertoire du personnel sectionnaire parisien en l'an II*, Publications de la Sorbonne, 1985 (more than 70% of these militants were subjected to Thermidorean or consular repression).

9. A NEW STATE?

Why did the French Revolution result in the establishment of a personal dictatorship?

1. Louis Bergeron, *L'Épisode napoléonien: Aspects intérieurs, 1799–1815*, Le Seuil, 1972, 7–31; cf. also Jean Tulard, *Napoléon*, Fayard, 1977, 115–129; Jean-Pierre Bertaud, *La France et Napoléon, 1795–1815*, Messidor, 1987. See a good study by John Dunne, "What Differences Does a Decade Make?: Recent Works in Napoleonic Studies," *E.S.R.*, 1980, 383–392. Louis Bergeron has dealt again with the problem of "Napoleon or the post-revolutionary state," in Colin Lucas, ed., *The Political Culture of the French Revolution*, Pergamon, 1988, 437–441.

2. Donald M. G. Sutherland, *France 1789–1815*, 336–340, 356–362. Marcel Dorigny has recently shown, in fact ("La formation de la pensée economique de Sieyès d'après ses manuscrits (1770–1789)," *A.H.R.F.*, 1988, 17–34), the degree to which this author and brumaire profiteer was a strong supporter, even before the Revolution, not of liberalism, but of a strong state that was organized from the top down and of a civil society that was authoritarian in nature.

3. Harold T. Parker, "The Formation of Napoleon's Personality: An Exploratory Essay," *F.H.S.*, 1971, 6–26. Cf. another work by the same author, "Napoleon reconsidered: An Invitation to Inquiry and Reflection," *F.H.S.*, 1987, 142–156, where he stresses the necessity of integrating the psychological study of Napoleon with a study of the changes in French society and its values between the *ancien régime* and the beginning of the nineteenth century. See also Dorothy Carrington, *Napoleon and His Parents on the Threshold of History*, Viking, 1988. See a good portrait of Bonaparte in F. Furet, *Dictionnaire critique*, 216–229. There are perhaps several rash judgments in the work by Desmond Seward, *Napoleon and Hitler: A Comparative Biography*, Harrap, 1988.

Was the administrative centralization achieved by the Revolution and Napoleon a carryover from the ancien régime?

1. Louis Bergeron, *L'épisode napoléonien*, 32–64.

2. Jean Tulard, *op. cit.*, 129; Michel Bruguière, *Gestionnaires et Profiteurs de la Révolution: L'Administration des finances françaises de Louis XVI à Bonaparte*, Olivier Orban, 1986, 49–72.

3. *Ibid.*, 73–90.

4. *Ibid.*, 90–106.

5. *Ibid.*, 106–137.

6. *Ibid.* 138–159.

7. *Ibid.*, 160–193.

8. Harold T. Parker, "Two Administrative Bureaus Under the Directory and Napoleon," *F.H.S.*, 1965, 150–169; Clive H. Church, "The Social Basis of the French Central Bureaucracy under the Directory, 1795–1799." *P.P.*, 1967, 59–72; *Revolution and Red Tape: The French Ministerial Bureaucracy, 1770–1850*, Oxford, 1981.

9. Edward A. Whitcomb, "Napoleon's Prefects," *A.H.R.*, 1974, 1089–1118.

10. Donald M. G. Sutherland, *France 1789–1815*, 344–347. Isser Woloch ("The Fall and Resurrection of the Civil Bar, 1789–1820," *F.H.S.*, 1987, 241–262) has recently begun a study of the movement of French civil society from an old system in 1789 to a new one by the beginning of the nineteenth century. This occurred alternatively through the adoption of very liberal views and decentralization and then through the return to much stricter state control.

Did Napoleon's regime eliminate all opposition?

1. Louis Bergeron, *L'épisode napoleonien*, 95–118. See a good study by Brigitte Sarlichen-Lange and Franz Knopstein, "Les Idéologues avant et après Thermidor," *A.H.R.F.*, 1988, 35–59. She shows the depth of their involvement in anti-Montagnard politics and their effort to explain the Revolution's terrorist deviation as a betrayal of the Enlightenment. Harvey Mitchell, "Tocqueville's Mirage or Reality?: Political Freedom from Old Regime to Revolution," *J.M.H.*, 1988, 28–54, has studied the critical analysis by Tocqueville of the Ideologues' failure to achieve a liberal outcome for the Revolution.

2. Donald M. G. Sutherland, *France 1789–1815*, 340–344.

3. *Ibid.*, 347–354, 362–365.

4. *Ibid.*, 376–380.

5. *Ibid.*, 390–397. For a good recent study, see Isser Woloch, "Napoleonic Conscription: State Power and Civil Society," *P.P.*, 1986, 101–129. For a study on this entire question, see the magisterial work by Alan Forrest, *Déserteurs et Insoumis sous la Révolution et l'Empire*, Librarie Académique Perrin, 1988.

10. A NEW SOCIETY?

Did the Revolution ruin the French economy?

1. Alfred Cobban, *Le Sens de la Révolution française*, Julliard, 1984, 86–96.

2. Florin Aftalion, *L'Économie de la Révolution française*, Hachette, 1986, 250–255.

3. René Sédillot, *Le Coût de la Révolution française*, Perrin, 1986, 149–267. For a confirmation of these views, see William M. Reddy, *The Rise of Market Culture: The Textile Trade and French Society, 1750–1900*, Cambridge University, 1984, 61.

4. François Crouzet, *De la supériorité de l'Angleterre sur la France. L'économique et l'imaginaire, XVII-XXe siècles*, Perrin, 1985.

5. *Ibid.*, 248–279.

6. *Ibid.*, 22–89; D. K. Cohen, "The Vicomte de Bonald's Critique of Industrialism," *J.M.H.*, 1969, 482–484; Humphrey Jennings, *Pandaemonium: The Coming of the Machine as seen by Contemporary Observers*, Deutsch 1985.

7. Jean-Claude Perrot, "Les publications françaises d'économie politique (XVIIe-XVIIIe siècles)," *B.S.H.M.*, no. 1, *B.S.H.M.*, 21–26; Robert Forster, "Obstacles to Agricultural Growth in Eighteenth-Century France," *A.H.R.*, 1970, 1600–1615; Emmanuel Le Roy Ladurie, "Pour un modèle de l'économie rurale française au XVIIe siècle," *C.H.*, 1974, 5–27; P. O'Brien and C. Keyder, *Economic Growth in Britain and France, 1780–1914*, 1978.

8. P. Viles, "The Slaving Interest in the Atlantic Ports, 1763–1792," *F.H.S.*, 1972, 529–543; Robert Louis Stein, *The French Slave Trade in the Eighteenth Century: An Old Regime Business*, University of Wisconsin, 1979; Jean Tarrade, "Le groupe de pression du commerce à la fin de l'Ancien Régime et sous l'Assemblée constituante," *B.S.H.M.*, no. 2, 1970, 23–26; Richard B. Du Goff, "Economic Thought on Revolutionary France, 1789–1792: The Question of Poverty and Unemployment," *F.H.S.*, 1966, 434–451.

9. Jean-Claude Perrot, "Voies nouvelles pour l'histoire économique de la Révolution," *A.H.R.F.*, 1975, 30–65.

10. Albert Soboul, in Fernand Braudel and Ernest Labrousse, ed., *Histoire économique et sociale de la France*, Vol. III, P.U.F., 1976, 3–64; Hubert Bonin, "La Révolution française a-t-elle brisé l'esprit d'entreprise?", *L'Information historique*, 1985, 193–204; Denis Woron-

off, *L'Industrie sidérurgique en France pendant la Révolution et l'Empire*, Éditions de l'École des hautes études en sciences sociales, 1984.

11. Louis Bergeron, *L'Épisode napoléonien: Aspects intérieurs, 1799–1815*, Le Seuil, 1972, 178–214.

12. Jean Tulard, *Napoléon*, Fayard, 1977, 261–276; Albert Soboul, *op. cit.*, 65–133; *La Civilisation et la Révolution française*, Vol. III, *La France napoléonienne*, Arthaud, 1983, 117–226, 347–405; Donald M. G. Sutherland, *France 1789–1815*, 380–384. For a good recent study by Denis Woronoff, see "La Révolution a-t-elle été une catastrophe économique?", *L'Histoire*, no. 113, July–August 1988, 110–114. Cf. also Guy Lemarchand, "Du Féodalisme au Capitalisme: À propos des conséquences de la Révolution sur l'évolution de l'économie française," *A.H.R.F.*, 1988, 171–207. The best study, in fact, appears to be that of Louis Bergeron in *Econorama 88–89*, Nathan, 1988, 36–44. He notes successively that "the suppression of the fiscal and juridical obstacles to the circulation of goods" merely represented the proclamation "of the liberty to enjoy that which did not exist yet"; that "the Revolution and the Empire left France alone with its national market; and that both led to economic development that *was not based* on mass production and the production of military equipment."

Did the French Revolution result in a renewal of the elites?

1. Alfred Cobban, *op. cit.*, 97–105.

2. Jean Sentou, *La Fortune immobilière des Toulousains et la Révolution française*, "Mémoire et documents," XXIV, Commission d'histoire économique et sociale de la Révolution française, 1970.

3. Louis Bergeron, *op. cit.*, 65–91, 130–146. Less than 10 percent of the French nobility emigrated, according to Patrice Higgonnet (*Class, Ideology and the Rights of Nobles During the French Revolution*, Harvard University, 1981, citied by T. C. W. Blanning, *The French Revolution, Aristocrats versus Bourgeois?*, Macmillan, 1987, 44). More than one thousand officers from the nobility served the Republic in 1795, including approximately one hundred generals. (*ibid.*). The Count of Puisaye, who was in charge of the counterrevolution in the west, served the Revolution faithfully, until the summer of 1793 (M. Hutt, *Chouannerie and counter-revolution: Puisaye, the Princes and the British Government in the 1790s*, Vols. 2, 1983, cited *ibid.*).

4. *Ibid.*, 146–172. Gail Bossenga has recently noted ("La Révolution française et les corporations: trois exemples lillois," *A.E.S.C.*, 1988, 405–426) that it was the state under Napoleon that had to impose economic liberalism on local civil servants and *the industrial sectors*.

5. Jean Nicolas, "Le ralliement des notables au régime impérial dans le département du Mont-Blanc," *R.H.M.C.*, 1972, 92–127; Jean Tulard, *op. cit.*, 241–260, 325–334; Albert Soboul, in Fernand Braudel and Ernest Labrousse (ed) *Histoire économique et sociale de la France*, Vol. 3, P.U.F., 1976, 54–60, 124–133; "La grande propriété foncière à l'époque napoléonienne," *A.H.R.F.*, 1981, 405–418; *La France napoléonienne*, 150–159, 320–431.

6. Robert Forster, "The Survival of the Nobility During the French Revolution," *P.P.*, 1967, 71–86; C. Brelot, *La Noblesse en Franche-Comté de 1789 à 1808*, Les Belles Lettres, 1972; Michel Simonot, "L'opinion publique en Côte-d'Or et la question des émigrés," *B.S.H.M.*, no. 4, 1985, 2–8; François Koerner, "La noblesse auvergnate et l'émigration sous la Révolution et l'Empire (1789–1815)," *L'Information Historique*, 1987, 133–139; Robert Forster, "The French Revolution and the 'new' elite," in J. Polenski, ed., *The American and French Revolution*, 1980.

7. Béatrice Fink, "Un inédit de Benjamin Constant," *XVIIIᵉ Siècle*, 1982, 199–218; Ulrich Ricken, "Louis-Sébastien Mercier et ses deux nouveaux paris," *XVIIIᵉ Siècle*, 1972, 301–313; Jean Meyer, in *L'Europe à la fin du XVIIIᵉ siècle*, 1985, 425ff.

8. Louis Trénard, "Un notable lyonnais pendant la crise révolutionnaire: Pierre-Toussaint Dechazelle," *R.H.M.C.*, 1958, 201–225. See a good biography by Richard A. Lebrun, *Joseph de Maistre: An Intellectual Militant*, McGill-Queen's University, 1988, about a man who, like many others, went from an aristocratically inspired liberalism to total support for the counterrevolution.

9. Stuart Woolf, "Les bases sociales du Consulat: Un mémoire d'Adrien Duquesnoy," *R.H.M.C.*, 1984, 596–618.

10. Donald M. G. Sutherland, *France 1789–1815*, 366–369.

11. *Ibid.*, 384–390.

12. Hubert Bonin, article previously cited, *L'Information historique*, 1985, 198–201.

Did the French Revolution change the condition of the popular classes?

1. Melvin Edelstein, "Mobilité ou immobilité paysanne? Sur certaines tendances conservatrices de la Révolution française," *A.H.R.F.*, 1975, 446–477; *"La Feuille villageoise," Communication et modernisation dans les régions rurales pendant la Révolution*, "Mémoires et documents," XXXIV, Commission d'histoire économique et sociale de la Révolution française. 1977; Jean Vassort, "Mobilité et enracinement en Vendômois au tournant des XVIIIᵉ et XIXᵉ siècles," *A.E.S.C.*, 1983, 735–768; Jean-Pierre Jessenne, "Le pouvoir des fermiers dans les villages d'Artois (1770–1848)," *A.E.S.C.*, 702–734; *Pouvoir au village et Révolution: Artois 1760–1848*. Presses universitaires de Lille, 1987.

2. Albert Soboul, *op. cit.*, 61–64, 116–118; *La France napoléonienne*, 145–249; Louis Bergeron, *L'Épisode napoléonien*, 173ff.; Jean Tulard, *op. cit.*, 246–248; Françoise Fortunet, "Le Code rural ou l'impossible codification," *A.H.R.F.*, 95–112. The Soviet historian Anatoly Ado (*Krest'yanskoe dvizhenievo Frantsii vo nemya velikoy burzhiarnoy revoluitsii Kantsa XVIII veku*, 1971), who greatly influenced the most recent ideas of Albert Soboul on this subject, has argued that in destroying the seignorial regime the French peasantry prepared the way for capitalism. G. van der Heuvel (*Grundprobleme der französischen Bauernshaft 1730–1794*, 1982) is, quite correctly, much less sure about this point. An overall study of agricultural and rural society such as that of P. Léon, ed., *Histoirè économique et sociale du monde*, Vol.III, *Inerties et révolutions (1730–1840)* (A. Colin, 1978), leads one to conclude that the real destroyer of the *ancien régime* in the French countryside was the railroad.

3. Peter M. Jones, " 'La République au village' in the Southern Massif Central, 1789–1799," *The Historical Journal*, 1980. 793–812; "Political Commitment and Rural Society in the Southern Massif Central," *E.S.R.*, 1980 337–356; "The Rural Bourgeoisie of the Southern Massif Central: Contribution to the Study of the Social Structure of 'Ancien Régime' France," *Social History*, 1979 65–83; *Politics and Rural Society: The Southern Massif Center c. 1750–1880*, Cambridge, 1985.

4. Daniel Roche, *Le Peuple de Paris: Essai sur la culture populaire au XVIIIᵉ siècle*, Aubier, 1981; "Cuisine et alimentation populaire à Paris," *XVIIIᵉ Siècle*, 1982, 7–18; Albert Soboul. "Problémes du travail au XVIIIᵉ siècle. L'apprentisasge: réalités sociales et nécessités économiques," *S.S.*, 1964, 449–466; Claude Petitfrère, "Les Lumières, la Révolution et les domestiques," *B.S.H.M.*, 1986, no. 4, 10–15.

5. Olwen Hufton, *Bayeux in the Late Eighteenth Century: A Social Study*, 1967; *The Poor of Eighteenth-Century France, 1750–1789*, Oxford University Press, 1974.

6. Mahne Erpeldinger and Claudine Lefebvre," Les misérables sous la Révolution (districts de Lille et de Douai)," *A.H.R.F.*, 1974, 164–186; Alan Forrest, "The Condition of the Poor in Revolutionary Bordeaux," *P.P.*, 1973, 147–177.

7. Alan Forrest, *The French Revolution and the Poor*, St. Martin's, 1981. For Isser Woloch's more optimistic view, see "From Charity to Welfare in Revolutionary Paris," *J.M.H.*, 1986, 779–812. But Paris does not represent all of France, just as the entire Revolution cannot be reduced to its Jacobin period.

8. Albert Soboul, *La France napoléonienne*, 60, 117–124, 251–317.

9. Louis Bergeron, *op. cit*, 174–177; Jean Tulard, *op. cit.*, 248–254. William H. Sewell, Jr., has pointed out (*Work and Revolution in France: The Language of Labor from Old Regime to 1848*, Cambridge University, 1980) this corporatist continuity among French workers before and after 1789. Lynn Hunt and George Sheridan, in their recent critique of this author ("Corporatism, Association and the Language of Labor in France, 1750–1850," *J.M.H.*, 1986, 813–844), rule out even the beginning of any kind of "class consciousness" during this period.

11. A CULTURAL REVOLUTION?

Did the Revolution de-Christianize France?

1. The best study from this new perspective is by Michel Vovelle, *La Mentalité révolutionnaire. Société et mentalités sous la Révolution française*, Messidor, 1985. This can be compared with René Pillorget, "The Cultural Programme of the 1789 Revolution," *History*, 1985, 386–396.

2. Jean de Viguerie, *Christianisme et Révolution: Cinq leçons d'histoire de la Révolution française*, Nouvelles Éditions latines, 1986, 256–260, 7–226.

3. *Ibid.*, 226–256. Roger Chartier (*XVIIIᵉ Siècle*, 1986, 57) has recently called into question the value of Restif's observations about the popular class's reading of the Bible. For invaluable information about the complexity of religious reactions to the Revolution in one particular case, see *Un fondateur dans la tourmente révolutionnaire, Pierre de Clorvière (1735–1820)*, Colloque du Centre Sèvers, 1985, in *Christus*, no. 131, 1986, special edition.

4. Serge Bianchi, "La déchristianisation dans le district de Corbeil," *R.H.M.C.*, 1979, 256–281; Jean Dumont, *La Révolution française ou les Prodiges du sacrilège*, Criterion, 1984, 181–510; Daniele Menozzi, *Letture politiche di Gesù dall'Ancien Régime alla Rivoluzione*, Brescia, Paideia Editrice, 1979; "La Bible des révolutionnaires," in Yvon Belaval and Dominique Bourol, eds., *Le Siècle des Lumières et la Bible*, Beauchesne, 1986, 677–695; Anne Sauvy, "Lecture et diffusion de la Bible en France" *ibid.*, 27–46; Louis Pérouas, "Sur la déchristianisation: Une approche de la pratique pascale sous le Directoire. Le cas de la Cresue," *R.H.E.F.*, 1986, 295–299. Frank-Paul Bowman (*Le Christ des barricades, 1789–1848*, Le Cerf, 1987) has recently emphasized again the importance of the revolutionary image of Jesus during this period.

5. Guy Lemarchand, "L'Église appareil idéologique d'État dans la France d'Ancien Régime (XVIᵉ–XVIIIᵉ siècles)," *A.H.R.F.*, 1979, 250–279; Louis Trénard, *Lyon, de l'Encyclopédie au préromantisme: Histoire sociale des idées*, 2 vols., P.U.F., 1958; Michel Péronnet, "Les censures de la Sorbonne au XVIIIᵉ siècle: base doctrinale pour le clergé de France," in François Lebrun and Roger Dupuy, eds., *Les Résistances à la Révolution*, Imago, 1986, 27–36; Michel Morineau, "Raison, Révolution et contre-révolution," *ibid.*, 284–291; Yves Fauchois, "Les évêques émigrés et le royalisme pendant la Révolution française," *ibid.*, 386–395; Mona Ozouf, "L'idée et l'image du régicide dans la pensée contre-révolutionnaire; l'originalité de Ballanche," *ibid.*, 331–341; Gérard Gengembre, "Bonald: La doctrine pour et contre l'histoire," *ibid.*, 342–351; Daniel Ligou, "Le président Nicolas Jansson: une vision contre-révolutionnaire," *ibid.*, 376–385; Édouard Guitton, "Aspect de la conversion (1790–1802)," *XVIIIᵉ Siècle*, 1982, 151–165; Jean-Louis Vieillard-Baron, "Phénoménologie de la conscience religieuse," *ibid.*, 167–189.

6. Louis Bergeron, *L'Épisode napoléonien: Aspects intérieurs, 1799–1815*, Le Seuil, 1972, 24–28, 48–50, 215–224; cf. Pierre Bénichou, *Le Sacre de l'écrivain, 1750–1830*, José Corti, 1973. See some interesting remarks about reform by A. Benoist, "Le corps pastoral et les protestants poitevins face aux idées nouvelles et à la Révolution (1760–1803)," *Bulletin de la Société des Antiquaires de l'Ouest et des Musées de Poitiers*, no. 2, 1987, 117–152. This points out that the initial supporters of the Revolution did not foresee its slide toward an anti-Christian outlook, during which they became momentarily paralyzed before rallying, *before the Brumaire*.

7. Donald M. G. Sutherland, *France 1789–1815*, 354–356, 369–374.

8. Claude Langlois and Timothy Tackett, "A l'épreuve de la Révolution (1770–1830)," in François Lebrun, ed., *Histoire des catholiques en France*, Privat, 1980, 215–289; Louis Châtellier *L'Europe des dévots*, Flammarion, 1987; Dominic Aidan Bellenger, *The French Exiled Clergy in the British Isles After 1789: An Historical Introduction and Working List*, Bath, Downside Abbey, 1987. See a remarkable study by Bernard Plongeron in the fourth part of the volume he edited, *Le Diocese de Paris, Vol. 1: Des origines à la Révolution*, Beauchesne, 1987.

9. William R. Everdell, "The 'Rosières' Movement, 1766–1789: A Clerical Precursor of the Revolutionary Cults," *F.H.S.*, 1975, 23–36.

10. P. M. Jones, "Parish, Seigneurie and the Community of Inhabitants in Southern Central France during the Eighteenth and Nineteenth Centuries," *P.P.*, 1981, 74–108; "Quelques formes élémentaires de la vie religieuse dans la France rurale (fin xviiie et xixe siècles)," *A.E.S.C.*, 1987, 91–115; cf. J.-L. Le Floch, "Les luttes d'une paroisse pour conserver son identité: Plonivel" in "Riante Cornouaille," *Les Cahiers de l'Irvise*, no. 3, 1987, 118–126.

Did the French Revolution undermine the traditional family?

1. René Sédillot, *Le Coût de la Révolution française*, Perrin, 1986, 11–37; Louis Bergeron, *op. cit.*, 119–129; André Armengaud, in Fernand Braudel and Ernest Labrousse, ed., *Histoire économique et sociale de la France*, III, Vol. 3, P.U.F., 1976, 161–187. See a good study of the demographic heritage passed on to the Revolution in Jacques Dupâquier, *Histoire de la Population française*, Vol. II, *De la Renaissance à 1789*, P.U.F., 1988. Jacques Gélis, *De la Sage Femme au Médecin: Une nouvelle conception de la vie*, Fayard, 1988, shows (219–23) that in matters relating to childbirth the Revolution represented continuity rather than a rupture with the past.

2. Donald M. G. Sutherland, *France 1789–1815*, p. 383; Jacques Dupâquier and Christine Berg-Hamon, "Voies nouvelles pour l'histoire démographique de la Révolution française," *A.H.R.F.*, 1975, 3–29; Claude Langlois and Timothy Tackett, *op. cit.*, 274; Jean-Claude Sangoï, *Démographie paysanne en bas Quercy (1781–1872): Familles et groupes sociaux*, Éditions du CNRS, 1985.

3. Jacques Godechot, *Les Institutions de la France sous la Révolution et l'Empire*, P.U.F., 1968, 237–249.

4. *Ibid.*, 433–439, 693–696. In keeping with others and with one type of American model, Lynn Hunt ("The Rhetoric of Revolution in France," *History Workshop*, no. 15, 1983, 78–94) sees, with perhaps a certain lack of caution, the signs of a rejection of paternal authority in the revolutionary French rhetoric of 1789 and after. For an excellent recent study, see Jacques Mullier, "Droit et Morale Conjugale: essai sur l'histoire des relations personnelles entre époux," *R.H.*, no. 563, 1987, 35–106, regarding the evolution of the situation from the *ancien régime* to the nineteenth century.

5. Albert Soboul, *La Civilisation et la Révolution française*, Vol. III, *La France napoléonnienne*, Arthaud, 1983, 13–20; Donald M. G. Sutherland, *France 1789–1815*, 374–376; Arlette Farge and Michel Foucault, *Le Désordre des familles: Lettres de cachet des archives de la Bastille*, Gallimard/Julliard, 1982, 374–363.

6. André Armengaud, *op. cit.*, 180; Roderick G. Phillips, *Family Breakdown in Late-Eighteenth-Century France: Divorces in Rouen, 1792–1802*, Clarendon, 1981; Dominique Dessertine, *Divorcer à Lyon sous la Révolution et l'Empire*, Presses universitaires de Lyon, 1981.

7. J. F. Traer, *Marriage and the Family in Eighteenth-Century France*, Cornell, 1980; I. A. Hartig, "Révolution et communautés familiales: témoignages et représentations," *A.H.R.F.*, 1982, 59–70; Colette Piau-Gillot, "Le discours de Jean-Jacques Rousseau sur les femmes et sa réception critique," *XVIIIe Siècle*, 1981, 317–333; David Williams, "The Fate of French Feminism," *Eighteenth Century Studies*, 1980, 37–55; Paule-Marie Duhet, *Les Femmes et la Révolution, 1789–1794*, Julliard, 1971.

8. Jane Abray, "Feminism in the French Revolution," *A.H.R.*, 1975, 43–62; Louis Devance, "Le féminisme pendant la Révolution," *A.H.R.F.*, 1977, 341–375; L. Kelly, *Women of the French Revolution*, Hamish Hamilton, 1987; Elisabeth Guibert-Sledziewski, "La femme/objet de la Révolution," *A.H.R.F.*, 1987, 1–16; Nina Rattner Gelbart, *Feminine and Opposition Journalism in Old Regime France: 'Le Journal des dames,'* University of California Press, 1987.

9. Olwen Hufton, "Women and the Family Economy in Eighteenth-Century France," *F.H.S.*, 1975, 1–22. Jacques Peret ("Famille et société à Poitiers à la fin du xviiie siècle," *111e Congrès national des sociétés savantes*, Vol. II, Poitiers, 1986, 7–21) has recently portrayed the family of the popular class as a precarious unit. Cf. Gay L. Gullickson, *Spinners and Weavers of Aussay: Rural Industry and the Sexual Division of Labor in a French Village, 1750–1850*, Cambridge University, 1987.

10. Olwen Hufton, "Women in Revolution, 1789–1796," *P.P.*, 1971, 90–108; Alix De-

guise, *Trois Femmes: Le monde de Mme. de Charrière*, Slatkine, 1985; Albert Soboul, "Madame Tallien, in *Portraits de révolutionnaires*, Éditions sociales, 1986, 299–310. In a recently defended thesis (cf. *A.H.R.F.*, 1987, 219–223) Dominique Godineau presents a more optimistic view about the durability of militant feminism (cf. *A.H.R.F.*, 1987, 219–223) in "Femmes des milieux populaires parisiens pendant la Révolution (1793–messidor an III)." See a good recent study by Marie-Hélène Bourquin, *Monsieur et Madame Tallien*, Libairie Académique Perrin, 1987. Also see the excellent book by Dominique Godineau, *Citoyennes Tricoteuses: Les femmes des milieux populaires à Paris pendant la Révolution française*, Alinea, 1988.

Did the French Revolution create a new man?

1. Michel Vovelle, *La Mentalité révolutionnaire; 1789–1799, la Révolution française. Images et récit*, 5 vols., Livre-Club Diderot, 1985–1987; Serge Bianchi, *La Révolution culturelle de l'an II: Élites et peuple (1789–1799)*, Aubier, 1982; "Vie quotidienne et Révolution française," *Historiens et Géographes*, no. 303, March 1985, 661–671; Michel Sonenthez, "Les sans-culottes de l'an II: repenser le langage du travail dans la France révolutionnaire," *A.E.S.C.*, 1985, 1087–1118. For a well-informed and subtle critique, particularly of the work of Serge Bianchi, see Marianne Caron-Leullier, "La Revolution culturelle: concept et réalité," *Bulletin de la Commission d'histoire de la Révolution française*, 1984–1985, 201–214. She shows that this new model, favored by the admirers of the year II, is neither more valid than the old Jacobin one nor more "popular" in character.

2. William H. Sewell, Jr., article previously cited, *J.M.H.*, 1985, 76–79; Michel de Certeau, Dominique Julia et Jacques Revel, *Une politique de la langue: la Révolution française et les patois*, Gallimard, 1975; Hans-Ulrich Gumbrecht, Hans-Jürgen Lüsenbrink, and Rolf Reichardt, "Histoire et langage: travaux allemands en lexicographie historique et en histoire conceptuelle," *R.H.M.C.*, 1983, 185–195; Hans-Jürgen Lüsenbrink, and Rolf Reichardt, "La Bastille dans l'imaginaire social de la France à la fin du XVIIIe siècle (1774–1799)," *ibid.*, 196–234; Hans-Ulrich Gumbrecht, "Chants révolutionnaires, maîtrise de l'avenir et niveau du sens collectif," *ibid.*, 235–256; Olivia Smith, *The Politics of Language, 1791–1819*, Oxford, 1985. See good recent studies of recent cases in the special March 1988 issue (no. 116) of *Mots Textes Ordinateurs Sociétés* called "La Langue de la Révolution française." Cf. also Jean-Claude Bonnet, ed., *La Carmagnole des Muses: L'homme de lettres et l'artiste dans la Révolution*, Armand Colin, 1988. This collection clearly shows the persistence during this time of previous genres and reputations in the midst of undeniable new developments brought about by political upheavals. Cf. Beatrice Didier, *La Littérature de la Révolution française*, P.U.F., 1988.

3. Lynn Hunt, *Politics, Culture and Class in the French Revolution*, University of California Press, 1984, 1–119. For an interesting study on one particular point, see Claude de Langlois, "Les Dérives vendéennes de l'imaginaire révolutionnaires," *A.E.S.C.*, 1988, 771–797.

4. Robert Darnton, "Révolution sans revolutionnaires," *New York Review of Books*, January 31, 1985, 21–23: Jacques Guilhaumou, article previously cited, *B.S.H.M.*, no. 3, 1986, 8–15; Marc-Élie Blanchard, *Saint-Just et Cie: la Révolution et les mots*, A. G. Nizet, 1980; Marie-Hélène Huet, *Rehearsing the Revolution: The Staging of Marat's Death, 1793–1797*, University of California Press, 1982; Jean-Claude Bonnet, ed., *La Mort de Marat*, Flammarion, 1986; Marcel David, *Fraternité et Révolution française*, Aubier, 1987; Daniel Arasse, *La Guillotine et l'Imaginaire de la Terreur*, Flammarion, 1987; Antoine de Baecque, "Le sang des héros: figures du corps dans l'imaginaire politique de la Révolution française," *R.H.M.C.*, 1987, 553–586.

5. Daniel Milo, "Le nom des rues," in Pierre Nora, ed., *Les Lieux de mémoire*, Vol. II, *La Nation*, Vol. 3, Gallimard, 1986, 283–315; Antonio Sergi, "*Phèdre*, corrigée sous la Révolution," *XVIIIe Siècle*, 1974, 157–165; B. Baczko, "Le complot vandale," in *Le Temps de la réflexion*, IV, Gallimard, 1983, 195–242; Jennifer Harris, "The Red Scape of Liberty: A Study of Dress Worn by French Revolutionary Partisans, 1789–1794," *Eighteenth Century Studies*, 1981, 293–312; Claude Langlois, "Le vandalisme révolutionnaire," *L'Histoire des bibliotheques publiques en France de la Révolution à 1939*, Promodis, 1987 emphasizes the destruction of French books wrought by the Revolution. In addition to this, see the proceedings of the colloquium "Livre et Révolution" organized in May 1987 and published in 1989, in

Mélanges de la Bibliothèque de la Sorbonne, new series, no. I. Jean-Marie Goulemot (*La Quinzaine Littéraire,* no. 508, May 1–15, 1988) has noted, in reconsidering Robert and Elisabeth Badinier's *Condorcet,* to what extent their hero in his biases, rigidities, and awkwardness incarnates the failings of Enlightenment thought. This thought was often marked, as in his case, by an excessive abstractness and "a complete insensitivity to reality." The cultural failure of the Revolution was also a defeat by Enlightenment thought.

6. Jean Starobinski, *L'Invention de la liberté, 1700–1789,* Skira, 1964, 100–104; "La fête révolutionnaire (colloque de Clermont-Ferrand, 24–26, 1974)," *A.H.R.F.,* 1975, 337–430; Mona Ozouf, "Symboles et fonctions des âges dans les fêtes de l'époque révolutionnaire," *A.H.R.F.,* 1970, 569–593; "De Thermidor à Brumaire: le discours de la Révolution sur elle-même," *R.H.,* 1970, 31–66; *La Fête révolutionnaire, 1789–1799,* Gallimard, 1976, 7–74.

7. *Ibid.,* 75–340. Recent confirmation comes from Bruno Benoît, "Les fêtes révolution-naires à Lyon," *C.H.,* 1987, 101–121. Étienne François and Rolf Reichardt ("Les formes de sociabilité en France du milieu du XVIIIe siècle," *R.H.M.C.,* 1987, 453–472) must acknowl-edge (*ibid.,* 463, n. 50) the fact that traditional "forms of village festivities [were] at their height" right after the Revolution and that Michel Vovelle's model on this point is not applicable to France as a whole (*Les métamorphoses de la fête en Provence de 1750 à 1820,* Flammarion, 1976). For a complete treatment of this question, see Étienne François, ed., *Sociabilité et societe bourgeoise en France, en Allemagne et en Suisse (1750–1850)* Éditions Recherche sur les Civilisations, 1988.

8. Mark K. Derning and Claudine de Vaulchiez, "La loi et ses monuments en 1791," *XVIIIe Siècle,* 1982, 117–130; Dominique Poulot, "Naissance du monument historique," *R.H.M.C.,* 1985, 418–450; R. Mortier, "La transition du XVIIIe au XIXe siècle," *XVIIIe Siècle,* 1982, 7–12; François Laforge, "Illusion et désillusion dans *l'Émigré* de Sénac de Meilhan," *XVIIIe Siècle,* 1985, 367–385; Pierre Escoube, *Sénac de Meilhan (1736–1803),* Librairie académique Perrin, 1984. Françoise Dion-Ségala has recently pointed out ("Une contradiction chez Helvétius: l'herbivore et le carnivore," *XVIIIe Siècle,* 1986, 325–335) the final pessimism this *philosophe* expressed in his work *l'Homme,* published in 1774. Diderot had fought this, in the name of an anthropological optimism that Condorcet was able to retain despite the revolutionary tumult that would affect everyone, including himself (cf. Jean-Paul Frick, "Con-dorcet et le problème de l'histoire," *ibid,* 337–358). But the Revolution seemed to show that ignorance of melancholy historical facts was at the root of Enlightenment illusions. This was to be, in fact, the origin of the already romantic vision of *décadence* that was associated with Benjamin Constant (cf. Markus Winkler, *Benjamin Constants Kritik der Franzosischen Auf-klarung,* Berne 1984). For a different perspective, see Henri Coulet, "Révolution et roman selon Mme de Staël," *Revue d'Histoire Litteraire de la France,* 1987, 638–660. See an in-valuable study by Christopher Greene on "Alexandre Lenoir and the *Musée des Monuments français* during the French Revolution," *F.H.S.,* 1981, 200–222. These observations have recently been confirmed in Jean-Claude Bonnet's collection *La Carmagnole des Muses.* He shows the cultural ambivalence toward museums displayed by a revolution that both conserved and purged items at the same time and that safeguarded ancient monuments as soon as they were dismantled. Jay Fliegelman has noted correctly (*Prodigals and Pilgrims: The American Revolution Against Patriarchal Authority 1750–1800,* Cambridge University, 1982, 230) that the French Revolution's unnecessary violence and ultimate failure showed *to its contemporaries* above all the frightful consequences of an ideology adrift and a utopianism that indulged in vague principles based on a universal idealism.

9. Jeremy D. Popkin, *The Right-Wing Press in France, 1792–1800,* University of North Carolina Press, 1980; D. G. Charlton, *New Images of the Natural in France: 1750–1800,* Cambridge University, 1985; John McManners, *Death and the Eighteenth,* Oxford, 1981; Daniel Roche, "Sciences et pouvoirs dans la France du XVIIIe siècle (1666–1803)," *A.E.S.C.,* 1974, 738–748. Jacques Marx, "Catéchisme philosophique et propagande éclairée au XVIIIe siècle," in J. Marx, ed., *Propagande et Contre-Propagande Religieuses* (Éditions de L'Université de Bruxelles, 1987, 121–144), has analyzed the successors of the Enlightenment leaders in all their lack of originality and their simplistic behavior.

10. François-Georges Pariset, "Problèmes posés par le néo-classicisme français," *B.S.H.M.,* no. 2, 1973, 2–4; George Levitine, *The Dawn of Bohemianism: The "Barbu" Rebellion and Primitivism in Neoclassical France,* Pennsylvania State University, 1978; Ronald Paulson,

Representations of Revolution (1789–1820), Yale University Press, 1983; "Revolution and the Visual Arts," in R. Porter and M. Teich, eds., *Revolution in History*, Cambridge University, 1986, 240–260; Jean-Jacques Lévêque, *L'Art et la Révolution française*, Neufchâtel, Ides et Calendes, 1987. Michel Vovelle, ed., *Les Images de la Révolution française*, Publications de la Sorbonne, 1988. See a balanced recent study by Luc de Nanteuil, *Jacques-Louis David*, Éditions Le Cercle d'Art, 1987. This can be supplemented by Philippe Bordes, "La fabrication de l'histoire par Jacques-Louis David," in *Triomphe et Mort du Héros: La Peinture d'histoire en Europe de Rubens à Manet*, Musée des Beaux-Arts de Lyon, 1988, 110–119. See also Antoine de Baecque, *La caricature revolutionnaire*, and Claude Langlois, *La caricature contre-revolutionnaire*, Presses du C.N.R.S., 1988. Philippe Bordes has pointed out (cf. *Triomphe et Mort du Héros*, 389) the astounding request by David, who in 1798 considered redoing his painting *The Tennis Court Oath* and proposed to the Directory that its *actual* figures be replaced by much more interesting ones for the sake of posterity. An admirable sketch of artistic conditions in France and in Europe at the time of the revolutionary era can be found in Jean Starobinski's *1789: Les Emblèms de la Raison*, Flammarion, 1979.

11. Marcel Dorigny, "Les girondins et Jean-Jacques Rousseau," *A.H.R.F.*, 1978, 560–583; Françoise Brunel and Myriam Reváult d'Allonnes, article previously cited, *XVIIIᵉ Siècle*, 1982, 108–113; Jean-Claude Perrot, article previously cited, *A.H.R.F.*, 1975, 50–53; Diego Scarca, "Rousseau e il primitivismo tra Rivoluzione e Impero," *Studi Francesi*, 1985, 243–262; Sergio Moravia, "La société d'Auteuil et la Révolution," *XVIIIᵉ Siècle*, 1974, 181–191; Marc Regaldo, "Lumières, élite, démocratie: La difficile position des idéologues," *ibid.*, 193–207; Martin S. Staum, *Cabanis Eighteenth and Medical Philosophy in the French Revolution*, Princeton University, 1986; "The Class of Moral and Political Sciences, 1795–1803," *F.H.S.*, 1980, 371–396; "The Enlightenment Transformed: The Institute Price Contests," *Eighteenth Century Studies*, 1981, 153–179; Louis Bergeron, *op. cit.*, 224–230; Albert Soboul, "Utopie et Révolution francaise," in Jacques Droz, ed., *Histoire Générale du Socialisme*, P.U.F., Vol. I., 1972, 195–254. Aesthetics was one of the privileged realms of the primitivism that was dear to the hearts of certain intellectuals of the revolutionary era, according to the invaluable observations of P. Rosenblum, *Transformations in Late-Eighteenth-Century Art*, Princeton University, 1967. This has subsequently been confirmed by later research.

12. Maurice Agulhon, *Pénitents et Francs-Maçons de l'ancienne Provence*, Fayard, 1968, 319–322; Jean-Marc Chouraqui, "Le 'combat de Carnaval et de Carême' en Provence du xviᵉ au xixᵉ siècle," *R.H.M.C.*, 1985, 114–124; Albert Soboul, *La France napoléonienne*, 241–249, 311–315; Michel de Certeau, Dominique Julia, and Jacques Revel, "Une ethnographie de la langue: l'enquête de Grégoire sur les patois," *A.E.S.C.*, 1975, 1–41; Jean-Pierre Goubert, "L'art de guérir: Médecine savante et médecine populaire dans la France de 1790," *A.E.S.C.*, 1977, 908–926; Matthew Ramsey, *Professional and Popular Medicine in France, 1770–1830*, Cambridge University, 1988. Knut Thielsen has noted (*Die Sprachepolitik der französischen Revolution und die katholische Kirche*, Erlangen, 1987) that the preachers of "southern France where the influence of the royalists was greater" still spoke in a provincial dialect.

13. Donald M. G. Sutherland, *France 1789–1815*, 369; Roger Chartier, Marie-Madeleine Compère, and Dominique Julia, *L'Education en France du xviᵉ au xviiiᵉ siècle*, Sedes, 1976; Louis Trénard, "Manuels scolaires au xviiiᵉ siècle et sous la Révolution," *Revue du Nord*, 1973, 90–111; Dominique Julia, "L'enseignement primaire dans le diocèse de Reims à la fin de l'Ancien Régime," *A.H.R.F.*, 1970, 233–257; Georges Minois, "L'enseignement secondaire en Bretagne à la fin de l'Ancien Régime: l'exemple de Tréguier," *R.H.*, 1980, 297–317; Gérard Chianéa, "L'enseignement primaire à Grenoble sous la Révolution," *C.H.*, 1972, 121–160; J. Vassort, "L'enseignement primaire en Vendômois à l'époque révolutoinnaire," *R.H.M.C.*, 1978, 625–655; Emmet Kennedy and Marie-Laurence Netter, "Les écoles primaires sous le Directoire," *A.H.R.F.*, 1981, 3–38; Charles R. Bailey, "Municipal Colleges: Small-Town Secondary Schools in France Prior to the Revolution," *F.H.S.*, 1982, 351–376.

14. Philippe Marchand, "L'enseignement secondaire dans le département du Nord au lendemain de la Révolution et la loi de floréal an X," *A.H.R.F.*, 1974, 235–266; Louis Trénard, "Les écoles centrales," *XVIIIᵉ Siècle*, 1982, 57–74; Catherine Merot, "Le recrutement des écoles centrales sous la Révolution," *R.H.*, 1985, 357–382; Mona Ozouf, *L'École de la France: essais sur la Révolution, l'utopie et l'enseignement*, Gallimard, 1984. Françoise Mayeur expresses relatively optimistic views in L. H. Parias, ed., *Histoire générale de l'enseignement et*

de l'éducation en France, Vol. III, *De la Révolution à l'école republicaine (1789–1939)*, Nou-velle Librairie de France, 1981, 25–89; it is true that she is interested particularly in principles and in several key innovations such as the *École polytechnique*. See an admirable geographical study of these phenomena in Dominique Julia et al., *Atlas de la Révolution française*, Vol. II, *L'Enseignement 1760–1815*, Éditions de L'E.H.E.S.S., 1987. She shows convincingly on this point the powerlessness of revolutionary utopianism in the face of the inertia and constraints inherited from the past. Oliver Devaux, *La Pique et la Plume: L'Enseignement à Toulouse pendant la Révolution* (Eché, 1988) has recently confirmed the destructive and negative record of the Revolution in this area.

15. Joël Cornette, "La personne, l'histoire et le récit: le destin de Benoît Lacombe, pro-priétaire, négociant et révolutionnaire (1783–1819)," *R.H.M.C.*, 1985, 541–590; *Un révo-lutionnaire ordinaire, Benoît Lacombe, négociant, 1759–1819*, Champ Vallon, 1986; Nicole Castan, "Le public et le particulier," in Roger Chartier, ed., *Histoire de la vie privée*, Vol. III, *De la Renaissance aux Lumières*, Le Seuil, 1986, 413–451.

12. AN IDEOLOGICAL LEGACY?

Does the shadow of the Revolution color contemporary French politics?

1. René Rémond, *La Vie politique en France*, Vol. I, *1789–1848*, A. Colin, 1965, 5–101.

2. *Ibid.*, 102–163.

3. *Ibid.*, 164–183.

4. *Ibid.*, 184–204; Michel Winock, *La France hexagonale*, Calmann-Lévy, 1986; Patrick Bresart, *Paroles de la Révolution: Les Assémblées Parlementaires 1789–1794*, Minerve, 1988.

5. René Rémond, *op.cit.*, 207–414; Jean-Clément Martin, "La Vendée, région-mémoire," in Pierre Nora, ed., *Les Lieux de mémoire*, Vol. I, *La République*, Gallimard, 1984, 595–617; "La Vendée entre Révolution et contre-révolution: L'imaginaire de l'histoire," in François Lebrun and Roger Dupuy, eds., *Les Résistances à la Révolution*, Imago, 1987, 406–416.

6. Rainer Riemenschneider, "Les libertés locales entre libéralisme et jacobinisme," *B.S.H.M.*, no. 2, 1983, 13–19; Henri Dubief, "Daniel Encontre a été robespierriste," *Bulletin de la Société d'histoire du protestantisme français*, 1971, 279–301; François Furet, "Burke ou la fin d'une seule histoire de l'Europe," in François Lebrun and Roger Dupuy, eds., *op. cit.*, 352–361; Albert Soboul, "Paul-Louis Cournier et la Révolution française: Notes de lecture," *A.H.R.F.*, 1973, 528–538.

7. David H. Pinkney, *Decisive Years in France*, 1840–1847, Princeton University, 1985; Raymond Huard, "Souvenir et traditions révolutionnaires: Le Gard, 1848–1851," *A.H.R.F.*, 1984, 565–587.

8. Albert Soboul, "Pour le centenaire de la Commune de Paris. De l'an II à la Commune de 1871: La double tradition révolutionnaire française," *A.H.R.F.*, 1971, 535–553; "Some Problems of the Revolutionary State, 1789–1796," *P.P.*, 1974, 52–74.

9. Hélène Papadopoulos, "Deux lettres inédites de Buonarroti," *A.H.R.F.*, 1971, 615–621; Saint-Just, *Pages choisies*, introduction by Jean Cassou, Les Éditions du Point du Jour, 1947, I–XXIX. See the special July 15, 1939, issue of *Europe* (whose chief editor was Jean Cassou) devoted to the French Revolution for a good example of the ideological frenzy from which hardly anyone except Georges Lefebvre escaped. This attitude was well summed up by Jean Bruhat when he asserted that the "Jacobinism of today . . . is bolshevism" (*ibid.*, 530). Romain Rolland, Lucien Febvre, Georges Friedman, Edouard Dolléans, Pierre Trahard, etc. contributed to this issue.

10. Marcel David, *Fraternité et Révolution française*, Aubier, 1987, 276–294; Raoul Gir-ardet, in Pierre Nora, ed., *op. cit.*, 33 (cf. "Les Français jugent leur histoire," *L'Express*, August 19–25, 1983). Confirmation comes from a recent SOFRES poll in the *Figaro* magazine in *L'État de l'Opinion, clefs pour 1988*, Le Seuil, 191. The results showed that three out of four French people believe that the Revolution was a positive thing; that it was best symbolized by the Declaration of the Rights of Man and the citizen; and that it was superior to the American and Soviet revolutions. The same proportion supported the abolition of the mon-

archy, but condemned the Terror and the execution of the king. La Fayette and Bonaparte are by far the most popular figures on the "hit-parade of heroes." Cf. a study in depth on these feelings by Gérard Bellouin, *Entendez-vous dans nos mémoires? Les Français et leur Révolution*, La Découverte, 1988. Stendhal was ahead of everyone when he confided to the son of La Fayette at the death of his father in 1834 that the "Revolution's purest individual has just disappeared" (*Siècle*, 1988, 419).

Did the French Republic originate from the Revolution?

1. Claude Nicolet, *L'Idée républicaine en France (1789–1924): Essai d'histoire critique*, Gallimard, 1982, 7–114.

2. *Ibid.*, 115–361.

3. *Ibid.*, 361–507.

4. François Furet, *La Gauche et la Révolution française au milieu du XVIIIe siècle: Edgar Quinet et la question du jacobinisme (1865–1870)*, Hachette, 1986; Edgar Quinet, *La Révolution*, Belin, 1987; Pierre Nora, ed., *op. cit.*, 136.

5. *Ibid.*, 139–193, 247–289, 353–378.

6. *Ibid.*, 381–472.

7. *Ibid.*, 523–560, 651–659; cf. Philippe Nieto, *Le Centenaire de la Révolution Dauphinoise: Vizille, un mythe républicain*, Presses Universitaires de Grenoble, 1988. The death of Edgar Faure and his replacement by Jean-Noel Jeanneney in May 1988 as the head of the official mission to commemorate the bicentennial does not seem to have significantly changed its fundamental orientation. The ambiguity of this orientation was pointed out strikingly by Marcel Gauchet and Regis Debray during the December 5, 1987, debate in the senate presided over by Laurent Fabius (summary by Solidarités Modernes, 42 Bd. Raspail, Paris).

8. Mona Ozouf, *La Fête révolutionnaire, 1789–1799*, Gallimard, 1976, 340; Serge Bianchi, *La Révolution culturelle de l'an II: Élites et peuples (1789–1799)*, Aubier, 1982, 291–295; Lynn Hunt, *Politics, Culture and Class in the French Revolution*, University of California Press, 1984, 123–236. See some interesting remarks by Peter McRhee, "Electoral Democracy and Direct Democracy in France 1789–1851," *European History Quarterly*, 1986, 77–96, on the slow passage toward democracy in France from the Revolution into the nineteenth century, during which time voter participation grew progressively.

9. Jean-Claude Bonnet, ed., *La Mort de Marat*, Flammarion, 1986, 413–443; Françoise Brunel and Geneviève Coulmy, "Chronique théâtrale," *A.H.R.F.*, 1971, 466–470; Michel Pertué, article previously cited, *A.H.R.F.*, 1981, 663.

Can modern revolutions be traced back to the one in 1789?

1. John G. A. Pocock, *Virtue, Commerce and History*, Cambridge University, 1985, 282; William H. Sewell, Jr., article previously cited, *J.M.H.*, 1985, 81–84; Boyd C. Shafer, *Forces of Nationalism: New Realities and Old Myths*, Harcourt, 1972; Jacques Godechot, "Nation, patrie, nationalisme et patriotisme en France au XVIIIe siècle," *A.H.R.F.*, 1971, 481–501; Pierre Nora, ed., *Les Lieux de mémoire*, Vol. II, *La Nation*, 3 vols., Gallimard, 1986; *Littérature et Révolution française*, Annales Littéraires de l'Université de Besançon, no. 354, Belles-Lettres, 1987.

2. Marc Richir, "Révolution et transparence sociale," in J. G. Fichte, *Considérations sur la Révolution française*, Payot, 1974; W. Markow, "I giacobini dei paesi absburgici," *S.S.*, 1962, 493–525; Sander Lukacsy, "L'historiographie de la Révolution française et les intellectuels hongrois (1810–1849)," *A.H.R.F.*, 1973, 264–284; G. Nicolae Liu, "La Révolution française et la formation de l'idéologie révolutionnaire et républicaine chez les Roumains," *A.H.R.F.*, 1986, 285–306; Thomas P. Saine, *Black Bread–White Bread: German Intellectuals and the French Revolution*, Columbia University, 1988. See some interesting remarks by Hans-Jürgen Lüsebrink and Rolf Reichardt on "L'écho de 1789 en Allemagne," in XVIIIe *Siècle*, 1988, 259–275. Fichte wrote in 1799 that "for every rational man, there can be no doubt that the principles that are the foundation of the French Republic and of republics based on it are the only ones that are capable of guaranteeing the dignity of man" (in F. Furet and M. Ozouf, *op. cit.*, 964). The greatest English writers of the nineteenth century, from Blake to

Hardy, were also fascinated by the French Revolution. Cf. Burton R. Friedman, *Fabricating History: English Writers on the French Revolution*, Princeton University, 1988. On the immediate impact of the Revolution, see Seamus Deane, *The French Revolution and Enlightenment in England, 1789–1832*, Harvard University, 1988.

3. Rolando Minuti and Mauro Moretti, "Aspect de la réflexion sur l'histoire nationale dans la culture postrévolutionnaire," in François Lebrun and Roger Dupuy, eds., *op. cit.*, 362–375; Franco Della Peruta, "La Révolution française dans la pensée des démocrates italiens du Risorgimento," *A.H.R.F.*, 1977, 664–676; Claudio Giovannini, "Mito della Révolution française e scientismo nella 'Plebe' dei Primi Anni," *S.S.*, 1981, 345–369.

4. René Sédillot, *Le Coût de la Révolution française*, Perrin, 1986, 279–282.

5. W. Markov, "Jacques Roux e Karl Marx: come gli 'enragés' entrarono nella 'sacra famiglia,' " *S.S.*, 1965, 41–54; Hans-Peter Jaeck, *Die französische Bügerliche Revolution von 1789 im Frühwerk von Karl Marx, 1843–1846*, Akademie Verlag, 1979; Ferenc Fehér, "La Révolution française come modelli della concezione marxiana della politica," *S.S.*, 1983, 377–396; Tony Judt, *Le Marxisme et la Gauche française, 1830–1981*, Hachette, 1987.

6. Victor Daline, "Lénine et le jacobinisme," *A.H.R.F.*, 1970, 89–112.

7. Theda Skocpol, *States and Social Revolutions: A Comparative Analysis of France, Russia and China*, Cambridge University, 1979; Lynn Hunt, *op. cit.*, 205–211; Ferenc Fehér, "The French Revolution: Between Class Identity and Universalist Illusions," *Review*, Vol. VIII, no. 3, 1985, 335–351.

8. *Ibid.*, 342–347. See also Jaroslav Krajci, *Great Revolutions Compared: The Search for a Theory*, Wheatsheaf, 1988. For brilliant observations on the entire problem, see Jean-Marie Domenach, "Révolution et Modernité," *Esprit*, June 1988, 25–36.

CONCLUSION

1. Donald M. G. Sutherland, *France 1789–1815*, 438–442. Trotsky noted in 1922, no doubt to justify a situation in the USSR that was similar to that in France from 1789 to 1799, that the greatest revolutions generally have "as a first result ruin and want" (*Cahiers Léon Trotsky*, no. 30, June 1987, 87).

2. François Lebrun and Roger Dupuy, eds., *Les Résistances à la Révolution*, Imago, 1987, 11–15, 469–474; Norman Hampson, "La contre-révolution a-t-elle existé?" *ibid.*, 462–468.

3. Yves-Marie Bercé, *Histoire des croquants*, Le Seuil, 1986, 349. Robert Griffiths (*Le Centre Perdu: Malouet et les "monarchiens" dans la Révolution française*, Presses Universitaires de Grenoble, 1988) has recently shown how this moderate wing of the counterrevolution easily rallied, in the person of Bonaparte, to a type of power that it had sought since the prerevolutionary era and that was both strong and reformist. See important observations, moreover, by Roger Chartier in *Le Monde* of July 1, 1988, where he contrasts the "illusion of politics" that was dear to the voluntarism and messianism of the French Revolution and that was the undeniable cause of a profound division with the "fundamental continuities that stem from long-standing cultural divisions and inequalities in development."

4. Valérie Quinney, "The Problem of Civil Rights for Free Men of Color in the Early French Revolution," *F.H.S.*, 1972, 544–557; Claude Wanquet, "Histoire d'une Révolution: La Réunion (1789–1803)," *A.H.R.F.*, 1979, 495–506; Thadd E. Hall, "Thought and Practice of Enlightened Government in French Corsica," *A.H.R.*, 1969, 880–905; François Pomponi, "Sentiment révolutionnaire et esprit de parti en Corse au temps de la Révolution," *A.H.R.F.*, 1971, 56–87, Anne Perotin-Dumon, *Être jacobin sous les Tropiques*, Société d'histoire de la Guadeloupe, 1985; " 'Sous ce soleil brûlant': recherches sur les jacobins des Antilles," *Bulletin de la Commission d'histoire de la Révolution française*, 1984–1985, 23–44. (She stresses the importance of the temporary abolition of slavery in so far as it led to the development of a "Jacobinism of color.") Cf. Yves Benot, *La Révolution française et la fin des colonies*, Éditions La Decouverte, 1988. Anne Pérotin-Dumon, "Les Jacobins des Antilles, ou l'esprit dans Îles-du-Vent," *R.H.M.C.*, 1988, 275–304, has recently confirmed that these militants were often

"foreigners," notably from southern France. These lower-class whites remained "colonists" during the Revolution as they had been under the *ancien régime*.

5. Jean-Clément Martin, *La Vendée et la France*, Le Seuil, 1987. Jean Boutier has recently confirmed ("Un autre Midi: Note sur les sociétés populaires en Corse (1790–1795)," *A.H.R.F.*, 1987, 158–175) François Pomponi's brilliant analysis of an island where the spirit of partisanship was clearly stronger than a truly democratic interpretation of the Revolution. Cf. also the remarkable special issue of *Provence historique* (Vol. XXXVI, Part 148, April–September 1987) entitled "Midi rouge et Midi blanc: Les antagonismes politiques sous la Révolution française et leur héritage dans le Midi méditerranéen." Consult also Michel Brunet, *Le Roussillon: Une société contre l'État 1780–1820*, Association des publications de l'université de Toulouse-Le-Mirail/Editions Eché, 1986. See the interesting volume *Actes du Colloque International de Besançon: Région, Nation, Europe, unité et diversité des processus sociaux et culturels de la Révolution française*, Université de Besançon, 1988. It is significant that the best part of *L'État de la France pendant la Révolution*, Éditions La Découverte, 1988, edited by Michel Vovelle, is without a doubt the section concerning *regional* subjects (pp. 323–414). Louis Bergeron and Jean Luc Moyand also are editing for the bicentennial the *Histoire Provinciale de la Révolution française*, Éditions Privat. This will involve twenty volumes. *The Legend of the Revolution* was the subject of an interesting colloquium at Clermont-Ferrand in June 1986 whose proceedings were edited by Christian Croisille and Jean Ehrand, Publications de la Faculté des Lettres de Clermont-Ferrand, 1988.

6. John Lynch, *The Spanish-American Revolutions, 1808–1826*, Norton, 1986, 416. For an analysis of the relationship between political ideology and historical knowledge regarding the French Revolution, see an interesting recent effort in *Cahiers Bernard Lazare*, nos. 119–120 that was pointed out by Pierre Lepape in *Le Monde* of April 1, 1988.

INDEX

ABOUT THE AUTHOR

Born in Lyons in 1932, the author received his B.A. from the University of Lyons and his Ph.D. from the Sorbonne. Currently the Professor of Modern History at the University of Social Sciences, Grenoble, he is the author of *L'amour en Occident a l'époque moderne* and *Les mythes chrétiens de la Renaissance aux Lumières*. He lives in Grenoble.